Canadian Political Debates:

Opposing Views on Issues that Divide Canadians

Christopher Dunn

M&S

Canadian Cataloguing in Publication Data

Dunn, Christopher J.C., 1948-

Canadian Political Debates

Includes bibliographical references and index.

ISBN 0-7710-2930-6

1. Canada – Politics and government – 1984-1993.*   2. Canada –
Politics and government – 1993-   .* I. Title.

FC630.D85 1994   971.064'7   C94-930834-X
F1023.2.D85 1994

McClelland & Stewart Inc.
The Canadian Publishers
481 University Avenue
Toronto, Ontario
M5G 2E9

1 2 3 4   98 97 96 95

Typesetting by M&S, Toronto
Printed and bound in Canada

Contents

To my wife Hilda,
whom I love like the earth loves the rain

Preface

A book is always a joint project, even in cases where there is only one author. The genesis of this work owes much to Michael Harrison, the former Managing Editor, College Division, who encouraged me to write the piece and collaborated in shaping it. The staff of McClelland & Stewart guided it expertly and efficiently to a smooth finish. Richard Tallman proved a meticulous copy-editor and separator of academic wheat from linguistic chaff.

I had the good fortune to receive funding to hire research assistants from the Memorial University Undergraduate Career Experience Program (MUCEP) as well as from the Challenge summer student employment program of Employment and Immigration Canada. This enabled me to work with some very bright students: Sara Rich, Garry Sullivan, Susan Patten-Boulos, Derrick Hynes, and Brian Taylor. I am grateful indeed for their help.

Comments and reviews were sought at various stages regarding certain chapters of the book from Joan Boase, David Close, Robert Coutts, James Feehan, Chris Harris, David Laycock, Adrian Tanner, and Michael Wallack. Their considerable wisdom and perspective were appreciated. I, of course, accept responsibility for any errors of fact or interpretation.

Introduction

This book reviews controversial Canadian political issues in a dialectical fashion. Points made in support of a certain stand in one chapter are directly criticized in the companion chapter. "Debates" readers in Canadian politics have of course been published before. However, the articles in them were invariably written by several writers who were writing for purposes other than being included in an anthology. The reader is left to try to make explicit connections between often uneven material. Frustration rather than clarification can result.

This book grew from a conviction that much existing political and public policy material is unnecessarily one-sided. It sometimes features biases clothed in academic jargon or is presented in such a way as to downplay the possibility of alternative views or options. The present work tries to broaden the perspective of readers without dictating a certain course of thought or action.

Canadian Political Debates is also intended to be a source book for those who are new to the field of Canadian politics and who want something a little more than the usual "structures and cultures" approach. It does not attempt to replace but to supplement this approach. The basic information usually given in an introduction to politics is here presented in a different guise. It comes into play as part of an ongoing political controversy, immediately accessible, so to speak.

One question is considered in each "part" to the book and each part consists of three sections. The part introduction outlines the basic concepts, prevalent theories, and historical landmarks that tend to dominate discussion in the policy area. The next section argues the affirmative to the question using a variety of categories. The last section argues a negative response to the question, using the same categories insofar as they are appropriate.

Continuing Canadian Controversies

The political controversies covered here are certainly not new. There is a basic similarity in national political debates over the years. The subordinate place of provinces in the national federation was systematically disputed in the 1870s and 1880s by Oliver Mowat and Honoré Mercier. The question of whether Quebec needed to remain in a colonial and then a national framework dominated by English-speaking Canadians goes back in some respects to the Rebellions of 1837-38 in Lower Canada. It has certainly been a sub-theme in Quebec politics for much of Canadian history, especially in recent years. The Progressives and related farmer-labour groups made direct democracy a major issue after the First World War, and the spirit of citizen participation reappeared in Canadian life with the New Left. The social democratic movement, plagued by doctrinal and political division, has never ceased to wonder if its latest incarnation – be it the Co-operative Commonwealth Federation, the New Democratic Party, or other short-lived parties – has a secure future. Free trade, or "reciprocity" as it was called in the last century and in the early years of this century, is an issue that has arisen every generation or two since 1854 because Canadians divide over the cultural implications of trade. Bilingualism disputes are simply a reflection of the ongoing dispute about the nature of the Canadian identity; Henri Bourassa would have called it "pan-Canadianism" around the turn of the century. Aboriginal self-government and rights and freedoms disputes were latent disputes until very recently, but they, too, are part and parcel of the debate about the meaning of Canadian identity.

Controversies in the 1993 General Election

The Canadian general election of 1993 demonstrated the durability of these issues – and others – in the Canadian dialogue. Most of them featured the pro and con debates familiar to contemporary Canadian discourse, but, perhaps predictably, the debates did not offer much meat for rational dialogue. The significant stakes involved in these issues demand that Canadians carefully consider the choices that they have been called upon to make. This book attempts to aid in that task. First, however, to get a sense of how issues are framed in the heat of *political debate,* we review the controversies that surfaced during the 1993 election.

The Quebec Question

The "Quebec question" was a clear campaign issue, but few, other than the Bloc Québécois, cared to acknowledge it. The Bloc was a small grouping of ex-Conservative cabinet minister Lucien Bouchard and seven other Quebec nationalists who had broken from the Liberal and Conservative parties. Theirs was the novel policy of promoting Quebec secession using the instrumentality of the national Parliament. The election saw them arguing, as before, that sovereignty was the only option left to Quebec after the defeat of the Meech Lake and Charlottetown Accords. Some sort of economic association would be in the interests of both Quebec and the rest of Canada and there could perhaps even be a shared Parliament. The other side of the argument was presented by the Reform Party. It would deny the economic tie to Quebec and offer a vision of a "New Canada" of strict provincial equality. This is essentially a negation of traditional Quebec nationalist demands and would effectively force Quebecers to make a once-and-for-all choice about their connection to Canada. The other parties avoided specifics on the constitutional question.

The Welfare State

The election's social policy debates featured many variations, but two themes were predominant: that the limits of the welfare state had been met or passed; and that there was a need for further elaboration and infilling of social citizenship rights. The first theme was explicitly enunciated by the Reform Party and implicitly mooted by the Conservatives. The Reform Party opted for the principle of needs-based social programs over universal ones. It suggested deep cuts in old age security payments, unemployment insurance, and transfers to provinces. The Conservatives, the governing party prior to the election, hinted at these or similar solutions by establishing a Human Resources "super-department," by undertaking a secret review of social policy programs, and by refusing to talk about social policy reform for much of the election. On the other side of the debate was the case provided by all the other parties: that the social programs should be maintained or expanded. The Liberals promised a national child-care program, expanded literacy training, Aboriginal initiatives, and a youth corps. The New Democrats maintained the need for a national child-care program, expanded social housing and student loans, and stability in transfers to provinces.

Canada as a Dependency Society

A sub-theme of the election was the question of whether or not federal programs fostered dependency on government. A secret internal document prepared by Employment and Immigration Canada was obtained by the *Globe and Mail* and released during the 1993 election. The document used language very similar to that in speeches by Human Resources Minister Bernard Valcourt, blaming the current unemployment and welfare programs for fostering "dependency" among recipients. There was too much emphasis on "passive income support" and too little on incentives to work.[1] Both the Conservatives and Reformers would have redesigned the unemployment insurance program to have it serve only the temporarily unemployed, rather than depressed regional economies. The Reformers took the theme of dependency culture a few steps further, however, stating that subsidies provided to business and interest groups had to be massively slashed along with a reduction of $1.5 billion in transfer payments to provinces. The Liberal Party "Red Book" (page 21) used virtually the same "dependency" terminology as did the Conservatives but appeared not to draw the same conclusions about levels of funding. Instead, Liberal leader Jean Chrétien "made funding for existing social service programs and transfer payments to provincial governments a sacred trust" and stated that he would negotiate a five-year commitment on transfers to the provinces.[2] He also announced a $6 billion tri-level intergovernmental infrastructure (public works) plan to provide new employment, of which the federal government would spend a third. The other parties joined with the implied Liberal policy and effectively rejected the theme of Canada as a dependency society.

Provincial Power and Prerogatives

Although the subject of degrees of provincial power – whether it was too much or too little – was never argued in the abstract, it became the backdrop to the health care controversy that flared during the election. The Reform Party announced itself opposed in general to the use of the federal spending power and more disposed to allow the provinces tax room to fund their constitutional responsibilities. In the case of health care, the Reformers suggested changing the Canada Health Act to permit provinces to make their own decisions about user fees, physician extra-billing, and the use of private insurance for health care. The Bloc Québécois also favoured provincial control of health care delivery, including the right to set user fees. The Liberals, on the other hand, pronounced themselves against user fees and in favour of universal medicare, uniform services provided in each province, and more federal leverage in medicare than had been the case under the Conservative government. In short, the Liberals favoured the traditional use of the spending power in the health field, a position not unlike that of the other parties.[3] They also showed no inclination to change their historical approach to intergovernmental relations other than promising to reduce duplication in federal-provincial program delivery.

Immigration

Immigration in a sense became a code word for the issue of Canadian multiculturalism and the relative weight that people from non-traditional sources of immigration should play in shaping Canadian culture. The actual division in the election was between (1) an expansive level of immigration and mixing economic with humane considerations, and (2) a restrictive level of immigration with a more exclusive focus on the potential economic benefits for Canada. Most parties agreed on the first option, pegging the desirable level of immigration at about a quarter-million people per year. The Reformers, by contrast, chose the second option and gave 150,000 as the target figure. The voters seemed to be able to decipher what the leaders were saying in code: that the issue was between conservative and fundamental change in the status of traditional charter groups in Canadian society.

The Free Trade Deals

Division on the two free trade deals, the Canada-U.S. Free Trade Agreement (FTA) and the North American Free Trade Agreement (NAFTA), was significant, although not as pronounced as during the 1988 general election. In 1988, the Liberals had opposed the free trade agreement and the Conservatives, having negotiated it, supported it. (The NDP policy on the subject was nebulous, but negative.) In the 1993 election the Conservatives were still very much the unabashed free-traders in favour of NAFTA, again having struck the deal. Ranged foursquare against the deal were the NDP and the National Party. The Liberal Party's business wing had convinced the party that free trade frameworks were inevitable and so Liberal opposition to NAFTA (it had to rationalize its stand in 1988) was more rhetoric than reality. A *Globe and Mail* editorial caught Liberal Red Book bafflegab on NAFTA very nicely:

> The Liberals promise to "renegotiate both the FTA and NAFTA." Abrogation is promised "if satisfactory changes cannot be renegotiated." At the same time, "if a Western Hemisphere free trade bloc evolves," the Liberals would "work to build common Western Hemisphere institutions" to oversee it. Huh?[4]

Liberal trade critic Roy MacLaren called the lack of a meaningful subsidies and anti-dumping code the "great flaw," the "black hole" at the centre of NAFTA.[5] Presumably, NAFTA had ceased to be as major an issue as it had been during the 1980s. However, there was just enough ambivalence in support for it to make it a potential future issue for Canadian politics.

The Peace Dividend

The Cold War effectively ended with the fall of Communist regimes across Eastern Europe and the Soviet Union in the late 1980s and early 1990s. This development caught Canadian parties in the horns of a dilemma. Would they support the continued level of military build-up that had characterized the Cold War or would there be a beating of swords into ploughshares – the so-called "peace dividend" – which called for a redirecting of defence spending into domestic purposes. The Conservatives seemed unwilling to entertain the notion of such a paradigmatic shift and used peace-keeping activities in Somalia and Bosnia-Herzegovina to justify a fairly static defence outlook. The peace dividend issue became symbolically enmeshed in the Conservative plan to purchase forty-three EH-101 state-of-the-art military helicopters. The EH-101, which one wag said might be mistaken for a university course in Canadian slang, became a significant albatross around Conservative Prime Minister Kim Campbell's neck. All the other parties except the Reformers maintained they would completely scrap the helicopter deal and redirect military expenditures into peaceful uses. Paradoxically, however, the parties had no clarification to bring on the question of Canadian participation in international peacekeeping activities, which itself required expensive technological and military retooling. By the end of the election it was clear that defence and foreign policy had become latent issues of division for Canadians.

Why This Approach

This book assumes an intrinsic value in investigating opposing points of view in depth. It may be instructive to note what use some Western intellectuals have seen in such exercises. They include the prevention of absolutist majoritarianism, the seeking of

truth, the recognition of the limits of knowledge, and the understanding of change.

Alexis de Tocqueville

Although Alexis de Tocqueville was ultimately optimistic about
the condition of democracy in 1830s America and its future in the
rest of the world, he was alive to its dangers. *Democracy in America,*[6]
published in 1835, saw the tyrannical side to majority opinion and
has been rightly interpreted as a universal warning about confor-
mity in behaviour and opinion.

The decided majority is a more formidable barrier to liberty of
opinion than exists in the most despotic state. This is because
majority opinion achieves an absolute authority that is both physical and moral in nature; it acts on both actions and wills in a
democracy, whereas the despot tends to rely merely on the prohibition of action. In the tyranny of democratic republics, "the body is
left free, and the soul is enslaved."[7] The overwhelming desire for
equality, a natural concomitant of democracy, overshadows the
love of liberty. The freedom to be different and to think differently
is of less value where people find more security in equality of fortune and practical knowledge. If free institutions ever foundered in
America, it would be because of the omnipotent majority.[8]

The answer, of course, was not to hinder liberty but to place
obstacles before tyranny. The difficulties were not insurmountable; the solutions lay in varied attempts to resurrect individualism.
The implications for an observer of, and participant in, political
debates are clear.

John Stuart Mill

The classic statement on the value of integrating opposing
viewpoints came in John Stuart Mill's essay "On Liberty." In this,
one of his most lyrical essays, Mill distinguishes four reasons for
valuing freedom of opinion and freedom of speech.[9]

The first reason is that any opinion that is silenced may in fact be
the truth. Those who silence it are wrongfully claiming infallibility
and harming the future well-being of mankind. They effectively
put themselves in a position of judgement without hearing the
other party's case.

The second reason is that prevailing opinions seldom contain the whole truth, but only parts of it. The only way to elicit the remainder of the truth is to let adverse opinions collide. Mill said that "on every subject on which difference of opinion is possible, the truth depends on a balance to be struck between two sets of conflicting reasons."[10] The rational approach to controversy is the suspension of judgement, in anticipation of strong arguments from the proponents of each side. If those holding opposing views cannot be found, mental discipline consists of imagining what they might say and debating them internally. Like Cicero, Mill felt that "he who knows only his own side of his case, knows little of that."[11]

The third reason is that the holder of even a true opinion will not comprehend the rational grounds for holding it, merely maintaining it like a prejudice, unless he vigorously contests it. "Not the violent conflict between parts of the truth, but the quiet suppression of half of it, is the formidable evil; there is always hope when people are forced to listen to both sides; it is when they attend only to one that errors harden into prejudices, and truth itself ceases to have the effect of truth, by being exaggerated into falsehood."[12] Judgement should follow the judicial model, which insists that both sides have advocates and that they be fully heard.

The fourth is that not actively entertaining opposing viewpoints will deprive the truth of its salutary effect on the character and conduct of the individual. The prevalence of dogma crowds out conviction. The personal meaning of the truth will suffer, if not disappear. All of these considerations argue for a sympathetic hearing of opposing viewpoints. They are, needless to say, valuable approaches in a debates reader.

Karl Popper

The work of philosopher Karl Popper relates "critical rationalism" and the advance of knowledge in social and scientific affairs. Critical rationalism is akin to the scientific attitude. It is based on the idea that nothing is exempt from criticism: everyone is liable to make mistakes, and the quest for certainty is a mistaken one. A rationalist is one who has faith in reason, not only one's own, but even more so that of others. One will reject all claims to authority and believe oneself an intellectual:

only insofar as he is capable of learning from criticism as well as from his own and other people's mistakes, and that one can learn in this sense only if one takes others and their arguments seriously. Rationalism is therefore bound up with the idea that the other fellow has a right to be heard, and to defend his arguments. [13]

The search for truth is not, however, a mistaken one; it is just that we may never be certain that we have in fact found it.

We can *learn*, we can *grow* in knowledge, even if we can never *know* – that is, know for certain. Since we can learn, there is no reason for despair of reason; and since we can never know, there are no grounds here for smugness, or for conceit over the growth of our knowledge. [14]

The sources of knowledge, for Popper, are therefore many, but none is superior to any other. Tradition, reason, observation, intellectual intuition, imagination, and other sources are important but not ultimately authoritative. [15] That is, they are not immune from critical examination. As we learn, we learn that we do not know much. This state of "learned ignorance" is humbling but, in the end, enlightening. "While differing widely in the various little bits we know, in our infinite ignorance we are all equal." [16] The adoption of such Socratic wisdom is a useful approach to bring to a study of policy controversies in Canada.

The Dialectic of History

Even if one remains unimpressed by the case for dialogue established by the previous thinkers, there is a certain utility in examining contesting policies. It consists of seeing history as the unfolding of a dialectic. Opposites combine to form more inclusive unities. The philosopher Hegel posited that every concept had its own opposite contained within it and that this provided the universal dynamic of change. He named this dynamic the "dialectic" to honour the origins of the idea in the work of Plato and other Greek philosophers. The dialectic had a triadic structure to it, usually described in terms of the thesis, antithesis, and synthesis. The thesis is the original position, within which is embedded a contradiction that will destroy it, yielding its antithesis, or opposite. The thesis and antithesis are then united in a higher unity or synthesis, a new development. The triad then becomes the thesis of another triad. Change is in this way a continuous process.

Hegel never claimed to see the future by using this dynamic. However, for the social scientist it does provide some clues as to what might be the future shape of change. Politicians often try to reconcile opposites, and the result of such efforts is often a surprise even to them. Examining arguments that contradict each other might lead one to guess what solutions may transpire, or else allow one to construct a solution to problems that bridges the positions. This certainly is not a complete guidance to political problem-solving; but it is a useful one.

The Critical Observer

This book is not intended to force the reader into an "either/or" situation in specific Canadian policy dilemmas. It very well might be that the observer finds certain of the arguments compelling. This is natural. Yet it may be useful to consider some flaws and fallacies that may occur in some of the arguments when trying to come to a personal resolution of the issues.

1. *The false dichotomy.* The false dichotomy occurs when the reader is asked to choose between two alternatives that may not exhaust the available options or that ignore the possibility of overlap.
2. *The post hoc fallacy.* The *post hoc* fallacy (*post hoc, ergo propter hoc*) mistakes sequence for consequence. It maintains that simply because B occurred after A, therefore A was the cause of B.
3. *The reductive fallacy.* The reductive fallacy consists in reducing an obviously complex network of causation to a simple cause. It may also involve assembling a chain of causes in an inappropriate fashion.
4. *Fallacies of irrelevant evidence.* Such fallacies introduce material that does not argue to the issue in question. The most notable fallacies are the *ad hominem* (argument

against the arguer's prestige rather than the argument), the
ad misericordiam (appeal to pity, or the personal plight of
the subject), and the *ad antiquitam* (appeal to the ages, or
the supposed wisdom of the ancestors).
5. *The argument from authority.* The argument from authority
consists in basing one's judgement on the word of experts,
rather than reasoning through the problem itself.

These are merely a few of the pitfalls in argumentation that can
occur. The reader is advised to turn to the relevant literature for a
more intensive investigation. [17] These few are presented merely to
arm the reader with an initial scepticism to hack his or her way
through the thicket of affirmative and negative arguments about to
be encountered. Good luck!

Notes

1. "Overhaul of UI, welfare proposed," *Globe and Mail*, October 7, 1993.
2. "Liberal leader has had it easy," *Globe and Mail*, September 30, 1993.
3. "Fear keeps health care feuding to a minimum," *Globe and Mail*, October 4, 1993.
4. "What was that mandate again?" *Globe and Mail*, October 25, 1993.
5. Roy MacLaren, "Setting new rules for NAFTA," *Globe and Mail*, October 12, 1993.
6. Alexis de Tocqueville, *Democracy in America*, 2 vols. (New York: Alfred A. Knopf, 1953).
7. *Ibid.*, vol. I, p. 264.
8. *Ibid.*, p. 269.
9. John Stuart Mill, *Three Essays* (Oxford: Oxford University Press, 1975).
10. *Ibid.*, p. 46.
11. *Ibid.*
12. *Ibid.*, p. 64.
13. K.R. Popper, *The Open Society and its Enemies* (Princeton, N.J.: Princeton University Press, 1966), p. 238.
14. *Ibid.*, p. 383
15. Karl R. Popper, *Conjectures and Refutations: The Growth of Scientific Knowledge* (New York: Harper and Row, 1965), pp. 27-29.
16. *Ibid.*, p. 29.

17. See, for example, David Hackett Fischer, *Historians' Fallacies: Toward a Logic of Historical Thought* (New York: Harper and Row, 1970); and Ruggero D. Aldisert, *Logic for Lawyers: A Guide to Clear Legal Thinking* (Deerfield, Ill.: Clark Boardman Callaghan, 1992). Books dealing with policy analysis and critical thinking are also advised.

PART ONE

Is There an Inherent Right of Aboriginal Self-Government?

The question of an inherent Aboriginal right of self-government can be argued strongly from both the affirmative and negative positions. The arguments fall into some predictable patterns: constitutional, philosophical, historical, pragmatic, and financial. What both sides share, however, is a conviction that the question is one of the most important facing Canada today.

Other than the "Quebec question," Aboriginal self-governance has been the most contentious constitutional issue in Canada over the past decade and more. Its non-resolution helped defeat the Meech Lake Accord, and the self-governance package in the Charlottetown Accord contributed to the latter's appearance of complexity and open-endedness.

This introduction will examine the meaning and context of inherency, and its basic legal and political theory. (For simplicity's sake, the inherent right of self-government will be referred to here as the *inherency argument* or simply *inherency*.)

Inherency as a Right

No universally accepted definition of the term "inherent right of self-government" exists. Its essence seems to come to light when its alternatives are considered. The important thing is that its proponents consider it a *right*. A commentary by the Royal Commission on Aboriginal Peoples says that inherency has mostly to do with consideration of the *source* of self-government:

> If the right [of Aboriginal self-government] is inherent, it is viewed as originating, not from the constitutional provision, but from sources within the Aboriginal nations. On this view, the constitutional provision serves to recognize, delimit, and protect the right rather than create it. [1]

An inherent right is therefore an existing rather than a created right. The Royal Commission's paper is valuable because it examines concepts other than source, such as *scope* (circumscribed by the powers of other governments in Canada, versus uncircumscribed) and *status* (subordinate to the powers of other governments, versus sovereign within its sphere). According to the Commission, all three of these issues (source, scope, and status) are conceptually independent of each other, which is a fine point that not all analysts make. (Nevertheless, according to the Royal Commission, inherent self-government, to be realistic in Canada, must be a circumscribed and sovereign right.)

Inherency versus Contingency

The alternative to inherency is called the *delegated* or *contingent right* of Aboriginal self-government. Delegated self-government is granted by state levels of government, whereas inherent self-government does not depend on the will of governments, for it simply recognizes an ancient right that Aboriginals have never abandoned. Contingency implies changing the application of self-government by negotiation; inherency can never be negotiated out of existence, although it can be ignored. Contingency implies a standard form or, at the most, a limited range of forms of Aboriginal government; inherency means sensitivity to the many forms of government required by the First Nations. A heavy implication of municipal or quasi-municipal status for Aboriginal governments applies under the contingency approach; by contrast, the logic of a "third order of government" is attached to the inherent right.

Inherency versus Independence

Analysts must also take care to distinguish inherency from other terms, such as *independence* and *self-management*. As Clark says, self-management or self-administration can include the "function of managing or administering laws made by some other body politic; 'self-government' however . . . means making one's own laws, laws that can have precedence over the laws of outside lawmakers when the laws conflict."[2] Independence is not what most Aboriginals intend in their drive for inherency; in keeping with the circumscribed/uncircumscribed distinction, Aboriginal leaders see First Nations jurisdictions limited by the necessity to co-exist with other levels of government in Canada. Aboriginal jurisdictions will be both interdependent and overlapping (concurrent) with other governments. There are, of course, certain exceptions, like the Six Nations Confederacy, which does in fact maintain an historical claim of unbroken independence vis-à-vis the Canadian state.

Legal and Political History

The legal and political history of inherency must be understood before one is in a position to judge the relative wisdom of Aboriginal self-government. The pre-contact pattern of Aboriginal governance must be understood, and various historical and legal occurrences of particular significance must also be examined.

In pre-contact North America, self-governance or Indian sovereignty was practised under a number of forms. A quasi-federal system called the Haudenosaunee (Five Nations)[3] Confederacy featured a matriarchal system of choosing chiefs, as well as councils of chiefs meeting in super-tribal councils with legislative, executive, and judicial powers.[4] On the west coast, tribes used the potlatch, a ceremony involving songs, speeches, and lavish gift-giving, which had governmental implications, particularly in relations between the major self-governing house groups of the society. The potlatch affirmed important decisions. There were also simpler, more consensual forms. Aboriginal people clearly possessed power over their own lives.

The Royal Proclamation of 1763 was in a sense Canada's first constitution. It established a governmental system for the colonies seized from France; but its importance has been more enduring for Aboriginals in Canada. It provided that Indians in "unceded" lands would not be molested or disturbed by settlers, and that lands the Indians wanted to sell must first be offered to the British Crown. The Proclamation has never been repealed. It is regarded by many observers as a kind of "charter" of Aboriginal rights because it implied the continuance of the sovereignty that the First Peoples enjoyed before contact. Others disagree, as the following chapters will discuss.

The federation of the Canadian colonies in 1867 brought with it a whole new era of complexity in Aboriginal-white relations. The Constitution Act, 1867, established in section 91(24) that the "Indians, and lands reserved for Indians" were under federal jurisdiction. Based on this authority, Parliament passed a series of "Indian Acts." Successive Indian Acts since 1876 have defined "Indians" for the purposes of the Act and outlined the specific methods of federal management of Indian people, but not of Inuit or Métis. Inuit, because they are not on reserves, are not covered by the Indian Act definition, but they have been deemed by the Supreme Court of Canada to be Indians within the meaning of section 91(24).[5]

The importance of the Indian Act, at least for our purposes, is that it began, first in 1876 (consolidated legislation) and then in subsequent revisions, to establish a style of government based on Western democratic assumptions. Ultimately this came to mean limited internal government by elected band councils on reserves. Band government was overseen for most of early Canadian history by an Indian agent, whose major job was to act as a conduit for the will of the federal administration, usually as the chairman of the council itself. Traditional Indian government, involving consensual decision-making and male-female balance, was disallowed. The new form of government was so restrictive and so clearly against the direction of Indian history that it was often secretly supplanted by a covert form of traditional government on the reserves.

Although the restrictions on Indian decision-making were lifted somewhat by amendments to the Act in 1951, 1985, and 1988, it still remains a highly restrictive instrument, a fact that even the federal policy-makers admit.

In recent decades a series of government and government-instigated studies of Aboriginal affairs moved the Native dossier closer to the forefront of the Canadian policy agenda. In 1966, the report of the Hawthorn Commission heightened concern about the generally impoverished state of Indian life. It maintained that the main policy problem was the lack of community-level self-governing institutions and recommended reserve municipal status and greater provincial involvement in services to reserves.[6] The report advocated maintaining the special status of the Indians, whom it called "citizens plus" (having normal Canadian citizenship plus being charter members of the Canadian community).[7]

In 1969 the federal Liberal government issued a policy statement that generated so much Aboriginal opposition that it provided the impetus for modern Native political consciousness. Inspired in part by a fear of being branded segregationist in an era of civil rights consciousness, the White Paper of 1969 urged the ending of the reserve system and the transfer of Indian lands to Indian people. The Indian Act would be repealed, provinces would be expected to serve Indians on a basis of equality with other citizens, and the programs of the Department of Indian Affairs and Northern Development (DIAND) dealing with Indian affairs would be wound down over a five-year transitional period. Bitter opposition by Natives highlighted an ambiguous attitude toward the Indian Act: it was unsatisfactory, but it was better than nothing, which is exactly what they interpreted the White Paper as offering. Indians agreed that they were indeed "citizens plus." The policy was officially retracted in 1971.

Two important developments followed in short order, one stemming from the politically embarrassing circumstances of the failed federal initiative, the other from the courts. On the political front, the federal government began direct funding of national and local Aboriginal organizations and used them as sole bargaining agents for their respective Aboriginal constituencies.

On the judicial front, the *Calder* decision of 1973 recognized that Aboriginal title or right to land in the case of the Nishga of British Columbia had survived European settlement; however, the

Supreme Court split on the issue of subsequent extinguishment.[8] Prime Minister Trudeau was apparently impressed by the legal implications flowing from the judgement.[9] In August of 1973 the federal government announced its intention to negotiate Aboriginal land title claims (a new comprehensive form of treaty) in areas of Canada where no treaties had been previously concluded. These developments laid important groundwork for later progress toward self-government.

The Penner Report of 1983 heralded the modern tenor of Native-state relations. This Report of the Special Committee on Indian Self-Government showed how far the level of dialogue had evolved in little more than a decade. The political dynamics of the previous constitutional settlement had necessitated attention to the unfinished Aboriginal agenda. Although not mentioning the notion of inherency *per se,* the report recommended the constitutional entrenchment of the Aboriginal right to self-government. The federal government would first occupy areas of legislative competence under s. 91(24), then vacate them after negotiations with new Indian governments.

The report, although not implemented in its original form, marked a new attention to negotiation on the basis of mutual respect with Aboriginals. A series of relatively significant steps followed during the 1980s: revisions to the Indian Act in 1985 and 1988; the inauguration of limited self-government as a part of a comprehensive land claims settlement (the Cree-Naskapi [of Quebec] Act, 1984); the inauguration of a municipal-model self-government with the Sechelt band in British Columbia [the Sechelt Indian Band Self-Government Act, 1986].

As well, the Liberal government in 1982 ended a federal-provincial constitutional reform process by inviting Britain to pass a new Constitution Act. Its two provisions of central importance to Aboriginals were sections 25 and 35, the latter of which was amended in 1983:

25. The guarantee in this Charter of certain rights and freedoms shall not be construed so as to abrogate or derogate from any aboriginal, treaty or other rights or freedoms that pertain to the aboriginal peoples of Canada including
    (a) any rights or freedoms that have been recognized by the Royal Proclamation of October 7, 1763; and

(b) any rights or freedoms that now exist by way of land claims agreements or may be so acquired.

35. (1) The existing aboriginal and treaty rights of the aboriginal peoples of Canada are hereby recognized and affirmed.

(2) In this Act, "aboriginal peoples of Canada" includes the Indian, Inuit and Métis peoples of Canada.

(3) For greater certainty, in subsection (1) "treaty rights" includes rights that now exist by way of land claims agreements or may be so acquired.

(4) Notwithstanding any other provision of this Act, the aboriginal and treaty rights referred to in subsection (1) are guaranteed equally to male and female persons.

Another section, s. 37, provided for a constitutional conference on Aboriginal matters; when it was not deemed a success, three more meetings were provided for in the constitution. However, these were also unsuccessful from the standpoint of the Aboriginals and they turned their collective attention to the larger constitutional reform process, which began in 1987. The Meech Lake Accord, a clear example of the "government" agenda that executive federalism has a tendency to generate, largely ignored Aboriginal concerns. The Charlottetown Accord of 1992, however, was formulated with the Aboriginals acting as equal partners on the Aboriginal sections (after much pressure) and provided for recognition of inherent self-government with details to be worked out between federal, provincial, and Aboriginal representatives. This Accord, like the one before it, contained a multiplicity of proposed constitutional amendments and changes. It was defeated in a national referendum in October of 1992.

Notes

1. Canada, Royal Commission on Aboriginal Peoples, *The Right of Aboriginal Self-Government and the Constitution: A Commentary* (Ottawa, February 13, 1992), p. 16.

2. Bruce Clark, *Native Liberty, Crown Sovereignty: The Existing Aboriginal Right of Self-Government in Canada* (Montreal and Kingston: McGill-Queen's University Press, 1990), pp. 6-7.

3. The sixth nation joined after contact.

4. Wendell H. Oswalt, *This Land Was Theirs: A Study of the North American Indian* (New York: John Wiley and Sons, 1966), p. 337, as quoted in Michael D. Mason, "Canadian and United States Approaches to Indian Sovereignty," *Osgoode Hall Law Journal,* 21 (1983), p. 425.

5. *Re Eskimos* [1939] SCR 104.

6. H.B. Hawthorn, ed., *A Survey of the Contemporary Indians of Canada: A Report on Economic, Political, Educational Needs and Policies* (Ottawa: Queen's Printer, 1966).

7. *Ibid.,* p. i.

8. *Calder v. British Columbia* [1973] SCR 313.

9. Douglas Saunders, "Pre-Existing Rights: The Aboriginal Peoples of Canada," in Gerald-A. Beaudoin and Ed Ratushny, eds., *The Canadian Charter of Rights and Freedoms,* second edition (Toronto: Carswell, 1989), p. 717.

Chapter 1

Arguments for the Inherent Right of Self-Government

The inherent right of Aboriginal self-government was, is, and ever shall be. Those who oppose it betray a regrettable lack of sophistication in matters constitutional, philosophical, historical, pragmatic, and financial. The time has come for Canadians to rectify one of the most glaring injustices in our national life.

Constitutional Arguments

Constitutionally, there can be little doubt that an Aboriginal right of self-government exists at present and in fact has always existed. When the question of self-government is approached in this manner, it appears less threatening. It is merely a matter of arranging mechanisms to accommodate what is already a firm constitutional responsibility.

The Development of Aboriginal Law

One way of dealing with the inherency question is to review the development of Aboriginal law in a chronological manner. This leaves us with a comprehensive review that stresses the reinforcing nature of successive legal landmarks. The contemporary streams in international law have rather long historical tributaries. Contemporary writers are now making reference to legal concepts in Aboriginal law that stretch back millennia. Basing land title on continuous use and possession was an element of natural law in Roman times, a part of the Justinian Code, and an important concept in feudalism and common law.[1] Legal historians who are inspired by the work of the monk Bartolome de Las Casas (1484-1566) remind us that his theories about the non-extinction of the sovereignty of the Amerindians were not explicitly repudiated by the Spanish Court. His contention was that the interpretation by Spain and Portugal of the papal bulls of 1493, as licence to have dominion over the New World, was not justified. Instead, Las Casas urged that dominion over the Natives was permissible only by virtue of their willing consent.[2]

United States law recognizes and assigns a distinct significance to the pre-contact Aboriginal practices. Chief Justice John Marshall in *Worcester v. Georgia* (1832) established the foundation for a domestic common law of Aboriginal self-government. What is particularly interesting is his description of the interaction between Europeans and Indians:

> America, separated from Europe by a wide ocean, was inhabited by a distinct people divided into separate nations, independent of each other and of the rest of the world, having institutions of their own, and governing themselves by their own laws. It is difficult to comprehend the proposition, that the inhabitants of either quarter of the globe could have rightful original claims of dominion over the inhabitants of the other, or over the lands they occupied; or that the discovery of either by the other should give the discoverer rights in the country discovered, which annulled the pre-existing rights of its ancient possessors.[3]

Partly from the logic of the case (and others), U.S. Aboriginal groupings came to be referred to as "domestic dependent nations" enjoying status as political entities with jurisdiction to govern their own internal affairs.[4] The state retained ultimate sovereignty over the land, but the Indians were to enjoy possession (use) of lands that they occupied, which in turn implied a measure of tribal sovereignty in internal and tax matters and some immunity from federal and state law.

In the Canadian context, the right in common law to continued self-governance was bypassed by domestic legislation. However, there is little dispute with the fact that successive governments have agreed that existing patterns of politics and social life could not be disrupted with impunity. Just what level of protection was to be accorded to them was a matter for instruments other than common law, like the Royal Proclamation of 1763. The point is that British North America was never treated as an "empty land" over which settlers had pure and unfettered jurisdiction. Some degree of respect for the original inhabitants was due. This approach is in keeping with contemporary thought in international law as well.

The Royal Proclamation of 1763 is an historical constitutional landmark of particular significance. The Royal Proclamation was an exercise of the King's *prerogative power,* which established the first constitutional framework for the newly conquered British territories in North America and set the pattern for the imperial approach to Indian affairs. This approach granted the Indians the right to occupy their lands already inhabited and prohibited non-Natives from occupying lands that had not been properly ceded to the imperial authorities. The specific wording of the Proclamation was indicative of a relatively cautious approach by Britain, which ultimately proved advantageous to the Aboriginal population:

> the several Nations or Tribes of Indians . . . should not be molested or disturbed in the Possession of such Parts of Our Dominions and Territories as, not having been ceded to or purchased by Us, are reserved to them, or any of them, as their Hunting Grounds . . . but that, if at any Time any of the Said Indians should be inclined to dispose of the said Lands, the same shall be Purchased only for Us, in our Name, at some public Meeting or Assembly of the said Indians, to be

held for that Purpose by the Governor or Commander in Chief of our Colony respectively within which they shall lie.[5]

Bruce Clark has argued that "by not molesting or disturbing these political entities [Indian nations], one necessarily leaves them in a self-governing condition."[6] The legal protection of tribal land entailed the legal protection of tribal sovereignty. The Royal Proclamation was never repealed. Neither were the *constitutional common law* precedents favourable to the concept of inherency. These established that only Parliament could have subsequently derogated from Aboriginal rights, which, with the exceptions of crimes and offences legislation, it did not; that colonial governments could not do this either unless mandated to do so by "great seal instruments" constituting the colonial governments, which did not happen; and that Aboriginal peoples had rights in the pre-Confederation era that subsequently continued after Confederation. In addition, in 1989 the Supreme Court recognized that "the law of Aboriginal title is federal [constitutional] common law and may well be entrenched in the constitution by virtue of ss. 35 and 52."[7]

As well, in statutes of the British Parliament, there were multiple cases of continuance of the principles established in prerogative law. "Most important, these statutes also constituted the powers of the federal and provincial governments, such that it is integral to those powers that they were inceptively counterbalanced by the Aboriginal right implicitly affirmed in the same legislative instruments."[8] The federal and provincial governments are not sovereign governments but are subordinate to the constitution, able to exercise powers delegated to them in the constitution. The constitution entrenches Aboriginal rights, including inherency, that are changeable not by governments acting alone but in concert under the appropriate amending procedure.

Where the Royal Proclamation and more than two centuries of statute and case law established a strong cumulative precedence for the inherent right of self-government, the Constitution Act, 1982, stands as a formidable historical landmark in the long march toward full recognition of inherency. The principal section of the Constitution Act of importance here is s. 35(1), which recognizes existing Aboriginal and treaty rights in Canada. Section 35(1) provides a few avenues along which inherency might travel. Some legal scholars have argued that Aboriginal self-government is included within the meaning of "aboriginal rights" and that this will one day be recognized judicially. Alternatively, "treaty rights" might be interpreted to include the right of inherency. Whatever the arrangement, the constitution clearly states that these rights are beyond the reach of the s. 1 "limitations clause," and therefore Parliament and the courts cannot justify weakening them by balancing them against the civil liberties of other Canadians.

The Royal Commission on Aboriginal Peoples views section 35 as an important element in a long chain of constitutional developments affecting Aboriginals, but not the determining one. Its discussion paper on constitutional matters emphasized that the inherent right of self-government has a firm basis in existing Canadian law, even after the defeat of the Charlottetown Accord and its inherency clauses. It demonstrated that Canadian law was not the only basis for inherency.[9] Its original foundation was the autonomous status of Aboriginal nations at the time of contact; treaties were signed on the tacit premise that Aboriginals enjoyed internal self-government; and there developed a common-law doctrine of Aboriginal rights that drew upon the practices and conceptions of all parties, both European and Aboriginal, over the course of contact.[10] In spite of these important qualifications, section 35 signifies an important confirmation of inherency. It does several things, according to the Royal Commission:[11]

- It has far-reaching structural significance, confirming historically defined and distinct constitutional entities that enjoy collective political rights not dependent on racial characteristics.
- By entrenching Aboriginal and treaty rights in the constitution [s. 35(1)], it provides substantial immunity from federal and provincial legislation, meaning that Aboriginal governments will not be presumed subordinate to other governments in the exercise of these rights. Neither, however, will they be presumed supreme. In cases where external laws and Aboriginal laws conflict, Aboriginal laws will *generally* prevail, except in cases where courts establish a transcending constitutional standard favouring external legislation.

- It recognizes the concurrent (overlapping yet independent) nature of federal and potential Aboriginal legislative powers in respect to s. 91(24) matters in the Constitution Act, 1867. Sections 91(24) of the 1867 Act and 35(1) of the 1982 Act are held to have essentially equivalent scope.
- It provides for the prospective (future) application of the phrase "existing . . . treaty rights" in section 35(1). This is the result of reading subsections (1) and (3) of section 35 together, with special attention to the words "for greater certainty" in 35(3). Therefore, land claims settlements are not the exception, but an example of the future-oriented nature of the section. Treaties concluded *after* 1982 will be covered and entrenched.

The Significance of Treaties

Treaties and the *treaty process* are significant to understanding inherency, since "treaties serve as the only definitions of Indian-White relationships acquiesced to by Indians."[12] They are also important because they span a lengthy period – from the conquest of various Indian nations right up to the present time. They formed a large part of the conceptual framework of the Aboriginal sections of the Charlottetown Accord of 1992.

There were various types of treaties. The earliest colonial treaties in North America involved military alliances, trading arrangements, and peace and friendship (non-aggression) agreements. (In the peace and friendship agreements, the parties made pledges of mutual aid or neutrality in conflicts, while deeming Indian hunting, fishing, and trapping rights to be protected.[13]) The later treaties typically dealt with land cession or extinguishment of land entitlement. Although most of the discussion of treaties here relates to the land cession treaties, the earlier peace and friendship agreements are important because they offer strong evidence of the acknowledgement of the self-governing nature of Aboriginal groups and consequently have some legal relevance today.[14]

The treaty process itself is suggestive of, but not definitive of, inherency. As Nakatsuru says, in Canada the courts have not appreciated the bilateral nature of the treaty-making process, tending to see it as largely an exercise in contractual agreement. However, "the American approach, which accepts the international character of these [treaty] documents, would seem to indicate that Indian treaties do affirm a right to Indian Government."[15] It is thus a matter of "judicial attitude" toward the process that matters.

In addition, the treaty process implied the continuation of traditional Aboriginal leadership and, therefore, of Aboriginal self-government. "The treaties do not indicate either Crown or Indian intent that Indian powers of self-government should be surrendered to the Crown," says Mason. Even chief Crown negotiators like Alexander Morris, who saw a mission to "civilize" Indians as an implicit mission of the treaties, never suggested that treaties meant the end of self-government.[16] Whyte notes that there was no express surrender of Indian self-government by the treaties:

> There is in the form of the treaties (the bands were represented by chiefs and headmen chosen by the Indians 'in open council') and in the very act of treaty-making (which implies the existence of a separate people capable of being responsible in their political character for any violations of their promises) some recognition of the Indian tribes as independent political entities.[17]

Of course, as both Mason and Whyte point out, the treaties could be interpreted broadly, as instruments having international overtones, or narrowly, as mainly contractual instruments creating obligations and duties for the Crown and the Indians. Certainly, the former approach would be more promising for the acceptance of inherency. However, even the latter theory could save inherency. Mason points out that self-government was not one of the matters explicitly bargained away in the "numbered treaties" (those after Confederation):

> The treaty language indicates that Indians did not give up the power to govern at least the farming reserves. It is doubtful that the Indians understood that the treaties incorporated Anglo-Canadian law by reference. They [the Indians] probably meant to keep power to punish Indian crimes which occurred on the reserve. Looking to the language of the agreement, the surrounding circumstances and the

understanding of the parties, Indians contracted to give up much less self-governing power than the Dominion assumed. [18]

The unfortunate aspect of the "contract" approach to inherency, however, was that once the treaties were adopted, the federal government, as the more powerful party to them, considered itself to have the right to abrogate their content and spirit.

Philosophical Arguments

If the constitutional case for inherency is interesting, then the philosophic case for it is imperative. Will Kymlicka offers a useful counter to the assumption that liberal theory is at its base incompatible with communitarian streams of thought. [19] Not only are the two reconcilable, but the synthesis of the two offers a compelling argument for inherent self-government. Little Bear, Boldt, and Long simply maintain that group rights are the pathway to self-government. Thomas Berger suggests, on the other hand, that tolerance may be the philosophic key to employ.

Kymlicka on Aboriginal Self-Government

Too often, says Will Kymlicka, liberal and communitarian thinkers have ignored the areas of commonality, with liberalism fearing that deviating from the principle of strict equality of individual rights would lead to differentiated classes of citizens, and communitarians confusing the protection of the community with the protection of a specific *character* of the community. In fact, "membership in a cultural structure is what enables individual freedom, what enables meaningful choices about how to lead one's life." [20]

The commonality starts when one realizes that the individual never acts in a context that is totally divorced from the community. There is an aspect of social formation to our interests; our interests are not set pre-socially, with society only to be used to pursue our own ends. The ability to lead a moral life depends on the ability constantly to question the appropriateness of one's goals and to do so on one's own initiative. The cultural community gives one the structure to survive the confusing variety of possibilities and resources at one's disposal, pointing out and sometimes obviating the dangers of their unregulated use. Restrictions on individual behaviour are desirable, as long as they are merely temporary restrictions that mitigate the shock of change in the character of a threatened culture and do not halt its ultimate progress to a fully liberal society.

Aboriginal self-government seems imperative once one takes such a perspective. Collective political rights are like a collective insurance scheme: the individual members covered do not have more resources at their control than other Canadians, but the community has a pre-emptive power to negate decisions that weaken the community's existence. Even if it fails in its protective task, the logic is similar. "To ensure that they could re-establish the community, Aboriginal people would need a legal status different from that envisaged in any non-political insurance model."[21]

Little Bear et al. *on Group Rights*

A defence of inherency does not only rely on the notion of balance between individualism and communitarianism. In the eyes of some Aboriginals, the philosophic case rests solely on group rights.

> Self-government is seen by Indians as necessary to preserve their philosophical uniqueness. They seek self-government so that they can develop their own institutions and shape laws to reflect their traditional cultural values. They do not want merely a European-Western model of government that is run by Indians; rather, they want an Indian government that operates in accordance with traditional principles and customs, one that rests on a spiritual base and emphasizes group, not individual, rights.[22]

Moreover, the group that is to achieve this inherent right of self-government is to do so on the basis of *equality*. Indian people demand political, economic, and socio-cultural equality with the rest of Canadian society.[23] This view is not necessarily opposed to that of Kymlicka; the difference is one of perspective and elaboration of analysis.

Chartrand on Legitimacy

Paul L.A.H. Chartrand offers arguments focusing on political legitimacy and Aboriginal government.[24] Past attempts at governance have lacked legitimacy because of two erroneous assumptions about Aboriginals: (1) that they constitute a disadvantaged racial minority; and (2) that commitment to the liberal concept of individual equality demands equal treatment of all Canadians regardless of race. These two assumptions have had hurtful results. Viewed as racial entities and not the "nations" or distinct political communities that they are, both in legal doctrine and self-concept, Aboriginal groups were denied participation in the constitutional creation of Canada. Liberal equality has historically valued a standard form of citizenship, considering separate political systems likely to lead to denial of the rule of law, or separate and unequal status, or both.

These assumptions, Chartrand insists, must be discarded. The reasons are numerous. For one thing, section 35.1 of the Constitution Act, 1982, recognizes a third set of constitutional actors; and it is obviously impractical to base Aboriginal identity on biological or racial characteristics, since scientists would end up deciding constitutional status. For another, "separate status" is not the desired aim of Aboriginal leaders; the aim is merely the maintenance of "unique ways of organizing society and promoting human values."[25]

As well, Aboriginal people contest the legal and political legitimacy of the Canadian constitution. Full political participation demands both negotiation and formal agreement by Aboriginals as constitutionally recognized peoples. This has been lacking, as indicated by the failure of the "section 37 conferences" of the 1980s.[26] The "other" side to legitimacy – other than in Canadian institutions, that is – is that Aboriginal representation must rest on traditional bases of consensual, community-based decision-making, not on the divisive strategy of "state recognition" of group and issues.

Berger on Tolerance

A final philosophic argument is based simply on the notion of tolerance. Although addressing the matter of inherency only tangentially, Thomas Berger noted that attempts to accommodate minorities in Canada are important and relevant to the contemporary world. They show that the races, cultures, and religions that coexist within a federal state should, by extension, be able to coexist at the international level.[27] In a later article Berger saw the inherency right as simply the logical culmination of entrenching Aboriginal and treaty rights in the constitution in 1982.[28]

Historical Arguments

The historical arguments that surround the inherency question are not meant to be considered in isolation from but complementary to the preceding ones. They involve the original inhabitants thesis and the record of international law.

The Original Inhabitants Thesis

The original inhabitants thesis, as partial a defence as it is, still strikes a resonant chord with reasonable observers. Because of their prior occupation of the land, Aboriginal governments would have the power to exclude various rights of other actors, much in the same way that contemporary states have the power and international recognition to enforce exclusionary policies on other states. Saunders offers one version of it:

> Aboriginal rights to land flow from the prior occupation of Canada by Aboriginal populations. They are, logically, part of the package of rights which the tribes had before European colonization. A full recognition of Aboriginal rights would involve (a) the recognition of Aboriginal self-government, (b) the recognition of customary Aboriginal law, (c) the recognition of Aboriginal land rights, and (d) the recognition of land-based rights, such as those of hunting, fishing and trapping.[29]

The Federation of Saskatchewan Indians has supported the historical primacy/self-government thesis by noting that before contact Indians inhabited North America as distinct nations that recognized each other as such. It has stated that "in asserting their political rights on the basis of their historical primacy as the Aboriginal peoples of the land, Indians of today are doing no more than is contained in the notion of nations as they have always understood it and as it is recognized in international law."[30]

Of course, the courts and governments have not seen the matter of Aboriginal rights in this fashion and have, in fact, tended to concentrate on the matters of land rights and hunting, fishing, and trapping rights. Section 35 jurisprudence may, however, come to include self-government and customary law implications. Since not all land in Canada was occupied by Aboriginals, or at least some of it was occupied for a relatively short time before contact, the original inhabitants thesis seems destined to serve primarily as a political justification rather than as an element of constitutional law.

The Record of International Law

International law offers aid to the inherency thesis in an indirect but effective way. Lyon indicates the relevance of the international community:

> [The] right of self-determination goes beyond s. 35 of the Constitution Act, 1982. . . . It is founded ultimately in the UN General Assembly's 1960 Declaration on the Granting of Independence to Colonial Countries and Peoples. That document denies the use of inadequacy of preparedness as a pretext for delaying independence and calls on all states to observe the Declaration on the basis of respect for the sovereign rights of all peoples and their territorial integrity. [31]

Since it is so generally stated, this presumably refers to a political theme rather than a legal one, but it is obviously a valid point.

Anderson goes further. She argues that Canada is accountable for certain matters under international law even though it has not explicitly ratified international documents to that effect. [32] Human rights have both an *erga omnes* and a *jus cogens* effect. The first refers to a human right becoming part of customary international law and therefore being unimpeachable by government. The latter refers to a principle of international law so fundamental to a people that any subsequent relinquishment of it has no effect and no treaties can extinguish it. Anderson applies international law to investigate the broad rights of Saskatchewan Indians, in particular, their right to self-determination. This right is said to depend on such international milestones as the United Nations Charter, Articles 1(2), 55, 73, and 74, which delineate the equal rights and self-determination of peoples; the Declaration of the Granting of Independence to Colonial Countries adopted by the UN General Assembly in 1960; and the Montevideo Convention of 1933,

Article 1 of which formulated the basic tests of statehood. "The principle of self-determination," Anderson points out, "has made a full transition from a political concept to a legal right in conventional and customary international law." [33]

Menno Boldt makes perhaps the most compelling case flowing from international sources, at the same time acknowledging the practical difficulties involved. [34] He stops short of calling for the adoption of self-government, relying instead on the concept of "peoples' rights" enshrined in the UN Charter of Rights (Article 55) and the covenants inspired by it. However, much of his analysis is applicable to the self-government question.

For example, the International Covenant on Human Rights, to which Canada is a signatory, commits Canada to the principle that "all peoples have the right of self-determination [and to] freely determine their political status." Canada has unfortunately made use of the lack of legal precision in the term "peoples" to avoid recognizing the self-determination of its own indigenous people. However, by the historic, cultural, legal, political, and humanitarian standards implicit in the UN Charter, Canadian Natives must have among the strongest claims in the world to identity as peoples. Continued possession of ancestral lands, collective expression of cultural identities, the recognition of special status implicit in the Royal Proclamation and subsequent instruments, special laws and administrative arrangements in the Canadian state, and need to preserve unique and threatened world cultures are just some of the standards that Boldt cites to support the peoplehood thesis. [35]

Pragmatic Arguments

Principles and history aside, simple pragmatism dictates that rapid and significant advances be made on the Aboriginal dossier. First of all, the process of expanding the autonomy of Native peoples is developing a powerful and irreversible logic of its own. Next, civil order requires a solution to the problem of the legal place of Canada's First Nations. A third point is simply that constitutional negotiations have demonstrated that Aboriginal governments are within grasp, that the reservoir of good will is there in Canada to make them work.

The Irreversible Logic of Aboriginal Autonomy

Current drives toward Aboriginal autonomy are in all likelihood irreversible, and it is unthinkable of doing other than bringing them to their logical conclusion. The report of the Penner Special Committee of the Canadian House of Commons suggested in 1983 that Indian governments may have implicit and unrecognized legislative powers and recognized that the surest way to effect permanent change in the relationship between Natives and the federal government was a constitutional amendment entrenching First Nation governments as a "distinct order of government in Canada, with their jurisdiction defined."[36] The Coolican Report of 1985 was instrumental in changing the federal government's approach to self-government in the context of land claims settlements to one of flexibility and wider acceptance of Aboriginal resource management.[37] From its creation in 1966 onward, but in an accelerated process under the Mulroney government, the Department of Indian Affairs and Northern Development (DIAND) has increasingly used *devolution* in its policy design and administration responsibilities with band councils. About 70 per cent of DIAND's $2.5 billion budget is administered by band councils,[38] and government officials have strongly hinted that the long-term intent of the government is to turn the department into an intergovernmental agency or one that specializes in fiscal transfers to self-governing bodies.

Moreover, there are currently in operation some examples of self-government, albeit limited in nature, that escape from the strictures of the Indian Act. These negotiated arrangements show the willingness of federal and provincial governments to grant self-government in fact even when they may not be willing to accept it in constitutional theory. The Cree-Naskapi (of Quebec) Act, 1984, was federal legislation that replaced Indian Act band council governance patterns with that of band corporations enjoying a heightened measure of self-management. The Sechelt Indian Band Self-Government Act, 1986, established what has come to be known as a modern "municipal" model of negotiated self-government. Analogous measures are currently being negotiated across Canada by federal and Aboriginal representatives.

Together, these developments represent a cumulative drive toward greater autonomy for Aboriginals. They are graphic evidence that the old pattern of band governance is on the way out. The Aboriginal negotiators in 1992 successfully moved the discussion far beyond the plane of contingency. Any government in the future that believes it can reverse the trend to inherency might as well command the sea to be still.

Civil Order

Civil order ultimately requires a solution to the inherency question. Native leaders caution that community antagonisms may spill over if negotiated settlements of the inherency question are not forthcoming. The Oka crisis in 1990 stemmed in large part from the non-recognition of Mohawk notions of sovereignty deriving from membership in the Six Nations Confederacy. As Bruce Clark put it:

> By purporting to override the Indians' claim to self-government, Quebec and now the Federal government have exceeded their constitutional jurisdictions.
>
> Given the appropriate legislation and legal precedents, it can be argued that the legalities of the Oka situation are transformed. From a constitutional law perspective, the Indians have been defending a legitimate jurisdiction, and the Quebec police and the Canadian army have illegally been enforcing their governments' usurpation of that jurisdiction.
>
> To that extent, Quebec and Canada have been lawbreakers. They have broken the social compact that constitutes the first and founding principle of Canadian constitutional law.[39]

Public Opinion

The most compelling argument from the standpoint of the policy-makers should be that public opinion has never been as supportive of Native self-determination as it is today. The role played by the Native Manitoba legislator Elijah Harper in the demise of the unpopular Meech Lake Accord provoked an outpouring of good will from ordinary Canadians toward the needs of the First Nations. Poll results showed a marked support for Aboriginal self-government in particular. Even in the aftermath of the failure of the

Charlottetown Accord, which promised a form of inherency, Grand Chief Ovide Mercredi of the Assembly of First Nations said Canadians had stressed to him that their opposition to the package had been based on other considerations.

A First Nations Province?

One of the ideas currently being discussed by observers sympathetic to the idea of Aboriginal inherency is that of establishing a First Peoples Province or a First Nations Province (FNP).[40] This would be a territorially dispersed province enjoying the normal accoutrements of a Canadian province: a single legislature, control over relevant electoral law, the capability of electing MPs from multi-reserve constituencies, and a full range of provincial regulatory and fiscal powers. Presumably, this new province would come into being by amendment as provided for in the Constitution Act, 1982. This would be one method of achieving significant (inherent?) sovereignty for Aboriginals, and it would also respond to the needs of non-Aboriginal Canadians for familiar landmarks in the reform process.

David J. Elkins says that a dispersed First Nations Province would be both a pragmatic and a popular innovation in Canada.[41] An Aboriginal premier could serve effectively in smoothing over intergovernmental or interracial tensions. The addition of one more province of medium size – 4 to 5 per cent of the population of Canada – would not upset the amending process very markedly. Provinces would become more internally homogeneous with the shifting of Aboriginals to their own province (although they would not necessarily be compelled to fall under its jurisdiction), making the reaching of provincial consensus on constitutional matters easier.[42]

The Several Roads To Inherency

Regardless of the fate of the "First Nations Province" idea, there remain several workable alternative methods of implementing inherency. Indeed, a discussion paper of the Royal Commission on Aboriginal Peoples reminds Canadians that since self-government means different things to different Aboriginal groups, there can be a variety of patterns or models employed. The guiding principles and techniques that the Commission offers to assist implementation of inherency seem pragmatic enough.[43] The first is group initiatives. Since external efforts at implementation would reflect a continuing loss of control, even if well-intentioned, communities should determine their own approach. Under s. 35(1) a group could assume control over "core areas" (matters central to the welfare of the community but not involving spillovers to other communities, regions, or the national government) while leaving "non-core" areas to intergovernmental negotiations. Care would be taken to avoid legal vacuums.

Treaties and other agreements are the second avenue to implement inherency. Self-government "treaties," honouring the traditional ways of Crown-Aboriginal interaction, could apply on either a general or particular basis. Political accords (like the Charlottetown Accord) could outline framework agreements committing the partners at a moral and political level, if not at a legally enforceable constitutional level.

The last avenue is federal government action to amend or remove legislation restricting self-government. Such legislation might also create mechanisms for negotiation of self-government or transition to self-government. The legislation would of course be premised on an inherent, not delegated, right.[44]

Financial Arguments

Two financial arguments serve to conclude the case for the inherent right of self-government. Simply, the costs of *not* introducing inherency are likely to be astronomical; and the costs of introducing it are overestimated.

Reasonable Costs

To cast the idea of self-government in terms of a First Nations Province, as Elkins does, allows one to see the costs of inherency in perspective. Since the land on which the roughly 2,000 reserves in ten provinces are situated do not actually belong to the provinces, in effect the provinces would not suffer any loss of territory. They may in fact be compelled to transfer territory through land claims settlements, but this they would have to do whether or not an FNP existed. A First Nations Province would initially, but not indefinitely, be classified as a "have-not province," since the size of current land claims settlements imply that some parts of the province would be quite well off; in fact, some internal redistribution may serve the role currently played by equalization payments.[45]

The aforementioned forms of devolved federal government programming also have fiscal implications. Boldt, although he does not approve of the strategy, notes that the federal government, under the guise of what it calls "self-government," is "devolving to band/tribal councils responsibility for services and programs on reserves under budget caps. The underlying plan is to make the same amount of money go further by requiring band/tribal councils to be more restrained, judicious, and efficient in their spending."[46] The process of fiscal discipline already begun could carry over to a new type of self-government regime. Certainly the management training that has begun is a necessary first step. Of course, the training alone is insufficient. The reneging on developmental assistance to Aboriginals that has taken place must be reversed, and indigenous politicians in a self-governing system are necessary for this to work.

The Costs of Inaction

The costs of inaction must also be factored in, and related in a humane way to the other conceptual problems in the matter of Aboriginal governance. Adrian Tanner offers a simple course in logic in regard to pragmatic and financial arguments:

> Either Aboriginal people are to be governed under a regime that takes account of their distinctive cultures, or they are to be placed under the laws and programs of application to everyone. Since Aboriginal people are a minority in Canada, if you decide it is best for them to have a separate system, it has to be one that is consciously provided for. This can be done in one of two ways: either it is designed and run for them by others, or they design and run it themselves. The above gives three logical possibilities: 1. Aboriginal people are governed by the same system as the majority; 2. a special

system designed and controlled by the majority; 3. a system they design and run themselves. In Canada we have already tried both 1. and 2.[47]

A system designed and run by Natives has never been tried in Canadian history; however, it is reasonable to consider it the precondition to independence and self-sufficiency.

Aboriginal people in Canada, who have for a couple of centuries had either system 1 or 2, are demonstrably disadvantaged, socially and economically. People living under either type of administration are caught in cycles of poverty and dependency and have serious social breakdown. Moreover, this condition appears to be self-perpetuating. Any analysis I am aware of which tries to account for this phenomenon of social breakdown points to the undermining of culture and traditions, government dependency and a resulting lack of self-respect. It seems to me that inherent (i.e. not provided as a gift, but as a right) self-governing powers are the precise conditions which could avoid these problems, by providing the conditions for people to take responsibility for themselves.[48]

The costs of inaction are the repetition of the past; and, as Santayana reminds us in his famous aphorism, those who do not remember the past are doomed to relive it.

The inherent right is an unextinguished right. It has survived contact, conquest, and Confederation. Its roots are grounded in Aboriginal history and spirituality and are strengthened by treaties, Canadian constitutionalism, and international law. Moreover, recognition of inherency is a pragmatic measure, and will end over a century of undemocratic and illegitimate governance.

Notes

1. Olive P. Dickason, "Concepts of Sovereignty at the Time of the First Contacts," in L.C. Green and Olive P. Dickason, eds., *The Law of Nations and the New World* (Edmonton:University of Alberta Press, 1989), p. 249.
2. *Ibid.*, p. 205. There were four relevant papal bulls issued in 1493. The most significant was that of May 4, 1493.
3. 6 Peters 515 (1832).

48   *Canadian Political Debates*

4. Bruce Clark, *Native Liberty, Crown Sovereignty: The Existing Aboriginal Right of Self-Government in Canada* (Montreal: McGill-Queen's University Press, 1990), p. 16.

5. As quoted *ibid.*, pp. 37-38.

6. *Ibid.*, p. 9. Clark notes a number of possible bases for inherency: domestic common law, constitutional common law, prerogative legislation, and statute law. See especially *ibid.*, pp. 11-12, 58.

7. Clark quotes *Wewayakum Indian Band v. Canada* (1989), 92 NR 241; [1989] 1 SCR 332. Sub nom *Roberts v. Canada.*

8. Clark, *Native Liberty, Crown Sovereignty*, pp. 84-85.

9. Canada, Royal Commission on Aboriginal Peoples, *Partners in Confederation: Aboriginal Peoples, Self-Government and the Constitution* (Ottawa: Minister of Supply and Services, 1993). It emphasized that the inherent right exists not only by virtue of Canadian law, but also by reference to international law, natural law, treaties, and the laws, constitutions, and spiritual beliefs of particular Aboriginal groups.

10. *Ibid.*, pp. 20, 40-41.

11. *Ibid.*, pp. 29-30, 35-36, 38-39, 46.

12. Michael D. Mason, "Canadian and United States Approaches to Indian Sovereignty," *Osgoode Hall Law Journal*, 21 (1983), p. 434.

13. James S. Frideres, *Native Peoples in Canada: Contemporary Conflicts*, third edition (Scarborough, Ont.: Prentice-Hall, 1988), p. 86.

14. My thanks to anthropologist Adrian Tanner of Memorial University for highlighting this point.

15. Shaun Nakatsuru, "A Constitutional Right of Indian Self-Government," *University of Toronto Faculty of Law Review*, 43 (1972), pp. 72-99.

16. Mason, "Canadian and United States Approaches," p. 426.

17. John D. Whyte, "Indian Self-Government: A Legal Analysis," in Leroy Little Bear, Menno Boldt, and J. Anthony Long, *Pathways to Self-Determination: Canadian Indians and the Canadian State* (Toronto: University of Toronto Press, 1984), p. 107.

18. Mason, "Canadian and United States Approaches," p. 436.

19. Will Kymlicka, *Liberalism, Community and Culture* (Oxford: Clarendon Press, 1989).

20. *Ibid.*, p. 208.

21. *Ibid.*, p. 194.

22. Little Bear, Boldt, and Long, eds., *Pathways to Self-Determination*, p. xvi.

23. *Ibid.,* pp. xvi-xvii.
24. Paul L.A.H. Chartrand, "Aboriginal Self-Government: The Two Sides of Legitimacy," in Susan D. Phillips, ed., *How Ottawa Decides 1993-1994: A More Democratic Canada?* (Ottawa: Carleton University Press, 1993).
25. *Ibid.,* p. 239.
26. *Ibid.,* pp. 240-41.
27. Thomas Berger, "Towards a Regime of Tolerance," in Stephen Brooks, ed., *Political Thought in Canada* (Toronto: Irwin Publishing, 1984).
28. Thomas Berger, "Voting Yes and making a life for the country," *Globe and Mail,* October 15, 1992, p. A31.
29. Douglas Saunders, "The Rights of the Aboriginal Peoples of Canada," *Canadian Bar Review,* 61 (1983), pp. 328-29.
30. The 1980 draft statement of the Federation of Saskatchewan Indians, as quoted in Whyte, "Indian Self-Government," p. 103.
31. Noel Lyon, *Aboriginal Self-Government: Rights of Citizenship and Access to Governmental Services,* Background Paper No. 1, Aboriginal Peoples and Constitutional Reform Series (Kingston, Ont.: Queen's University Institute of Intergovernmental Relations, 1984), p. 9.
32. Ellen Anderson, "The Saskatchewan Indians and Canada's New Constitution," *Journal of International Affairs,* 36 (1982), pp. 125-48.
33. *Ibid.,* p. 130.
34. Menno Boldt, *Surviving As Indians: The Challenge of Self-Government* (Toronto: University of Toronto Press, 1993).
35. *Ibid.,* pp. 47-52.
36. Canada, House of Commons, Special Committee on Indian Self-Government, *Indian Self-Government in Canada,* Second Report to the House, October 20, 1983, pp. 43-44.
37. Murray Coolican, *Living Treaties: Lasting Agreements,* Report of the Task Force to Review Comprehensive Land Claims Policy (Ottawa: DIAND, 1985).
38. Augie Fleuras and Jean Leonard Elliott, *The Nations Within: Aboriginal-State Relations in Canada, the United States and New Zealand* (Toronto: Oxford University Press, 1992), p. 80.
39. Bruce Clark, "Indian heroes, government outlaws," *Globe and Mail,* September 26, 1990.
40. The idea appears to have originated in an article by Thomas Courchene in 1990. Thomas Courchene, "How about giving natives a province of their own?" *Globe and Mail,* October 18, 1990. For a more

detailed exposition, see Thomas Courchene and Lisa M. Powell, *A First Nations Province* (Kingston, Ont.: Queen's University Institute of Intergovernmental Relations, 1992).

41. David J. Elkins, "Aboriginals and the Future of Canada," in Douglas Brown, ed., *Aboriginal Governments and Power Sharing in Canada* (Kingston, Ont.: Queen's University Institute of Intergovernmental Relations, 1992).

42. *Ibid.*, pp. 59-62.

43. Royal Commission on Aboriginal Peoples, *Partners in Confederation,* pp. 41-48.

44. *Ibid.*, p. 48.

45. Elkins, "Aboriginals and the Future of Canada."

46. Boldt, *Surviving As Indians,* p. 227.

47. Adrian Tanner, correspondence with the author, June 7, 1993.

48. *Ibid.*

Chapter 2

Arguments against the Inherent Right of Self-Government

There is no inherent right of Aboriginal self-government in Canada today. Whatever self-government that existed before contact has been effectively extinguished. The constitutional grounds for it simply do not exist. Moreover, the philosophical and historical implications that would flow from it would be extremely regressive. It is an unworkable and expensive idea.

Constitutional Arguments

Although the arguments proposed by the proponents for inherency are in tune with today's political culture, they are not convincing from the more rigorous perspective of constitutional law. The proponents of inherency indeed tend to shade their constitutional points with cultural overtones that have little place in constitutional argumentation.

The Development of Aboriginal Law

The landmarks of constitutional development have the opposite significance to that suggested by the proponents. This is apparent when one looks at pre-contact Aboriginal government, the Royal Proclamation of 1763, Canadian legislation pertaining to Aboriginals, and the Constitution Act, 1982.

The Aboriginals of pre-contact America did in fact enjoy self-government in the fullest measure of the term, yet it is problematic to suggest that pre-contact sovereignty had implications for the post-contact era. The major counter to the argument of pre-contact significance of Aboriginal sovereignty is the *principle of intertemporal law*. This is a central tenet of contemporary international law, which was given its major enunciation in international matters in the *Island of Las Palmas Case* of 1928, an international arbitration award.[1] It specifies that the validity of claims in law is to be determined by the rules of international law in force at the time that the act or right occurs initially, rather than by the retroactive effect of newly developing doctrines. The relevant law in effect at the time of the conquest of North America was of course the law of the European conquerors. This European law subsequently became the foundation of universal international law, so it is doubly important.

The basic tenets of international law at the time of contact have been ably outlined by Professor L.C. Green.[2] State practice, legal experts, and leading cases all coincided to bolster the Europeans' claim to lawful sovereignty over the New World they had conquered. The Papal Bull of May 4, 1493, and subsequent documents of international force made no mention of rights of possession by the original inhabitants of the New World. On the other hand, symbolic acts of possession, such as the erecting of crosses and the burying of coins, were considered to be essential acts in the assertion of sovereignty by the state actors of the time. French, English, Spanish, and Russian discoverers all performed them.[3] By these acts, therefore, rule passed to the monarch in whose name the settlement took place, providing that the lands had not previously been settled by nationals of another European monarch.[4]

The assertions of sovereignty, Green says, were bolstered by a number of doctrines put forward by Spanish, German, and French legal experts at the time of conquest. One such doctrine was that of *terra nullius,* unoccupied lands, which maintained that unoccupied territory could be acquired merely by occupation, as opposed to conquest or other measures. Original inhabitants, being outside of civilized society, did not possess rights of ownership. A second doctrine was that of the necessity to *spread the gospel,* and incidentally to engage in agriculture and trade, with the Natives obligated to acquiesce in these processes. The third doctrine, which in a sense cancelled out some of the more questionable aspects of the above two, was simply that of *positivism.* No matter what the exact source of title, whether by discovery, conquest, or colonization, and no matter how unjust it might have been initially, long and uninterrupted possession by one European nation pre-empted any lawful claim by another, based on general consent and the realization of mutual utility.[5]

In regard to delegated rights, and with reference to the import of such cases as *Worcester v. Georgia,* Green simply observes that "it should be remembered that, as the classicists pointed out, over a period of time even what had been wrongly established could eventually constitute a good title, especially in the absence of any strong opposition, which accords with the maxim *quieta non movere.*"[6] Along the same lines, Crawford explains that:

> Neither did the Canadian courts follow Marshall CJ's example in declaring tribes to be domestic dependent nations, or to have any of the attributes of sovereignty, however qualified. . . . While Indian structures of government remained, in the form of chiefs, council meetings and (in some cases at least) established constitutions, as a matter of historical fact there was no recognition of Indian tribes as a 'distinct political society separated from others' or as a separate state.[7]

Instead of admitting that there was a category of governmental rights internal to the Indian nations, of an original or unextinguished nature, Canadian law assumed from the start that whatever rights Indians enjoyed were delegated to them.

Thus, the Royal Proclamation of 1763 does not hold the same significance for opponents of inherency that it does for its proponents. Crawford gives a pithy description of the results of over two centuries of jurisprudence on the subject:

[The Royal Proclamation's] concern was not to confirm or establish these rights to self-government but rather to regulate the procedures for the cession of lands and trade with the Indians. Thus, notwithstanding the views of the Privy Council in the *St. Catherine's case,* the Royal Proclamation did not establish aboriginal rights on North America: it assumed them.[8]

Even if, as Nakatsuru has maintained, the Proclamation did signify the British intention to recognize Aboriginal governments, it "nowhere specifies in what ways or to what extent, apart from non-molestation of Indians in possession of their lands, the right to self-government is to be protected or guaranteed."[9] All the Royal Proclamation did, in short, was to regulate Indian-European interactions and protect the Indians from interference by settlers.

Green offers an even more detailed critique of the "Proclamation as Indian Charter" thesis. His points are many, and will therefore be presented in summary form.

1. The Proclamation was an internal Crown document, with no significance in international law.
2. The language of the Proclamation is plainly meant to regulate relationships between Indians and private individuals, and not to establish rights against the Crown on the part of the Indians.
3. The Proclamation was not a "charter" for the use of the Indians but a public policy decision based on "grace." Any one of three alternatives could have been used by the British to achieve ownership of Indian lands: the right of conquest; executive expropriation (although this was counter to common law, it was not impossible); and surrender by agreement. The last alternative was plainly the model for the Proclamation, and it was chosen for political reasons.
4. The Proclamation's insistence that lands that Indians wish to sell must first be offered to the Crown does not signify Indian title against the Crown. "In the light of the overall character of the Proclamation it is clear that this is really a reference to the common law right of English citizens holding lands not to be expropriated without compensation . . . ."

5. The reference in the introduction of the Proclamation to acquisitions in America secured by the Treaty of Paris (1763) meant that the British Crown secured *all* rights, including sovereignty, that France had possessed previously. Indians had no sovereign rights under French rule and did not have them under English rule; all they could possess were non-sovereign rights.

6. In English land law, the ownership of all land resides with the Crown, while all that a private subject can enjoy are rights or "title." That the lands "reserved" to Indians, in the terminology of the Proclamation, were not foreign (and hence under Crown authority) was to be seen in the "police power" provision of the Proclamation, which allowed colonial officials to seek fugitives from justice in the reserved lands without notifying the Indians.[10]

Canadian legislation pertaining to Aboriginals supports this limited view of the Royal Proclamation, and is indicative of such a restricted role for Aboriginals that it amounts to a negation of the self-government right. Successive Indian Acts have progressively limited the freedom of manoeuvrability of Indian bands. The federal minister is given an extremely wide range of powers; in contrast, band powers are reduced to less than those of a municipality in Canada. The paternalism of the Act is evident in its many provisions that treat Indians as incapable of protecting or fending for themselves, most especially in financial matters. A particularly significant modification to the Act came with the addition of section 88 in 1951, which allows for the application of provincial laws to Indian reserves, provided these laws are not inconsistent with any treaty or federal law or rule. "The effect of section 88 is to incorporate provincial laws by reference . . . [and] to reduce any enclaves of freedom or non-regulation which might have otherwise existed."[11] The general pattern of Indian Act legislation is thus inconsistent with claims of Aboriginal sovereignty. If it did exist in domestic common law, it would plainly have been reduced to insignificance.

Neither does the recognition of the "existing Aboriginal and treaty rights of the Aboriginal peoples of Canada" in section 35(1) of the Constitution Act, 1982, imply that the Aboriginal rights so mentioned include that of self-government. The operative word in this constitutional phrase is "existing," and from what has just been discussed, self-government certainly is not an existing right. Moreover, as Crawford has mentioned, "the reference in section 35(1) to aboriginal rights is clearly a reference to the common law rules which recognise certain rights of Indian and Inuit groups by reference to their status as self-governing communities before colonialization."[12] The courts have refused to recognize that these common-law rules extend to matters of self-government. Aboriginal rights are therefore to be found in jurisprudence relating to private law, rather than in the public law.

The Significance of Treaties

Contrary to the proponents of inherency, treaties are not supportive of self-government. This pertains for both aspects of the *treaty thesis*: that the process itself was indicative of a nation-to-nation relationship and that the contents of the treaties often revealed areas of non-interference by the British and Canadian governments.

A process is indicative of the status of one of the contracting powers only to the extent that the contents of the agreement arrived at by the process do not directly contradict the status. As Crawford points out, "the treaty provisions themselves being inconsistent with the plenary internal self-government which was the basis from which United States Indian tribes began, there seems to be no obvious starting point for determining the extent of any rights of autonomy or self-government."[13] As well, any claim to international status arising from the treaty process is doubtful, given that international treaties have no validity in Canadian law unless they are specifically incorporated by Canadian law. There has been no specific incorporation of any "international aspect" arising from the Canadian treaty process.

The contents of the treaties also betray a restrictive role for the Indians. Mason has pointed out, in defence of the treaties, that the numbered treaties' silence on the administration of farming lands indicated a retention of that aspect of sovereignty for Indians. He also observes that their injunction to the Indians to "obey and abide by the law" did not necessarily mean abiding by Anglo-Canadian law. At the very least it is not clear, even if Anglo-Canadian law were accepted, that it included the power to deal with crimes and disputes.[14] Mason's contentions are, of course, untenable. The language of the treaties does not give clear jurisdiction over land to Indians, let alone clarify that it relates to the concept of self-government. It is conceivable that the absence of mention in the treaties was simply meant to allow for traditional landholding patterns to continue; and in respect to law, it is clear that British law was to pertain, in the absence of any logical alternative.[15]

Philosophical Arguments

Strong philosophical arguments can be marshalled to counter the drive to inherency in Canada. They involve a reaction against "groupism" and "ghettoization." The philosophical stances of individualism and unhyphenated Canadianism are no longer in vogue, but this does not destroy their validity. One of the most compelling philosophical arguments against the concept of inherency is simply that it is in radical opposition to the liberal equality upon which our country is based. Inherency would have harmful impacts on both the Aboriginals themselves and on the larger Canadian society.

The Federal White Paper on Indian Policy

A now often ignored document – and if it is discussed, it is only to dismiss it – is the federal White Paper on Indian Policy of 1969. If people would actually take the trouble to read it, they would find a sincere case for integration of Aboriginals into the Canadian mainstream. Although the gist of the White Paper is that the Indian Act should be abolished to achieve this integration, its logic could be taken one step further, to the inherency question.

The argument is that the Indian Act has retarded the development of Aboriginal Canadians as citizens: rather than participating fully in the larger society, they have been shut out of it. The authoritarian and paternalistic role of the federal government in Indian life prevented Indians from developing their own communities and forging a relationship with the governments of provinces in which they live. The reserve system kept Indians out of the economic mainstream as well, in underdeveloped rural settings in the midst of a technological urban environment. The separation of Indian people and the lack of opportunities for intercultural exchanges have bred discrimination; discrimination breeds discrimination. Indian people have a fundamental right to full participation in Canadian society.

> To argue against this right is to argue *for* discrimination, isolation and separation. No Canadian should be excluded from participation in community life, and none should expect to withdraw and still enjoy the benefits that flow to those who participate. [16]

It is difficult to see how inherency would promote the broad participation of Aboriginals in Canadian life. Presumably the reserve would be an important foundation for the land base, and the question of rural/economic separateness would remain. Also, a largely ethnic-based political community does not appear to be conducive to intercultural exchange. Aboriginal governments would not allow for political participation in the affairs of provincial government, but instead for political battles with them on the intergovernmental front.

History-based Groupism

Inherency would also harm the larger society. Basically, inherency is a political theory founded on *group rights,* and it displays blindness to the individualism central to Western society. As Bryan Schwartz says, "there is an inherent crudeness in any political philosophy that makes the group a unit of ultimate importance." [17] Groups make comparisons aimed at achieving equal distribution difficult, since they are usually unequal in size, frequently have arbitrary or intersecting memberships, and vary according to the voluntariness of membership.

Examples abound in Aboriginal affairs. The previously complicated method of identifying membership in Indian bands was changed in 1985, but it did not erase the practical difficulties inherent in classifying the offspring of Indian/non-Indian marriages. Even if membership is not a problem, justice may be. The majority may impose illiberal or tyrannical decisions on individuals who never had a choice about their belonging to a self-governing

Aboriginal unit; and the principle of inherency has no obvious answer to the real problem of disputes between history-based group rights and individual rights. Neither has it any clear direction to offer in the case of intersecting or cascading memberships. Should Aboriginal women's rights dominate over "Aboriginal rights" in the context of self-government? What is the order of primacy in group rights in Canada – are French-Canadian rights trumped by inherency rights? There are no clear answers to these questions.[18] The only solution seems to be a divisive and ugly power struggle at the group level.

First Nations and the Canadian State

National integrity is another issue. With Aboriginal units calling themselves "nations" and claiming rights that generally belong to international actors, the validity of the Canadian state is called into question. Thomas Flanagan says that, contrary to the apologists for Aboriginal groups, the use of the term "First Nations" *does* have overtones of sovereignty. Nations do not necessarily possess statehood, but this is an integral aspect of their evolution. Even at a more moderate level, nationalism means making demands, and Aboriginal demands may be inconsistent with the needs of the larger polity. Reflecting on the recommendations of Penner Report of 1983, which now seem modest by comparison with contemporary Aboriginal demands, Flanagan said that they would create

> self-governing Indian communities with powers far in excess of those held by provincial governments. Indian First Nation governments could determine their own 'citizenship' and would provide to their members almost all services now delivered by federal or provincial governments. Indian governments would furthermore be largely exempt from judicial review in the courts, including civil liberties protected in the Canadian Charter of Rights and Freedoms. The essence of a federal system is that the citizen is directly affected by two governments in a scheme of divided jurisdiction. By this criterion, Indian First Nations would virtually secede from Canadian federalism. They would become enclaves within

the Canadian state, receiving fiscal subsidies but in other respects constituting *imperia in imperio*.[19]

In contemporary times, when the integrity of the Canadian nation is in question, it does not seem a viable option to create institutional competitors to it.

The Question of Asymmetrical Federalism

Canadian federalism seems incapable of accommodating the degree of complexity that would seem to be central to inherency. Frank Cassidy has said, in an approving way, that one of the implications of inherency in Canada is "federacy or asymmetrical federalism."[20] This would provide a way of integrating Indian and non-Indian governments. However, the Canadian people have twice rejected the notion of asymmetrical federalism as a philosophical basis for Canadian federalism, once by public opinion polls with the Meech Lake Accord (1987-90) and once by referendum with the Charlottetown Accord (1992). One of the proposals defeated in the referendum of 1992 was the asymmetry implied in the Accord's "inherent right of self-government" proposals.

Trudeau on Nationalism

One should not ignore the effect that the political philosophy of Pierre Elliott Trudeau has had on the mainstream of Canadian political thought. Here one deals with a bit of an anomaly, for Trudeau the practical politician sometimes acted in contradiction to Trudeau the political philosopher. One of the marks of this contradiction was that by 1984 the same Prime Minister who had told Indians in 1969 that they had to assimilate into Canadian society now seemed willing to experiment with Aboriginal self-government. However, the earlier Trudeau had the greatest impact on public attitudes in Canada. The statements about the dangers of French-Canadian and Aboriginal nationalism can be abbreviated as follows:

1. Nationalists are politically reactionary because they define the common good in terms of an ethnic group instead of

the whole society; nationalistic governments therefore tend to intolerance, discrimination, and even totalitarianism.

2. The state should not be the instrument of a cultural vision; cultures should have only the viability they can garner at the level of the individual, acting freely rather than being coerced by the majority.

3. One section of society should not make a treaty with another section of society; Aboriginal rights should be honoured only to the extent there has been a contract between Indians and the Crown.

4. A long history of injustice is not a basis upon which to decide Indian policy in Canada, since multiple other groups have been discriminated against as well and it is beyond the capacity of any state to right all historical wrongs. As President Kennedy stated, "we will be just in our time."[21]

The Issue of Balance

Balance is important to any consideration of inherent self-government. In a well-functioning society, institutions have to balance majority rights against minority rights. This would seem to involve a movement toward significant restraints on self-government; the strongest restraints that could be countenanced under this consideration are *contingent* or state-defined self-government rights. Although he is plainly sympathetic to Aboriginal self-rule, Whyte lists such limitations on it that they would scarcely allow true self-government. Parliament should intervene (1) when the rights of third parties outside the Aboriginal unit are threatened, (2) when the rights or opportunities of the non-voting or non-participating members of the unit are in danger, (3) when *other* Aboriginal rights, for example the rights of Aboriginal women, are in danger, and (4) when it is necessary to protect members of the unit from themselves even when this involves restraining freedom of choice.[22]

Historical Arguments

The record of historical injustices against Native people is indisputable. Yet there is no logical tie between them and the acceptance of an Aboriginal right of inherent self-government.

The Original Inhabitants Thesis

The lack of logic, or in some cases of elementary historical accuracy, is evident in the "original inhabitants thesis" of inherency proponents. Logically, if the occupancy of territory gave rights to exclude newcomers, Canadian immigration policy would long ago have doomed Canada to settlement along a thin strip of land in eastern Canada. Since Canada as a whole has opened the advantages of the country to increasing numbers of newcomers, then Aboriginals can be expected to do the same thing.

The founding of self-government solely on the original ownership of land is a problem in both history and logic. Even a self-government advocate like Kymlicka does not see a case arising from it. He rejects it because it does not provide a reason why all citizens should not share in the resources of a country. A fatal flaw is its silence on the question of why Aboriginal groups who lack title to land should have self-government. [23]

The Effect of International Law

Much is made of the statements of international bodies in the argumentation for the inherent right. Various documents are cited, ranging from the International Covenants of the United Nations to the Helsinki Declaration of 1975. All share a similar flaw if they are to be used as a centrepiece in the inherency argument. The principle of self-determination has not been integrated by statutory or constitutional means into the mainstream of the Canadian political system. This is a *sine qua non* for international law to have effect in the Canadian context. At any rate, the use of "peoples" in the various international texts seems a clear reference to colonial contexts, which is not the situation of a developed liberal-democratic country like Canada.

Pragmatic Arguments

When one moves beyond the lofty principles that dominate the debate on inherency and begins to consider the day-to-day realities of implementing inherency, the results are sobering. A host of practical difficulties seem not to have been considered by the proponents of the inherent right.

The Macdonald Royal Commission of 1985 had several concerns about formulations of self-government based on "territorialism." Territorialism, which it said was a common tenet of proponents of self-government, assumes "the existence of a land base or a territorially defined jurisdiction."[24] There were problems with a "land-based approach."

- Such government is exclusionary, likely to overlook the interests of non-status Indians and Métis who do not live on reserves or Crown land settlements; and approximately 75 per cent of Natives lack a land base, the Commission estimated.

- Disparities among the many bands (579) and reserves (2,000+) – as to population, land base, natural resources, personal wealth, and remoteness – yield problems, such as diseconomies of scale, that are not easily solved by amalgamation.

- The village-type size and economy of most of the reserves (average size: 516 people) would seem to doom them to a status of permanent economic dependency, both after land claims settlements and after fiscal transfers and land grants.

- The intergovernmental complexity that would result is unthinkable. Special powers for some communities and not for others would mean an inordinately complicated negotiating and bargaining system among the three orders of government; and Aboriginal associations are no substitutes, since they lack legislative and executive authority.

The Royal Commission meant only to bring "realism" to discussions of self-government. However, its comments indicate a general lack of pragmatism implicit in the inherent right idea.

Financial Arguments

As if the foregoing considerations were not enough, the financial arguments against inherency are substantial. The arguments are simply that the potential costs are overwhelming and that the country's fiscal situation is too alarming to allow further deterioration. The current level of services is in danger, let alone any future demands on the federal state.

Overwhelming Costs

The potential costs associated with self-government are massive and open-ended. This is borne out by looking at the text of the Charlottetown Accord of 1992. In a context where one would expect some specificity in the fiscal arrangements to undergird inherency, none could be offered. The Consensus Report on the Constitution of August 28, 1992, suggested that Aboriginals constitute a third order of government and that the two other orders, federal and provincial, should negotiate in good faith to establish the inherent right of self-government. All that was said about finances, however, was this (in part 45): "The negotiations would focus on the implementation of the right of self-government, including issues of jurisdiction, lands and resources, and economic and fiscal resources." This is far too open-ended a concept for most Canadians to accept.

However, some of the preliminary indications of the magnitude of costs associated with the implementation of inherency are already available. One is the creation of Nunavut, a new territorial government in the eastern Arctic carved out of the Northwest Territories. It is designed to give the Inuit a form of self-government, in this case territory-based instead of race-based, with installation beginning in 1999 and full powers accorded by 2008. (It is in fact a race-based government because the Inuit form the majority of residents of the eastern Arctic.) The Inuit relinquish Aboriginal title to the central and eastern Arctic and get many of the powers of a province over the area, including subsurface mineral rights. Yet precision eludes the commentaries on the deal. One story commented:

In addition to controlling development and hunting in an area half the size of Alberta, as well as receiving payments from the government over 14 years that will add up with interest to more than $1-billion, the Inuit have secured Ottawa's agreement to finance the administrative and startup costs of a new territory. Mr. Siddon [federal Minister of Indian and Northern Affairs] said the government has yet to work out those costs in any detail.[25]

Presumably, this will not all be done with new money; some of the financing of the new territory will come from existing NWT financing. Nevertheless, the lack of precision is worrying.

An important additional consideration is that the general population will bear the costs for the new government. A Coopers and Lybrand study of Nunavut's costs says that after 2008, Nunavut will cost $84 million more a year than it currently costs to run the eastern Arctic under the NWT framework, and the population of the new territory will not be able to contribute tax revenues to run the extensive new government that is envisaged.[26] When one stops to consider that the Inuit are the smallest of the Aboriginal groups and that a multitude of analogous situations are waiting for solution, the potential costs of inherency are staggering. This is happening in a country facing a debt-to-GDP ratio that is one of the worst in the industrialized world.[27]

It is therefore highly unrealistic to expect the Canadian people to accept the arguments for inherency that have surfaced in the last decade or so. They are founded on fairly flimsy historical and philosophical grounds. The financial implications appear not to have been clearly thought through. As with so many other areas of Canadian politics and constitution-making, perhaps the best hope for progress lies not in comprehensive change but in the strategy of incrementalism and the education of public opinion.

Notes

1. 2 RIAA 829, 845 (Judge Huber).
2. L.C. Green and Olive P. Dickason, eds., *The Law of Nations and the New World* (Edmonton: University of Alberta Press, 1989).
3. *Ibid.*, pp. 7-17.

4. *Ibid.*, p. 38.
5. *Ibid.*, pp. 17-81.
6. *Ibid.*, p. 113.
7. James Crawford, *Aboriginal Self-Government in Canada*, A Research Report for the Canadian Bar Association, Committee on Native Justice, January, 1988, pp. 31-32.
8. *Ibid.*, p. 39.
9. *Ibid.*, p. 40.
10. Green and Dickason, *The Law of Nations and the New World*, pp. 99-105.
11. Crawford, *Aboriginal Self-Government*, p. 48.
12. *Ibid.*, p. 40.
13. *Ibid.*, p. 39.
14. Michael D. Mason, "Canadian and United States Approaches to Indian Sovereignty," *Osgoode Hall Law Journal*, 21 (1983), pp. 434-37.
15. Crawford, *Aboriginal Self-Government*, pp. 36-37.
16. Canada, Department of Indian Affairs and Northern Development, *Statement of the Government of Canada on Indian Policy, 1969* (Ottawa, 1969), p. 8.
17. Bryan Schwartz, *First Principles, Second Thoughts: Aboriginal Peoples, Constitutional Reform and Canadian Statecraft* (Montreal: Institute for Research on Public Policy, 1986), p. 36.
18. *Ibid.*, ch. 1.
19. Thomas Flanagan, "The Sovereignty and Nationhood of Canadian Indians: A Comment on Boldt and Long," *Canadian Journal of Political Science*, 28, 2 (June, 1985), pp. 372-73.
20. Frank Cassidy, "The Governments of Canadian Indians," *Policy Options* (July, 1989), p. 29.
21. Pierre Elliott Trudeau, "Remarks on Aboriginal and Treaty Rights. Excerpts from a Speech Given August 8th, 1969, in Vancouver, British Columbia," in Peter A. Cumming and Neil A. Mickenberg, *Native Rights in Canada*, second edition (Toronto: General Publishing, 1972), p. 332. See also Pierre Trudeau, *Federalism and the French Canadians* (New York: St. Martin's Press, 1968), pp. 151-81.
22. John D. Whyte, "Indian Self-Government: A Legal Analysis," in Leroy Little Bear, Menno Boldt, and J. Anthony Long, *Pathways to Self-Determination: Canadian Indians and the Canadian State* (Toronto: University of Toronto Press, 1984), pp. 109-10.
23. Kymlicka, *Liberalism, Community and Culture* (Oxford: Clarendon Press, 1989), pp. 158-59.

24. Canada, Royal Commission on the Economic Union and Development Prospects for Canada, *Report,* Volume Three (Ottawa: Minister of Supply and Services, 1985), p. 368.
25. Miro Cernetig, "Accord sets up new Inuit territory," *Globe and Mail,* October 31, 1992, p. A4.
26. As cited in Jeffrey Simpson, "Paying for native self-government: If Nunavut's the model, it's a big tab," *Globe and Mail,* February 4, 1993, p. A20.
27. Business Council on National Issues, *Canada's Looming Debt Crisis and How It Can Be Avoided* (Ottawa, April, 1993), p. 13.

PART TWO

Was the Charter Worth It?

A country does not lightly enter into major new constitutional arrangements. Yet Canada has had *three regimes* for the protection of rights and freedoms in Canada. The eras in question covered 1867 to 1960, 1960 to 1982, and 1982 to present. The perceived deficiencies of the first two regimes led to the third. It will be our task here to assess the arguments, pro and con, about the wisdom of this move. It should be noted, however, that the protections involved in these three regimes were to a large extent cumulative rather than mutually exclusive, as section 26 of the Canadian Charter of Rights and Freedoms made explicit.

1867 to 1960

The first civil liberties regime in Canada involved *parliamentary protection* in the style of the United Kingdom: relatively unfettered parliamentary supremacy. The judiciary was anxious not to stray from its traditional adjudicative role into a legislative role. Of course, the courts did "legislate" to some extent as the umpire of the federal system; federalism demands judicial review to keep intergovernmental rivalries under control. Canadian courts largely followed the lead of British courts, deferring to the wisdom of the legislature in the matters of civil liberties and human rights. As in Britain, the best defence of rights was seen to be a concerned and educated citizenry exerting influence on their elected representatives.

There was but a meagre collection of legal strategies with which to challenge public power. One was to rely on the *division of powers*. This involved attempting to convince the courts that the law being challenged was *ultra vires* (beyond the legislative jurisdiction of) the government enacting it. Another was to purport that there was an *implied bill of rights* in the preamble of the British North America Act. This meant, in effect, that the rights and freedoms enjoyed by British citizens at the time of Confederation in 1867 had been transferred to the Canadian context by the preamble's description of a "Constitution similar in Principle to that of the United Kingdom" for Canada. Another approach concentrated on a concept with strong but not exclusive roots in the British tradition called *"the rule of law."* This maintained that the state could perform only those actions specifically permitted by law, that only individuals empowered by such laws could execute them, and that no one was above the law, regardless of station in life.

These approaches were theoretically attractive but ambiguous in practice. Although all of the above techniques were available to lawyers and courts, the division of powers became the most common tool. Most of the landmark civil liberties cases – and they were notably few in number – the courts decided on this narrow basis.[1] Even when it was not used, the powers technique formed the core of the decision, as in *Saumer*.[2] The other approaches were only applicable to a few relatively isolated situations.

Civil liberties activists, not surprisingly, were dissatisfied with this situation. They perceived it to be anachronistic in an era of big government and its attendant intrusiveness. The odds were stacked in favour of a public sector staffed with individuals capable of inflicting injustices backed up with a battery of public sanctions.

1960 to 1982

Nor were civil liberties proponents completely satisfied with the Canadian Bill of Rights introduced in 1960. It had a number of structural and political flaws. It was a *statutory*, not a constitutional, bill of rights, and by that token it was not beyond the reach of the legislature. The executive and legislature, who were implicated in the infringement of liberties in the first place, had the additional capacity to change the very rules of the game. As well, it applied only to the federal level of government, since Prime Minister John Diefenbaker's original conception of a pan-Canadian bill had been stymied by provincial opposition. Since more infringements had occurred at the provincial level than at the federal,[3] the exclusion of provinces was perceived as a worrying development. The fact that provinces had themselves introduced bills of rights (since 1971) or human rights codes (since 1962) was not seen as a telling argument. Like the federal Bill of Rights, the provincial bills were statutory in nature, hence liable to be changed by ordinary law; and the codes regulated relations between one individual and another, not between government and the individual. Still another troubling aspect of the 1960 Bill was its *lack of a remedies clause,* which would allow judges not only to identify infringements of civil liberties but also to mandate what measures would be necessary to correct such conditions. The last problem was that no clue was given in the Bill about its status in relation to the traditional doctrine of *parliamentary supremacy.* Its language was ambiguous on the subject, not revealing if the Bill of Rights was meant to be a canon of interpretation, a "matter and form" guide, or an instrument capable of overriding the will of Parliament.[4]

1982 to the Present

The realization was also dawning by end of the 1960s that a bill of rights could have significance beyond the merely legal. Matters that the rest of the world accorded paramount importance could no longer be so casually dealt with by Canada's governments. As well, the growing national crisis engendered by the Quebec question and "province-building" called for a variety of symbols to counteract the estrangement of Canadians from their national government.

The timing of the introduction of the Charter of Rights and Freedoms was, in light of these historical developments, fortuitous. The Charter that was ultimately agreed upon, after much federal-provincial wrangling, had several elements. One category involved *entrenched rights*. Democratic rights, official language rights, mobility rights, and minority language education rights were included in the constitution with few qualifications. The same could not be said for the fundamental freedoms, legal rights, and equality rights, which were subject to the section 33 *"override."* This enabled legislatures to pass legislation in conflict with these rights and freedoms in the Charter as long as the legislation expressly declared that it shall operate "notwithstanding" a provision included in sections 2 or 7-15 of the Charter.

One important Charter clause needs mention: section 1, the so-called "limitations clause." Rights and freedoms are not absolute; they collide with one another in the real world. In recognition of this, the Charter explicitly provided for judicial discretion in applying the Charter's protections. Section 1 says the Charter "guarantees the rights and freedoms set out in it subject only to such reasonable limits prescribed by law as can be demonstrably justified in a free and democratic society."

The Charter, and the broader Constitution Act, 1982, of which the Charter is a part, explicitly corrected several perceived gaps in the previous Bill of Rights. The Charter was *constitutional,* part of the "supreme law of Canada," said section 52 of the Constitution Act, 1982. It applied to *both levels of government,* as dictated by section 32 of the Charter. The Charter had a *remedies clause,* s. 24(1). The Constitution Act dealt squarely with the *issue of parliamentary supremacy* that the Bill of Rights had evaded, noting in section 52 that "any law that is inconsistent with the provisions of the Constitution is, to the extent of the inconsistency, of no force or effect." As well, the override clause was a compromise between entrenchment and parliamentary sovereignty.

Notes

1. *Union Colliery Company of B.C. v. Bryden* [1899] AC 580.
2. *Saumer v. Quebec and A.-G. for Quebec* [1953] SCR 299.
3. Walter Tarnopolsky, "A Constitutionally Entrenched Charter of

Human Rights – Why Now?" *Saskatchewan Law Review*, 33, 4 (Winter, 1968), p. 249.

4. A canon of construction merely establishes guidelines for statutory interpretation. A "matter and form requirement" is a requirement imposed by a legislature upon itself to respect procedural restraints in the passage of legislation. A legislature cannot bind itself as to substantive or policy matters, but it can bind itself as to the "manner and form," that is, the kind of legislative process involved in the passage of future legislation. Parliamentary supremacy means that a present Parliament cannot bind a future one and that the legislative power is superior to the executive and judicial powers of government. For more on the conundrum presented by the Canadian Bill of Rights, see Peter W. Hogg, *Constitutional Law of Canada,* 3rd edition (Toronto: Carswell, 1992), sections 12.3(b), 32.3(c), 32.5.

Chapter 3

Arguments Favouring the Charter

The Charter of Rights and Freedoms has captured the imagination of a new generation of Canadians. Its opponents are out of step with progressive thought in the twentieth century. Their views need urgent refutation in Canada, lest the sense of crisis that has settled over general constitutional discussions in Canada be expanded to include the Charter as well. The case for the Charter can be made on the grounds of history, national integrity, ideology, the international context, philosophy of law, and the institutions of governance.

History

History provides a fertile ground for demonstrations of the need for constitutional rights. Especially relevant are considerations of the federal decline and the Canadian rights record.

The Federal Decline

Recent years have witnessed the diminishing relevance of the federal government and the decline of national cultural symbols. The post-World War Two era saw first the rise and then the decline of federal influence on public policy. No significant federal welfare state shared-cost legislation was passed after the Medical Care Act of 1966. Aggressive provincial governments, aided by burgeoning bureaucracies, sought new ways of establishing links with their electorates and in doing so splintered the existing national consensus. National symbols were losing some of their potency in the wake of the American cultural invasion. Prime Minister Trudeau wisely perceived that a new symbol, the Charter, could remind Canadians of the values they coveted and at the same time rescue the federal government from the danger of growing irrelevancy.

The Canadian Rights Record

In addition, a new sense of *realism* was dawning about the Canadian rights record. There were few major glories to celebrate and many bleak moments to contemplate. What glory is there in a record showing that Canada:

- excluded Indians and Chinese from the franchise in 1885;
- blocked entry to Sikhs aboard the *Komagata Maru* in 1914 in Vancouver harbour rather than let them land and begin immigration procedures;
- displayed a long history of anti-labour violence, especially in Winnipeg in 1919 and Regina in 1935;
- detained innocent Japanese Canadians in the 1940s due to wartime paranoia;
- at various times successfully declared membership in the Jehovah's Witnesses and the Front de libération du Québec to be illegal;
- featured growing discrimination against minorities in the larger cities of Canada?[1]

Canadians read often of the activism of the U.S. Supreme Court in racial matters but could only point to one case in which the Canadian Supreme Court had used the Canadian Bill of Rights to declare legislation unacceptable in regard to the Natives of

Canada, the *Drybones* case of 1970. The much-vaunted parliamentary supremacy and British rights heritage seemed to have failed, just when they were needed most.

National Integrity

One of the most potent arguments for an entrenched charter in Canada was, and still is, the notion of national integrity. National integrity in turn can be thought of as including a number of considerations in recent Canadian history: realistic theories of federalism, the requisite components of nationhood, the capacity to solve long-standing cleavages, and a balanced context for national institutions.

Theories of Federalism

Realistically, only two theories of federalism can be considered conducive to the goal of national unity. One is *centralist federalism,* which holds that national objectives – those common to all Canadians – can only be set and accomplished by a government elected by the entire country. Provincial governments are chosen by electorates shaped and driven by different historical imperatives, and governments must of necessity reflect these imperatives. The narrower the constituency, the narrower the statesmanship. The other theory, *intrastate federalism,* holds that the various centrifugal (provincializing) tendencies in Canada's federalism can be accommodated by strengthening the capacity of national institutions to deal with them in a decisive and accountable way. The legislative, executive, and judicial institutions of the federal government, if reformed so as to heighten their representativeness of socio-political forces in Canada, will contribute toward dispute resolution at the national level, rather than at the regional or even intergovernmental level. That is, of course, if the "centralist" variant of intrastate federalism is used.[2]

The Charter contributes to both of these theoretical frameworks. It contributes to centralized federalism by providing a system of rights that is almost completely uniform across the country, except in rare instances where a government will opt out of its application to certain areas of public policy. As well, the initiation of the Charter has rekindled interest in the Supreme Court as a national institution, and every attempt at constitutional reform after 1982 has focused giving provinces representation in one way or another in the selection or workings of the Court.

Of course, centralized federalism, like any other theory, is of little intrinsic value if the ends for which it is being used are not themselves of value. As well, practical politicians do not always act in the thrall of any one theory exclusively. One must hasten to add that, because of political compromise, the Charter reflects not only centralism but also *provincialism* – mainly in the section 33 override clause but also in analogous provisions: mobility rights (ss. 6[3] and 6[4]), equality rights (s. 15[2]), and minority language education rights (s. 23[1][a]). Still, to the extent that national values, such as democratic rights, bilingual education rights, general mobility rights, and official bilingualism in Ottawa, Quebec, and New Brunswick, are reflected in the Charter, and certain matters, such as historical Aboriginal rights, the multicultural heritage, and other existing freedoms, are protected from the Charter, the Charter is of inestimable value in nation-building. Even the "overridable" sections (2, 7-14, 15) are related strongly to national integrity because they express process and substantive values that are important to a majority of Canadians.

Overcoming Cleavages

One way to foster the unity of a country is to provide for a system of cross-cutting cleavages, rather than having cleavages that reinforce one another. The greater the extent of reinforcing cleavages, the greater the degree to which various social divisions compound one another and the greater the general fractiousness of the country will be. Accordingly, they are to be counteracted if possible by astutely designed constitutional reforms.

The Charter contains a number of provisions that aim to encourage the cross-cutting dynamic in Canadian society. Some of the most important, at least for committed federalists, are those dealing with language rights. Their basic purpose is to guarantee that the federal state, not just the Quebec state, nurtures the official languages in minority contexts. In particular, Quebec is deprived of its ability to exacerbate federal-provincial tensions by its historic claim to be the voice of French Canada. The mobility rights set forth in the Charter discourage a provincial government from establishing employment barriers that may stem from language- and culture-related motives. An analogous effect is achieved in the case of equality rights. Quebecers who feel that the Charter is merely an instrument of Anglophone domination would do well to examine it more closely. A number of Quebec-sensitive protections are built into the document. Section 23(1)(a) allows Quebec to stream children of immigrants into French-language education in the province. Section 15 does not have language as one of its prohibited discriminations, as does the Quebec Charter (the statutory analogue to the federal document), yet Quebecers should appreciate the commitment to official bilingualism in ss. 16 to 22. Like all provinces, Quebec has the right to invoke the protective mantles of ss. 1 and 33. In general, Quebec courts and litigants have made substantial use of the Charter[3] and Quebec public opinion appears to be in favour of the Charter.

The Context of the Charter

The nationalizing dynamic is also encouraged by the general context of the Charter. Civil liberties questions can now be phrased in terms of constitutional matters rather than in terms of the more nationally disruptive division of powers. Where civil liberties cases are decided by the power allocation technique, one government inevitably loses power to another. As well, some matters that were previously settled in the highly fractious forum of the First Ministers' Conference are now the purview of a national court, which itself acts as a centralizing influence on the courts below it. In fact, there is growing evidence that politicians themselves may prefer the selective use of the courts in matters with intergovernmental overtones in order to maintain their own prestige or resources, or both.

Perhaps the most important context for the Charter is its symbolic grounding in the notion of popular sovereignty. One of the peculiarities of Canada's original constitution was that it almost totally ignored the relationship between government and citizens, such a relationship being implicit in the inherited British style of government. It instead emphasized two other types of relationship: between the powers of government (legislative, executive, and judicial) and between governments. Totally ignored, and in fact deemed non-essential by the political elites, was what has come to be considered a prime function of constitutions in Western societies: the expression of the highest values and collective aspirations of the nation. The immediate popularity of the Charter was testimony to its functional role as an important national symbol of rule by the people.

As well, the Charter bolsters sovereignty because it is an instrument of inclusiveness. It allows many sectors to recognize themselves constitutionally. Ian Greene says that the public hearings of the Molgat-MacGuigan Committee of Parliament marked the point where the Canadian public began to present demands, previously thought of as "political," in terms of "human rights";[4] this represented a new level of rights consciousness in Canada. Inevitably, there will be "ins" and "outs" in any constitutional arrangement, but since the Charter has come into effect, few groups in society have claimed that they have been excluded from consideration by the Charter. More often the demand has been for incremental additions to already existing Charter protections.

Canadian Liberalism

Lastly, the Charter seems compatible with popular sovereignty because both its contents and its rationales are in keeping with the liberalism that is the primary characteristic of Canadian political culture. Trudeau's famous rationale for a "people's package" – to give ordinary Canadians the ability to challenge government actions – hinted broadly at the notion of an expanded popular sovereignty. Knopf and Morton reveal the basic assumptions about *inherent rights* that underlay the new package:

> A charter emphasizes the sovereignty of the people because the idea of rights entails the notion that government exists to serve the people. This connotation of the term "rights" may be traced to the state-of-nature teaching with which it was originally associated. According to that doctrine, rights are pre-political goods, the protection of which is the primary reason that people consent to government. Although the idea of a state-of-nature is no longer in vogue, the perception of rights as inherent in human beings as such, rather than as a grant from government to its citizens, retains its vigour, as does the corollary that government exists to protect rights.[5]

This is a powerful component of the cultural appeal of the Charter, and politicians and others will interfere with it at their peril. The idea of culture is fairly closely connected to a discussion of the ideological appeal of a constitutionalized bill of rights.

Ideology

There are strong ideological bases for supporting the adoption of constitutionalized rights. One of the interesting things about the 1982 package is its *appeal across ideologies*. The Charter includes a mixture of classical liberal individual rights and significant collective rights. Collective protections can be found in sections dealing with language rights, Aboriginal matters, and the multicultural heritage, plus the identities highlighted by equality rights and the sexual equality arrangements. (It should be remembered that women achieved sexual equality in the Charter with comparative ease, whereas in the U.S. the Equal Rights Amendment failed its ratification threshold of thirty-eight states, by three). All of these are rights over which the ideological streams in today's Canada do not hold particular sway. Modern liberalism and social democracy may differ on the methodology of reaching the aims implicit in these rights, but not on the aims themselves.

Progressive Decisions

Critics among the left contribute considerable significance to the several Supreme Court decisions in the late 1980s that went against progressive forces in Canadian society. Yet the list of decisions that empower sections of Canadian society in ways not possible before 1982 grows year by year. Most observers agree that the Supreme Court has been forced to give more procedural leeway to the accused and the convicted. The Court has also ruled (in *Singh*) that fundamental justice involves the right to an oral hearing in refugee determination hearings; any subsequent narrowing of refugee procedures was legislative, not court-induced. The pro-choice option on abortion, if not given explicit confirmation of its approach, was at least accorded significant encouragement in the *Morgentaler* decision that decriminalized abortion. In the *Ford, Devine,* and *Manitoba Language Rights* cases, the rights of official language minorities in Quebec and Manitoba were given a substantial enunciation, albeit on different grounds. A challenge by the right, claiming the unconstitutionality of the compulsory payment of union dues in an agency shop arrangement in the public sector, was beaten back in the Court's *Lavigne* decision of 1991. Admittedly, it also raised the possibility that in the future "freedom of association" in the Charter would be interpreted to include freedom *from* association, putting in danger certain closed shop and union shop arrangements.[6]

The Role of the Minority

Even where a majority of the Court rules against a progressive element, there has often been a strong minority ready to support it. Minorities can serve the function of keeping a constitutional doctrine vital enough to be of use to further litigants pursuing related legal points. David Beatty maintains such a view after his review of the first two periods of Supreme Court decisions (1984-86 and 1986-89).[7] One of the useful aspects of the "liberal" minority on the Court was to remind the "conservative" majority of the correct methodology of judicial review: that which the Court itself had established in the first period, especially in the *Oakes* decision. Accordingly, it was reminded to maintain the "purposeful" approach to the rights and freedoms of the Charter. Specifically, Beatty says, they highlighted the importance of following the two stages of *Oakes* (first the interpretive stage and then the justification phase) in their proper order, so as to give strength to the valuable "alternative means" principle.[8]

The International Context

The international context provides a powerful reason for initiating and maintaining a constitutionalized system of liberties. Canada does not exist in an international vacuum. It cherishes its ability to affect world events by displaying leadership in regard to political morality. The international dimension includes the role of international obligations, the example of other sovereign states, and the question of North American continentalism.

International Obligations

Canada is an important member of several international organizations, and its adoption of the Charter was a long-overdue recognition of values important to the world community. It is arguable that without some constitutional expression of human rights, Canada could not have lived up to its obligations. The United Nations is the organization with the most symbolic importance to the nation. The list of UN agreements to which Canada was a party grew steadily after the Second World War: the UN Charter (1945), the Universal Declaration of Human Rights (1948), the International Covenant on Civil and Political Rights (1976), and the International Covenant on Economic, Social and Cultural Rights (1976). Canadian John Peters Humphrey, a professor of international law from McGill University, drafted the original Universal Declaration of Human Rights and was the first director of the UN Division of Human Rights, a post he held for twenty years; Humphrey aided the inauguration of sixty-seven international conventions and several national constitutions that embodied the values and standards of the Declaration. [9] Yet his own country possessed no written charter of rights. Alan Cairns says that all this activity had a powerful effect on Canada:

> The Charter, the Universal Declaration, and subsequent covenants not only provided domestic groups with a powerful rights rhetoric legitimated by its UN origins but also suggested the criteria by which performance could be judged. In a forum such as the United Nations, it was obviously politically preferable for a state to employ written instruments, such as a Charter, to confirm its formal compliance with its UN obligations, than to try and explain that a parliamentary regime might better protect rights than a regime with a hollow charter designed for external consumption. That same international pressure put federalism as well as parliamentary supremacy on the defensive: Canadian legislative response to international commitments requiring provincial action could not be undertaken by the federal government acting alone. [10]

Canadian Human Rights Commissioner Gordon Fairweather testified to the Special Joint Committee on the Constitution in 1981 that Canada could not meet such international obligations without the introduction of an entrenched charter affecting both levels of government. [11] Similar dynamics were at play, on a lesser scale, in the Commonwealth scene.

Other Sovereign States

The example of other sovereign states helped Canada accept the diminution of legislative sovereignty inherent in rights entrenchment. These states, presumably concerned about the same prerogatives as Canada, voluntarily yielded a portion of their sovereign power to give meaningful expression to various international rights regimes. Twenty-three European states have ratified the European Convention on Human Rights since 1953, no states have withdrawn from this so-called "Strasbourg Law," and the number of protocols covered by the Convention has grown steadily. As the European Court of Human Rights becomes more interventionist in its judgements on the Convention, therefore, the adhesion to the Convention has grown. There are also domestic bills of rights and/or constitutional review of legislation in Germany, Italy, Austria, Portugal, Spain, Greece, France, Cyprus, Turkey, Japan, Malta, and Sweden. [12] Philip Zylberberg says that these patterns demonstrate the functional value of such judicial review in Western democracies: to symbolize the rule of law to the citizenry and thus to inspire confidence in constitutional government. [13] Canada, in enacting the Charter and diminishing its sovereignty, was merely joining the modern world.

Americanization?

Of course, the United States also has a constitutional Bill of Rights, and this fact presents problems of a special sort for Canada. Many Canadians experience a slight *frisson* of nationalistic fear when they hear comments like that of Seymour Lipset, who says that the Charter is "perhaps the most important step that Canada has taken to Americanize itself." [14] They need not.

In the first place, it should once again be noted that the move to constitutionalized rights is an international concept. The United States may have led the pack in the introduction of such a system, but this does not mean that the notion of rights will forever be identified as an American phenomenon. America was the first nation in the world to adopt federalism, but no country becoming federal in nature has ever hesitated in doing so out of a fear of becoming "Americanized"! Canada was responding to international rather than to specifically American examples.

Second, such critics are misusing terminology. For a country to be "American" in nature, it should be "presidential." This Canada most assuredly is not. Our system is built on the principle of the fusion of powers between the executive and the legislature, while the American system is premised on the separation of legislative, executive, and judicial powers, all moderated by a related principle of checks and balances that allows each branch of government to share in the functions of the others. This basic difference has not been changed since 1982, despite the obvious growth in the scope of judicial review. Judicial review is not inconsistent with either system.

Third, the Charter is a distinctive Canadian document. It includes rights and freedoms that are a result of our collective experience as Canadians; moreover, many of these guarantees are not to be found in the United States Constitution. There are both general and particular differences.

In general, Canada has had much more sympathy for the needs of particular groups and much less of a tendency to draw a dichotomy between individualism and collectivism. Tolerance has marked the Canadian way. Military service exemptions were granted over Canadian history to Quakers, Mennonites, and Hutterites; collective settlement patterns were allowed to Mennonites and Hutterites in western Canada; and welfare state universalism was bent to allow for the particular concerns of Hutterites and old-order Mennonites over old age pensions, family allowances, and social insurance.[15] Sikhs wear turbans in the most honoured and symbolic of Canadian institutions, the Royal Canadian Mounted Police. Canadians have allowed groups, most notably Aboriginals, to press their claims to constitutional negotiating rights without serious objection. One cannot imagine the same dynamics taking place in the United States, or affecting the process or contents of constitution-making to the same degree. In Canada, however, the Charter was simply one more attempt to accommodate the predominant individualism of the political culture with the specific circumstances of groups in society.

When it comes to specifics, many differences can be isolated in the respective bills of rights of the two countries. The American Constitution, of which the Bill of Rights is a part, does not have a specific limitations clause, a judicial remedies clause, recognition of historic Aboriginal rights, a multicultural heritage interpretive section, a sexual equality clause, or an override clause.[16] These are to be found, of course, in the Charter in sections 1, 24(2), 25, 27, 28, and 33. There are also a variety of more particular constitutional protections that are absent in the U.S. Constitution.[17] (It must be acknowledged, however, that some of these protections have entered American jurisprudence through judicial interpretation.) The Canadian approach is recognition that perceiving individualism and collectivism as opposites may create a false dichotomy: meaningful individualism often cannot be expressed except through the medium of collective protections. All in all, therefore, it seems misleading to term the Charter an "Americanizing" document.

Philosophy of Law

Supporters of the entrenchment of rights may also find support in various aspects of the philosophy of law. However, this body of literature yields up arguments for the other side as well. Proponents of entrenchment also find that disputes about rights fall into a larger category of disagreements about the proper place of judicial review itself.

The Place of Judicial Review

The basic dispute over judicial review revolves around the degree to which decisions about public affairs should be taken by the courts as opposed to legislative majorities. Barry Strayer offers several reasons why judicial review is compatible with parliamentary democracy.[18] First, it has never been assumed in democracies that rules should consistently mirror majority views; the electoral system, parliamentary arrangements, and durations of legislatures are testimony to this fact. Second, Canadians have given tacit approval to constitutional norms that were undemocratically arrived at and bolstered by judicial decisions; moreover, they frequently resist opening these norms to the threat of short-term legislative change. Third, judges may indeed be chosen undemocratically, but their job is to follow the last available expression of the democratic will. In fact, their job further involves reminding democratic majorities of the durable obligations that they have willingly undertaken. Fourth, judicial decisions often involve the expression of value judgements, but this is unavoidable because of the vague and general way that constitutional documents are written, to heighten their flexibility. "The danger of legislative power being 'transferred to the judiciary' has been much exaggerated," concludes Strayer. "Even in its most activist form, judicial review is interstitial, sporadic, and fortuitous." [19]

Constitutional Rights

The question of whether the courts should be trusted with the adjudication of constitutional rights is therefore a subset of the larger question about the appropriateness of judicial review. In the former area, however, courts have a number of strong arguments going in their favour. They can be separated into two classes: one discussing the judicial role, the other the question of democratic theory.

1. The judicial role

A number of characteristics of the judicial role make it an admirable bulwark of constitutional rights. One is that traditionally in Canadian society there has been considerable consensus on the use of judges as *teachers of morality*. This is testified to by the generally high standing in public opinion of the judiciary in comparison with the legislative and executive branches of government. Enmeshed as they are in political compromise, the legislature and executive are almost by definition tainted in the eyes of the public. Rights decisions of the courts will stimulate public interest and discussion and yield greater acceptance of rights in general.

Another characteristic of the judiciary is its traditional *focus on the individual* in the context of society. Legislatures in our complex contemporary world cannot act in terms of specifics or they would soon self-destruct from overwork. Logically, there has to be a place where the individual can turn for redress of rights infringements. Assessing the rights of the individual against society, or vice versa, is a job that Canadian courts did long before 1982. Surely they could be trusted to do so afterwards.

The nature of *judicial reasoning* is itself a cogent argument for the courts' role in the rights field, as opposed to parliamentary leader-ship. Courts aim at the standardization of rules; legislatures are driven by the political rationality of re-election, which may occasionally result in a distortion of the rules. Courts are committed to the refinement of logic;[20] legislatures are driven by a variety of imperatives ranging from nationalism to individual greed.

2. Democratic theory

The question of democratic theory is particularly challenging for the courts and their defenders, but here there have been some forceful defenders of judicial review. The work of legal philosophers, of course, is not always completely transferable between countries. However, some useful points can apply in the case of Canada.

Ronald Dworkin has been able to accommodate both democracy and judicial review in one conceptual framework. He notes that many observers fall prey to a "statistical" conception of democracy, equating it with political decisions made in a merely aggregative way, one by one. A "communal" conception of democracy, on the other hand, is based on the shared ideals of members of the community, but in an integrated, not a monolithic, fashion. This means that there is a collective unit of responsibility, but not a collective unit of judgement. Integrated collective action further implies the principle of participation (that each has an unfettered ability to make an impact on political decisions), the principle of stake (that each has equal concern in political outcomes), and the principle of independence (that each has a responsibility for moral and ethical judgement, and therefore the state must encourage and not dictate such judgement). "Disabling provisions" such as rights charters, which limit the structural powers of majorities, are therefore democratically justified if they are "edicts of political or moral principle" that reflect the principles of integrated collective action. Thus, structural arrangements are not synonymous with democracy, and we need have no qualms about the judicial review of constitutional rights.[21]

Dworkin further assuages worries about judicial review by distinguishing between the domain of "policy" and the domain of "principle." Much of the opposition to judicial review comes from the fact that unelected judges make new law where the existing positive law is inapplicable to the novel issues raised by a particular case. Rightly so, says Dworkin, if in fact the "law" in question is policy, which is "a compromise among individual goals and purposes in search of the welfare of the community as a whole."[22] This is to distinguish it from principle, which is a proposition that describes rights. An argument of principle attempts to establish individual rights in the context of social goals: a claim is a right if it has a certain "threshold weight," or withstanding power, against collective goals in general.[23] The business of majoritarian legislatures is to weigh collective goals against each other, but that of the courts is to assess arguments of principle. They are insulated from majoritarian pressure and thus able to render more just decisions where individual rights are concerned. Dworkin's points, of course, have to be modified by adding reminders about the balance of individualism and collectivism inherent in the Charter, but they are useful when considering that substantial part of the Charter that deals with individual rights.

Another way to deal with the conundrum of tension between sovereignty and democracy is to demystify sovereignty. This is in essence what the Special Joint Committee on the Constitution of Canada argued in its *Report* of 1972 when it denied that parliamentary sovereignty is any more sacrosanct a principle than is respect for liberties. It noted that sovereignty was already limited by federalism, and perhaps by natural law and a common-law Bill of Rights as well. An additional limit would not be an absolute one, for "a Bill of Rights constitutes rather a healthy tension point between two principles of fundamental value, establishing the kind of equilibrium among the competing interests of majority rule and minority rights which is in our view the essence of democracy."[24]

Peter Russell some time ago made a very convincing argument for constitutionalizing a bill of rights. He reminded us that the whole drift of Western political philosophy has been to promote the shift of power from the governors to the governed. A bill of rights continues this tradition, and is indeed necessary in the new world of bureaucratic tyranny that the expansion of government has given us. "We do not possess as much democracy as we are capable of enjoying," he said, and suggested new institutional forms to correct occasions where citizens could not make their demands felt on executive government.[25]

Institutions of Governance

The specific dynamics involved in Canadian institutions of governance also provide a compelling case for constitutional liberties. Here a great deal of caution is warranted, because Canadian public opinion is deeply divided on both the analysis of the institutional deficiencies of Canadian government and the correct solutions to these deficiencies. However, if one phrases one's analysis in terms of general tendencies, some resolution of the difficulties may be possible.

Canadian Views of Institutional Reform

In general, Canadians agree with the British style of government they inherited, but they feel it could use a great deal more democratization. They condemn the practice of virtually uncontrolled cabinet domination of the legislature. The legislature, however, does not get off lightly, for the public has begun to demand that it accommodate itself to various forms of direct democracy, especially in constitutional matters. Secrecy in the preparation of major policies raises serious objections, even outrage, as the free trade and Meech Lake episodes demonstrated. The courts, for their part, are also seen to be in need of more democratization. Canadians have come to see judicial appointments as highly political in nature as a result of the increased profile and importance of judicial review in recent decades. Calls for various forms of a "representative judiciary" have abounded in recent constitutional debates.

The Charter as Instrument of Democratization

The introduction of the Charter has not alleviated Canadians' distaste for all aspects of the institutional framework of the country, but it has gone a significant distance toward this end. First, the Charter was sold successfully as an instrument of democratization by the Trudeau government and retains the democratic image even today. The main democratic aspect of the Charter is that it provides the ordinary citizen with a power analogous to the reference procedure. The power to refer matters to courts for their opinion is one enjoyed by governments, and *only* by governments. Governments in Ottawa and the provincial capitals historically could catapult their concerns about public policy to a forum where they would be dealt with authoritatively (if not strictly in a judicial sense) by the courts. Now the public can approach the same effect. Surely this is significant democratization.

Cabinets

Cabinet domination is limited somewhat simply by the fact of entrenchment. Yet it may also be limited in other, more subtle ways. The Charter has provided a standard to guide the drafting of legislation and can logically be expected to provide a check on intrusive lawmaking. Courts have not only provided commentaries on substantive rights but have also provided implicit guidance on the form that sustainable legislation might take, once they have rendered particular legislation inoperative.

Legislatures

Although the courts have not made any moves in the direction of direct democracy, they have, by virtue of their Charter decisions, helped to supplement the previously narrow nature of legislative decisions. Courts do not "second guess" the legislature (a familiar critique).

> Institutionally, judicial review has a functional role in reweighing legislative choices with a different focus. Because courts are looking at statutes from the constitutional standpoint, they are asking themselves somewhat different questions than the legislature. Where the legislature asks itself what is best for *society* as it conceives it, the court reviews that enactment on the basis of what is best for *democracy* as it conceives it. The difference is subtle, but may be real.[26]

Courts accordingly serve a *complementary role* to that of legislatures. The court is therefore the ally of the legislature in the struggle for institutional relevance.

The Judiciary

The Charter is mute on the issue of democratization of judicial appointments. However, it does include a certain spirit of democracy. It provides in s. 33 an override measure to allow legislatures to enact legislation that the legislative majority may find necessary in the area of fundamental freedoms, legal rights, and equality rights. This allows an active expression of majority rights. As well, s. 1, by referring to "a free and democratic society," suggests that the experience of other democratic societies in the world is a relevant consideration when courts are trying to decide the constitutionality of government limits on Charter rights and freedoms. So the Charter is no stranger to the democratic urge and is in keeping with the significant democratization of Canadian society in the 1980s and 1990s. The high turnover rate of Supreme Court judges indirectly serves the cause of democratization by allowing governments to make appointments in tune with public sentiment.[27]

It should always be remembered that the Charter is a *supplement* and not a replacement for the statutory and quasi-judicial human rights instruments that have thrived in the post-war period. Section 26 notes that "other rights and freedoms" are not to be affected by the Charter. Also, other less blunt approaches to rights, such as the valuable educative roles of ombudsmen and human rights commissions, are not affected. One might even suggest that their existence is assumed, as parts of a comprehensive rights regime.

The Charter certainly is "worth it." It is the expression of the highest aims of liberal democracy in the twentieth century. In a sense, it is the constitution that Canadians deserved but never got until very late because of the cloying remnants of colonialism. It is one of the signs of political maturity among sovereign nations that only the weak-hearted among Canadians could not abide. It was an idea whose time had finally come. Indeed, the wonder is not that Canadians now have the Charter of Rights and Freedoms but that such a legal document to codify and protect the rights of all Canadians took so long to appear out of the turf-protecting maze of executive federalism.

Notes

1. For elaboration on these incidents, see Thomas R. Berger, *Fragile Freedoms: Human Rights and Dissent in Canada* (Toronto: Clarke Irwin, 1981); Brooke Jeffrey, "The Charter of Rights and Freedoms and Its Effect on Canadians," Background Paper for Parliamentarians, Library of Parliament, Canada, June, 1982.

2. For the difference between "centralist" and "provincialist" variants of intrastate federalism, see Donald V. Smiley and Ronald Watts, *Intrastate Federalism in Canada* (Toronto: University of Toronto Press, 1985).

3. Andrew Heard, "Quebec Courts and the Charter," paper presented to the annual meeting of the Canadian Political Science Association, June, 1992.

4. Ian Greene, *The Charter of Rights* (Toronto: Lorimer, 1989), p. 39.

5. Rainier Knopf and F.L. Morton, "Nation-Building and the Canadian Charter of Rights and Freedoms," in Alan Cairns and Cynthia Williams, Research Coordinators, *Constitutionalism, Citizenship and Society in Canada* (Toronto: University of Toronto Press, 1985), p. 146.

6. *Lavigne v. OPSEU* [1991] 2 SCR 211. Peter Hogg believes the Courts would interpret freedom of association in relation to section 1 of the Charter and thus save the closed and union shop, at least where the Charter applies – in arrangements stipulated by statute or where there is a public employer – but this is a matter of conjecture. See Hogg, *Constitutional Law of Canada*, section 41.3(f).

7. David Beatty, *Talking Heads and the Supremes: The Canadian Production of Constitutional Review* (Toronto: Carswell, 1990).

8. *Ibid.*, ch. 4.

9. James Patrick Sewell, "A World Without Canada: Would Today's United Nations Be the Same?" in John English and Norman Hillmer, *Making a Difference? Canada's Foreign Policy in a Changing World Order* (Toronto: Lester Publishing, 1992), p. 190; and André Picard, "Crusader Created 'conscience of mankind,'" *Globe and Mail*, December 9, 1992, p. A7. The Declaration, which included groundbreaking social and economic rights like the rights to health care, education, and a job, has been called the "Magna Carta of mankind" by Eleanor Roosevelt, and the "conscience of mankind" by Pope John Paul II.

10. Alan Cairns, *Charter versus Federalism: The Dilemmas of Constitutional*

92   *Canadian Political Debates*

Reform (Montreal and Kingston: McGill-Queen's University Press, 1992), p. 29.

11. As cited in Jeffrey, "The Charter of Rights and Freedoms and its Effect on Canadians," p. 8.

12. Philip Zylberberg, "The Problem of Majoritarianism in Constitutional Law: A Symbolic Perspective," *McGill Law Journal*, (1992), pp. 68-78.

13. *Ibid.*, pp. 79-80.

14. Seymour Martin Lipset, *Continental Divide* (London: Routledge, 1990).

15. From Khayyam Paltiel, as quoted in David J. Elkins, "Facing Our Destiny: Rights and Canadian Distinctiveness," *Canadian Journal of Political Science*, 22, 4 (December, 1989), p. 709.

16. Dennis Stone and F. Kim Walpole, "The Canadian Constitution Act and the Constitution of the United States: A Comparative Analysis," *Canadian-American Law Journal*, 2, 1 (Fall, 1983).

17. *Ibid.*

18. Barry L. Strayer, *The Canadian Constitution and the Courts: The Function and Scope of Judicial Review* (Toronto: Butterworths, 1988), ch. 2.

19. *Ibid.*, p. 55.

20. See, for example, Ruggero D. Aldisert, *Logic for Lawyers: A Guide to Clear Legal Thinking* (Deerfield, Ill.: Clark Boardman Callaghan, 1992).

21. Ronald Dworkin, "Equality, Democracy, and Constitution: We the People in Court," *Alberta Law Review*, 28, 2 (1990), pp. 324-46.

22. Ronald Dworkin, *Taking Rights Seriously* (Cambridge, Mass.: Harvard University Press, 1978), p. 85.

23. *Ibid.*, pp. 90-92.

24. Canada, *Report* of the Special Joint Committee of the Senate and the House of Commons, (Ottawa: Information Canada, 1972), pp. 18-19.

25. Peter H. Russell, "A Democratic Approach to Civil Liberties," *University of Toronto Law Journal*, 19 (1969), p. 131.

26. Zylberberg, "The Problem of Majoritarianism," p. 59.

27. Since 1977, nine judges have retired from the Supreme Court before the mandatory retirement age of seventy-five. See "Judges reasons for leaving bench are varied," *Globe and Mail*, August 10, 1992, p. A8.

Chapter 4

Arguments in Opposition to the Charter

The Charter of Rights and Freedoms is a failure. It has only maintained and deepened the worst aspects of Canadian history – elitism, lack of accountability, arbitrary rule, and a host of other characteristics associated with an unjust society. If progress is defined in terms of improving the lot of the most unfortunate in society, then the Charter must be viewed as a misguided and misunderstood mistake, a wrong turn on the long road of Canadian history.

History

The history of Canadian politics and jurisprudence tells a tale that should have given Charter drafters and commentators cause for concern. Relevant considerations include the history of progressive reform in Canada, the traditional function of Canadian courts, and the pattern of recruitment and training. As well, although the length of experience with the 1982 package is relatively short, the American historical record may provide additional insights into the wisdom of constitutional rights.

Sources of Progressive Reform

Progressive reform in Canada has been a product not of the courts but of the legislatures and cabinet leadership. The creation and continuation of this country has always been, above all, an act of *political will.* Canada initiated welfare state reforms in most cases sooner than the United States, and in some cases, such as national health insurance, to the exclusion of it.[1] The advances made by labour were accorded legitimacy by successive governments, in many cases provincial ones. The courts, on the other hand, were silent in the face of flagrant violations of fundamental justice. In *Cunningham v. Tomey Homma* (1903) the Judicial Committee of the Privy Council upheld the right of a provincial legislature to disenfranchise citizens of Japanese and Chinese ancestry. In the *Japanese Canadians Case* (1946) the Committee refused to strike down federal orders-in-council enacted during the war that evacuated Canadian citizens of Japanese ancestry from the west coast, confiscated their property, placed them in concentration camps, and pressured them to be "repatriated" to Japan. The inappropriate use of the War Measures Act to accomplish these measures was questioned by neither the Supreme Court nor the Judicial Committee.[2] During the War Measures Act imposition of 1970 the Supreme Court could not be stirred to restrain the questionable incarceration policies of the federal cabinet. Its decisions on the Bill of Rights of 1960 were characterized by rampant confusion and sloppy draughtsmanship.

Traditional Role of Courts

The traditional role of the courts in Canada prepared it poorly for any significant role in assuring liberties. Historically, the function of the courts has been *adjudicative* in nature. This means that the courts have had the responsibility for establishing legal meanings in actual disputes between individuals or between individuals and the state. The structures and resources of the court were aptly suited for dealing with adjudication. Here the adversary process pits two sides against each other, each of which has the responsibility for providing the judge with whatever information is needed to decide the case at hand. The judge is not expected to perform a research function. Now, with the Charter, the rules of the game have changed dramatically and caught the judiciary off guard. Judges are expected to deal with issues that are better left to political philosophers and social scientists.

Judicial Recruitment and Training

The pattern of judicial recruitment and training has stressed qualities that do not particularly qualify judges for the expanded role thrust on them by the Charter. Recruitment of judges is especially important because, as James Mallory has pointed out, "the social values articulated by the courts will reflect the prevailing values of their [the judges'] formative years."[3] Even at so elevated a post in society, it is too much to ask of human nature to expect that judges overcome the intellectual prejudices that result from *elite formation*. There is, as Peter Russell has termed it, a "social class" background to the Canadian judiciary.[4] Of the first fifty justices to serve on the Supreme Court of Canada, only two were born into working-class backgrounds.[5] Most judges today are male, middle-aged, married, of established religions, come from families with upper middle-class (business or professional) backgrounds, are of British or French ethnicity, and earn salaries vastly in excess of those of average Canadians.[6] Is it any wonder that many of the first generation of Charter decisions were to the benefit of corporations, while none were to labour's benefit?

Nor did the unrepresentative nature of judicial appointments improve under Prime Minister Brian Mulroney. Russell and Ziegel found that the judicial appointments of the first Mulroney government showed a continuation of the patronage or political favouritism that had marked the Trudeau and Turner appointments.[7] Of 228 appointees, 108 – or 47.4 per cent – had a known political association with the Progressive Conservative Party and a quarter (24.1 per cent) were actively involved in Tory political circles. The pattern was particularly strong in the case of courts of appeal and provincial supreme courts. As the authors noted, the threat of ideological imbalance is even more serious when the courts have an important policy role with Charter interpretation.[8] There has been significant resistance to measures to democratize judicial appointments, or even to make them more non-partisan/meritorious in nature.

American Rights Jurisprudence

The record of American judicial interpretation should especially have given Canadian reformers pause. In the United States a constitutional Bill of Rights did in fact exist, but it had proved not to be a major factor because of judicial conservatism. At times the judiciary itself blocked the enhancement of human rights and the quality of life, and indeed added to national disunity. In the *Dred Scott* case, the U.S. Supreme Court struck down an attempt by Congress to limit the expansion of slavery in the new territories with its "Missouri Compromise," a decision that led indirectly to the American Civil War. In *Plessy v. Ferguson,* the Court in effect sanctioned racial segregation by instituting the "separate but equal" doctrine. In spite of the efforts of state and federal legislatures in the late 1800s to the late 1930s to regulate the marketplace to limit hours of work, establish minimum wages, control child labour, and empower unions, they were often powerless in the face of Supreme Court opposition. The Court found support for many of its backward decisions in the "due process" clause of the American Bill of Rights.

The Court started following public opinion only after 1937, when President Roosevelt threatened to stack it with liberals. After World War Two, there was an extended period of progressive decisions under Chief Justice Earl Warren, but this gradually tapered off in intensity. The Court, in fact, became quite right-wing during the 1980s when President Reagan was able to fill it with those who shared his ideological outlook. Progressive periods in American rights jurisprudence have been notable for their brevity.[9] If the country with one of the longest-operating bills of rights in the world cannot use it to bring about substantive improvements in the quality of life of its citizens, then the case for entrenchment is weak indeed.

National Integrity

Canada could not and cannot afford the introduction of any complicating factors in its contemporary national unity troubles, especially a Charter introduced over the strenuous objections of a major partner in Confederation. As well as exacerbating the "Quebec question," the Charter has harmed national integrity by operationalizing inappropriate visions of federalism, changing the way Canadians see themselves, and leading to significant Americanization of Canadian jurisprudence and society.

Quebec and the Charter

As long as Quebec is dissatisfied about the history and the effects of Charter introduction, there can be no meaningful national unity. Quebec federalists do not work from the same assumptions as federalists in the rest of Canada. They are formed by a different historical context and react to different contemporary political pressures. Insensitivity to such imperatives outside Quebec will only spell the ultimate defeat of nation-building as it has been traditionally conducted in Canada. The nature of the Charter's introduction demonstrated basic misunderstandings about federal-provincial relations in a dualistic society.

One important reality is that Quebec nationalism has coloured favourable views of federalism that exist in the province. Supporters of the federalist option in Quebec tend to favour the so-called "dualist" view of Canadian federalism. *Dualist federalism* means that Canada was founded by two linguistic groups, the English and the French – the "charter groups," as the two founding peoples are often called. Each charter group has a political duty, perhaps even a moral duty, to make no changes to the constitution that upset the delicate balance between the two groups; changes must be made as a result of consultation and compromise between the two. The ultimate aim is to build a Canada where both can flourish in harmony.

The nature of the Charter's introduction in 1981-82 destroyed the nation-building effects that might otherwise have resulted. One important aspect of the Charter was that it constitutionalized a language policy of the Trudeau government that at best was largely peripheral to Quebec's concerns and at worst was a direct attack on

the right of Québécois to establish an education regime responsive
to the demographic imperatives facing the province. To many Quebecers, the rights and freedoms included in the document were
merely a *cheval de Troi* for the language provisions. This interpretation is bolstered by a look at the Charter. Most of the crucial rights
and freedoms sought by the English-Canadian intervenors in the
legislative hearings were made subject to the legislative override,
but the topic of central importance to Quebec, language, was not.

In addition, outside the Charter, two of Quebec's demands – a
veto over major constitutional change and compensation for
powers ceded by provinces to the federal government – were ignored or sidetracked by collusive federal-provincial bargaining.[10]
As Daniel Latouche says:

> None of the provincial actors felt obliged to conclude that the
> absence of Quebec, whatever the government in place, was
> sufficient reason to call off the whole deal. The participation
> of Quebec in the constitutional process was judged with a dif-
> ferent set of criteria than that of the other provinces. . . . The
> 1982 Constitution was not a conspiracy but an act of state-
> making and nation-building [of Canada-outside-Quebec].
> For Quebecers this is particularly difficult to admit, since it
> implies that they are not necessarily the centre of Canadian
> existence.[11]

Small wonder indeed that the government of Quebec, under Premier René Lévesque, initiated a blanket override from 1982 to
1985, using section 33 as a shield against all Charter challenges to
its public policies, or that successive Quebec governments have
adopted constitutional strategies aimed at moving Canada toward
a more dualistic conception of rights and freedoms.

Inappropriate Vision of Federalism

The vision of federalism toward which Canada is moving as a result
of the Charter is inappropriate. The Charter was initially opposed
by a substantial majority of the provinces in 1981-82. They perceived it to be a *nationalizing* (standardizing or centralizing) influence that would weaken many of the political advantages of living
in a federal state. There is some reason to believe this interpretation. A statistical study of the Supreme Court of Canada's first 100

Charter decisions (1982 to 1989) demonstrated that there was a roughly even quantitative impact of the Charter on federal and provincial statutes (eleven of the nineteen statutes nullified were provincial), but an uneven qualitative impact. Most of the federal statutes nullified involved procedural issues and not important matters of public policy, whereas most of the invalidated provincial statutes concerned important issues and were invalidated on substantive grounds. Quebec, at five, had the highest number of nullifications. The authors of this study concluded: "The greater impact of the Charter on provincial law-making . . . supports earlier predictions about the potential of the Charter to act as a force for policy uniformity throughout Canada."[12]

Canadian Political Culture

The Charter is beginning to change Canada's political culture, and not for the better. Canadian politics has never been easy to describe, but some general characteristics are indisputable. Much of our history has been marked by a general trust in the political and administrative elites of the country. Canadians have also shown a basic faith in the democratic process. Unfortunately, the Charter has worn away at these pillars. Canadians are more litigious. "Many people [in Canada] have come to believe that for every social ill there must be a legal remedy and, more important, that they can find a just resolution of their claims in the courtroom."[13] They are losing faith in the power of organized politics as the principal means to establish political gains. One study of women's experience in charter litigation ends on this optimistic note: "The Supreme Court of Canada is the first Court in the world to adopt the reality of social disadvantage as a basis for constitutional equality analysis. It will, as a result, be the first Court which will have the opportunity to change it."[14] Political life is a continual struggle, and anything that mystifies that reality is unhealthy.

The introduction of the Charter has weakened national unity and integrity. Its method of introduction was fundamentally flawed and contributed in a major way to national disunity. Its design and early interpretation suggest it is anti-federalist in effect.

Ideology

One can find some of the strongest arguments against the introduction of the Charter along the ideological plane. Judicial review is inherently protective of the status quo. Judicial review of rights, therefore, can be expected to involve the justification of already existing privileges. Certainly women, labour, and various social action groups have seen little cause to celebrate since 1982. Corporations, on the other hand, have benefited from Charter-based court decisions.

Labour and the Charter

Those optimistic enough to believe that the Charter marked a new era of opportunities for labour in Canada have been disappointed. Charter drafters did not include explicit rights of collective bargaining among the more traditional liberal protections. Despite this gap, some observers professed to see possibilities in the "freedom of association" provision in section 2. Supreme Court pronouncements on the meaning of s. 2, however, have not borne out this expectation. The most famous cases (among many) touching on labour issues are three decided in 1987 that have been dubbed the "labour triad."[15] Together these established that the Charter did not protect any of the classic tools of unions, namely strikes, collective bargaining, and picketing. The right to associate the Court defined merely as an individual's right to associate with others in common pursuits. Unions did not have a new and distinct type of group rights; groups had only those collective freedoms that were constitutionally protected for each individual. Right-to-strike legislation was a matter of policy that only legislatures were competent to judge. As well, in the *Dolphin Delivery* case, the Court in essence found that the Charter's freedom of expression guarantee did not extend to private-sector labour disputes because of their private law nature.

Corporations

Corporations, however, did benefit. The courts have granted them status as "individuals" in the language of the Charter, and this has expanded their freedom to move at the same time that the unions' freedom to manoeuvre was being restricted. Corporations have achieved standing to initiate Charter actions and are able to use the Charter to challenge various aspects of state regulation.[16] In light of the fact that the Charter was sold to Canadians as an exercise in democracy, this is a peculiar result indeed. Yet, it is not a surprising result, given the social background of the judges, the general meaning of "individualism" in liberal economic theory, and the general role of courts in Canada.

Other Groups

Other groups in society found the Charter less than fulfilling as well. Aboriginal people wanted self-government, an inherent right that had been guaranteed since the Royal Proclamation of 1763. Instead, they got a more limited statement of rights that the wording of the Constitution Act, 1982, implicitly admitted with its promise of subsequent constitutional conferences to study Aboriginal complaints. However, the courts in *Sparrow* hinted that even the Aboriginal rights clause (s. 25) would be interpreted as if those rights fell under the s. 1 guidelines, even though they were explicitly protected in the Charter.[17] In the case of women's rights, the *Morgentaler* decision destroyed the criminalization of abortion as outlined in the former s. 251 of the Criminal Code, but it did not explicitly recognize a woman's right to an abortion.

The International Context

The Charter has contributed to the disproportionate influence of American jurisprudence on the Canadian courts. On the other hand, Charter supporters overemphasized the importance of the international context as an imperative in moving toward a Charter.

American Influence

American influence on Canadian jurisprudence and society is becoming disproportionate as a result of Charter influence. Although the Supreme Court has not to date embraced American judicial decisions as the main guide to Charter interpretation, one can see certain inroads being made by the American outlook. Robert Martin has given a very forceful argument about the U.S.

influence. His basic point is that by its spill-over effect and its constant exaltation of the "individual" in legal philosophy, judicial decisions, and law school teaching, the American system is colouring how Canadians see the state and its possibilities. If the individual is glorified, then its antimony, the state, is seen as a malevolent force to be overcome. This, quite simply, is not the way Canadians have traditionally seen the role of the state. [18]

International Obligations

Those who argue that the Charter was necessary in order to respond to international pressures are mistaken. What was necessary was that each country respond with sincere measures of civil liberties enhancement within the context of its own specific constitutional traditions. The Universal Declaration of Human Rights notes only that the signatory states commit themselves to the "promotion of universal respect for the observance of human rights and fundamental freedoms." The International Covenant on Civil and Political Rights is more explicit about the country-specific methods of implementation. It states in Article 2, Section 1 that each signing party undertake "to take the necessary steps, in accordance with its constitutional processes and with the provisions of the present Covenant, to adopt such legislative or other measures as may be necessary to give effect to the rights recognized in the present Covenant." As well, Canadian courts have traditionally laboured under the rule of construction that international covenants are interpretive aids subject to being overridden by express domestic legislation to the contrary. [19] It seems likely that Canadian negotiators considered this to be the logical implication of signing such measures, not a full-fledged constitutional charter binding both federal and provincial governments in Canada.

Another elemental but important point needs to be made about the constitutionalizing of rights and the international context. A country may indeed have a bill of rights included in its constitution but still lack the cultural and institutional context to make it work. Canada did not have a constitutional charter for most of its history; the U.S.S.R. did. Yet Canada was vastly more sensitive about human rights than was the Soviet Union. In a world where civil liberties violations are rampant, it does not seem realistic to argue that Canada's international image depended on qualitative differences between the statutory or constitutional nature of its rights protections.

Philosophy of Law

Legal writers and philosophers have been very critical of the idea of constitutional rights. Both specific critiques of the judicial role and more generalized bodies of rights theory are relevant here.

The Place of Judicial Review

Extensive judicial review is fundamentally inconsistent with democratic principles. This is not to deny that it should exist at all. It is, of course, unavoidable in a federal state, and the constitutionality of ordinary legislation needs to be established from time to time. A constitutional bill of rights, however, invites a degree of judicial interference that is counter-productive to a working democracy. *Parliamentary supremacy* is a superior route to rights decisions because it implies accountability, closeness to the public mood, demonstrated progressiveness, and an escape from elitism. The Charter has swung the pendulum too far to the undemocratic, anti-majoritarian side.

A critique of constitutional rights logically begins with a survey of the weaknesses of judicial review. The interesting aspect of such an approach is that both mainstream and socialist writers have established a body of literature critical of the principle. Mainstream writers made several criticisms of judicial review while adoption of a Charter was under active consideration. D.A. Schmeiser was particularly worried, pointing to several difficulties. First, U.S. legal history shows that judges are prone to prejudice and fondness for establishment values. Second, judicial review is contrary to the traditional Canadian constitutional principles of responsible government and sovereignty of the people. Third, the prestige of the courts may suffer as citizens learn of conflict between judges and discover evidence of judicial errors. [20]

D.V. Smiley pointed to the general advantages of using legislatures over courts in the pursuit of social reform. First, legislatures control their own agenda, but courts are merely reactive in nature.

Second, legislatures could express themselves in general terms or with great specificity, to suit the intended public, whereas courts yield complex decisions understandable to very few people. Third, legislatures have broad powers of enforcement, as opposed to the narrow judicial measures. Fourth, legislatures can call upon a wider range of research or evidence than can the courts. All of these considerations weigh against excessive use of judicial review.[21]

Socialists, too, have a case against judicial review. Robert Martin suggests several hypotheses about the role of the Supreme Court of Canada. The starting point is to realize that the state is a means to protect the dominant class, but it has relative autonomy, or substantial independence, in the pursuit of class interests. Judges, by birth or socialization, are members of the dominant class. Judges contribute to class interests mainly on the ideological front, but to do so effectively they must maintain the appearance of neutrality. However, most writing on the Supreme Court has been very shallow, attributing only superficial titles like "liberal," "conservative," "activist," or "non-activist," to the individual judges, when of course they can be many of these things, depending on the particular case. More appropriate titles might be "positivists" – mere instruments of the written law, which judges maintain to be – and "dominant class" – which judges have in fact belonged to, as evidenced by past decisions on labour, women, and police issues.[22]

Constitutional Rights

On the more specific issue of constitutional rights, there are also a variety of criticisms that should be made regarding the place of the courts. The general criticisms of constitutional rights are apparent upon reflection. One is that the definition of rights tends to be *time-bound,* and the protected rights may lose their relevance as new generations express new concerns. Property, for example, was a matter that dominated discussions of rights and public policy in the last century. In 1982 it was not included in the constitutional package, and few voices were raised in complaint.

As well, there may be *false expectations* raised about the nature of protection accorded to rights. Rights documents, especially if they are lengthy and complicated, will inevitably involve balancing and limitations placed on the specific liberties guaranteed in them.

Most Canadians ignore or downplay the importance of the so-called "limitations clause" (s. 1), which basically allows judges to put their own "spin" or interpretation on the rights in question. In other words, if the courts do find a rights infringement, they may excuse it by reference to a "test" or set of criteria *they* devise and implement. The courts, not the legislatures, rank rights in relation to one another. Despite judicial efforts to paint the existing tests for s. 1 in terms of a strict logic, legal literature is increasingly critical of both this alleged logic and the consistency with which it is being applied. [23] This may dim some of the enthusiasm that various Canadians feel for the Charter.

In addition, there is the problem of *inclusion and exclusion.* Inevitably, there will be "ins" and "outs" as far as constitutional protections and protected groups are concerned. The non-protected groups or interests will feel upset and spend much of their valuable organizing time and money in an attempt to achieve "Charter status." Because of recurrent bouts of constitutional reform in Canada, there will be incessant efforts to add to the list of protections. The constitutional negotiations of 1990 to 1992 were an example of the "rights bandwagon effect" in operation. In trying to achieve constitutional status for elements of the welfare state and the environmental movement, proponents of the "Social Charter" seriously overburdened the negotiating process. When combined with an amending formula that is relatively flexible, as is presently the case, rights movements can harm the legitimacy of the constitutional process.

Democratic theory also provides arguments to counter entrenchment of constitutional rights. The so-called *majoritarian argument* is the most common appeal to democracy. It holds that to the greatest extent possible, public decisions should be made by elected majorities and kept out of the hands of the courts. The courts' purview would extend only to the most absolute and inalienable rights. Part of the majoritarian rationale is that the institutional characteristics of legislatures and courts differ. Legislatures are elected and thus not far out of tune with the public mood, and they therefore have a strong incentive to be accountable. Judges in Canada are appointed, tenured, can serve virtually for life (until mandatory retirement at age seventy-five), and can be removed from office only for very serious reasons. [24] Judges thus have no incentive, and indeed no mandate, to be accountable.

Democracy is, at its base, majority rule, and anything that interferes with this imperative is by definition anti-democratic.

Majorities as represented by legislatures should especially make decisions about rights because of the vague way that statements about rights are generally phrased. A useful rule of thumb is that the greater the ambiguity in legal concepts, the greater the amount of judicial legislation. Judges are enabled to decide matters of public policy by applying their own values and cannot be held accountable.

Those who doubt that judges are involved in policy-making, who maintain that they mechanically apply readily identifiable positive law, should review contrary evidence. They could consider the prevalence of dissents in the decisions of the higher courts in Canada. Dissenting opinions in Charter decisions have been especially common in the Supreme Court of Canada since 1986.[25] Those who see judges as neutral and unbiased might also consider the intense efforts by provinces in constitutional talks from the mid-1980s on to achieve better "representation" on the Supreme Court as well as a role in the appointment of justices. Plainly, they saw policy implications. As well, the literature suggests that judicial ideology, rather than mere partisanship, is a determining factor in the choice of judges.[26]

Implicit in the work of Michael Mandel is a theoretical framework that is fairly common to the socialist legal community in Canada. Mandel sees the Charter as a form of *legitimation*. This means that it acts as a way of making existing social relations acceptable, when in reality they are unequal and unjust. Judicial decisions are analogous to philosophy; both justify social power without making reference to concrete benefits. Both ignore certain realities, such as the diminution of freedom and voluntariness that occurs because of social relations. "Crimes committed under various compulsions (self-defence, necessity, duress, insanity) are excused, but the relative compulsions of class or lack of property are deemed not to affect the legal voluntariness of actions."[27] The "principle-policy" distinction made by Dworkin is used by judges to disguise their legislative function. Judicial activism is justified with relation to principle, judicial self-restraint by reference to policy. The real answer is to address power relations in society by power means, and not the more illusory route of the courts and the Charter.[28] This is an appeal to democracy, but phrased in a socialist way.

Institutions of Governance

Cabinet members and legislators, of all people, should have realized the threat to their legitimacy that the new Charter implied, but they did not. Perhaps they did not want to. Yet, unmistakeably, the Charter has weakened the potential of the institutions of government.

Cabinets

Cabinets may find their *leadership,* one of their fundamental roles, usurped under the new Charter. There is an incentive under a Charter regime to look to the courts, rather than to government, as one's protector. This is somewhat ironic, given the historical antipathy of the courts to regulatory regimes.

Legislatures

The Charter has affected *legislative vitality.* One sees an increasing tendency for legislatures to turn over to the courts some of the "no-win" issues of Canadian politics. A short list of the subjects of Supreme Court decisions is testimony to this fact: Quebec language of education; Quebec commercial signs; Ontario separate school funding; Sunday shopping in Ontario and Alberta; and, of course, abortion. Politicians now perceive political rationality as knowing when to refer matters to the courts.

Citizen quiescence is the logical end of Charter politics. Everything about the legal system is calculated to induce in the layperson a feeling of awe, and above all, of powerlessness. The cost of litigation places the process out of reach of all but the wealthiest in Canadian society. There are disincentives to self-representation. Both judges and lawyers dress in garments that are evocative of an earlier, absolutist era. How this system could be touted as an instrument of citizen participation and democracy in the first place is almost beyond comprehension.

The Legal System

The legal system, paradoxically, is also suffering. The Charter is clogging the business of the Supreme Court, edging out the traditional subject matters with which it dealt. Provincial appeal courts are becoming the "court of last appeal" in a *de facto* if not a *de jure* sense.[29] The courts of appeal route may thus be robbing Canadian jurisprudence of a useful body of precedent in certain areas, such as civil law.

The justices themselves seem to be suffering as well, both mentally and physically. Since 1988 four Supreme Court justices have resigned before mandatory retirement age (Willard Estey, 1988, at sixty-eight, after eleven years of service; Gerald LeDain, 1988, at sixty-three, after four years; Bertha Wilson, 1991, at fifty-seven, after nine years; and William Stevenson, 1992, at fifty-eight, after a mere two years). In all but Estey's case, "Charter stress" – the vastly increased workload and expectation level that came in the Charter era – appears to have been a contributing cause.[30]

The Charter was most assuredly not "worth it." It has sapped the vitality of representative government. It has compromised the traditional democratic ethos of Canadian society and culture. It is a centralizing, Americanizing, elitist, and right-wing instrument. The rest of Canada should have joined Quebecers in flying flags at half-mast when it was proclaimed on April 17, 1982.

Notes

1. See, for example, David B. Robertson and Dennis R. Judd, *The Development of American Public Policy: The Structure of Policy Restraint* (Glenview, Ill.: Scott, Foresman and Company, 1989), ch. 3.

2. Thomas R. Berger, *Fragile Freedoms: Human Rights and Dissent in Canada* (Toronto: Clark Irwin, 1981), ch. 4.

3. J.R. Mallory, "The Courts as Arbiters of Social Values," in David P. Shugarman and Reg Whitaker, eds. *Federalism and Political Community* (Peterborough, Ont.: Broadview Press, 1989), p. 293.

4. Peter H. Russell, *The Judiciary in Canada* (Toronto: McGraw-Hill Ryerson, 1987), p. 164.

5. George Adams and Paul J. Cavaluzzo, "The Supreme Court of Canada: A Biographical Study," *Osgoode Hall Law Journal* (1969), p. 84.

6. *Ibid.* See also Ian Greene, *The Charter of Rights* (Toronto: Lorimer, 1989), pp. 66-69, for a digest of available research on judicial backgrounds.

7. Peter H. Russell and Jacob S. Ziegel, "Federal Judicial Appointments: An Appraisal of the First Mulroney Government's Appointments and the New Judicial Advisory Committees," *University of Toronto Law Journal,* 41 (1991), pp. 4-37. (There had, however, been a modest improvement in the percentage of women appointees to the bench.)

8. *Ibid.,* p. 25.

9. Alan Borovoy, *When Freedoms Collide: The Case for Our Civil Liberties* (Toronto: Lester and Orpen Dennys, 1988), p. 203.

10. Claude Morin, *Mes premiers ministres* (Montréal: Boréal, 1991).

11. Daniel Latouche, "Canada: The New Country From Within the Old Dominion," *Queen's Quarterly,* 98, 2 (Summer, 1991), p. 11.

12. F.L. Morton, Peter H. Russell, and Michael Withey, "The Supreme Court's First One Hundred Charter of Rights Decisions: A Statistical Analysis," Occasional Papers Series, Research Study 6.1, Research Unit For Socio-Legal Studies, University of Calgary, n.d.

13. Robert Martin, "The Charter and the Crisis in Canada," in David E. Smith *et al., After Meech Lake: Lessons for the Future* (Saskatoon: Fifth House Publishers, 1991), p. 126.

14. Kathleen E. Mahoney, "The Constitutional Law of Equality in Canada," paper presented to the International Canadian Studies Conference, Jerusalem, May, 1992, p. 37.

15. *Reference Re Public Service Employee Relations Act,* [1987] 1 SCR 313, (1987), 38 DLR (4th) 161; *Public Service Alliance of Canada v. Canada,* [1987] 1 SCR 424, (1987), 38 DLR (4th) 249; *Retail, Wholesale and Department Store Union v. Saskatchewan* [1987] 1 SCR 460, (1987), 38 DLR (4th) 277

16. Robert Martin, "Ideology and Judging in the Supreme Court of Canada," *Osgoode Hall Law Journal,* 26, 4 (1988), p. 827. See also *R. v. Big M Drug Mart Ltd.,* [1985] 1 SCR 295.

17. Michael Mandel, *The Charter of Rights and the Legalization of Politics in Canada* (Toronto: Wall and Thompson, 1989), p. 255.

18. Martin, "Ideology and Judging in the Supreme Court."

19. William F. Pentney, "Interpreting the Charter: General Principles," in Gerald-A. Beadoin and Ed Ratushney, *The Canadian Charter of Rights and Freedoms,* second edition (Toronto: Carswell, 1989), p. 61.

20. D.A. Schmeiser, "The Case Against Entrenchment of a Canadian Bill of Rights," *Dalhousie Law Journal,* 1, 1 (September, 1973), pp. 15-50.

See also D.A. Schmeiser, "The Entrenchment of a Bill of Rights," *Alberta Law Review,* 19 (1981), pp. 375-83.

21. Donald Smiley, "Courts, legislatures, and the protection of human rights," in Martin L Friedland, *Courts and Trials: a Multidisciplinary Approach* (Toronto: University of Toronto Press, 1975), pp. 97-98.

22. Martin, "Ideology and Judging in the Supreme Court."

23. See, for example, Norman Siebrasse, "The *Oakes* Test: An Old Ghost Impeding Bold New Initiatives," *Ottawa Law Review,* 23, 1 (1991), pp. 99-131; Ruth Colker, "Section 1, Contextuality, and the Anti-Disadvantage Principle," *University of Toronto Law Journal,* 42 (1992), pp. 77-112.

24. Some of these reasons involve conventions of the constitution. See Andrew Heard, *Canadian Constitutional Conventions: the Marriage of Law and Politics* (Toronto: Oxford University Press, 1991), ch. 6, especially pp. 121-25.

25. David Beatty, *Talking Heads and the Supremes: The Canadian Production of the Constitutional Review* (Toronto: Carswell, 1990), ch. 3.

26. Mandel, *The Charter of Rights,* pp. 95-96 and *passim.*

27. *Ibid.,* p. 58.

28. *Ibid.,* pp. 50-58.

29. See, for example, a review of the activities of the Manitoba Court of Appeal in the *Winnipeg Free Press,* July 21, 1992, pp. A1, B10.

30. *Globe and Mail,* August 10, 1992, pp. A1, A7.

PART THREE

Do Canadian Provinces Have
Excessive Power?

One of the major themes of Canadian federalism for the past thirty years has involved provincial and, to a lesser extent, federal demands for new powers. Demands for new provincial powers usually emphasized dichotomous choice. Citizens were asked to choose between strong provinces and a strong central government, between centralization and decentralization, and between the historical records of different levels of government.

Activity on the division of powers generated a considerable body of scholarly literature on the subject. The literature, while often acknowledging that wider conceptualizations of federalism were possible, also tended to drift toward discussions of the relative merits of centralization and decentralization. A review of this literature will give us an idea of the variety of grounds for both sides of the centralization-decentralization question. While many Canadians feel it would be best to have both a strong national government and strong provincial governments, such an arrangement presents immense conceptual difficulties. Here the arguments for both sides will be presented in their traditional dichotomous fashion. [1]

A few caveats are appropriate at the beginning. References are made to recent history and to current controversies, but the following two chapters do not purport to deal with them in any substantive way. They do not deal specifically with the role of Quebec in Confederation, although some of the "solutions" may be applicable to the Quebec question. The major focus is merely a review of arguments for and against the idea that provinces already have enough power in Canadian federalism.

One finds that the arguments about overreaching provincial powers cover constitutional politics, modern Canadian constitutional theory, international and domestic economic factors, social policy considerations, and comparative politics. There have been strong arguments on either side of the centralist-provincialist divide.

Provincial Power in Historical Perspective

The agenda for Trudeau-era constitutional reform usually placed division of powers questions at the bottom of the list, after entrenchment of rights and institutional reform. The failed Meech Lake process advanced the division of powers question more to the forefront, although in rather oblique fashion. The question of provincial power shares – in both the *de jure* and *de facto* senses – became an important item in constitutional talks once again. The question of whether or not to increase provincial power has, of course, already been with us for some time.

Quebec and Power Claims

In the modern era the drive for power was spearheaded by the Jean Lesage government in Quebec in the early 1960s. Quebec was particularly successful in the areas of pension policy and the 1965 opting-out provisions. Quebec continued to push for reform of the division of powers during the 1968-71 constitutional conferences of first ministers, challenging the federal agenda for the talks. The first ministers considered changes in the division of taxing and spending powers in 1969, as well as federal and provincial roles in the field of income security and social services. In June, 1971, Quebec made some radical proposals for reallocation of federal and provincial responsibilities for social security; the Victoria Charter of 1971 made some limited concessions to Quebec in this area and others, but Premier Robert Bourassa ultimately rejected the Victoria agreement.

The Increase of Claims for Provincial Power

In the mid- to late 1970s other provinces joined the call for new powers. Now requested were provincial controls of varying degrees over a sizeable list of matters: immigration, language, resource taxation, the declaratory power, annual first ministers' conferences, creation of new provinces, culture, communications, the federal spending power, equalization, reservation and disallowance, implementation of treaties, fisheries, natural resources, and appointment of judges of the provincial supreme courts. Consideration of *other* aspects of federal power was to follow this as well! The other provinces had joined Quebec in the challenge to the federal agenda. What they did not get from this list in the 1980-82 and 1987 constitutional negotiations – and they got some items[2] – they continued to seek on the judicial, regulatory, fiscal, and policy fronts.

The Meech Lake Accord

The Meech Lake Accord was negotiated in 1987 and failed in 1990 for political and constitutional reasons. To many, the Accord appeared an opportunity for provinces to obtain powers that had eluded them in past constitutional rounds. To others, it was simply the constitutionalizing of federal-provincial practices that had developed in the past few decades and did not constitute any major departures. Probably the truth lies somewhere between these two poles; at the very least it would have meant an increase in provincial status and an ability to constrain the federal authorities. Certainly it indicated that the *compact theory* of Canadian federalism, which states that the provinces had created the federal government and hence shared a loosely defined equality of status in matters of constitutional amendment and national policy, had a new lease on life. The Accord, if implemented, would have constitutionalized federal-provincial immigration agreements, thus allowing them a modicum of security from unilateral change. It would have allowed provinces to submit names for the federal appointment of senators and Supreme Court judges, making it a *de facto* joint process. The spending power of the federal government, which allowed Parliament to spend but not regulate in areas of provincial jurisdiction, was to be constitutionalized but narrowed. Up to three provinces could opt out from new shared-cost programs and receive compensation if they undertook programs or initiatives compatible with national objectives. There would also be constitutionalization of that pantheon of provincial influence, the federal-provincial conference – once yearly, on each of the constitution and the economy. The amendment formula reached in 1982 would have been made more rigid by increasing the items falling under the unanimity (or all-government approval) clause.

The only section of the Meech Lake Accord that explicitly stated that no change in the division of powers was involved was the "linguistic duality and distinct society clause." This involved still another theory of Canadian federalism with provincial power overtones, the *dualism theory*. The clause reflected dualism by defining Canada in terms of English and French language groups. It also gave Quebec a rather mysterious mandate to "preserve and promote" the distinct identity of Quebec, mysterious because the other governments were only given the responsibility to "preserve" linguistic duality and because of the aforementioned non-derogation clause. Quebec nationalists scorned the duality/distinct society clause as offering Quebec no new powers, while English-Canadian nationalists saw a panoply of new initiatives arising from it that would be unavailable to provinces other than Quebec.

Post-Meech Developments

In the spring of 1991 the Allaire Committee of the Quebec Liberal Party demanded that Quebec be given exclusive control of twenty-two jurisdictional matters; and this new emphasis on the division of powers was echoed by the Quebec National Assembly's Belanger-Campeau Commission. Perhaps seeking to mollify Quebec without violating the principle of provincial equality, the federal government's proposals of September, 1991 – *Shaping Canada's Future Together* – suggested recognizing exclusive provincial jurisdiction over tourism, forestry, mining, recreation, and municipal affairs, as well as sharing authority in such areas as manpower training, culture, and immigration. Of course, these suggestions were counterbalanced by some centralizing provisions in the federal package. Reflecting a Trudeau-era theme, the federal proposals suggested a new head of federal power, called section 91A, allowing the Parliament of Canada exclusive power to pass laws for the efficient functioning of the economic union, subject to approval by a new "Council of the Federation," a "two-thirds – 50 per cent" provincial approval threshold, and an opting-out provision.

The Charlottetown Accord

The Charlottetown Accord of August 28, 1992, showed to what extent the provincial drive for power had affected the constitutional bargaining process. Section III of this Accord (dealing with "roles and responsibilities") would have generated one of the most thoroughgoing modifications of federal and provincial powers in Canadian history. Part of it dealt with the federal spending power, part with the allocation of constitutional powers, and part with assorted constitutional issues.

The federal *spending power* was to achieve constitutional status, but it was to be heavily qualified. A constitutional provision would state that Canada would provide reasonable compensation to any province choosing not to participate in a new Canada-wide shared-cost program established by Ottawa in areas of exclusive provincial jurisdiction, where the provincial program or initiative was compatible with national objectives. The legal text released later in October, however, specified that the "national objectives" would in fact be jointly set by the federal and provincial governments as part of a "framework" (jointly established) to guide the use of the federal spending power.[3] Once developed, moreover, this framework would become a "designated multilateral agreement" and receive constitutional protection. The constitution therefore would be amended to provide for designated agreements, which, as described in the Charlottetown Accord, meant that (1) federal and provincial legislatures would pass identical legislation to give effect to bilateral or multilateral intergovernmental agreements, (2) the agreements would have a maximum life of five years during which they were immune to unilateral change, and (3) they would be renewable by a similar process.

The sections dealing with allocation of constitutional powers involved a detailed outline of new provincial prerogatives. Labour market training was to be identified as an area of exclusive provincial jurisdiction; the federal government would retain responsibility for job creation and unemployment insurance. Exclusive provincial jurisdiction would be "recognized and clarified" by constitutional amendment in regards to culture, but with an undefined and continuing federal role. Such exclusive jurisdiction and amendment would also be the case for what intergovernmental argot had deemed the "six sisters" – forestry, mining, tourism, housing, recreation, and municipal and urban affairs – except that in these six areas the provincial legislatures would have the power to constrain federal spending through justiciable intergovernmental agreements undertaken as designated agreements. Such an agreement would require the federal government either to maintain its spending in the area or to vacate the area, transferring compensation to the province. In the latter case the feds would be kicked off the front porch, but leave behind the money.

The federal government would have an obligation to negotiate agreements in certain areas. This was to be accomplished by constitutional amendments in the areas of immigration and regional development. As well, there would be harmonization of telecommunications policy and constitutionalized protection of the results.

The Accord would have put certain issues to rest. The federal power of reservation and disallowance would be repealed. The federal declaratory power (section 92 10(c) of the 1867 constitution) would be limited. Its use would require provincial legislative authorization.

The Charlottetown Accord was therefore something of a landmark in the drive for increased provincial power. It demonstrated that provincial power was the price to be paid for the achievement of federal objectives, such as Quebec's acceptance of the constitution and measures to ensure the Canadian common market.

Provincial Power in Theoretical Perspective

There have been many investigations of the question of division of powers and related matters; they have employed a wide variety of values in their attempts to chart the future of the Canadian federation.[4] However, for the sake of simplicity, it is convenient to mention only two categories of approach: on the one hand, those that are elaborate as to the values to be sought in federalism and that outline detailed changes to the division of powers; on the other, those that posit relatively few values and do not advocate detailed changes to the division of powers. We call the first the Pepin-Robarts Model and the second the Macdonald Commission Model, after the work of two federal commissions: the Pepin-Robarts Task Force of 1979[5] and the Macdonald Royal Commission on the Economic Union and Development Prospects for Canada of 1985.[6] The two models will be examined in greater detail in the following two chapters. For the time being, it is sufficient to comment that the Pepin-Robarts reasoning is supportive of more provincial power and the Macdonald Commission reasoning points toward resisting such provincial demands.

Notes

1. Those who prefer a more synthetic approach to the division of powers question would find the approach of Mintz and Simeon an interesting one. See Jack Mintz and Richard Simeon, *Conflict of Taste and Conflict of Claim in Federal Countries,* Discussion Paper No. 13 (Kingston, Ont.: Institute of Intergovernmental Relations, Queen's University, 1982). The main attraction of this approach is that it refuses to make generalized statements; instead, it accounts for the relative impact of different types of issues, different sizes of province, and different states of provincial wealth.

   Mintz and Simeon distinguish between two types of interregional conflict. The first is "conflict of taste," which refers to the extent to which regional majorities have preferences about public policies different from, or incompatible with, those of other regional or national majorities because of different social or cultural values (pp. 2-4). The second is "conflict of claim," which refers to the competition between regions (provinces) who share certain values but who disagree on the distribution of wealth between them; in order for one region to get what it wants, it must obtain it, or its equivalent, from other regions who want the same things (pp. 4-5).

There are "efficient" solutions to "conflicts of taste" in the sense that in federalism, responsibilities (like health, welfare, and education) can be allocated so as to respond to the desires of regional majorities and to minimize interference or vetoes from other majorities. There are no "efficient" solutions possible in "conflicts of claim" since the usual objective is the maximization of regional welfare rather than national welfare. Conflicts of claim may take the form of competition for investment, interprovincial trade barriers, arguments over relative shares of resource wealth, or hostility to central government policies that discriminate against the region in question in favour of other regions. Although conflicts of claim have existed since Confederation they are becoming increasingly salient. Many disputes supposedly about conflicts of taste may in fact be conflicts of claim in disguise.

There are few clear rules in regard to defining when national or regional majorities should carry the day. All that Mintz and Simeon offer as guidance is that federal and provincial bargainers should all aim at *system maintenance.* They should avoid systematic coercion of specific regions and attempt to balance regional wins and losses even when this means departing from majority rule. National integration in the final analysis depends on the principle of mutual advantage.

2. For example, the right to indirect taxation over resources in section 92A, a constitutionalized role in the amending process, and the right to opt out of certain Charter protections by invoking the section 33 override clause.

3. See the *Draft Legal Text* of the Charlottetown Accord, October 9, 1992, sections 37 (1)(a) and 93C (2).

4. A few are as follows: Canada, 28th Parliament, 4th Session, Special Joint Committee on the Constitution of Canada, *Final Report* (Ottawa, 1972); Canadian Bar Association, Committee on the Constitution, *Towards a New Canada* (Montreal, Canadian Bar Foundation, 1978); Quebec Liberal Party, Constitutional Committee, *A New Canadian Federation* (Montreal, January 9, 1980) ("The Beige Paper"); Garth Stevenson, "The Division of Powers," in Richard Simeon, ed., *Division of Powers and Public Policy* (Toronto: University of Toronto Press, 1985); M.H. Sproule-Jones, *Public Choice and Federalism in Australia and Canada* (Canberra: Centre for Research on Federal Financial Relations, Australian National University,

Research Monograph No. 11, 1975); Anthony Scott; "An Economic Approach to the Federal Structure," *Options,* Proceedings of the Conference on the Future of the Canadian Federation, University of Toronto (Toronto: University of Toronto, 1977).

5. Canada, Task Force on Canadian Unity, *Report,* 3 vols. (Ottawa: Minister of Supply and Services, January, February, and March, 1979). The main report is *A Future Together: Observations and Recommendations* (January, 1979).

6. Canada, *Report of the Royal Commission on the Economic Union and Development Prospects for Canada,* 3 vols. (Ottawa: Minister of Supply and Services, 1985).

Chapter 5

The Provinces Have Too Much Power

Canadian provinces have far too much power. Enlightened politicians and academics have occasionally drawn our attention to this fact, but the forces of provincialism have been able to divert attention away from it. Canadians would do well to remind themselves about the effects of provincialism and the advantages of a strong central government. This chapter proposes to do just this by reviewing constitutional politics, international and domestic economic factors, social policy considerations, and Canadian federalism in a comparative context.

Constitutional Politics

Provinces have blocked needed constitutional change and have weakened constitutional arrangements that had bona fide reasons for being installed in the first place. They have weakened provisions that allocate foreign affairs to the national government and that provide for an economic common market within the Canadian union. Provinces should not be accorded more of a hammerlock on future constitutional change.

The Process of Constitutional Reform

Provinces have hindered constitutional modernization in Canada. The provinces of Ontario and Quebec jointly hindered agreement on amendment formulas in the constitutional negotiations of 1927, 1936, and 1950. Claiming prerogatives arising from their sizable population and economic power, they demanded *de facto* or *de jure* veto powers through either unanimity provisions or provisions that accorded them special rights. Saskatchewan opposed the Fulton formula of 1961 and Quebec effectively torpedoed the Fulton-Favreau formula of 1964 and the 1971 Victoria Charter. The eight dissident provinces very nearly defeated the 1979-82 constitutional renewal process.

Provinces bring a narrow provincialism to the process of constitutional reform. The increasing power of the provinces in the area of constitutional reform has had a variety of negative effects. One is the pursuance of constitutional renewal, predominately through executive federalism: secretive and definitive bargaining by federal and provincial political elites, upon which provinces have insisted as a condition of constitutional renewal. It has resulted in an unjustified appropriation of power by the provincial and federal authorities.

As Alan Cairns has recounted, governments are appropriating power that not so long ago was decentralized to popular groups. The federal government in the 1968-to-1982 rounds of constitutional negotiations very effectively contrasted the rights of people (the Charter) with the provinces' "selfish pursuit of governmental advantage"[1] and relegated the question of division of powers to a category of secondary importance. Referendums were suggested as deadlock-breakers in cases of constitutional impasse between governments. The citizens' voice in constitutional change began to be seen as a necessary complement to those of governments, whose collective authority and legitimacy were definitely waning.[2]

Citizen groups established along non-territorial cleavages are not likely to be as deferent to government in matters of constitutional renewal.

The Constitution is no longer an affair of governments. In addition to the governments' Constitution, which tends to focus on federalism, there is a citizens' Constitution which the Charter symbolizes. A central task for the constitutional theory and practice of future decades is to find ways in which these two visions, warring in the bosom of the Canadian Constitution, can be reconciled.[3]

Former Prime Minister Trudeau has given implicit approval to this "government versus the people" distinction. He contrasts the "legal country" of Canada, that is, a Prime Minister desirous of electoral victory and provincial premiers "all panting to increase their powers," and the "real country" of Canada, namely "the unorganized coalition of Canadian individuals and groups scattered across the nation, for whom Canada is more than a collection of provinces to be governed through wheeling and dealing."[4] Trudeau argues that the real country shared his antipathy to the values inherent in the Meech Lake Accord.

The Internal Common Market

Provinces have blunted constitutional directives as to an internal common market. Section 121 of the Constitution Act, 1867, says that "All articles of Growth, Produce or Manufacture of any of the Provinces shall, from and after the Union, be admitted free into each of the other Provinces." However, as is well known, provinces have erected a wide variety of barriers to the free flow of interprovincial commerce, such as technical and product standards, procurement policies, and conditions set on the sale of raw natural resources. Until prevented by section 6 of the Constitution Act, 1982, provinces also engaged in analogous restrictions to the mobility of labour in Canada. The reason for these blockages was purportedly to promote development – to design economic policies that would enhance provincial employment and per capita income, decrease net out-migration, and expand forward, backward, and final demand linkages in the area of staple goods.

Such restrictions, however, are contrary to economic efficiency, and they are contrary to the specific intent of the Fathers of Confederation. The Canadian Manufacturers' Association has estimated that such internal barriers cost Canadians $6.5 billion annually. Clearly, regional development policies should be de-emphasized at the provincial level, at least those that feature inter-provincial trade barriers.

The Division of International Responsibilities

Although the 1867 constitution, the British North America Act, was unclear on the division of international responsibilities in Canadian federalism, there is some indication in section 132 ("Empire Treaties") that Ottawa was intended to play the major role in international treaties and undertakings. Since the *Labour Conventions Case* of 1937, of course, the responsibility has been effectively curtailed: Canada did not have the right to conclude an international treaty committing a province to carry out the matter agreed to therein if it fell within provincial jurisdiction. Left ambiguous in this 1937 Judicial Committee decision, however, were the respective rights of the federal and provincial governments to negotiate international agreements, and Quebec has at times asserted its right to do so. Given the vast range of provincial transnational activity, it is not beyond the realm of possibility that other provinces one day might claim similar privileges.

It is instructive to review the federal defence of "one voice" in international affairs during the heyday of the controversy in the late 1960s:

Ottawa's case was that the prerogative power to enter into international arrangements and to conclude agreements binding in public international law resided in the federal executive alone. . . . The federal authorities made much of the point that Canada had a single international personality and that the United Nations and its specialized agencies, as well as other international associations and international law, drew a very sharp line between jurisdictions which were sovereign states and those which were not. The general case was made that "foreign policy is indivisible" although in the

Canadian circumstances this did not preclude the provinces in cooperation with the federal government from being involved in international affairs.[5]

With some exceptions this has continued to be the status quo stance of the federal government.

It was given a new twist in the case of negotiation of international trade agreements; during the Canada-U.S. Free Trade Agreement negotiations in the late 1980s, federal spokespersons implied that their right to conclude the FTA rested on the federal trade and commerce power and related constitutional sources of power, and that provinces would be bound by the results.[6] The subliminal message in Ottawa's defences of its international role is that provinces have enough of an international presence, and perhaps too great a one. The Macdonald Royal Commission offered a more explicit defence for federal predominance in international trade negotiations:

> Unless the negotiating parties in international negotiations can fully commit their own countries to abide by the agreements signed, they will have only limited ability to secure concessions. Informal undertakings made by provinces . . . to comply with negotiated international agreements will not solve the problem.[7]

Canadian Constitutional Theory: The Macdonald Commission Report

The Macdonald Royal Commission took a different approach than did the Pepin-Robarts Task Force to the philosophy of federalism, and this yielded a different set of prescriptions for federal and provincial powers. The *Report* can be seen as having a kind of laissez-faire outlook on the division of powers and, if not patently hostile to increased provincial powers, it provides one of the best counter-arguments to these demands.

In fact, the Commission offers a somewhat conflicting theory of federalism. Volume One of the *Report* seems to promote the value of "competition" over co-operation.[8] However, in Volume Three, the Commission argues for "balance":

We Canadians must seek to establish balance in our federal institutions. We must try to find middle ground between unregulated competition and implausible harmony, and between accountability of governments to citizens and collaboration among governments.[9]

This balance is to be exercised within the "spirit of the Constitution," which is said to be self-restraint by both orders of government.

The Commission, evidently choosing the notions of balance and self-restraint as its operative guides, resisted the urge to modernize or specify aspects of the division of powers (other than in the area of regional development). It noted that the present constitution is a useful record of the collective experience of Canadian society, that any attempt to codify the division of powers would be a dauntingly controversial topic in an era of interwoven policy areas, and finally that any specific reallocation of powers, rather than clarifying matters of jurisdiction, would run the distinct risk of obsolescence.[10]

The Commission could see no outstanding case for either increasing centralization or advocating decentralization. "Disentanglement" or returning to "watertight compartments" might reduce the costs of decision-making; but *overlapping authority* and *de facto concurrence* were, on balance, more attractive. Governments would "compete" to respond to the needs of citizens. However, some mechanisms allowing flexibility would be valuable: delegation, establishing First Ministers' Conferences in the Constitution, creating "third-party bodies" to facilitate intergovernmental relations, and establishing three ongoing federal-provincial "ministerial councils" in the fields of finance, economic development, and social policy.[11]

International and Domestic Economic Factors

International and domestic economic factors are another major argument against giving provinces increased powers. The federal government should have the predominant power to define economic strategy toward our increasingly influential international competitors and to minimize harmful economic competition between provinces. International trade and economic questions must therefore be considered in tandem with domestic industrial policy when contemplating who the major governmental actors should be.

Economic Strategy

Peter Leslie has suggested that from about 1960 to 1984 the federal government operated on such a rationale, in what he called "a third national policy":

> [Federal] initiatives were mainly aimed at strengthening and transforming the manufacturing sector to meet foreign competition in domestic and external markets, although (somewhat inconsistently) it frequently had recourse to various forms of protectionism to sustain failing industries and firms. . . . In one variant of the policy the government seemed ready to make the resource industries subservient to the needs of manufacturing; in another . . . the resource industries were to be the main motor of economic development, and manufacturing was to be built up by maximizing its linkages with primary production. Both variants called for an activist or interventionist federal government and required affirming and augmenting its powers over the economy. [12]

This "interventionist-nationalist" approach, as Leslie calls it was abandoned and replaced by the "liberal-continentalist" option of the Mulroney Conservatives.

During the interventionist period it was also clear that restrictions on foreign ownership were considered an important part of a federal economic role. A federal economic development statement of 1981 repeated with approval the preamble to the centralist Foreign Investment Review Act of 1974, which identified as a matter of "national concern" the extent to which foreign control of industry, trade, and commerce had affected Canadians' control over their own economic environment. [13]

The Trudeau government in 1981 saw itself in a leading role in economic development, having "a special responsibility for preserving and strengthening the integrity of the economic union." [14] This it interpreted as resisting balkanization of the Canadian market and promoting joint federal-provincial economic development planning. Joint planning did not imply joint implementation, however, and for the rest of its mandate the federal government was to focus increasingly on unilateral federal initiatives in major projects, regional development, and the search for international markets.

There were substantial advantages to the federal approach, as Hugh Thorburn noted. It would promote efficiency by obviating the need for constant intergovernmental compromise, by favouring the provinces that were best located in respect to economic development opportunities, and by encouraging internal population migration. Thus would Canada be better able to do economic battle with foreign unitary governments.[15]

Comprehensiveness

Other than a desire for coherence in international economic strategy, other factors may militate in favour of federal leadership in economic development. Michael Jenkin saw the need for comprehensiveness as the main reason for federal predominance. Provinces would miss opportunities not of immediate interest to them individually or collectively, and at any rate they often lack the resources or capacity to seize opportunities quickly and effectively.[16]

Tom Kent says that contemporary provincial regional development should have only restricted, relatively modest components. These are the improvement of education and training, the offsetting of negative economic change on communities, and research and development assistance to small-scale enterprises that would engage in import substitution and export activity. The major hope for equality of opportunity across the nation, however, rests with the federal government. Only if it has the capacity to manage the economy for higher levels of employment are economic redistribution and a better regional balance of employment and income possible.[17]

Superior Powers

Federal leadership in development stems from the simple fact that federal development policies have the capacity to frustrate provincial policies. Provided, of course, that the government possesses the political will, federal regulatory and taxation powers may be sufficient to counteract provincial economic and resource policies springing from constitutional sources of power, and even from the new section 92A of the Constitution Act, 1982, which added new provincial powers over natural resources and extended provincial taxation powers in relation to them. This the National Energy Policy conclusively demonstrated, says Leslie.[18]

Public Opinion

As well, Leslie suggests, political support may not always be forthcoming for provincially led development. It will not be attractive in resource-poor provinces. Boom-and-bust cycles may lead both public opinion and producers to welcome federal policies of stabilization. Even after prolonged periods of prosperity, when the expected economic diversification promised by provincial governments does not materialize, public faith in provincial leadership may flag.[19]

Social Policy Considerations

Still another set of arguments against giving provinces increased powers in Canadian federalism centres on social policy. Certain social functions – especially *redistribution* and *citizenship rights* – are better performed by national rather than by subnational governments.

Redistribution

Redistribution is manifestly a federal responsibility. A complex argument to this effect has been enunciated by Dan Usher, who proposed that a "contractarian" (citizen-centred) approach to the question of division of redistributive powers reveals three principles: relative efficiency, balance, and harmony.[20] Efficiency is understood to be maximization of real national income; balance is allowing linguistic, racial, or religious minorities a certain area of self-determination; and harmony is the achievement of minimum conflict by means of a strict apportionment of rights. Usher suggested that all arguments based on these principles are valid for all citizens, but that these same citizens will weight them differently according to their own different circumstances throughout the country. For example, consideration of balance would probably be foremost in the assignment of many redistributive responsibilities by French Canadians; for English Canadians, considerations of harmony would probably predominate.[21]

By and large, however, the weight of Usher's argument points toward federal administration. Direct federal redistribution *links together all donors and recipients* in Canada; redistribution authority limited to provinces would probably lead to limited concern by people in rich provinces for their brethren in poorer provinces.[22] Choosing equalization grants as a surrogate for redistribution, in order to compromise between French and English Canadians, is no answer; equalization may not in fact always result in redistribution.

Citizenship Rights

A.W. Johnson perceives citizenship rights to be the appropriate purview of the federal government.[23] Constitutions, he says, should do three things: define rights and freedoms, establish a system of governance, and strengthen the bonds of nationhood.

Strengthening the *bonds of nationhood* depends on the strength of feeling that a people has for the nation, which in part depends on the degree of commonality of benefits enjoyed by all members of the nation and in part on a sense of association with national institutions. The benefits of citizenship in Canadian history have, for example, been programs like medicare, hospital care, old age pensions, disability allowances, access to higher education, and the Trans-Canada Highway. Most of these were established either by a federal-provincial shared-cost program operating under federal standards or by constitutional amendment to allow federal assumption of a previously provincial responsibility.

An initiative like the Meech Lake Accord threatened both the commonality of benefits and Canadians' affinity for national institutions. Meech's endowing of provincial governments with the right to opt out of nationalizing amendments, or of new shared-cost programs, with federal compensation, would have seriously attenuated the possibility for national "sharing" or commonality of benefits.[24] The Charlottetown Accord would have had analogous effects. In other words, provincial efforts to seek more power over social programs, by deviating from national norms, should be resisted.

Canadian Decentralization in a Comparative Context

Another argument against giving provinces more power is that Canada, in terms of comparative politics, is already a highly decentralized federation. The general line of reasoning is as follows: (1) provinces have more power in Canada than do other subnational units; (2) they should thus be satisfied with this state of affairs; (3) even if they are not, we have something to learn from the political stability of the more centralized federations.

Riker has argued that "among the more or less centralized federations of the modern world, most writers would agree that Canada is about as decentralized as one can get."[25] "Political centralization" for him means shifting the locus of decision-making to the central government from constituent units; "partially centralized federalism" – the case in Canada – means constituent governments making many significant political decisions and operating according to a meaningful "provincial rights" doctrine.[26] Of course, the main correlate of political centralization/decentralization is the party system. "The Canadian party system as a whole is just about as decentralized as it can be to match a federal union that is increasingly decentralized in order to keep Quebec content."[27]

Others see Canada's comparative decentralization largely in fiscal terms. Albinski noted some years ago that constitutional and political factors had rendered Canadian federalism far more devolutionary than Australian federalism, requiring substantial transfers from Ottawa to the provinces.[28] Canadian provinces, in contrast to Australian states, had wider tax bases, which were also more stable and more accessible; and they were not as subject to federal priorities in their borrowing activities. A contemporary analyst of Canadian and Australian fiscal federalism says that there is significance in the fact that in the early 1950s Australian states declined the return of income tax powers originally taken from them during the Second World War, whereas Canadian provinces pressed the federal authorities to allow them a greater share of direct tax fields. The struggle for fiscal independence is the ultimate *symbol of sovereignty.*[29]

In summary, the case for rejecting increased provincial power claims is rather striking. The provinces have stymied constitutional reform, and they offer no compelling theoretical arguments for increasing their power. The economic tools of the federal government override the provincial ones. As well, there are overwhelming social and cultural reasons for trusting the national government rather than provincial ones.

Notes

1. Alan C. Cairns, "The Limited Constitutional Visions of Meech Lake," in Katherine E. Swinton and Carol J. Rogerson, eds., *Competing Constitutional Visions: The Meech Lake Accord* (Toronto: Carswell, 1988), p. 257.

2. *Ibid.*

3. *Ibid.*, p. 259.

4. Pierre Elliott Trudeau, "The Values of a Just Society," in Thomas S. Axworthy and Pierre Elliott Trudeau, eds., *Towards a Just Society: The Trudeau Years* (Markham, Ont.: Viking, 1990), pp. 383-84.

5. Donald V. Smiley, *Canada in Question: Federalism in the Eighties*, 3rd edition (Toronto: McGraw-Hill Ryerson, 1979), p. 48.

6. Canada, Standing Senate Committee on Foreign Affairs, *Constitutional Jurisdiction Pertaining to Certain Aspects of the Free Trade Agreement* (Ottawa, May, 1988).

7. Canada, *Report of the Royal Commission on the Economic Union and Development Prospects for Canada*, vol. 3 (Ottawa: Minister of Supply and Services, 1985), p. 153.

8. *Ibid.*, vol. 1, p. 68.

9. *Ibid.*, vol. 3, p. 252.

10. *Ibid.*, pp. 254-55.

11. *Ibid.*, pp. 399-400.

12. Peter M. Leslie, *Federal State, National Economy* (Toronto: University of Toronto Press, 1987), p. 137.

13. Government of Canada, *Economic Development for Canada in the 1980s* (Ottawa, November, 1981).

14. *Ibid.*, p. 10.

15. H.G. Thorburn, *Planning and the Economy: Building Federal-Provincial Consensus* (Ottawa: Canadian Institute for Economic Policy, 1984), p. 202.

16. Michael Jenkin, *The Challenge of Diversity: Industrial Policy in the Canadian Federation* (Ottawa: Science Council of Canada, August, 1983), p. 172.

17. Tom Kent, "Regional Development in Hard Times," lecture delivered to Department of Political Science, Memorial University, February 16, 1990.

18. Leslie, *Federal State, National Economy*, pp. 176-77.

19. *Ibid.*, p. 177.

20. D. Usher, "How Should the Redistributive Power of the State be Divided between Federal and Provincial Governments?" *Canadian Public Policy*, VI, 1 (Winter, 1980), pp. 16-29.

21. *Ibid.*, p. 26.

22. *Ibid.*, p. 29.

23. A.W. Johnson, "The Meech Lake Accord and the Bonds of Nationhood," in Swinton and Rogerson, eds., *Competing Constitutional Visions*, pp. 145-53.

24. *Ibid.*, pp. 147-48.

25. W.H. Riker, "Federalism," in F.L. Greenstein and N.W. Polsby, *Handbook of Political Science* (Reading, Mass.: Addison-Wesley, 1975), pp. 132-33. The Canadian Bar Association used the argument about Canada's relative decentralization in its 1978 report *Towards a New Canada*.

26. Riker, "Federalism," pp. 132-33.

27. *Ibid.*, pp. 135-36.

28. Henry S. Albinski, *Canadian and Australian Politics in Comparative Perspective* (New York: Oxford University Press, 1973), pp. 382-83.

29. Kenneth Wiltshire, "Federal State/Provincial Relations," in Bruce W. Hodgins *et al.*, eds., *Federalism in Canada and Australia: Historical Perspectives, 1920-1988* (Peterborough, Ont.: The Frost Centre for Canadian Heritage and Development Studies, Trent University, 1989), p. 193.

Chapter 6

Provinces Do Not Have
Too Much Power

There are, of course, some effective parries to arguments that provinces have harmed national regeneration. They involve constitutional, economic, social, and comparative considerations. Canada must reject the straitjacket of excessive centralism and return to true federalist values.

Constitutional Politics

Critics often charge that there have been provincial roadblocks to constitutional reform. One might respond that modern reform efforts have been characterized by a remarkable degree of *provincial consensus*. In the Victoria Charter episode of 1971 only Quebec demurred; this was again the case in 1981 as negotiations ended on the repatriation package. Ontario gave up its historical claim to veto status (regarding amendments) as a way to clear a constitutional logjam in the early 1980s. Gordon Robertson has reminded us that "the Meech Lake Accord is the only arrangement since [constitutional] discussions began in 1968 to be approved by all 11 governments and so far by Parliament and eight legislatures."[1] Even the dissident provinces in the Meech Lake process were relatively conciliatory, most wanting to save the "essence" of the Accord (defined in various terms) and to make clarifying amendments. Provinces apparently take the need for "elite accommodation" relatively seriously.

The need for participatory constitutional negotiations is sometimes offered as counter to provincial power. This can be dismissed as oblivious to the lessons of Canadian history. The very characteristics of the executive federalism bargaining process that have been criticized – its secretiveness, its resistance to legislative alteration, its elitism – are in fact its virtues.

If one accepts the notion, as does S.J.R. Noel,[2] that Canada is a "consociational democracy," a term inspired by Arend Lijphart,[3] then the type of bargaining traditionally associated with constitutional negotiations begins to take on positive aspects. "Consociationalism" is both a descriptive and normative approach to the problems of limited identities and cultural fragmentation in stable democracies. It places the responsibility for the maintenance of the national political system with political elites. A process of "elite accommodation" overcomes cultural conflict and weak national consensus.

The leaders of the various subcultures will be successful practitioners of consociational democracy (1) if they can accommodate the divergent interests of their own subcultures; (2) if they can transcend cleavages and engage in common efforts with the elites of rival subcultures; (3) if they are committed to maintaining the national system; and (4) if they understand the perils of political fragmentation.[4] Masses are expected to follow their elites. The elites, in turn, discourage interaction between cultural fragments at the mass level as potentially destabilizing and counterproductive.

Noel has suggested some adjustments to the Lijphart model to make it applicable to Canada. The use of the term "subculture" is extended to include not only French Canada and English Canada but also distinct regions of Canada (Maritimes, Quebec, Ontario, the West) and even provinces. *Elite accommodation* therefore takes place at several levels: provincial representation on federal boards and commissions, interprovincial consultation among senior provincial bureaucrats, interprovincial ministerial bodies, federal-provincial conferences, and, especially, the federal cabinet. One particularly relevant conclusion he draws can be seen as an answer to Cairns's argument about the necessity for reconciliation of the "governments' constitution" with a "citizens' constitution":

> A decline of "elitism" in Canada and its replacement by a general acceptance of the Jacksonian myth of popular or "participatory" democracy may be detrimental to the maintenance of Canadian federalism if it leads to a situation in which the mass of the people are unwilling to accept the inter-elite accommodations made by their political leaders. If inter-elite accommodations must be popularly ratified they may be impossible to achieve.[5]

Of course, Cairns had suggested melding the two traditions of the "citizen" and "government" constitutions, not privileging the former; but the net effect of heightening the legitimacy of the citizen role in political and constitutional renewal is to decrease the legitimacy of the traditional mechanisms of leadership that have kept this fractious country together for so long. The tension raised by legislative hearings on the Meech Lake Accord is one example; the overwhelming defeat of the Charlottetown Accord in a national referendum is another.

The Internal Common Market

The argument that provinces harm the internal common market can be dismissed. Federal as well as provincial policies may result in a failure of national economic integration. Centralized regional development policies may hinder rather than facilitate economic adjustment to technological change and market conditions. The industrial structure may remain inappropriate to changing patterns of comparative advantage if it is propped up by ill-advised development grants. However, Canadian nationalists tend to turn a blind eye to such facts, and concentrate instead on "provincial protectionism."[6]

As well, such arguments overlook evidence of significant national and regional efforts to decrease interprovincial trade barriers.

The tempo of such efforts stepped up in the wake of the Canada-U.S. Free Trade Agreement. In June, 1994, the federal and provincial governments ended fifteen months of talks with an agreement to eliminate some important barriers between provinces. It includes reform of government procurement practices, a code of conduct on investment practices designed to prevent provinces "poaching" investment from each other, a dispute-settlement mechanism, and measures to increase labour mobility between provinces. The agreement aimed at a July 1, 1995, implementation date, with a further one-year delay in the case of municipalities, universities, schools, and hospitals.

The Division of International Responsibilities

Provinces both have and deserve a role in international arrangements. They have an implied role in treaty negotiation thanks to the silence of the Judicial Committee of the Privy Council, at least until this role is countermanded by the courts. Even the Macdonald Commission admitted this, pointedly arguing only for a "predominant," but not exclusive, federal role in negotiating and ratifying treaties and in co-ordinating Canada's federal and provincial international activities.[7] It recommended a constitutional amendment to provide that where treaties affecting provincial jurisdiction were negotiated, those sections placing obligations on provinces would only take effect upon the passage of resolutions in two-thirds of provincial legislatures representing over half of Canada's population. This would be a compromise between respecting the constitution and effective international participation.[8]

Canadian Constitutional Theory: The Pepin-Robarts Model

The case for increased provincial powers can certainly find some basis in modern Canadian constitutional theory. The unstated but clear implication of the Pepin-Robarts *Report*, for example, was that the provinces would get more powers in a renewed federalism. It is telling that Prime Minister Mulroney in 1991 said of the Task Force that "they were 15 years ahead of their time,"[9] plainly indicating that its reasoning was in tune with the major provincialist-leaning initiatives of the era, the Meech Lake Accord as well as a 1991 government White Paper and the 1992 Charlottetown Accord. As if to telegraph his message, Mulroney appointed Ronald L. Watts, a Queen's University political scientist and former member of the Task Force, as assistant secretary to the cabinet for constitutional affairs. It is also telling that the originator of the Task Force, Prime Minister Trudeau, flatly rejected the tenor and recommendations of the *Report*.

The Pepin-Robarts *Report* posited several "objectives" for constitutional reform [10] and outlined several "criteria" for distribution of powers. [11] It seemed to give special emphasis to the value of *accommodation* (or, alternately, *co-operation*) over that of conflict in intergovernmental matters. [12]

It saw the federal government's responsibilities – other than defence, foreign policy, and trade – as "combatting regional disparities, establishing appropriate minimum standards of living for all Canadians where appropriate, and redistributing income between individuals and between provinces." [13] Provinces were to take "the main responsibility for the social and cultural well-being and development of their communities, for the development of their economies and the exploitation of their natural resources, and for property and civil rights." [14] It suggested a vague list of exclusive (and occasionally concurrent) powers in a number of areas. Quebec was to be given powers necessary for the preservation and expansion of its distinct heritage – assigned to it alone or, preferably, to the provinces in general. [15]

The main implication (for the division of powers) of the Pepin-Robarts emphasis on accommodation and co-operation was a high degree of *categorization and specificity.* There was to be a "full enumeration" of federal and provincial powers under a continuum of seven categories. [16] Provinces could control language policy and there was to be greater decentralization of social and cultural policy; but to counter this there was more emphasis on economic integration. The federal spending power was to be protected, but the provinces had the right to opt out with compensation. Provincial consent for the use of the declaratory power was to be necessary. The residual power would now rest with the provincial legislatures. Reservation and disallowance were to be abolished. There would be a provincially appointed Senate and a regional veto system for constitutional amendments. The implications of Quebec's "distinctive culture" were that it should achieve powers in areas needed for its cultural survival, but that these powers should be generalized to other provinces as well. This would be done both by allowing intergovernmental delegation of powers and by placing the powers under concurrent jurisdiction with provincial paramountcy.

The Pepin-Robarts Report was remarkable for several reasons. It was the first federal report to respond in a positive way to long-standing provincial demands for more power. It demonstrated that stronger provinces were not necessarily contradictory to a strong federal system. It was the model for later honourable attempts at constitutional reform – Meech, the White Paper of 1991, and the Charlottetown Accord – whose proposals were remarkably like those of Pepin-Robarts. In short, it showed that the provincial demands for more authority in the federal system were not at all unreasonable.

International and Domestic Economic Factors
Economic Strategy

International factors may not always lead in the direction of greater economic policy centralization. Richard Simeon has stated that international constraints have diminished the advantages of belonging to a large, open-economy state like Canada. *External market forces*, not provinces, have limited the federal government's manoeuvrability in recent years, leading citizens to turn to subnational power centres. [17] David Milne has stated that Trudeau's unilateral, imposed federal industrial strategy was motivated more by a drive for federal power than by economic rationality; an international recession and acrimonious federal-provincial discord helped to lend such *dirigisme* a bad name and led to the market-oriented Free Trade Agreement. [18]

The Macdonald Commission *Report* noted in a similar vein that "while federalism does not entirely undermine, it certainly dilutes, our enthusiasm for a state-led, highly interventionist, industrial strategy." [19] However, in the particular area of *regional economic development* the Commission was willing to countenance provincial leadership and a merely supplemental federal role.

This emphasis on place prosperity is both understandable and defensible when it comes from a provincial government.

It should not, however, unduly concern the federal government. Commissioners believe that community preservation, to the extent that people want it, is ultimately the responsibility of citizens and of their local and provincial governments.[20]

The federal government would have no direct regional job creation role; it would only attend to overcoming regional productivity gaps and labour-market imperfections, as well as to building complementary links between provincial economies. There would, however, be a federal commitment to regional economic development grants; these would increase in the next few years but provinces would make the primary decisions as to their use.[21]

Many reasons have been suggested as to why provinces should play a lead role in regional and industrial development policies. The Macdonald Commission *Report* argues that one reason is that "the federal government has been unable to form a satisfactory link between its regional development responsibilities and its broader role in managing our national economy."[22] Constant reorganization of the federal regional development bureaucracy is a sign of the failure of the former type of policies. *National economic management* (as defined above) is said to have a better chance of serving the major aim that regional development seeks to serve in the first place: reducing regional disparities in wage gaps and employment-rate differences.

Superior Powers

Another reason for provincial leadership is simply that provinces have the tools to use in economic development and the disposition to use them. Not only are the powers available; they have been used aggressively, as a number of texts on provincial development policy have informed us. Provincial powers over economic development include the following:

- Various sections of the Constitution Act, 1867 (ss. 92(5), 92(13) 108, 109 and 117) give the provincial legislatures wide power over public property. This means, with regard to provincially owned natural resources, that provinces can directly produce or sell the resource, or grant leases for private companies to do so; they can also control the rate of production, the degree of intra-provincial processing (the "manufacturing condition"), and the selling price within the province; and they can collect fees, rents, or royalties on such resources. [23]

- They can engage in commercial activities through provincial crown corporations.

- Many of the powers complementary to actual industrial policy – those over the environment, labour, financial institutions, and land use – fall largely (though not exclusively) within provincial jurisdiction.

- In addition, of course, provincial spending and taxation powers have become potent instruments in the field of industrial policy.

The growing dependence on trade with the American market, an international factor that Canada could not ignore, moved it to enter into negotiations with the United States on the matter of free trade. Notably, the net result of the federal-provincial jockeying that preceded the Canada-U.S. trade negotiations was not political centralization but a form of joint national economic planning:

> In the end the provinces did not succeed in winning "seats at the table", although they were given assurances of consultation and regular monitoring of the process of negotiations every three months by the first ministers. Clearly the old federal claim to an exclusive role in defining the national interest in trade and economic matters and then simply projecting it onto the international scene was no longer tenable. [24]

Subsequent international trade and economic questions saw analogous monitoring structures established – even extended – as a result of constitutional necessity and the original free trade precedent.

Social Policy Considerations

Canadians should resist slotting redistribution so easily into the federal jurisdictional slot. For good measure, they might even deny that citizenship rights are the proper concern of constitution-makers. The drive to place social policy predominantly under federal jurisdiction raises serious objections.

Redistribution

Redistribution is not universally accepted as a federal responsibility (or even as a desirable policy). *Public choice* theorists, for example, are particularly consistent critics of watertight compartmentalization of constitutional responsibilities, social policy included. West and Winer have written what they call "a defence of decentralization." *Decentralization* can be viewed in two senses: "decentralization in the narrow sense of moving towards more scope and autonomy for subcentral jurisdictions; and decentralization in the broad sense, which also includes movement to a system of competing regimes."[25] Decentralization is preferable in the narrow sense, but their preference lies with the broader option. Broad decentralization reflects the authors' philosophic preference for James Madison's "compound republic," under which there is a need for "*overlapping* sets of political regimes operating *concurrently* upon the same constituencies."[26] A choice among political authorities replaces a monopoly of political authority, allowing citizens to establish sets of countervailing power.

In terms of redistributive policies, what once seemed vices are now deemed virtues. Usher had argued against provincial jurisdiction over redistribution to prevent people migrating to generous programs in specific provinces; West and Winer say that such migration would act as a healthy deterrent to provinces establishing divergent programs.[27] Whereas Usher argues for federal jurisdiction over redistribution to reduce conflict, West and Winer suggest that some "optional" tension emerging from a system of checks and balances is necessary to protect citizens from government power.[28]

Citizenship Rights Contested

The contention that the job of the constitution is to strengthen the bonds of nationhood, and more specifically to do this by assuring the federal provision of common benefits, does not pass unchallenged. One could look to Andrew Petter, now a British Columbia cabinet minister, for a different view.[29] There are, he says, two predominant values to be served by the Canadian constitution: *federalism* and *responsible government.* The federal spending power violates the political purposes of federalism by allowing national majorities to invade areas allocated to regional majorities under the constitution. It also violates responsible government by allowing the federal government to influence provincial policies, making the electors unable to determine what level of government is in effective control of various programs.[30]

Petter has also challenged the assumption behind the unconstrained use of the federal spending power: that national politics is inherently more progressive than provincial politics.[31] Provinces, he says, have been catalysts for reform during the past forty years in a number of social areas: hospital insurance, medicare, human rights codes, and public automobile insurance, to name but a few. Success in one province inevitably leads other provinces to implement the reform in question. As well, provincial governments have spurred the expansion and improvement of social programs that have eventually been adopted by the federal government.

Petter admits that opting out with compensation from federal shared-cost programs has some risks attached; but he feels that on balance there are compensating benefits likely in the areas of provincial experimentation and innovation. The national government by its very nature is preoccupied with mediating between regional, cultural, and linguistic interests; however, in the provincial context, social and economic matters are the focus. Despite the appearance in our day of conservative administrations and retrenchment, the general trend has been toward social progress. Certainly, succeeding administrations find it unwise to dislodge major social programs instituted by their predecessors. In short, "The lesson of Canadian history is that social progress is seldom attained all at once. It evolves from the small to the large. It must be fought for one piece at a time."[32]

Canadian Decentralization in a Comparative Context

A case can also be made from comparative politics that Canada's decentralization is a good thing. Hueglin suggests that whereas Canadian federalism is indeed more decentralized than that of the United States and Germany, the Canadian situation should be considered a strength instead of a liability.[33] To be sure, in the *political sphere*, there are in the United States and Germany substantial elements of "intrastate federalism," that is, state involvement in the national political substructures. German Laender instruct their delegates in the Bundesrat (Federal Council, or Upper House), who must vote as a bloc. The American Senate has two members from each state, thus offering a measure of representation for regional minority interests.

Yet centralization is the rule. In Germany "unitary federalism" (highly centralized federalism) has dominated since the late sixties due to joint economic and financial planning, more integrated law and order forces, and, finally, the conflict-avoidance governing style inherent in a centralized party system where the adoption of major policies requires all three parties to agree.[34] The U.S. style of "permissive federalism," which subordinates state power in a dominating federal grant system, achieves a centralizing dynamic as well.

The Canadian system, by contrast, features strong intergovernmental conflict with substantial provincial autonomy in the grant system. In addition to political substructures, the economic and cultural substructures also reveal a Canada less centralized than the other two countries; and all three substructures are at once interdependent and relatively autonomous, says Hueglin.

In the *economic sphere,* the U.S. federal government dominates because it collects most of the revenue and states spend most of it. A full 75 per cent of all federal grants are categorical (conditional); neither liberals nor conservatives have a meaningful agenda for shifting power to the states; and Congress is loath to let control over the purse slip from its grip. In Germany, economic interests – the interconnected financial and industrial sectors – are closely allied with the CDU and FDP political parties and with government and labour in a system of corporatist planning. The result is a focus on national rather than regional economic strategy. By contrast, Canada's tax-sharing, cost-sharing, and equalization are sensitive to provincial needs. "As long as the commitment to equalization remains intact, the Canadian polity can be regarded as living up to the federal yardstick of sharing and balancing regional group liberty with national individual liberty."[35]

In the *cultural sphere,* the institutions of federalism in general channel conflicts between capitalist fractions and between classes in ways that accommodate or deny regional identities. U.S. and German federalism, according to Hueglin, denies regional identities, the former by suppressing class conflict and promoting mass culture, the latter by interlocking (or "cartelizing") ideological blocks in the institutions of intrastate federalism. In both cases, potential legitimation crises loom as regional interests bypass national institutions and seek solutions elsewhere. However, because of Canadians' "dual loyalties" to the centre and to specific regions/provinces, the Canadian system is not as inherently unstable. "When compared to the potentially delegitimizing conflicts between economic centralism and societal bifurcation in West Germany [as it then was] or between federal supremacy and regional decline in the United States, the relative congruence of politics, economy and culture in Canada ought to be considered a strength and not a liability."[36]

To summarize, the provinces have been the defenders of important Canadian values, not the offenders. They have been largely responsible for inculcating in the Canadian psyche the notion of accommodation and compromise. They have trusted market forces rather than elitist *dirigisme*. They have, by and large, relied on their existing constitutional powers to promote economic development, rather than invading federal jurisdiction. They have refused to allow a distant Ottawa bureaucracy to dictate social policy in the name of some vague theory of the national interest. Their insistence on real and symbolic sovereignty has had the important side effect of preserving a spirit of tolerance and diversity in the Canadian polity.

Notes

1. Gordon Robertson, "Meech Mythology," *Globe and Mail*, March 13, 1990.
2. S.J.R. Noel, "Consociational Democracy and Canadian Federalism," *Canadian Journal of Political Science*, IV, 1 (March, 1971), pp. 15-18.
3. Arend Lijphart, "Consociational Democracy," *World Politics*, XXI, 2 (January, 1969), pp. 207-25.
4. *Ibid.*
5. Noel, "Consociational Democracy," pp. 17-18. Noel's point is, of course, awkwardly stated, since if elitism declines there may not be such inter-elite accommodations. What he no doubt means is that the nominal elites who would remain in place in a participatory

democracy would find themselves playing less important roles in maintaining the federal system.

6. Peter M. Leslie, *Federal State, National Economy* (Toronto: University of Toronto Press, 1987), p. 91.
7. *Ibid.*, pp. 149, 155.
8. *Ibid.*, pp. 154-55.
9. Graham Fraser, "Mulroney hints at constitutional plan: 1978 task force's decentralized vision of Canada praised at caucus meeting," *Globe and Mail,* April 11, 1991.
10. These were: reinforce central institutions, respond to provincial self-confidence, reflect Canadian duality, accountability, effectiveness, and efficiency. Canada, Task Force on Canadian Unity, *A Future Together: Observations and Recommendations* (January, 1979), p. 81.
11. These were national and provincial concerns, efficiency and effectiveness, consensus, continuity, and balance. *Ibid.,* p. 88.
12. *Ibid.,* pp. 81, 85, 86, 89.
13. *Ibid.,* p. 85.
14. *Ibid.*
15. *Ibid.,* pp. 85-86.
16. These were exclusive central powers, exclusive provincial powers, concurrent powers with central paramountcy, concurrent powers with provincial paramountcy, provincially administered central laws (a limited list), powers requiring joint action (also a limited list), and, finally, overriding central powers with specific limitations. The enumerated powers of sections 91 and 92 of the 1867 constitution, lacking a coherent theme to their arrangement, were to be rearranged into general domains of public activity, with more specific subject matters listed under them that could be then distributed exclusively or concurrently to the most appropriate level of government. *A Future Together,* pp. 88-89.
17. Richard Simeon, "Considerations on Centralization and Decentralization, in R.D. Olling and M.W. Westmacott, eds., *Perspectives on Canadian Federalism* (Scarborough, Ont.: Prentice-Hall Canada, 1988), p. 375.
18. David Milne, *Tug of War: Ottawa and the Provinces under Trudeau and Mulroney* (Toronto: James Lorimer and Company, 1986), p. 161.
19. Canada, Royal Commission on the Economic Union and Development Prospects for Canada, *Report,* vol. 1 (Ottawa: Minister of Supply and Services, 1985), p. 71.

20. *Ibid.*, vol. 3, p. 219.
21. *Ibid.*, pp. 219-20.
22. *Ibid.*, p. 215.
23. P.W. Hogg, *Constitutional Law of Canada*, Second Edition (Toronto: Carswell, 1985), pp. 572-73.
24. Milne, *Tug of War*, p. 152.
25. Edwin G. West and Stanley L. Winer, "The Individual, Political Tension and Canada's Quest for a New Constitution," *Canadian Public Policy*, VI, 1 (Winter, 1980), pp. 3-15. Mark Sproule-Jones takes a similar though more complex approach in *Public Choice and Federalism in Australia and Canada* (Canberra: Centre for Research on Federal Financial Relations, Australian National University, Research Monograph No. 11, 1975).
26. West and Winer, "The Individual, Political Tension and Canada's Quest," p. 7.
27. *Ibid.*, p. 8.
28. *Ibid.*, p. 9.
29. Andrew Petter, "Meech Ado About Nothing? Federalism, Democracy and the Spending Power," in Swinton and Rogerson, eds., *Competing Constitutional Visions*, pp. 187-201.
30. *Ibid.*, pp. 188-191.
31. Andrew J. Petter, "Meech won't stall social reform in the Provinces," *Globe and Mail*, June 30, 1987.
32. *Ibid.*
33. Thomas O. Hueglin, "Federalism in Comparative Perspective," in R.D. Olling and W.W. Westmacott, *Perspectives on Canadian Federalism* (Scarborough, Ont.: Prentice-Hall Canada, 1988), p. 29.
34. *Ibid.*, p. 24.
35. *Ibid.*, p. 27.
36. *Ibid.*, p. 29.

PART FOUR

Do Canada and Quebec
Need Each Other?

One of the striking characteristics of Canadian politics since the early 1960s has been the symmetrical development of linguistically based nationalisms. As Quebec nationalism grew in strength, so did English-Canadian nationalism, albeit without as much intensity. These two nationalisms were not solely dependent on each other for their development; other factors such as culture, ideology, and international affairs were to some degree also responsible. They have very little in common, save for this: they both maintain that Canada and Quebec do not "need" each other, if this means that deep compromises are the price to pay for continuing the Canadian federal union. One has only to remember the harsh and uncompromising tenor of many participants on radio phone-in shows in the last decade to be reminded of this great divide. However, as shall be seen, these two constitutional camps were not the only ones. Many Canadians agreed then and still agree that a reform of federal institutions and practices was needed.

This introduction and the ensuing two chapters will offer a focused review of recent literature on the Quebec-Canada question. In reviewing the "yes" and "no" sides to this question, the reader will note a general tendency toward reductionism. This is the case not only for descriptions of Quebec politics but for the politics of English Canada as well. The "yes" side will be synonymous with the arguments of those we call *renewed federalists*. The "no" side will be synonymous with the views of those we call *sovereignists*.

No attempt is made to draw fine distinctions between sovereignists, sovereignty-associationists, nationalists, and confederalists. If analysis tends to lead to a separate or "confederated" Quebec, it is sovereignist. The terms "English-Canadian nationalist" and "renewed federalist" are used to summarize, in perhaps arbitrary fashion, the other major streams of thought in Canadian federal theory. By exaggerating the similarities within schools of thought, we can establish the essence of their relative contributions to Canada's national debate.

It is significant that the party standings in the Canadian general election of 1993 reflected in a general sense the three main constitutional camps identified here. The renewed federalist option was reflected in the majority party, the Liberals, with their 177 seats. The sovereignist Bloc Québécois became "Her Majesty's Loyal Opposition" with fifty-four seats. The Reform Party, the main exponent of English-Canadian nationalism, became the next largest party grouping at fifty-two seats. These three parties altogether control 96 per cent of the seats in the Canadian House of Commons.

The parties' popular vote lent more geographical specificity to the constitutional camps as well. The Bloc Québécois captured 13.5 per cent of the vote nationally but almost half of the vote – 49.3 per cent – in Quebec. The Reform Party took 52.3 per cent of the Alberta vote, 36.4 per cent in British Columbia, 27.2 per cent in Saskatchewan, 22.4 per cent in Manitoba, 20.1 per cent in Ontario, 13.3 per cent in Nova Scotia, 13.1 per cent in the Yukon Territory, 8.5 per cent in New Brunswick, 8.4 per cent in the Northwest Territories, and 1 per cent in each of Newfoundland and Prince Edward Island. Reform did not field candidates in Quebec. The Liberals got well over half the popular vote in all four Atlantic provinces,

Ontario, and the NWT, 45 per cent of the vote in Manitoba, about a third in Quebec and Saskatchewan, and about a quarter in B.C., Alberta, and Yukon. [1]

The figures show an obvious concentration of sovereignists in Quebec, but if one adds the Quebec Liberal and Conservative votes together (33 per cent and 13.5 per cent), the federalist parties in Quebec approach the sovereignist numbers. English-Canadian nationalist votes, as represented by Reform, are concentrated in the three westernmost provinces, with diffuse but impressive support for this new party (founded in 1988) throughout the rest of the country. The federalist Liberals are strong if not dominant in most areas.

The implications are staggering for federal and provincial governments trying to come to some lasting solution of Canada's constitutional conflicts. The relatively balanced strength of different constitutional camps means that there will seldom be constitutional policies acceptable to significant numbers of Canadians. It is of course hard to predict if the relative power of these groupings will change over the long run, or if they signify a federation on the verge of collapse.

Recent English-French Relations in Canada

The crisis in national unity in a sense has always been present in Canada, with successive governments seeking to balance the needs of English and French Canada. The modern crisis, however, is the most profound in Canadian history. Table 1 gives a capsule history of the growing strength of sovereignist forces in Quebec.

Table 1
The Growth of the Sovereignty Option in Quebec

1960-1966   The Liberal government of Jean Lesage undertakes an intense modernization program ("the Quiet Revolution") touching most areas of provincial public policy. Many have since argued that the education and public service reforms created a newly trained Francophone middle class with a vested interest in Quebec sovereignty.

1965   Union Nationale leader Daniel Johnson publishes his political manifesto *Égalité ou Indépendance* demanding constitutional respect for the principle of "two nations" or, failing that, contemplation of independence. Johnson becomes Premier of a strongly nationalist Union Nationale government in 1966.

1966   Two separatist parties, the Rassemblement pour l'Indépendance Nationale (RIN) and the Ralliement National (RN), contest the provincial election and between them achieve almost 10 per cent of the popular vote.

1967   René Lévesque leaves the Liberal Party, in which he was a minister under Lesage, and proposes "sovereignty-association" – political independence but overarching economic ties – as the goal for *indépendantistes*. The next year he begins his own separatist party, which will ultimately become the Parti Québécois after amalgamating the various splinter independence groups.

1970   After a decade of sporadic political violence, the Front de Libération du Québec (FLQ) overextends itself in the so-called "October Crisis." Two FLQ cells kidnap a Quebec cabinet minister and a British diplomat. The Trudeau government invokes the War Measures Act. The body of the minister, Pierre Laporte, is soon thereafter discovered. Public opinion turns against extra-parliamentary methods of promoting sovereignty.

The PQ receives 23 per cent of the popular vote in the general election but only seven of the seats in the provincial legislature.

1973   The PQ popular vote increases to 30 per cent in the general election, but the party obtains only six of the 110 seats in the legislature. Lévesque fails to be elected.

1976   René Lévesque becomes the first PQ Premier of Quebec after the party gets 41 per cent of the popular vote and seventy-one of the 110 legislative seats. Lévesque had campaigned promising to hold a referendum on the question of sovereignty-association before negotiating it with Canada.

1977 The Quebec legislature passes its major *francisation* mechanism, the Charter of the French Language (Bill 101). This purports to make French the official language of the public and commercial sectors of the province.

1980 The promised referendum is held and the PQ attempt to obtain a mandate to negotiate sovereignty-association is defeated by a ratio of 60 to 40. The Francophone vote splits half and half.

1981 The April general election sees the PQ re-elected after distancing itself from the sovereignty option, with an increased popular vote of 49.3 per cent and eighty seats.

In November the other provinces and the federal government agree to a constitutional reform package that Quebec nationalists regard as having marginalized Quebec.

1982 The "Renérendum": in February, and in reaction to the December, 1981, PQ convention's endorsement of sovereignty without association, the entire PQ membership is called to vote, and at Lévesque's urging, massively supports the sovereignty-association policy.

1984 Lévesque announces that the sovereignty question will not be a platform in the next provincial general election. Defections from the cabinet and caucus indicate a serious split in the party.

1985 Lévesque resigns and Pierre-Marc Johnson becomes the new PQ leader in an innovative direct election by party members. In the December general election, Johnson also downplays the sovereignty question. The PQ government is defeated, slipping to 39 per cent of the popular vote and twenty-three seats.

1987 Johnson resigns and the more militant Jacques Parizeau, a former PQ Finance Minister who quit the cabinet in 1984, later becomes the new leader.

1989 The PQ improves in the general election; it gets 40 per cent of the popular vote and twenty-nine seats.

1990 The Meech Lake Accord, the "Quebec Round" that *souverainistes* have denounced but that is symbolically important to many Quebecers, fails to be adopted as a resolution in the Manitoba legislature. In the subsequent months, sovereignist feeling once again runs high.

1992 The Charlottetown Accord, arrived at by the first ministers as a reaction to the defeat of the Meech Lake Accord, is submitted to a national referendum. Sovereignist opposition to it helps to turn public opinion in Quebec against the Accord.

1993 Ex-Liberal Jean Allaire founds Parti de l'Action Démocratique du Québec, a new sovereignist party situated between the Liberals and PQ on the Quebec political spectrum. Allaire quits the party in 1994 and Mario Dumont becomes leader.

The sense of crisis about Canada-Quebec relations was heightened following the apparent convergence between the *souverainistes* and the more mainstream Liberal Party of Quebec following the failure of the Meech Lake Accord. The *souverainiste* analysis of Canada-Quebec links had gained progressively more sympathizers in the past two decades; a major indication of this is the language used by the constitutional documents of the Quebec Liberal Party.

The Beige Paper of 1980

The Quebec Liberal Beige Paper of 1980 maintained that the Parti Québécois (PQ) sovereignty-association project[2] was unrealistic and negative. It rejected the PQ's alarmist assessment of Canadian federalism, saying that "a realistic and honest evaluation of the Canadian federation can lead to only one conclusion – the assets far outweigh the liabilities."[3] Quebec plainly needed Canada. Canada offered it a vast geography rich in resource wealth, an internal common market where Quebec's manufacturing and dairy products enjoyed tariff protection, an equalization fund of which Quebec received almost half, and a federal order of government incorporating weights and counterweights that had made Canada "one of the countries which best guarantees individual liberty and collective rights, both in law and in practice."[4] It proposed a vision of a Canada open to Quebec. The latter would be a "distinct and unique" national community within the context of a federal system.

The Allaire Committee Report of 1991

Another report of the Quebec Liberal Party a mere eleven years later showed a striking shift in emphasis. The Allaire Committee cited "the chronic inability of Canadian federalism to renew itself."[5] It said that a radically different Quebec-Canada structure was necessary:

> Under the existing federal structure, the Quebec government lacks the essential powers it needs to enable Quebec to develop fully as a distinct society, as well as the tools to allow it to secure the future of the French fact in North America. The current structure fails to reflect the realities of Quebec and Canada, and gives rise to incoherence, abuse and duplication of government efforts. It frequently encourages inaction, exacerbates the crisis in public finances and perpetuates budgetary imbalances.[6]

Mr. Bourassa's Strategic Ambiguities

Commentaries by Robert Bourassa over the past decade were seemingly also indicative of a drift – albeit ambiguous – in the direction of a sovereignty option. In April, 1980, ex-Premier Bourassa campaigned against the PQ White Paper monetary and fiscal proposals in the referendum campaign of the day. He concluded that the inapplicability of the White Paper's economic proposals confirmed the necessity of maintaining federal ties between Quebec and the rest of Canada.[7] In February, 1985, as Liberal leader, Bourassa submitted a brief to the Macdonald Royal Commission arguing for a modernized federalism and strengthened Canadian economic union. He noted that the alternative to Canadian federalism was not a centralized unitary state but a mosaic of small unitary states, which would be weak both economically and politically. Federalism allowed Quebec to draw profit from a political and economic sphere covering a half-continent, a situation that would not be possible in the balkanized arrangement that would follow the demise of federalism. [8]

Yet in an addendum to the Report of the Bélanger-Campeau Commission on the Political and Constitutional Future of Quebec, Bourassa agreed "willingly" to the simultaneous consideration of both reorganized federalism and sovereignty for Quebec by committees of the Quebec National Assembly. [9] Quebec, it began to seem, did not necessarily need Canada, or did not need it in the same way, as was the case only years previously.

In hindsight, of course, it appears that Bourassa always was a federalist. He used ambiguities strategically to avoid alienating the nationalist sector in his province. Even when he stepped down as Liberal leader and Premier, he was much closer to what is here called "renewed federalism" than he was to sovereignty. He would say that Quebec does need Canada, but a Canada that is sensitive to Quebec needs.

English-Canadian Nationalism

Recent tensions in English-French relations have been spurred on by the dynamics of Quebec nationalism itself rather than by any impetus from English Canada. Yet, in Anglophone Canada, English-Canadian nationalists have pursued the question of the relative need of Canada and Quebec for each other. Previously, the "national question" tended to be the prerogative of Quebec nationalists.

English-Canadian nationalists are not all of the same political stripe, nor do they have one specific agenda. The net effect of their agendas, however, is to downplay the importance of the question, "Do Canada and Quebec need each other?" They claim a certain ennui with the national unity problem. Philosophically, some believe in a strict interpretation of individual equality (Charter dominance, hostility to the notwithstanding clause), some in provincial equality (symmetrical federalism), and still others in economic and cultural protectionism. Despite their dissimilar stances, they share a belief that Canadians should manifest an overarching sense of national community in certain fundamental aspects. If Quebec is not willing to honour those aspects, then sovereignty is an option for consideration. Emotionally, their reactions to

Quebec range from indifference to frustration to betrayal. There is a certain terminological overlap among them as well. On the left, some nationalists echo the *souverainiste* theme of Quebec-Canada incompatibility. Self-determination for Quebec has always been a strong theme among left-wing nationalists in English Canada, but events of the last decade have propelled some of them to lend a more positive sheen to the sovereignty option. Philip Resnick's recent books are a good example of the sense of betrayal among leftists in Canada.[10] *Letters to a Québécois Friend* notes that there has been a certain parallelism in the development of English-Canadian and French-Canadian nationalism. Canada's English and French societies were both committed to cultural defence, but by different means. Quebec moved from a long-standing rejection of modernity to a new nationalism beginning in the 1960s, in which language served the interests of class. The real winners of Quebec nationalism were the Francophone bourgeoisie who benefited directly and indirectly from state support. English-Canadian nationalism moved beyond foreign dependency to economic and cultural nationalism in the 1960s, and perceived the federal government as the protector of this vision. The late 1980s, however, showed a certain selfishness by Quebec nationalists. They demanded protection for their own cultural identity in Meech, but denied analogous protection to English-Canadian nationalists by swinging decisively behind free trade in the 1988 general election. "If we are to live together," Resnick says, "we will have to recognize the principle of reciprocity in our relationship."[11]

In *Toward a Canada-Quebec Union*, Resnick takes his analysis a few steps further. English-Canadian nationalism and Quebec nationalism are incompatible. The former insists on a strong Canadian government to enunciate a sense of nationhood; the latter seeks to weaken this government by open-ended constitutional demands and minimal commitment to the Canadian nation. A looser confederal arrangement is necessary. He calls this a "Canada-Quebec Union," a "condominium-type arrangement" where domestic parliaments in Quebec and Canada handle internal affairs and a new Union Parliament covers common citizenship and foreign affairs.[12]

Other leftist nationalists have voiced frustration with the constitutional struggles of past decades. Bela Egyed says it is to the benefit of both English Canada and Quebec that separation take place. Quebec would get full control of linguistic and immigration policy. The federal government would be free of the seemingly interminable political struggles with Quebec and free also to consolidate the consensus among English-Canadian nationalists since George Grant: economic independence from U.S. multinationals.[13] Reg Whitaker claims the Quebec-Canada constitutional agenda blocks the "Canadian agenda" of democratization and greater public participation because the former emphasizes elite accommodation. The state should preoccupy itself with the concerns of those who want "in," like Natives and residents of western and Atlantic Canada, rather than with the concerns of those who want "out."[14]

The Reform Party, an English-Canadian nationalist grouping on the right, has a specific view of national purpose and of the necessary implications that flow from this. One of the implications is that Quebec may or may not be a part of this nation.

The Reform Party's view of the nation is a negation of the one that has dominated national politics for the last quarter-century. Reform leader Preston Manning contrasts what he calls "Old Canada" and "New Canada." "Old Canada – the Canada defined as an equal partnership between two founding races, languages and cultures, the English and the French – is dying."[15] The period under the Act of Union, 1840, when this theory predominated, proved its unworkability. Confederation bypassed the "two nations" concept; it left the government of Quebec to deal with the "two nations" problem at the provincial level. The Liberal governments of Lester Pearson and Pierre Trudeau, however, resurrected this policy, "nationalizing" by official languages legislation what had been "provincialized" in 1867. It relegated nine million "other Canadians" to the status of second-class citizens, and of course it was during this period that the duality principle ebbed in Quebec itself. "New Canada" was implicit in the Confederation of 1867: Canada was to be a new nation from sea to sea. Manning contends that the populist thrust of the Reformers has enabled them to reach a redefinition of this new nation:

New Canada should be a balanced, democratic federation of provinces, distinguished by the conservation of its magnificent environment, the viability of its economy, the acceptance of its social responsibilities, and recognition of the equality and uniqueness of all its provinces and citizens.[16]

Implicit in this, and reiterated in other Reform Party speeches, are the nationalist themes of symmetrical federalism, equal individual rights, and no special status for Quebec. (Manning wants a strong national government and strong provincial governments.) During the Meech debate, Manning was alarmed by the implication that the "distinct society" clause implied rights and privileges for Quebec that were not enjoyed by other provinces.[17] Manning purports to desire a Quebec in the New Canada, but the latter "must be more than viable without Quebec."[18] He ran Reform candidates in the general election of 1993 in all regions but Quebec. Three alternatives, he says, would be preferable to the present divisive federal arrangements: (1) a "reconfederated Canada" with provincial equality and equal treatment of all Canadians; (2) a "constitutional duplex," meaning a more separate relationship for Quebec that is mutually acceptable to Quebec and English Canada; or (3) a decentralized Canada of more independent regions operating within a Canadian Commonwealth and Common Market.[19]

There are some things to notice here. One is the attempt to redefine the Canadian nationality. Second is that such an attempt provides little room for the Quebec of the last thirty years. The third is the apparent similarity of Manning's preferred options to those of the *souverainiste* school and the more radical of left nationalists. Manning's duplex replaces Resnick's condominium.

Federalists criticize the manipulation of the highly emotive term "provincial equality" by English-Canadian nationalists. They note that at times Newfoundland Premier Clyde Wells and Manning use it to signify the equality of provincial representation desired in a future reformed Senate, based on Triple-E principles.[20] At other times English-Canadian nationalists use it as a principle to justify the refusal to recognize Quebec as a distinct society; distinctness (or "special status") would imply that Quebec could have legislative status enjoyed by no other province. At still other junctures the nationalists use the banner of provincial equality to protest a constitutional veto for Quebec, either given to Quebec singly or, *de facto,* through a rigid unanimity provision in the amending formula. They fear that Quebec would in turn veto constitutional changes, like Senate reform, that are of vital concern to other areas of the country. Constitutional deadlock might ensue. Manning and Stephen Harper, Reform's former policy adviser, have implied that provincial equality also means identical provincial legislative authority.[21] In addition, they have tended to conflate the notions of provincial and regional equality, to be achieved by a cumulative process of provincial and national "constitutional conventions" (and a national referendum) based on populist principles.

"Provincial equality" is therefore a fundamentally ambiguous term, and English-Canadian nationalists make use of it to justify their favoured solution on a number of fronts. It can be used to support a flexible amending formula, Senate reform, and jurisdictional equality. Yet its major implication has been to deny any unusual recognition of Quebec's specificity.

Renewed Federalism

The second major stream of thought on the national question is the *renewed federalism* option. Renewed federalism, although one should not try to narrow it to any one example, is generally what was involved in the Charlottetown Accord. The proposed 1987 Constitutional Accord (the Meech Lake Accord) involved relatively restrained decentralization, but renewed federalism calls for a more thoroughgoing decentralization. We will investigate the meaning of this term presently, but first we examine the convergence of Canada's traditional federal parties toward the renewal option.

It may seem surprising, in light of their partisan rhetoric, to speak of the convergence of the constitutional strategies of the Liberals and Conservatives. In fact, there are surprising similarities between them.[22] In December, 1990, and February, 1991, Prime Minister Mulroney raised the possibility of a "profound redistribution of powers," with some federal powers going to provinces and some provincial ones being passed on to Ottawa.[23] In his testimony to the Bélanger-Campeau Commission, Jean Chrétien said that "nothing is sacred in the current division of power."[24] Both have stressed the elaboration of the Canadian economic union as a prime objective of any altered division of powers.[25] Both have criticized the inefficient overlap between federal and provincial powers and have suggested lessening it (Mulroney with more emphasis than Chrétien).

Liberal and Conservative stances on Quebec have contained a certain *rapprochement*. Both parties have countenanced some kind of asymmetrical relationship among Ottawa, Quebec, and the other provinces. Mulroney's first reaction to the "five conditions" the Quebec government insisted on in 1986 for its practical acceptance of the repatriated constitution was to warn premiers to avoid "paralyzing linkages" between their issues and the Quebec conditions (advice the premiers promptly neglected).[26] In February of 1991 Ottawa announced a new immigration agreement that evolved from the earlier Meech discussions, thereby allowing Quebec to perform functions that in other provinces were performed by the federal government.[27]

Current Liberal Prime Minister Chrétien has been lukewarm on Quebec asymmetry over the years, but he has not completely ruled it out. He told the Bélanger-Campeau Commission: "The modernization of Canadian federalism does not require a complete affirmation of the principle of total symmetry. Canadian federalism has always been sufficiently flexible to accommodate asymmetry in certain situations."[28] As well, Chrétien responded to questions following his testimony by insisting that he had favoured Quebec's original list of five demands.[29] This certainly implies asymmetry, if only to an extent. He has called for Quebec's right to veto over constitutional amendments, preferably in a Victoria Charter-style regional veto arrangement. One of Chrétien's objectives for a future division of powers is to honour regional diversity, "including the distinct character of Quebec society,"[30] which approaches Mulroney's terminology.[31] On May 26, 1991, Chrétien endorsed the constitutional program of the Quebec wing of the federal Liberal Party, which included recognition of "Quebec's distinct character," a Quebec role in protecting and promoting the French language, and the right to opt out of shared-cost programs with compensation. After the election of a Liberal government in 1993, Prime Minister Chrétien appointed Marcel Massé as Minister of Intergovernmental Affairs. Massé soon began meeting with provincial representatives to discuss possible reductions in federal-provincial program overlap, a development that may have asymmetrical overtones. In general, where questions of national unity (read: Quebec-Canada) policy are concerned, the two parties have tended to converge in the last few decades.

So is the Mulroney-Chrétien picture of reorganized federal and provincial powers equivalent to "renewed federalism"? It may certainly be the core of it, but the degree of change implied will depend partly on the tug-of-war between *souverainistes* and English-Canadian nationalists. As the mid-point between these two on the spectrum, renewed federalism will be the barometer of the strength of symmetrical and factionalist tendencies in Canada.

The evolutionary nature of the renewed federalism option must be stressed. A decade ago many of this school would have had Trudeauist tendencies: reluctant to discuss the division of powers, anxious to treat all provinces generally the same or at least to have options equally open to all provinces, and sympathetic to an activist nation-building and welfare-state role for Ottawa. Now this vision is not a realistic one; renewed federalism has become the middle ground and the Trudeau vision is the status quo that most agree must be shunted aside. A whole new group of analysts has begun to explore the permutations of renewed federalism.[32] Renewed federalism has a shifting content.

It is instructive to review what the Bélanger-Campeau Commission considers to be "renewed federalism" – its alternative to sovereignty. Renewed federalism, according to Bélanger-Campeau, *may* include recognition of Quebec's "right to be different" from the rest of Canada; the elimination of federal overlap and spending power in areas of exclusive provincial jurisdiction; the attribution of powers related to the social, economic, cultural, and linguistic development of Quebec; the transfer of related tax and financial resources; Quebec representation in common institutions; and either a Quebec veto over constitutional modifications or the right, "where applicable," to opt out, with compensation, from provincial transfers of jurisdiction to the federal government.[33]

The review in Part Three of the Charlottetown Accord shows that the renewed federalism option was its guiding inspiration. The Accord's version of renewed federalism was clearly not as radical as the Bélanger-Campeau version. Yet the Charlottetown Accord had obviously been affected by the Quebec thinking; it was the only constitutional agreement endorsed by the federal government since 1971 to have dealt with the question of the division of powers, a long-standing concern of nationalists in Quebec.

Despite their differences, common things concern sovereignists and English-Canadian nationalists, the modern "two solitudes": constitutional landmarks, language issues, the economic and fiscal benefits of political union, and the significance of international developments.

Notes

1. Popular vote figures are from Canada, Chief Electoral Officer of Canada, *Official Voting Results: Synopsis, Thirty-Fifth General Election, 1993* (Ottawa: Chief Electoral Officer of Canada, 1993), Table 9.

2. Gouvernement du Québec, Conseil Exécutif, *Québec-Canada: A New Deal* (Québec: Éditeur Officiel, 1979).

3. Constitutional Committee of the Quebec Liberal Party, *A New Canadian Federation* (Montreal, January 9, 1980), p. 10.

4. *Ibid.*, p. 12.

5. *A Quebec Free to Choose: Report of the Constitutional Committee of the Quebec Liberal Party*, for submission to the 25th Convention, January 28, 1991, p. 25.

6. *Ibid.*, p. 35.

7. Robert Bourassa, "L'Union monétaire et l'union politique sont indissociables," Les Québécois pour le non, avril 1980, p. 31.

8. "L'alternative au fédéralisme canadien n'est pas un État unitaire centralisé à Ottawa, mais une mosaïque de petits États unitaires plus ou moins indépendants, faibles et vulnérables économiquement, socialement, culturellement et politiquement. Une telle balkanisation rendrait bien sûr impossible la préservation de l'espace économique canadien. Le fédéralisme est ce qui permet au Québec de vivre 'sa différence' tout en tirant profit de ce qui, autrement, ne lui serait pas accessible, c'est-à-dire un espace politique et économique à la mesure d'un demi-continent." *Mémoire présenté par le Parti Libérale du Québec devant la Commission sur l'Union Économique Canadienne*, 24 février 1984, p. 10.

9. Commission sur l'avenir politique et constitutionnel du Québec, *The Political and Constitutional Future of Quebec* (Montreal, March 27, 1991). Hereafter cited as Bélanger-Campeau Report.

10. Philip Resnick, *Letters to a Québécois Friend* (with a reply from Daniel Latouche) (Montreal: McGill-Queen's University Press, 1990);

Philip Resnick, *Toward a Canada-Quebec Union* (Montreal: McGill-Queen's University Press, 1991).

11. Resnick, *Letters,* p. 66.

12. Resnick, *Toward a Canada-Quebec Union,* chs. 5, 6, 10.

13. Bela Egyed, "Quebec should separate so that the rest of Canada can unite," unpublished manuscript, Department of Philosophy, Carleton University, 1990.

14. Reg Whitaker, "Who Speaks for the Rest of Canada?" in Richard Simeon and Mary Janigan, eds., *Toolkits and Building Blocks: Constructing a New Canada* (Toronto: C.D. Howe Institute, 1991), pp. 92-96.

15. Preston Manning, "The Road to New Canada," an address to the 1991 assembly of the Reform party of Canada, Saskatoon, April 6, 1991, p. 2.

16. *Ibid.,* p. 10.

17. Preston Manning, "Reform Party Position on the Meech Lake Accord," news release, May 18, 1990.

18. Manning, "The Road to New Canada," p. 9.

19. Memorandum from Preston Manning to Premiers Grant Devine, Gary Filmon, Donald Getty, and William Vander Zalm re: "Proposals for Advancing the West's Constitutional Interests in the Post-Meech Period," July 13, 1990, p. 4. This "memorandum" was actually a news release.

20. Government of Newfoundland and Labrador, *Proposal for a Revised Constitutional Accord* (St. John's, March 22, 1990), p. 1; Manning, "Reform Party Position," p. 2.

21. Stephen Harper, "The Reform Vision of Canada," speech to the Party Assembly, Saskatoon, April 5, 1991; Preston Manning and Stephen Harper, "The Road to Conflict in Canada," *Globe and Mail,* June 28, 1990.

22. A fact not unrecognized by Jean Chrétien himself, who in December, 1990, half-jokingly accused Prime Minister Mulroney of cribbing from an advance copy of his own constitutional proposals for division of powers. See Graham Fraser, "Pitfalls at every turn for politicians," *Globe and Mail,* January 22, 1991, p. B24.

23. The later discussions of division of powers by the Prime Minister were outlined in "Notes for an address by Prime Minister Brian Mulroney to the Canadian and Empire Clubs of Toronto, February 12, 1991"; and "Speaking Notes for Prime Minister Brian Mulroney, Chambers

of Commerce, Quebec City, Quebec, February 13, 1991," Ottawa, Office of the Prime Minister, February, 1991.

24. Submission to the Commission on the Political and Constitutional Future of Quebec by the Honourable Jean Chrétien, MP, December 17, 1990, p. 40. Hereafter cited as Chrétien submission.

25. Fraser, "Pitfalls at every turn."

26. Andrew Cohen, *A Deal Undone: The Making and Breaking of the Meech Lake Accord* (Vancouver: Douglas and McIntyre, 1990), p. 82.

27. "Quebec calls immigration pact model for future," *Globe and Mail*, February 6, 1991; "Quebec heralds immigration agreement is a move to 'new vision of federalism,'" St. John's *Evening Telegram*, February 6, 1991.

28. Chrétien submission, p. 42.

29. Jeffrey Simpson, "Enter Mr. Chrétien, carrying the political baggage of years past," *Globe and Mail*, December 18, 1990. The "five demands" referred to were the five conditions that the new Quebec Liberal government announced, after being elected in 1985, as requirements for Quebec's acceptance of the Constitution Act, 1982. The five were "(1) recognition of Quebec as a distinct society; (2) a greater provincial role in education; (3) a provincial role in appointments to the Supreme Court of Canada; (4) limitations on the federal spending power; and (5) a veto for Quebec on constitutional amendments." P.W. Hogg, *Meech Lake Accord Annotated* (Toronto: Carswell, 1988), pp. 3-4.

30. Chrétien submission, p. 41.

31. Once bitten, twice shy: Mulroney's synonym for distinctness was "uniqueness." Gil Rémillard, Quebec's Intergovernmental Minister, "applauded the fact that the [May 14, 1991, federal] Speech from the Throne acknowledged Quebec's 'uniqueness,' which he said was synonymous with recognizing Quebec as a distinct society, one of the key demands of the failed Meech Lake Accord." Rhéal Séguin, "Ottawa given mixed message on federalism," *Globe and Mail*, May 15, 1991.

32. See, for example, Simeon and Janigan, eds., *Toolkits and Building Blocks*.

33. Bélanger-Campeau Report, pp. 48-49. We say "may" because the demands are introduced in this way: "The groups and individuals who commented on this solution indicated to the Commission the constitutional changes which they felt were necessary."

Chapter 7

The Argument for Quebec Sovereignty

Souverainistes, with reason, deny the adaptive and modernizing capacities of Canadian federalism. Constitutional history is replete with cases of intended or pathological insensitivity to the needs of the French minority culture. The language issue shows no sign of satisfactory solution under an Anglophone-dominated majority. Increasingly important is the fiscal quagmire that Quebec is attached to in the Canadian union. In addition, international politics illustrates the importance of localized responses to global imperatives.

Constitutional Issues

Constitutional landmarks have given rise to extensive *souverainiste* commentary. There is even a certain nostalgia for the brief period in the mid-nineteenth century under the Act of Union, 1840. The

PQ White Paper some years ago noted that parliamentary equality in the quarter-century before Confederation had provided the means of developing a Francophone elite, resisting assimilation of Francophones, and checking the territorial and commercial expansion of Anglophones.[1] Lately, Georges Mathews has echoed this theme.[2] In fact, save for Quebec's dwindling demographic importance, Mathews suggests that the legislative union model may even have been a more useful expedient historically than the federal one, offering important French-Canadian influence on the public service, general influence on public policy (for example, education), and a greater share of economic modernization. However, it is certainly not a tenable option at present.[3]

The Canadian federal regime established in 1867 is open to much criticism. Essentially, it has evolved in directions contrary to Quebec's expectations. One theory held by *souverainistes* is that a centralist constitution was imposed on Quebec when it had expected a legal structure allowing more autonomy especially for Quebec. Provincial autonomy was granted over language and religion but was bounded by countervailing federal powers of taxation, the declaratory power, disallowance, and paramountcy in concurrent fields, to say nothing of the residual power.

A more optimistic theory is that of "Canadian dualism." Dualism refers to the founding of Canada as a pact between the English and French. It implies equitably shared benefits and influence by both linguistic groups in the federal union and a special role for the provincial government of Quebec. However, the history of Canada contradicts the dualist foundation: the subsequent expansion of Anglophone commercial interests, the Riel affair of 1885, restrictive provincial language legislation in Manitoba in 1890, two conscription crises, and a host of other irritants. Sovereignists give special emphasis to these grievances as indications of a fundamental incompatibility between language groups.

In a more general sense, the Constitution Act, 1867 (formerly known as the British North America Act), is denounced as a Trojan horse for all sorts of federal invasions of provincial jurisdictions. Its cardinal weakness is its vagueness – a characteristic much beloved by Anglophile constitutionalists but anathema to Quebecers, who prefer specificity in constitutional matters. The archaic aspects of the constitution of 1867 have, moreover, given rise to extra-constitutional negotiations as an element of adaptability. Quebec cannot rely on negotiations in which it is but one of eleven partner governments, and will be forever condemned to accommodating English-Canadian needs rather than its own. Division of powers questions, for example, have never been seriously discussed in an executive federalism context to Quebec's satisfaction.

The intensity of criticism among *souverainistes* reached a new crescendo with the Constitution Act, 1982. It introduced a fundamental shift in power relations between Quebec and the rest of Canada. Daniel Latouche says:

> With the new Canadian constitution of 1982, the political connection between Quebec and the rest of Canada was profoundly changed. . . . In 1982, the rest of Canada decided to make Quebec a province like the others, a province that would not be able to appeal to the pretext of being different. . . . Meech Lake or not, they [English Canadians] now know they can function without Quebec. Pierre Trudeau proved that one could very well go over the heads of Quebec political authorities and make fun of all appeals to a sacred union [of Quebec and English Canada as equals].[4]

Wounded pride aside, *souverainistes* have functional reasons for a deep and abiding mistrust arising from the events of 1980-82.[5] They are many.

1. *Prime Minister Trudeau promised renewed federalism* if Quebec rejected the sovereignty-association message in the 1980 Quebec referendum. He implied the government would respond to traditional Quebec demands for decentralized federalism. However, almost nothing changed in the division of powers, the federal spending power continued unchecked, and there was no recognition of Quebec as a distinct society.

2. *Quebec exited from the constitutional agreement of 1982 empty-handed, in contrast to other provinces.* Some of the recent or traditional demands of other provinces – increased natural resource jurisdiction, protection of the principles of equalization and regional development, provincial equality in the new amending formula, Ontario's protection against enforced bilingualism – were honoured, but Quebec actually lost powers in the process.

3. *The Canadian Charter of Rights and Freedoms constrained or derogated from Quebec powers.* It introduced the "Canada clause" in regard to language of instruction, allowing Canadians from outside

Quebec the right to educate their offspring in English in Quebec. This was contrary to Bill 101, Quebec's language legislation, and even contrary to the spirit of the Constitution Act, 1867. The mobility clauses of the Charter prevent a "Quebec-first" employment policy if the province's unemployment rate exceeds the national average. It constitutionalizes an unrealistic definition of Canada as including official bilingualism and multiculturalism, bypassing reality: Canadian duality and Quebec's distinctiveness are neither mentioned nor protected. It is almost exclusively individualistic in its conception of rights, ignoring a long Quebec tradition of concern for collective rights.

4. *The amending formula of the Constitution Act, 1982, severely weakened Quebec strategically.* It ignored a consensus developed over fifty years of constitutional bargaining that Quebec had a right of veto over important constitutional amendments. Under the general amending formula, Quebec could not prevent the transfer of provincial jurisdictions to the federal Parliament. Provinces could refuse to transfer jurisdiction to Ottawa, but even where they agreed to they would only receive compensation if the transfers related to education and culture. The equality of provinces in the amending formula marked a step backwards in that it did not recognize basic realities of power relations arising from unequal population weights. Quebec has more than a quarter of the national population, but no analogous clout in the formula. As well, a single province could block Quebec's attempt to regain the veto since the amending formula could only be changed under the unanimity provision.

Independence-minded Quebecers see the Meech Lake Accord as a heroic act by a new Prime Minister anxious to reverse the trauma of 1982; but the outcome of the Meech episode is indicative of basic incompatibilities that were foreshadowed in 1982. Quebec had prioritized its previously overwhelming list of requests into a compact and relatively modest list of five minimum demands.[6] Yet English-Canadian public opinion was massively opposed to even this small list, bespeaking a systemic disregard for Quebec's security in the federation.

Even if Meech (or the companion resolution of June 9, 1990, "Meech II") had in fact been successful, problems apparently would have persisted. Pierre Fournier has listed some *souverainiste* concerns.[7]

1. The "distinct society" clause was placed in an ambiguous and probably weaker relationship to the linguistic duality clause, the Charter's multiculturalism provision (s. 27), and, for the matter, the Charter itself. Furthermore, the French language and culture were not mentioned as components of the distinctness of Quebec. The clause conferred no new powers on Quebec and did not recognize two nations in the Canadian state.

2. The spending power provision gave the federal government for the first time an unambiguous constitutional basis for invasion of provincial jurisdictions, imposing conditions in areas of exclusive provincial jurisdiction. A "distinct society" moreover should have protection against this in the form of a veto, but such was not present in Meech.

3. The general amending formula still existed in the constitution, and Quebec's veto rights were shared with other provinces in the proposed new section 41 of the amending formula. As well, the expanded s. 41 did not amount to a full veto for Quebec.

4. The Meech II process and results amounted to the weakening of already unacceptable compromise (Meech I). The majority of Canadians were plainly committed to the constitutional status quo, which amounted to a Charter of rights-based national identity and a strong federal government. Demands for various reforms (for example, Senate reform, minority protection) were merely secondary to protecting this basic status quo.

Language Issues

By some standards, the French language is under siege in Quebec. A review of demographic studies done for the Bélanger-Campeau Commission by Marc Termote is frank about the Quebec situation: "It's no longer a question of just knowing if Quebec will still speak French in a few generations, but as well how many Quebec men and women will be there to speak it."[8] Francophones in Quebec saw their relative share of the Quebec population return to 82.9 per cent in 1986 (the 1951 share), and Quebec contains today nearly 85 per cent of Canadians whose mother tongue is French and almost 90 per cent of French-language users in Canada. Yet these proportions are not the whole story. Except for immigration, natural increase is the only source of growth for the Quebec Francophone population, but the rapid drop in the Quebec birth rate has meant that natural increase is now approaching zero. The natural increase of allophones (neither French nor English as mother tongue) in Quebec exceeds that of both Francophones and Anglophones and is concentrated in the Montreal region, where the French population is predicted to fall a few percentage points from its 1981 census percentage of 59.9 per cent. Quebec's population as a proportion of the entire Canadian population has seen a downward drift from 29 per cent in 1951 to 25.8 per cent in 1986, and it is forecast to sink to 24 per cent in 2011.[9]

Language issues understandably rank high in the catalogue of Quebec nationalist causes and are usually connected to the independence issue. Daniel Latouche's critique of Quebec's permissive allophone policy suggests that political independence will assure the linguistic assimilation of Quebec immigrants, almost as an afterthought, as if the matter were self-evident.[10] Political economist Georges Mathews maintains that the federal government's policy of official bilingualism is unfair to Francophones since it effectively blocks the upper reaches of the federal civil service to unilingual Francophones. As well, alliances between English Canada and Quebec Anglophones over controversial aspects of language legislation (such as Bill 178 on the language of commercial signs) hinder the bilingualization of the latter and support Anglo indifference to French Quebec.[11] Sovereignty here is the implied solution to such problems. Pierre Fournier says that Quebec sovereignty is the only realistic solution to language problems in Quebec. The federal government historically has been more sympathetic to Anglo-Quebecers and to *francophones hors Québec* than to the Francophones within Quebec. Sovereignty would remove the harmful federal role in immigration, alleviate the need for ambiguous language legislation within Quebec and Canada, and reduce the insecurities of French Quebecers.[12]

Fiscal and Economic Issues

One striking aspect of the current *souverainiste* analysis is the extent to which it emphasizes the fiscal and economic problems of the current federal system. It is striking because this analysis has moved progressively closer to centre stage in nationalist argumentation. Quebec's economic future may suffer if the present arrangement continues, say the *souverainistes*; they were not able to say this convincingly in 1980. The economic gun to Quebec's head is not there any more.[13] The fiscal and economic critiques are wide-ranging.

1. *The federal debt.* Nationalists often emphasize that of the Group of Seven nations, only Italy is accumulating debt at a faster rate than Canada. The federal debt, it is noted, grew from $72 billion in 1980 to $352 billion in 1990.[14] The Quebec Chamber of Commerce wants an end to the present federal system, arguing that Ottawa's lack of control over spending and borrowing and its attendant budget deficits have destabilized the Canadian economy. A large accumulated debt has been a major factor leading to high interest rates and debt-servicing costs, which have in turn restricted business investment, destabilized provincial finances, and led to unilateral reductions in transfers to the provinces.[15] Quebec economist Pierre Fortin observes that "the contrast between the failure of the federal government to control its deficit and the success of the Quebec government in achieving budget balance is striking. This clearly adds to the relative discredit in which the central government is held in the province."[16] The Allaire Committee Report says simply that "the state of public finances is such that the federal government can no longer attend to the problems of the system or manage its internal contradictions."[17]

2. *The balance sheet.* Many nationalists view the federal system with an eye to profitability for Quebec, and the balance sheet has become less attractive in the past decade.[18] The secretariat of the Bélanger-Campeau Commission reviewed a number of Quebec and Canadian studies based on provincial economic accounts and they all showed essentially the same thing as its own studies: that "Quebec proved itself a net contributor to federal budgetary operations during the 1960s, and from the beginning of the 1970s until the mid-1980s it benefited substantially from federal operations, after that seeing its benefit from federal operations diminish in a considerable way."[19] Pierre Fortin says nationalists basically draw an egoistic lesson from fiscal federalism:

> federalism is sharing, and the Quebec debate takes place entirely outside these considerations. . . . Quebec is now realizing that its balance of costs and benefits in terms of national accounts are [sic] essentially zero with the federal government. So they say, well, we receive a lot of equalization payments but on the other hand Ottawa spends much less in

Quebec for other purposes, and therefore our balance is just zero so why not opt out?[20]

3. *Overlap.* Oft-cited among nationalists is a 1978 study by Julien and Proulx on the overlap of federal and provincial programs in Quebec.[21] There have also been a number of less methodical and/or political accusations of jurisdictional crowding. Overlap is said to distort accountability, engender contradictions between programs, and result in less than optimal use of public funds. Where the federal spending power is concerned, overlap submerges Quebec priorities; Ottawa even has the temerity to continue standards while lowering transfers.

4. *Regional development.* Lastly, *souverainistes* take aim at the regional development role of the federal state, a useful strategy since the alleviation of regional disparities has been an important rationale for federalism since the Second World War. The Allaire Committee criticized the Canadian record of industrial development programs and of equalization. Equalization apparently fostered dependency, not productivity, and did not provide comparable standards of service across Canada due to the fiscal crisis; as well, federal development programs often ignore the regions' own objectives.[22]

International Developments

Another aspect that has also moved closer to centre stage in *souverainiste* analysis is the relative importance of international developments. In the referendum campaign of 1980, Quebec *souverainistes* were effectively clubbed with the accusation that Quebec's economy was insufficiently developed to succeed in the international marketplace. Nationalists now have extensive arguments for Quebec's international competitiveness to augment their review of domestic federal inadequacies.

1. *Globalization.* The internationalization of competition has become a consistent theme of *souverainiste* analysis. PQ constitutional adviser Daniel Latouche told the Bélanger-Campeau Commission that globalization was the most important factor leading to a redefinition of the current constitutional debate and was the principal challenge facing Quebec.[23] Entire societies are now in competition with one another world-wide, and their success largely

depends on their capacity for social compromises and rapid adaptation to changing economic conditions. Yet federal-provincial competition in Canada has reduced Quebec's capacity to adapt to the new global imperatives. Canadian federalism has been a form of "political protectionism," which, like economic protectionism, had its day in Quebec. Sovereignty would give Quebec a greater range of policy instruments than those of a province; and Quebec's capacity to use them for purposes of adaptation – a requisite condition for success – is evident in the wide-ranging policy development that has been a characteristic of the Quebec state for thirty years.[24]

2. *Economic maturity*. Nationalists are not slow to draw conclusions from Quebec's new business culture. Pierre Fournier says that "In economic terms Quebec now has all the assets needed for political sovereignty; a strong, autonomous financial network, a broad industrial base controlled by Québécois, a healthy governmental financial structure, and reduced dependence on the federal government and the Canadian economy."[25]

3. *International economic integration*. Quebecers envision the Western world allowing progressively more mobility for international capital through economic integration, and some draw specific conclusions. Nationalists assume that since economic integration will continue despite political separation, Quebec's continued adhesion to the Canadian common market and North American free trade are likely. Possible retaliatory actions by Canadian partners seldom appear as real possibilities in nationalist literature. Commentators are anxious to put the so-called "federalization" of the European experience in perspective. Georges Mathews devotes a whole chapter of his *Quiet Resolution* to demonstrating that the common market is only "one-tenth supranationality and nine-tenths national sovereignty" and that the single "Europe" design of 1992 does not affect such aspects of national sovereignty as social policy, defence, and foreign policy. The lesson? "Greater economic integration does not necessarily lead to political unity."[26]

Sovereignists have therefore established a comprehensive argument covering both internal and external factors. They enter the contemporary debate with a certain serenity and self-confidence. Those Canadians who expect the old Quebec insecurities, which were somewhat in evidence in 1980, to emerge once again are in for a rude shock. Preparation for an independent Quebec should begin in all earnestness. PQ leader Jacques Parizeau, on the eve of the

Quebec general election of 1994, said, "Psychologically . . . I am already in another world."[27] These no longer seem like the words of a dreamer.

Notes

1. Gouvernement du Québec, Conseil Exécutif, *Québec-Canada: A New Deal* (Québec: Éditeur Officiel, 1979), p. 6.

2. Georges Mathews, *Quiet Resolution: Quebec's Challenge to Canada* (Toronto: Summerhill Press, 1990), p. 57.

3. *Ibid.*, pp. 57-58.

4. Daniel Latouche, *Le Bazar* (Montréal: Les Editions du Boréal, 1990), p. 201; my translation.

5. What follows is an amalgamation of points from *A Quebec Free to Choose: Report of the Constitutional Committee of the Quebec Liberal Party*, for submission to the 25th Convention, January 28, 1991, p. 12 (Allaire Report); Commission sur l'avenir politique et constitutionnel de Québec, *The Political and Constitutional Future of Quebec* (Montreal, March 27, 1991), pp. 28-31, 33-38 (Bélanger-Campeau Report); Latouche, *Le Bazar*, p. 164; Mathews, *Quiet Resolution*, pp. 67-76; and Pierre Fournier, *A Meech Lake Post-Mortem: Is Quebec Sovereignty Inevitable?* (Montreal: McGill-Queen's University Press, 1991), pp. 11-13.

6. Gil Rémillard, "Quebec's quest for survival and equality via the Meech Lake Accord," in Michael D. Behiels, ed., *The Meech Lake Primer* (Ottawa: University of Ottawa Press, 1989), pp. 28-42.

7. Fournier, *A Meech Lake Post-Mortem*, chs. II, V.

8. Marc Termote "L'évolution démolinguistic du Québec et du Canada," *Eléments d'analyse institutionelle, juridique et démolinguistique pertinents à la revision du statut politique et constitutionnel du Québec*, Document de travail, numéro 2, Commission sur l'avenir politique et constitutionnel du Québec, n.p., 1991, p. 276; my translation.

9. *Ibid.*

10. Latouche, *Le Bazar*, p. 286.

11. Mathews, *Quiet Resolution*, chs. 2, 7.

12. Fournier, *A Meech Lake Post-Mortem*, ch. VI.

13. At least apparently not, judging from the polls of business people. See Charles Macli, "Dueling in the dark," *Report on Business Magazine* (April, 1991), pp. 29-38. See also SOM – *Les Affaires* polls of Quebec business people in 1990-91.

14. Mathews, *Quiet Resolution,* p. 141. It is now closer to $400 billion.

15. *Rapport sur les aspects économiques sur l'avenir politique et constitutionnel du Québec,* Chambre de Commerce du Québec, Comité des Affaires Constitutionnelles, 24 septembre 1990, pp. 11-12.

16. Pierre Fortin, "How Economics is Shaping the Constitutional Debate in Quebec," in Robert Young, ed., *Confederation in Crisis* (Toronto: James Lorimer, 1991), p. 39.

17. Allaire Report, p. 20.

18. Mathews, *Quiet Resolution,* pp. 138-41.

19. Secrétariat de la Commission, "Analyse des activités fiscales et budgétaires du government fédéral. Evolution et comparisons inter-provinciales," *Elements d'analyse économique pertinents à la révision du statut politique et constitutionnel du Québec,* Document de travail, numéro 1, Commission sur l'avenir politique et constitutionnel du Québec, pp. 351-52; my translation. The Secrétariat also comments (p. 341) that although Quebec has benefited substantially from federal transfers, it has practically never obtained a share of federal expenditures relating to its share of the population.

20. Fortin, "How Economics is Shaping the Constitutional Debate," pp. 60-61.

21. Germain Julien et Marcel Proulx (sous la direction de Arthur Tremblay), *Le chevauchement des programmes fédéraux et québécois* (Québec: École nationale d'administration publique, 1978).

22. Allaire Report, pp. 21-22.

23. Daniel Latouche, "La stratégie Québécoise dans le nouvel ordre économique et politique international," *Les Avis des spécialistes invités à répondre aux huit questions posées par la Commission,* Document de travail, numéro 4, Commission sur l'avenir politique et constitutionnel du Québec, p. 605.

24. *Ibid.*

25. Fournier, *A Meech Lake Post-Mortem,* p. 105.

26. Mathews, *Quiet Resolution,* pp. 133-34.

27. Rhéal Séguin, "Parizeau means business," *Globe and Mail,* June 25, 1994, p. A4.

Chapter 8

Renewed Federalism for Canada

Advocates of renewed federalism stress the adaptive and modernizing capacities of Canadian federalism. This gives them a different view on constitutional landmarks, language, the economy, and international imperatives. The twenty-first century belongs to Canada.

Constitutional Issues

Renewal federalists tend to view the constitutional exercise as a question of balance. Their commitment to past constitutional landmarks is significant, but not unlimited. They see them as reference points or points of departure. Constitution-making is perceived essentially as an ongoing political process, with the interests of governments and citizen groups to be brokered. *C'est une constitution à refaire.* To some extent even the national purpose is to be negotiated.

The one constant is a commitment to federalism as a means of reconciling national rights and regional innovation. Renewed federalism reminds Quebecers about the general accomplishments of federalism in Canada. The case for Canadian constitutionalism can be reduced to a series of propositions.[1]

1. The Constitution Act, 1867, made provision for Quebec specificity in sections 93, 94, and 133, in various sections relating to representation, and in various miscellaneous provisions.

2. Certain *de jure* aspects apparently contrary to the spirit of federalism are included in the constitution (for example, the residual, disallowance, and senate/judiciary appointment powers), but these have not prevented a *de facto* flexibility in the assignment of federal and provincial roles in Canadian history. If fiscal relations are examined, Canada is in a decentralist phase at present.[2]

3. The silence of the constitution has actually redounded to the benefit of provinces like Quebec. Quebec has, for example, been able to establish international representation and introduce a range of policies in "grey areas" of the constitution. Constitutional ambiguity, of course, also allowed the federal government to introduce a range of intrusive shared-cost programs, but federal legislation later allowed Quebec to opt out from many of them, with compensation. Further mutual accommodation in the division of powers may also be expected.

4. Quebec Francophone complaints about being a minority in Canada must be balanced by the fact that Francophones are the majority in the Quebec state. There Francophones control wide social and economic powers, including large autonomy in language policy.

5. Despite being a minority of the Canadian population, Quebecers enjoy a kind of *de facto* dualism: they have sent their native sons to be prime ministers fifty-one out of the last 127 years; Francophones comprise 28 per cent of the federal civil service, slightly more than their proportional share of the population; one-third of Prime Minister Mulroney's order-in-council appointments were Francophones; a third of the Mulroney cabinet was from Quebec. Quebec has both "French power" and "Quebec nationalism."[3]

Despite their acceptance of the general constitutional framework, renewed federalists are not satisfied with the results of constitutional negotiations in the 1980s. They were sensitized to the message of Quebecers before or during Meech and persuaded by the country's fiscal realities to expect less of the national government. They were not alarmed by the relatively modest curbs on the federal spending power in Meech, nor by the federal-provincial partnership aspects implied in its immigration, Supreme Court, Senate, and executive federalism sections, nor by the openness to Quebec that was evident in the distinct society and amendment provisions.

Perhaps the constitutionalism of renewed federalism is best described as a state of mind rather than as a commitment to specific constitutional nostrums. Christian Dufour's comments are relevant here. He says that past directions, such as official bilingualism, multiculturalism, the Charter of Rights, and provincial equality responded to the "reality of the country" but were taken to extremes.

> But, beyond the reality of the country, beyond the ideal, Canada is foundering in an idealism, in the ideology of the ideal, that is constraining and compulsory. This is not surprising: in politics, idealism corresponds to losing touch with reality. It results from an inability to integrate some aspects of that reality.[4]

Trudeauist opponents of Meech, for example, suffered from a surfeit of idealism. Dufour says they should have remembered the essence of Canada:

> As for everything else, in the image of Canada, the [Meech] agreement was superbly imperfect and ambiguous – the first manifestation in a long time of that pragmatic spirit of compromise that has always been the basis of Canada in everything operational. . . . The Meech Lake Accord would have been what Quebecers and Canadians made of it.[5]

Indeed, Dufour's perspective sounds like that expressed by Prime Minister Brian Mulroney in February of 1991:

> In the last constitutional debate, the perfect became the enemy of the good. Had the same stringent tests of perfection been applied to the BNA Act as were applied to Meech Lake, the Fathers of Confederation might never have got Canada

off the drawing board and on the way to a nation. So in the next negotiation, let's ask what's practical. . . . Let's look at the common features of the various agendas, and let's look where the differences can be reconciled, for the good of all.[6]

Language Issues

Renewed federalism does not accept the Quebec nationalist line on language. To do so would imply the acceptance of sovereignty. The Conseil du Patronat, a leading big business association in Quebec, advocates renewed federalism.[7] It commissioned a study by economist André Raynauld to counteract some of the *souverainiste* propaganda on the disadvantages of federalism.[8] The findings were positive in language matters, where the important demographic issues were found to be numbers, concentration, and quality. The numbers of French-speakers in Canada increased from one million in 1871 to 6.4 million in 1986. French-speakers were concentrated in Quebec, Raynauld noted. Mother-tongue French comprised 79.7 per cent of Quebec's population in 1931, 82.8 per cent in 1986; in 1931, 85 per cent of Quebecers could speak French, but by 1986, 93.5 per cent could do so; and unilingual English were 13.8 per cent of the Quebec population in 1931, and only 5.7 per cent in 1986.[9] Federalism, therefore, did not prevent the *francisation* of Quebec. Nor did it deter an improved quality of life for Quebec Francophones, according to studies surveyed by Raynauld. Traditionally underrepresented in management, Francophones now occupy 80 per cent of management positions in Quebec. In 1987, 61.6 per cent of Quebec jobs were in establishments under the control of Francophones, as opposed to 47.1 per cent in 1961, and the French influence was relatively evenly spread across economic sectors.[10]

Fiscal and Economic Issues

The Conseil du Patronat also counters the *souverainiste* critique of the fiscal and economic record of Canadian federalism. Sovereignists have claimed that international economic integration is beneficial for Quebec but that political independence is a prerequisite to achieving concessions not possible inside the federation. Raynauld says that it is impossible to imagine a greater economic integration than that which is to be found within a single federal or unitary state. The sovereignists claim that North-South integration under free trade with the United States is more rational for Quebec than East-West integration with Canada. Raynauld replies that Quebec has more to gain if it increases *both* North-South and East-West trade, rather than substituting one for the other.[11] Finally, sovereignists claim that Canadian federalism is not profitable for Quebec and that federal policies are systematically prejudiced against Quebec. Raynauld shows, however, that a multitude of facts put these nationalist claims in disrepute. Quebec is more dependent on the internal Canadian market than are other provinces; in 1984 it "exported" 26.5 per cent of its manufactured goods and 55 per cent of its total finished goods to other provinces, whereas the respective percentages for Ontario were 17 and 35. In 1988, federal expenditures in Quebec exceeded the amount Ottawa received in Quebec taxes by $1 billion, although there has been a decline in net gains for Quebec in recent years from the previous average of $2.3 billion a year (in current dollars). Faced with losses of this magnitude, a sovereign Quebec would have to depress services or raise taxes. However, the balance sheet approach should not to be overemphasized, Raynauld explains; the important thing is the maintenance of a common market that enables the Canadian collectivity to produce an economic surplus based on the principles of regional specialization, economies of scale, risk-sharing, and maximizing the conditions of exchange with the rest of the world.[12]

International Developments

Reform federalists insist the net effect of international developments on Canadian federalism is integrative rather than disintegrative. Especially pertinent are the effects of globalization and the implications of recent European experience.

   1. *Globalization.* Jean Chrétien, now Canada's Prime Minister, has maintained that globalization, in concert with such other factors as economic integration, should compel countries like Canada to promote pluralism and eschew nationalism. Nationalism in the modern world tends to be strongest in countries not associated

with high levels of freedom and economic growth. Political integration in pluralistic societies, on the other hand, will be necessary to overcome the potentially harmful effects of economic integration (international harmonization of economic policies) and globalization (the extra-national organization of economic factors). As well, there will have to be a rethinking of the role of the state and of international agencies; they must be able to counteract the strong tendency of globalized multinationals to replace the social contract approach in most countries with a mere business culture. "Due to the pressures of interdependence, the importance of the nation-state has declined. . . . It has been replaced with the notion of pluralistic societies joined in a sovereign community."[13]

2. *European integration.* Reform federalists draw different conclusions from those of the *souverainistes* regarding the process of continuing European integration. They emphasize the abridgements of national sovereignty rather than the remnants of sovereignty. Prime Minister Mulroney stressed that a basic federalism is implicit in the approach of the Europeans to confer new powers on the Community in 1992:

> In all these fields, sovereignty will be shared by the Community – in other words, federal Europe – and member countries. . . . What Europeans are doing is clear: they are integrating and uniting politically in order to become more prosperous and secure, and to ensure progress. And they are heading towards shared sectoral sovereignty, rather than insisting on exclusive sovereignty.[14]

Sylvia Ostry, the ex-head of economics and statistics for the Organization for Economic Co-operation and Development (OECD), draws a conclusion from European integration opposite to that of Georges Mathews. The logic of international competitiveness pushed Europe beyond the Single European Act of 1985 to start planning for European Monetary Union (EMU).

> EMU is not, however, the end of the story. Largely triggered by the unification of Germany, a move to constitutional reform for European political union [EPU] was also launched in December [1990]. Although the timing of EPU is explained by the German situation, the push to further political

integration was an inevitable consequence of the powerful forces of economic integration. [15]

Such further economic and political integration transpired under two subsequent European initiatives: the passage of the "1992" program by Community legislation (foreseen in 1989), which removed many remaining economic barriers, and the Treaty on the European Union ("Maastricht Treaty") creating the European Union, which foresees greater political and economic convergence, especially in the areas of foreign, economic, and monetary policy. Chrétien forecast that Europe will evolve by the year 2000 to where Canada is now in terms of federalist design. Social and economic progress are being made by transferring, rather than maintaining, sovereignty. [16] *Souverainistes* are said to be out of step with major developments in the West.

Proponents of renewed federalism therefore exhibit flexibility on the federal design but not on the federal principle. They are willing to explore a reorganized division of powers but maintain that the obvious economic benefits and lessons from abroad do not allow for loosening the national framework. While attacking the sovereignists, however, they are themselves under attack from English-Canadian nationalists.

In addition, renewed federalism offers several general reasons why Canada needs Quebec. Among other things:

- Quebec represents a continuing reminder of the spirit of federalism in Canada.
- Quebec provides a useful and relevant model of a nation struggling to retain its cultural and economic integrity under conditions of duress, and is therefore the Canadian dilemma in miniature.
- Quebec has been a continuing deterrent to Canadian militarism.
- Our international image of moral leadership and peacemaking would suffer in the wake of an inevitably bitter breakup.
- Canadian influence in the GATT, NAFTA, the Group of Seven, the UN, and other international bodies might dwindle if our population drops.
- The Atlantic provinces would suffer from decreased

equalization, geographic isolation, and pressure to sub-
merge their identities in a larger union.
- Quebec is currently acting as a corrective to our economic
  and fiscal policy.

One question is unavoidable: what is the basic purpose of federalism in Canada? To an English-Canadian nationalist, it is apparently to enforce uniformity and balance. Reform federalists believe
that a different conception is required, one more in keeping with
the original purposes of Confederation. Federalism is about *protection.* Sometimes protection of a territorial grouping is possible
under conditions of symmetrical federalism. The alarm and fear
evident among sovereignists in the last decade are indications that
symmetrical federalism can no longer protect Quebec interests.
Asymmetrical federalism may be a response that neither English
nor French nationalists will accept, but renewed federalists see that
this is the only workable solution. Renewed federalism reflects a
spirit of tolerance that in recent years has too often been missing
between groupings, yet Canada has always been a country of paradoxes and contradictions, and in fact thrives on them. The paradox
of renewed federalism will ultimately create a political climate in
which all Canadians can thrive.

Notes

1. The following propositions are an amalgamation of material from the
   Chrétien submission, the Mulroney Toronto and Quebec City
   speeches (see Part Four introduction, notes 24 and 23), and Gilles
   Lalande, *In Defence of Federalism* (Toronto: McClelland and Stewart,
   1978), Part Two, chs. 1-3, as well as general information.
2. Chrétien submission.
3. The terms, but not their implications, are taken from Christian
   Dufour, *A Canadian Challenge – Le défi québécois* (Lantzville, B.C.,
   and Halifax, N.S.: Oolichan Books and The Institute for Research on
   Public Policy, 1990). The first Chrétien cabinet had only five of a
   twenty-three member cabinet from Quebec (22 per cent), but one has
   to consider that there were far fewer Liberal members (19) elected
   from Quebec in 1993 than was the case with Mulroney's available
   pool of Quebec members (63) in 1988.
4. *Ibid.,* p. 145.
5. *Ibid.,* p. 155.

6. Mulroney, Toronto address, February 12, 1991, p. 10.

7. "Business torn by Sovereignty," *Globe and Mail*, March 22, 1991, p. B1. See also "Quebec should stay: Report," *Globe and Mail*, October 19, 1990. The Conseil advocates a renegotiated federalism, with Quebec given additional powers over immigration, manpower, and social policy.

8. Conseil du Patronat du Québec, *Les enjeux économiques de la souveraineté*, Mémoire soumis au C.P.Q. par M. André Raynauld avec la collaboration de M. Jean-Pierre Vidal, October, 1990.

9. *Ibid.*, pp. 31-33.

10. *Ibid.*, pp. 34-40.

11. *Ibid.*, pp. 9-11.

12. *Ibid.*, pp. 11-31.

13. Chrétien submission, p. 25.

14. Mulroney speech, Quebec City, February 13, 1991, p. 4.

15. Sylvia Ostry, "Learning the real lessons from Europe," *Globe and Mail*, February 7, 1991.

16. Chrétien submission, p. 26.

PART FIVE

Does Canada Need
Radical Institutional Reform?

The critics of Canadian institutions of government have become increasingly vocal in recent years. Most observers admit that there must be changes made, but they differ on the degree of change required. Part Five investigates the case for radical alteration of institutions in the direction of direct democracy. In so doing, it reviews the record of older, less dramatic experiments in institutional renewal, experiments that have proved insufficient in the eyes of some Canadians. The older tradition is here called the parliamentary tradition and the more radical approach to change is called plebiscitarian (or radical plebiscitarian) reform.

The Parliamentary Tradition versus Radical Plebiscitarianism

The terms "parliamentary tradition" and "plebiscitarianism" allow us to categorize and to simplify, albeit in an arbitrary fashion, the various attempts to enhance the legitimacy of Canada's institutional framework in the last few decades.

The parliamentary tradition holds that the cabinet/executive derives its authority from the Crown, is accountable to the House of Commons, and is only indirectly accountable to the electorate. The plebiscitarian challenge is to stress that whatever the legal/ constitutional formalities, government should be primarily accountable to the electorate.

For parliamentarians, the tenets of representative and responsible government are the points of departure for discussions of institutional reform. They maintain that much can be accomplished by reforms at the margin, namely those that do not seriously impede the leadership of the executive.

Canadian parliamentary government is structured on the operative constitutional theory of *representative* and *responsible government*. Citizens elect members to *represent* them in the legislature, and the efficient executive (cabinet) is directly *responsible* to the legislature (and thus indirectly to the public). If the House demonstrates a lack of confidence in the executive by voting down major legislation or a budget, so the theory goes, the legislature can support a newly formed government or a general election can be imposed, the choice of which rests with the Crown's non-elected representative, the Lieutenant-Governor (provincial) or the Governor General (federal).

Generally, however, responsible government manifests itself in less dramatic ways. It has also been interpreted so as to imply the necessity for the government of the day to allow sufficient legislative opportunities for scrutiny and debate, to respond to criticism, and to disclose enough information to keep legislators and the public apprised of vital functions in government.[1]

Parliamentary traditionalists in the recent past have typically prescribed changes that loosen the executive's hold on the Commons in one place only to tighten it in others. They also proposed Senate reform, but suggested that provincial (or federal and provincial) executives choose the senators. They see no need for a fundamental change in the machinery of intergovernmental relations, especially in the potentially dangerous area of constitutional revision. Party discipline is seen as amenable to some relaxation, but ultimately this tradition is perceived to be necessary for national unity. No other social institution is considered as well suited to brokering the disparate interests of Canada's national communities as is the national political party.

Radical reformers are not convinced that such tinkering would work. They demand a more thoroughgoing overhaul of the institutional framework and see a more modest role for legislatures. They are not focused on the question of responsible government in the British mould, but in *redefining institutions*. They want an elected Senate, less party discipline, referendums, and even constituent assemblies to remake the constitution. Hence, the reforms the moderates suggest to bolster responsible government hold little attraction for the radicals. For the sake of simplicity and brevity, we are identifying the institutional program of the Reform Party of Canada and of Premier Clyde Wells of Newfoundland as that of "radical plebiscitarians."

The plebiscitarians hold that the promises of responsible government have not occurred in Canada. To the extent that disclosure and restraint are not honoured, executive dominance holds sway, responsible government is harmed, and legislatures drift further from the accountability that is the hallmark of healthy government.

The Declining Legitimacy of the Parliament-Centred Model

Despite the considerable efforts taken by advocates of the Parliament-centred model to increase the legitimacy of Canadian institutions in general,[2] the public has either misunderstood or not appreciated the nuances of the model. In fact, as we shall see, the legitimacy of the model has declined substantially in the last few decades.

The reasons for the decline are not hard to discern. In many senses, the perceived failures of the "Westminster model," as the combination of representative and responsible government is sometimes called, are due to the human failures of the main actors involved. It is an open question whether or not these failures are endemic to the model in question; but the simple fact is that the public perceives this to be the case, and so the legitimacy of the political system has suffered.

Dissatisfaction with the Westminster Model

The first reason for the decline in legitimacy of the parliamentary or Westminster model is simply that it did not afford Canadian citizens a role in the great dramatic changes in national policies in the 1980s and early 1990s. The introduction of the Goods and Services Tax, the Meech Lake Accord, and free trade first with the U.S. and then with Mexico were accomplished without significant public input. The title of an article on Aboriginal exclusion from the Meech process could well apply to the rest of the citizenry: "So what are we? Chopped liver?"

Parliamentary Pay and Perquisites

The relative decline in Canadian prosperity and the attendant competition for scarce resources have also indirectly affected politicians' status. There is a widespread feeling that the political stratum is not applying the same restraint to itself that it preaches for the rest of the population. Robert Fife and John Warren have condemned the duplicity of federal politicians of all partisan stripes in matters of pay and perquisites.[3] Their indictment of the Mulroney-era Parliament included the following:

- Cabinet has grown to a size (thirty-nine in 1991) that could not be excused by reference to workload and international comparisons.
- Tax-free allowances are expensive, anachronistic, and superfluous, and the uniform formula for staff and equipment is not tailored to the individual needs of members.
- Parliamentary pensions are markedly out of step with those of average Canadians and can be claimed during prime work years.
- "Double-dipping" allows retired politicians to continue to collect substantial pensions while ensconced in patronage positions in government.
- Federal conflict-of-interest guidelines, based as they are

on the Criminal Code, allow loopholes and potential abuse.

- The Senate and Commons Boards of Internal Economy determine allowances, travel, and benefits for parliamentarians in private, not in a public forum.
- Many "fact-finding missions" by parliamentarians are wasteful and may even be immoral if foreign countries seeking favours actually subsidize the travel, as has often occurred.

Prime Minister Chrétien has introduced changes attacking some of these problems, though incompletely. In 1994 his government announced initiatives it planned to introduce in the areas of parliamentary reform and economies.

- Study will be done on reducing the costs of operating Parliament.
- There will be a modification of the pension plan for MPs to establish a minimum age at which pensions can be paid.
- There will be an end to double-dipping.
- There will be less generous travel subsidies for MPs and family members.
- There will be a two-year legislated pay freeze for the Prime Minister, cabinet, and all other appointed and elected federal officials.

Some other measures were pure public relations gestures. These included charging an annual membership fee for fitness and massage services, eliminating free shoeshines and the picture-framing allowance, and placing restrictions on office renovations.

Chrétien also addressed the issue of cabinet size by reducing the cabinet to twenty-three members (himself included) and reducing by $13 million the budgets of ministers' offices. However, the reduction of the *ministry* was less dramatic, since he established a position analogous to those in Britain, France, and Australia, called the Secretary of State. There were to be eight secretaries of state to assist certain cabinet ministers in specific areas of their portfolios. They were to be members of the Privy Council but not of cabinet and are bound by collective responsibility. They are to earn 75 per cent of a cabinet minister's salary. The ministry therefore is still rather large, at thirty-one members.

In politics, however, perception is often reality for the public. There is a public feeling that the reforms do not go far enough. They look to the 1993 abolition of MLAs' pensions in Alberta, or to Manitoba's plan to make MLA salaries taxable, as meaningful reform. There may be strong functional reasons for certain types of politicians' expenses; but the perception is strong that "the buck stops here" has taken on a whole new meaning in Canadian political life. This negative perception has decreased the attractiveness of the Parliament-based model. It has engendered a feeling that general reform, rather than piecemeal change, is needed.

The Senate Expenses Case of 1993

In June of 1993 there occurred what can only be described as a defining moment for public attitudes toward the upper house. The Senate voted itself an increase in expense allowance of $6,000 because of an alleged shortfall in the current amount allotted for the living expenses for senators living outside of Ottawa. A national sense of outrage, focused on the senators' lack of comparative sacrifice in hard economic times, swept across the land. In July the senators returned to Ottawa to rescind their increase, but the harm to the institution's reputation, such as it is, appeared to be irreparable. A *Globe and Mail* article reported that "in recent weeks people have not been asking that the Senate be fixed at the fringes; they appear to be asking for abolition or wholesale reform."[4]

Political Morality

Outrage at the level of public morality has also affected the trust Canadians have in their political leaders. There have been charges brought against parliamentarians throughout Canadian history, but the visibility of the offenders appears greater in the modern era. All parties are touched to one degree or other, but chiefly the governing party appears culpable, at least in part because of greater media scrutiny and more opportunity to use political office for personal gain.

Summary of Federal Scandals Resulting in
Criminal Charges Since 1984

Conservatives
   Ten people charged with various offenses. Three acquitted on all charges. Five convicted on some or all charges. Two
cases before the courts.

Liberals
   Two people charged with various offenses. One case never
went to court because accused died. Other case dropped for
insufficient evidence.

New Democrats
   One person charged. Acquitted.

Bloc Québécois
   One person charged. No plea entered. Case before the
courts.

SOURCE: Canadian Press, June 18, 1993.

In fact, it appears that things are getting worse. Don McGillivray
commented as early as 1989 that the pace of ministerial resignations for various indiscretions or conflicts of interest had picked up
since 1984. There were 150 resignations from cabinet since 1867, of
which eighteen had been a result of legal problems, and nine of
these eighteen occurred during the Mulroney reign. "In other
words, in Canada's 122-year history, half of all the cabinet ministers resigning after brushes with the law, failures of discretion or
allegations of conflict of interest have quit the Mulroney Government."[5]

Patronage

Perhaps the most controversial element of modern institutional
government is political patronage. It is out of keeping with the mer-
itocratic tenor of modern Canadian society and is contrary to the
direction that Canadian governments themselves have set for the
federal civil service since the Civil Service Act of 1918 was introduced.

   Yet the federal government is awash in patronage at the top levels of the executive and judiciary. "Trudeau relentlessly used his
patronage powers," Jeffrey Simpson wrote in his major study on

the history of patronage in Canada. "To have served him almost guaranteed a patronage post if one was desired."[6] When the Tories assumed power in 1984 they found 3,300 Liberals in appointed positions.[7] While cultivating the image of the anti-patronage crusader during a 1984 campaign debate, Prime Minister Brian Mulroney was simultaneously appointing the chairs of national and provincial patronage committees.[8] He became an acknowledged master in the art of rewarding political friends with public positions, doubtless in numbers similar to those established by his Liberal predecessors. Stevie Cameron estimated that between mid-December, 1992, and early June of 1993, of the 655 appointments made by the Prime Minister, more than 500 were overtly partisan.

> Mr. Mulroney has given jobs to at least 10 of his former aides, nine former politicians, 12 failed Tory candidates from federal elections, six relatives of senior Tories and 33 high profile backroom organizers or party donors. The remaining jobs have gone primarily to party workers and riding fundraisers.[9]

Even the judiciary has not gone untouched by the hand of political cronyism. Russell and Ziegel found that of the 228 federal appointments to the bench during the first Mulroney term in office, 47.4 per cent had associations with the Conservative Party and 24.1 per cent were Tory activists. This continued the pattern of the Trudeau and Turner governments.[10]

The Increasing Legitimacy of the Plebiscitarian Model

The decline of the Parliament-centred model has given rise to a search for alternatives. The most coherent models available at present are those provided by modern plebiscitarians such as Preston Manning of the Reform Party and, to a lesser extent, Premier Wells of Newfoundland. "Coherent" refers to the internal consistency of the recommendations and their relationship to a wider supporting theory or larger body of reforms. Of course, in promoting their plebiscitarian vision of Canada, these actors have followed a tradition that was not as established and thoroughgoing but just as honourable as the Westminster model. (See Table 1.)

Table 1
Record of Canadian Direct Votes

Electoral Jurisdiction	Date of Voting	Issue
Canada	Sept. 29, 1898	Prohibition of liquor
	Apr. 27, 1942	Releasing of government from its 1940 promise of no conscription for overseas military service
	Oct. 26, 1992	Referendum on Charlottetown Accord, the constitutional renewal package of Aug. 28, 1992
B.C.	Nov. 25, 1909	Local option policy for liquor control
	Sept. 14, 1916	Women's suffrage
	Dec. 16, 1916	Prohibition of liquor
	Oct. 20, 1920	Temperance
	June 20, 1924	Beer by the glass
	June 1, 1937	Public Health Insurance
	June 12, 1952	Daylight saving time
	June 12, 1952	Regulating sale of liquor
	Aug. 30, 1972	Daylight saving time (provincially conducted plebiscite, but voting in five electoral districts only)
	Oct. 7, 1991 (two questions)	Recall
		Initiative
Alberta	July 21, 1915	Prohibition of liquor
	Oct. 25, 1920	Prohibition of liquor
	Nov. 5, 1923	Temperance
	Aug. 17, 1948	Ownership of power companies
	Oct. 30, 1957	Additional outlets for sale of liquor
	May 23, 1967	Daylight saving time
	Aug. 30, 1971	Daylight saving time
Sask.	Nov. 27, 1913	Approval of the Direct Legislation Act
	Dec. 11, 1916	Abolition of liquor stores
	Oct. 25, 1920	Importation of liquor into Saskatchewan
	July 16, 1924	Prohibition of liquor
	June 19, 1934	Sale of beer by the glass
	Oct. 31, 1956	Choice of local time zones
	Oct. 21, 1991 (three questions)	Balanced budget legislation
		Ratification of constitutional amendments by referendum
		Government funding of hospital abortions

Table 1 *(continued)*

Electoral Jurisdiction	Date of Voting	Issue
Manitoba	July 23, 1892	Prohibition of liquor
	Apr. 2, 1902	Prohibition of liquor
	March 13, 1916	Temperance Act
	June 22, 1923	Government control of liquor sales
	June 11, 1923	Amendments to Temperance Act
	June 28, 1927	Three questions on the sale of beer
	Nov. 24, 1952	Marketing of coarse grains
Ontario	Dec. 4, 1902	Prohibition of liquor
	Oct. 20, 1919	Four questions respecting repeal of the Ontario Temperance Act and sale of beer
	Apr. 18, 1921	Liquor importation referundum
Quebec	Apr. 10, 1919	Prohibition of beer and wine
	May 20, 1980	Sovereignty-association
	Oct. 1, 1987	Constitutional future of northern Quebec (voting in the region only)
N.S.	Oct. 25, 1920	Regulation of liquor sales
	Oct. 31, 1929	Retention of prohibition
P.E.I.	1878	Prohibition
	1901	Prohibition
	1929	Prohibition
	1940	Prohibition
	June 28, 1948	New Temperance Act
	Jan. 18, 1988	Fixed-link crossing
Nfld.	Nov. 4, 1915	Prohibition of liquor
	June 3, 1948	1) Responsible government 2) Join Canada, or 3) Stay under commission government
	July 22, 1948	1) Join Canada, or 2) Responsible self-government
N.W.T.	Apr. 14, 1982	Territorial division

SOURCE: Patrick Boyer, *The People's Mandate: Referundums and a More Democratic Canada* (Toronto: Dundurn Press, 1992), pp. 231-33, with revisions.

Reform Party Proposals

Perhaps the most radical set of institutional proposals to date has come from the Reform Party. Together they add up to a fundamental challenge to the Parliament-centred approach to policy-making in Canada.

Senate reform. Senate reform is one of the oldest platforms of the Reform Party: it was outlined early in a proposed draft amendment to the Canadian constitution prepared for the party in May, 1988.[11] It is also highlighted in the party's Blue Book, its statement of principles and platform.[12] The Senate would be elected for six-year terms at regular three-year intervals from senatorial districts designated by the provincial legislatures. Half the Senate would be elected each time. There would be equality of representation – as few as six and as many as ten from each province. In terms of powers, the Senate, except for the power to initiate money bills, was to be equal in power to the Commons, but it was not to be a confidence chamber (an upper house whose vote could lead to the defeat of the government). A Reconciliation Committee composed of equal numbers of members from the Senate and the Commons would seek compromises in case of disagreement between the two houses, with their reports to be considered by the two houses.

House of Commons reform. The Reformers address themselves not so much to the structure of the Commons itself but to the symbolic and fundamental aspects of the institution. The Commons would apparently be a much different place under a Reform government. There would be greater attention to constituency work and individual members, and much less on the prerogatives of Prime Minister and cabinet.

Elections would occur at fixed four-year intervals unless the government were defeated on an explicit non-confidence motion; and the defeat of government motions would not entail a government's resignation or dissolution – only an explicit vote for dissolution that would follow the defeated motion could force it.[13] Any imposition of bloc voting by a Reform Party caucus would be preceded by a free vote on the issue (and on bloc voting itself), with a simple majority to carry the day regardless of the leader's position; and such vote would be made publicly available.

Reformers seek to change electoral law to make MPs beholden to constituents and not to party leaders or executives. They would reduce the number and kind of orders-in-council, make use of parliamentary committees to review regulations, and fix maximum lengths of time by which by-elections must be held. The general purpose of the legislative arrangements is to focus members' loyalties primarily to their constituents. There would in fact be a "unified field" of representation blending together the delegate, mandate, and trustee theories of representation, with the mandate theory the starting point, but the other two theories active in the caucus context. [14]

Direct democracy. Direct democracy is for Reformers a key complementary aspect to reformed central institutions. Democracy for them is not a sporadic exercise at election time but a continuous process aided by referendums, initiatives, and recalls. These, of course, are the traditional instruments favoured by North American populist movements over the past century.

A Reform government would pass a National Referendum and Citizens' Initiatives Act making it possible for people or Parliament to begin a referendum process and to provide for binding or advisory referendums on important national issues. The threshold for approval is vague: the Blue Book says a simple majority of the electorate plus a simple majority in two-thirds of the provinces, but Manning later stated the last half of this double-majority principle to be "a majority in more than half of the jurisdictions affected." [15]

Citizens' initiatives would guard against government manipulation of the referendum process by allowing a certain threshold number of citizens – probably around 3 per cent of the electorate – to place a question or legislative proposal on the referendum ballot. The threshold is meant to discourage frivolous use of this instrument. The recall petition is designed to force the removal of a sitting member by the petition of a certain threshold of federal electors, as yet undetermined. It must, however, be quite high to prevent it being used as a purely partisan mechanism.

Constitutional amendment by democratic means. The amendment of the Canadian constitution would be subject to popular ratification. The threshold would be a simple majority of the electorate plus a simple majority in two-thirds of the provinces, including the Territories, according to the Blue Book. Again, there is ambiguity on the second part of the double majority: Manning later implied that it would be "a majority in some percentage of the constituent parts of the country." [16]

Constitutional conventions are also a part of the constitutional renewal package offered by Reformers. Conventions at the beginning of the process offer direct public input into the constitution-making process and are necessary because referendums do not provide enough of a sense of "ownership" of the final project. Such conventions should be held in English Canada and Quebec and among Aboriginals.

The Wells Proposals

The constitutional package suggested in 1991 by Premier Wells consisted of four distinct elements considered to be a linked package. The four elements of the package are:

- A triple-E Senate, that is, *elected,* with *equal* representation from all provinces, and having *effective* powers to protect provincial interests. The section 47 Senate suspensive override from the 1982 Constitution Act would be replaced by a requirement for a double majority in the Senate for the passage of amendments affecting culture, language, and the civil law system. One majority is Quebec and the other is the collectivity of the other provinces.
- The use of a referendum following a resolution approved according to the general amending formula, that is, by both federal houses plus five legislatures or by seven legislatures out of ten, having 50 per cent of the population. The Governor General would be required to issue a proclamation after the requisite approval by referendum. Referendums are to be used in cases of substantial amendment, uncertainty as to public opinion, failure of legislatures to act, "or when any political, economic or social circumstances warrant."
- The use of a constitutional convention (constituent assembly). Premier Wells was flexible on the organizational characteristics of this assembly; he was willing to compromise on representation and choice. Half of the convention would be chosen on a population basis; the other half of its membership would be divided equally between provinces. As to method of choice, it would be partly elected and partly appointed. Proposals from the

convention would go either to Parliament and legislatures under the general amending formula, or to a referendum. Constitutional conventions would be used where there is lack of consensus on how constitutional issues are to be addressed, where legislative issues are to be addressed, and where legislative discussions are not an option because of lack of agreement on the structuring of proposals.

- Adherence to the general amending formula with the three-year limit removed. The unanimity provision would be abolished.

Notes

1. T.A. Hockin, "Flexible and Structured Parliamentarianism: From 1848 to Contemporary Party Government," *Journal of Canadian Studies*, 14, 2 (1979), pp. 17-18.
2. The question of executive dominance has arisen in several recent task forces and committees, including the *Report* of the Royal Commission on Financial Management and Accountability (Lambert Report), 1979; the federal position paper, *The Reform of Parliament*, 1979; the various reports of the House of Commons Special Committee on Standing Orders and Procedures, 1982-84; *Reform of the Senate: A Discussion Paper*, issued in 1983 by Minister of Justice Mark MacGuigan; and the *Report of the Special Committee on Reform of the House of Commons* (McGrath Report), 1985. All have agreed on the need to reintroduce and reinforce the centrality of the legislature in the governmental system.
3. Robert Fife and John Warren, *A Capital Scandal* (Toronto: Key Porter Books, 1991).
4. Susan Delacourt and Geoffrey York, "Senators will display humility," *Globe and Mail*, July 10, 1993.
5. Don McGillivray, "Valcourt resignation creates bad precedent," *Toronto Star*, August 4, 1989.
6. Jeffrey Simpson, *Spoils of Power: the Politics of Patronage* (Toronto: Collins, 1988), p. 350.
7. Robert J. Jackson and Doreen Jackson, *Stand Up for Canada: Leadership and the Canadian Political Crisis* (Scarborough, Ont.: Prentice-Hall Canada, 1992), pp. 81-82.
8. Simpson, *Spoils of Power*, pp. 357-58.

9. Stevie Cameron, "Rewards: So long and thank you very much," *Globe and Mail*, June 5, 1993.

10. Peter Russell and Jacob S. Ziegel, "Federal Judicial Appointees: An Appraisal of the First Mulroney Government's Appointments and the New Judicial Advisory Committees," *University of Toronto Law Journal*, 41 (1991), pp. 4-37.

11. Reform Party of Canada, *A Proposed Draft Constitutional Amendment to Reform the Senate of Canada*, prepared by the Reform Party of Canada, May 17, 1988.

12. Reform Party of Canada, *Platform and Statement of Principles*, adopted August 14, 1988, p. 6.

13. Preston Manning, *The New Canada* (Toronto: Macmillan Canada, 1992), pp. 323-24.

14. *Ibid.*, p. 322.

15. *Ibid.*, p. 325.

16. *Ibid.*, p. 306.

Chapter 9

Direct Democracy Will Return Peace to the Kingdom

Canadians have come of age politically in the political and constitutional upheaval of the last few decades. No longer do acquiescence and deference characterize the "peaceable kingdom." Canada has undergone a sea change in its political culture and is now at ease with the concepts and instruments of plebiscitarian democracy. The arguments for direct democracy are philosophical, hypothetical, international, and political.

Philosophical Arguments

Philosophic rationales for plebiscitarian democracy are extremely rich and varied. They can be categorized in terms of the work of classical political theorists and the arguments of their modern democratic disciples. Direct democracy obviously relates to a political theory of participation. Here the contributions of Jean-Jacques

Rousseau and J.S. Mill are particularly insightful. Although they did not pronounce themselves on modern democratic institutions, the general drift of their work is of obvious interest to the modern reformers.

Classical Theorists

Jean-Jacques Rousseau has contributed much about the concept of participation to political theory. Although his thinking is not perfectly transferable to the modern industrial state, his thinking on the value of unmediated dialogue between the rulers and the ruled certainly is. Rousseau in *Social Contract* stressed that the best governance came in small political communities where the population could vote *en masse* for or against the policy in question and direct their rulers without interference from third forces. The theme of "no intermediate interests" has in turn been adopted by populists around the world.

Rousseau also emphasized the mutual gain to both the individual and society arising from participation. Society gains because general participation in decision-making assures the rule of law. "The problem," Rousseau said in one of his classic paradoxes, "is to find a form of association which will defend and protect with the whole common force the person and goods of each associate, and in which each, while uniting himself with all, may still obey himself alone, and remain as free as before" (*Social Contract*, I, vi). Each is one's own master and independent from others, and thus the law is made impersonal and easier to accept. By participation one also is "forced to be free." Pateman interprets this enigmatic clause of Rousseau's as referring to the way the citizen becomes shaped by others in the ways of freedom. "Unless each individual is 'forced' through the participatory process into socially responsible action then there can be no law which ensures everyone's freedom, i.e., there can be no general will or the kind of just law that the individual can prescribe to himself."[1] If institutions operate on a participatory basis they do not pose a threat to freedom. Rousseau is an obvious inspiration to plebiscitarians.

J.S. Mill tells us that one contribution of participation is the educative function it serves. The only way that one learns about democracy, he tells us, is to become involved in the process itself. A democratic process is necessary to yield a democratic result. Unfortunately, much of Mills's writing is marred by assumptions about (1) the superiority of the intellectually gifted and the institutional bias needed for them to share their experience and insight with the less gifted (who incidentally happen to be at the lower levels of government), and (2) his preference that the people of property enjoy weighted voting rights by virtue of their greater stake in the body politic.

However, most important for our purposes is his uncompromising commitment to the value of free speech; the squelching of even patently false opinions constituted a real harm to the public interest. His passionate defence of the liberty of the individual conscience has marked twentieth-century liberalism. His soul hovers above every hall where public-minded citizens gather to debate the latest referendum issue, and the tenets of Mill comfort the individual MP who has been punished by his or her caucus for deviating from the party line.

As to theory in support of the broader program of institutional change, one can look to antebellum America. John C. Calhoun suggested an arrangement called "concurrent majorities," which would require that laws be passed by a majority in each major interest or group in society, with each group possessing a veto on government actions. Despite the danger of anarchy, the people would avoid this great calamity by acting ultimately in the interests of the whole community and the common interest.[2] The concurrent majorities principle derives from a simple fact of life about federal societies: population characteristics are not evenly distributed throughout the society, and national majorities may oppress regional majorities unless prevented from doing so by institutional or other arrangements.

As Reg Whitaker has noted, the contemporary application of Calhoun's theory to Canada would imply a bicameral national legislature, with the upper house based on region or province rather than population and possessing the right of veto over legislation of a federal-provincial nature coming from the Commons upon initiative from the cabinet. It would also imply a concurrent majority as part of a referendum formula for amendments, namely a regional veto included in any popular ratification of constitutional amendments.[3] Certainly the triple-E advocates can claim some

202   *Canadian Political Debates*

kinship with Calhoun. There are as well elements of Calhoun in their demand for regional thresholds in constitutional or policy referendums.

Modern Disciples

The modern disciples of plebiscitarian democracy are too numerous to mention, but a sample review is helpful. The modern era for radical democrats begins with the American Progressive movement of the 1890s and continues, with some historical ruptures, until the present day.

Butler and Ranney begin their book *Referendums* by noting that the American Progressives claimed a number of anticipated benefits for direct democracy. One was the possibility of facing all issues, rather than just the ones that those in power or special interests preferred to deal with. Another was the chance to overcome the geographical and psychological remoteness of the capital city legislature, making policy more comprehensible by bringing government closer to the people. A third was the chance to overcome the secrecy of normal government decision-making by stressing elements of openness: ballots, speeches, and votes are available to all. Open government promotes honesty. Fourth, the popular will is expressed directly and accurately, without being filtered through a party or other intermediary. Most public policy is ambiguous as to its level of support in the community, and direct democracy is the proper antidote. A fifth point is that direct democracy overcomes apathy and alienation by putting control directly in every individual's hands. Sixth, the public interest is served when the public votes on issues; conversely, when special interests have influence, the public interest is harmed by their compromise and logrolling. Finally, direct democracy maximizes human potential: it accepts the model of the individual as a social animal and uses political participation in elemental democratic exercises as a building block to greater participation on other political fronts.

No Canadian has done more in the last few decades to promote plebiscitarian democracy than Conservative MP (and leadership candidate in 1993) Patrick Boyer.[4] For it he claims a number of philosophical benefits. Legitimization is an important one. Unmediated approval by the people gives the highest degree of legitimization possible, and legitimization should be the basic characteristic of most political decisions. Boyer also carries the familiar progressive/populist hostility to intermediary interests, who he says have, in the guise of special interests and lobbyists, recently gained "unwarranted prominence." He adds one uncommon point: that direct democracy would promote self-reliance and a sense of duty and help to overcome the preoccupation with "rights" so common in the new Charter age.

Political Hypotheticals

Much of the argument for plebiscitarian democracy features what one might call "political hypotheticals." (A hypothetical is a proposition that is structured "If . . . then.") That is, the attraction of some elements of direct democracy is tied to their capacity to overturn past political defeats *if they had been in place at the time*. The hypothetical is: "If X (bad) policy succeeded in the past in the absence of this democratic instrument, then X could be defeated (or modified) in the future with it in place – or even Y, which is analogous to it."

Law professor Howard McConnell's case for a triple-E Senate features many such hypotheticals.[5] One notable policy choice that traumatized western Canadians was the Mulroney cabinet's choice of Canadair of Montreal in 1986, rather than Bristol Aerospace of Winnipeg, for the CF-18 fighter maintenance contract despite Bristol's cheaper and technically superior bid. Westerners interpreted the choice as driven purely by electoral considerations and as auguring poorly their future lot in Confederation. However, says McConnell, an elected independent Senate unfettered by party discipline could have discussed the policy more rationally and fairly. Similarly, Quebec might have had more input into the constitutional package of 1982 if a truly "federal" Senate representing popular sentiment had been in place; the package would probably have looked different and at the same time would have enjoyed greater legitimacy.

Other conflicts would have been better dealt with by a new Triple E Senate. Among such disputes was the recent disagreement between Alberta and Ottawa over the taxation and regulation of energy [1973-1985]; the controversies between British Columbia and Ottawa, and between Newfoundland

(and some other Atlantic provinces) and Ottawa, over the ownership and control of mineral rights in the sub-soil under territorial waters and in the adjacent continental shelf; the dispute between Saskatchewan and the federal government over the rescinding of the "Crow Rate" for hauling grain, a dispute, indeed, with large ramifications for all of western Canada; the disputes between the provinces on both coasts and Ottawa over the fisheries; the disputes between New Brunswick and, incipiently, Manitoba, with the federal government and other provinces over the ratification of the Meech Lake Accord; and the ongoing dispute between Quebec and Ottawa over educational language rights (as well as related disputes on the rights of linguistic minorities both inside and outside Quebec); and other contentious political conflicts, all of which might more effectively be debated in a revised upper house. [6]

The revised upper house would have been able to consider both the local and national implications of national policy in these matters. As it was, the federal Parliament acted as a monolithic entity possessing a single will.

Premier Wells of Newfoundland offered an argument for Senate reform that was oriented toward hypothetical arguments. The clear implication from his speeches is that economic development would have occurred differently if there had been a triple-E Senate in place.

The overwhelming influence of the 60% of the members of the House of Commons who represent the two massive economic engines of central Canada is the *primary cause* of Ottawa adopting a symptom treatment rather than problem solving approach to correcting regional economic disparity. *Only with a Triple-E Senate* will we have the political ability to ensure national legislative jurisdiction is exercised and economic policy is developed and implemented in a manner that will provide for the equitable development of the economy across all parts of the nation. Real and sustained economic balance will only be achieved if and when we achieve political balance. [7]

The likely past, and future, result of Senate reform would be the application of a disparity factor, perhaps taking into consideration unemployment and earned income disparities, to national spending and national economic policy.

International Models

Decisions about the adequacy of Canadian institutions should not be taken without considering comparative politics. Several other nations have many of the same problems that we have and have benefited from the imaginative use of governing institutions. This section will examine the various categories of the plebiscitarian model – an elected upper house, less party discipline, direct democracy, and constitutional conventions – and evaluate how successful these have been in other countries. The results are much less disturbing than the Parliament-centred school would have us believe.

Elected Upper Houses

The United States Senate has been elected by direct popular state vote since 1913. Previous to the Seventeenth Amendment of that year, U.S. senators had been chosen by state legislatures. Now two are elected from each state and serve a six-year term. One-third of the Senate is up for re-election at each of the congressional elections, which take place every two years, where they are elected at the same time as the entire House of Representatives (the lower house) and a host of other elected positions. The principle of election for the Senate is territorial equality, while that for the House is representation by population, since larger states merit proportionately more members. Senators represent the entire state from which they are elected, while representatives are elected from single-member districts.

The Australian Senate is also elected on the basis of territorial equality. Each of the six states has twelve members and each of the two territories has two, for a total of seventy-six senators. The constituency in each case is the total electorate of the state or territory. The state senators, elected since 1948 on the basis of proportional representation, each serve a six-year term, with half of them up for re-election every three years. The term for territorial senators is three years. State legislatures choose senatorial replacements for vacated seats. By contrast, the House of Representatives comprises 148 members elected from single-member constituencies, with each serving a three-year term, unless there is a dissolution.

The constitution that created the Commonwealth of Australia in 1901 also created an effective Senate. It gave it equal powers with the House, with the exception of the initiation and amendment of money bills. Since the co-equality raised the possibility of conflict between the two chambers, the constitution provided for "double dissolution," that is, the dissolution of both houses. A joint sitting was the fallback provision in the case of continuing deadlock between the two houses after a new election and the continued failure of the two houses to agree. The joint sitting would make the final decision, but the numerical superiority of the lower house would give it an advantage in such a vote.

The relevance of the American and Australian examples to the Canadian situation should not be overlooked. Both of them allow for the derivation of distinctly national policy from the interaction between central and local interests. This should be of extreme interest to Canadians who are upset with the continuing population-based domination of the Commons and cabinet by central Canadians.

The net effect of the American arrangement is that dreamed of by the intrastate federalists: the American Senate becomes the forum for the blending of both national and territorial interests. Gibbins notes that the U.S. Senate has become a *centripetal* or national institution in the sense that its concerns are those shared by a community of interests, and it represents states *per se,* not state governments, and so does not promote constitutional decentralization. Ironically, the district basis of election has made the majoritarian House the *centrifugal* or decentralizing institution because it infuses local, often substate, interests into the national legislature.[8]

It is highly unusual for the Australian government to have a majority in both houses due to the strength of the minor parties in the Senate, which in turn is partially induced by the electoral system, whereby parties receive seats proportional to the percentage of votes they receive in an election. "Those minor-party and independent senators who have gained representation since the mid-1960's have all had strong regional variations in their bases of support, so that, at least in this sense, the Senate now mirrors a regional diversity not apparent in the House of Representatives."[9] Another lesson from the two countries is how to alleviate executive dominance. The Senate in Australia frequently holds hearings on matters the government of the day may find politically embarrassing, and it engages in detailed review of proposed legislation. Canada, says David Kilgour, could learn from the institutionalized check on prime ministerial power that this Senate provides with its encouragement of rival views of the national interest, informed debate, and compromise.[10] Sharman notes that the Australian example illustrates the need for a "running compromise" between upper house autonomy and the Westminster tradition of executive dominance of federal-state interaction and the legislative process. He concludes that Australia, at least, demonstrates that "bicameralism is the natural ally of federalism; both imply a preference for incremental rather than radical change, for negotiated rather than coerced decisions, and for responsiveness to a range of political preferences rather than the artificial simplicity of dichotomous choice."[11] Although Australia is perhaps the more relevant example, given the common British parliamentary heritage, the American model of separation of powers and a bicameral legislature shows that fragmentation of powers is not inimical to concerted action in international relations, military might, or technological progress.

Direct Democracy

The idea of direct democracy is alive and well in many other countries. The United Kingdom, for example, has used the referendum on three separate occasions: in 1973, to sound out the citizens of Northern Ireland on the question of continued adhesion to the United Kingdom; in 1975, on continuing Britain's membership in the European Economic Community; and in 1979 on the issue of devolution of power to Scotland and Wales. Despite the dependence on the theory of representative and responsible government, British politicians and political philosophers, including A.V. Dicey, Joseph Chamberlain, Arthur Balfour, James Bryce, Benjamin

Disraeli, Stanley Baldwin, and Winston Churchill, have been among the leading advocates of referendums.[12]

Australia has regularly used direct democracy to ratify constitutional amendments and settle national political debates. Of particular interest is the requirement in the Australian constitution that amendments pass a combination of legislative and democratic tests. Proposed amendments must ordinarily pass both houses of the national Parliament with an absolute majority and then be submitted to the electors in each state. Thereafter, the amendment must garner both a national majority of the electors voting as well as a majority of electors in a majority of states. In the case of one of the national houses twice rejecting the amendment that the other house has approved by an absolute majority, the Governor General, acting on the advice of the Prime Minister, may put the amendment to the people. Since the early 1900s there have been approximately forty amendments submitted to the Australian people, with conservative results: only eight have been ratified by the requisite double majorities.[13]

The Swiss, on the other hand, are bathed in direct democracy: both initiatives and referendums became staples of their politics after the Swiss confederacy was founded in 1848. There are both mandatory and non-mandatory referendums. The former are mandated by the constitution; the latter are referendums that take place after a certain threshold number of electors asks for a vote on legislation already passed by the legislature.

Referendums take place at the federal, canton (state), and community levels. All federal constitutional amendments proposed by the government are subject to mandatory referendums. However, if 100,000 signatures are collected within eighteen months on a citizens' initiative proposing a constitutional referendum, the people themselves can force a referendum on constitutional change. A majority of electors and cantons must agree to the amendment. If enough signatures are collected, legislative referendums can be forced on statutes that the federal government has already passed. At the canton and community levels, most constitutional and statutory decisions are subject to mandatory referendums, and there is also the possibility for citizen initiatives.[14] There have been about 350 national referendums between 1848 and 1990 and most often the proposals of the federal parliament are successful; by contrast, "since 1891 when the federal initiative in Switzerland was introduced, only eight initiatives have been endorsed by Swiss voters."[15]

The United States is as enthusiastic a user of direct democracy as Switzerland. Direct democracy is not employed at the federal level, but it is common at the state and local levels. Forty-nine states call for the ratification of amendments to their constitutions by referendums; it is possible in twenty-three states to have citizen-initiated referendums on constitutional amendments; and twenty-five states allow citizens to petition the legislature to hold referendums on laws already passed.[16] Between the years 1898 and 1976, 685 citizen-initiated referendums and about 1,800 referendums initiated by governments took place.[17] California has a particularly active initiative culture. There were 264 initiatives during the 1980s, which in turn was double the amount of the preceding decade and far more than in the decades before that.[18]

The Fifth French Republic, which came into being in 1958, has seen a number of government-initiated referendums. Article 89 of the constitution states that "the initiative for amending the Constitution shall belong both to the President of the Republic on the proposal of the Premier and to the Members of Parliament." There is hence no role for popular initiative. The government or parliamentary bill to amend the constitution must pass the two assemblies in identical form and comes into effect after approval in a referendum. Alternatively, however, a constitutional amendment may be approved by parliament convened in congress if there is a three-fifths majority of votes cast.

As well, Article 11 allows the President on the proposal of the government or on joint motion of the two assemblies to put to a referendum any bill dealing with the organization of public powers, involving the approval of a European Community agreement, or involving ratification of a treaty that may affect the functioning of institutions of government.

Although the role of the President is constitutionally not foremost, most French presidents have put their political status on the line in national referendums. The constitution of the Fifth Republic was approved by referendum on September 28, 1958, and was amended in 1962 to allow direct presidential election. There have been referendums on the Algerian policy (1961-62), regional government and senate change (1969), expansion of the European Economic Community (1972), and approval of the Maastricht

210 Canadian Political Debates

Treaty (1992). After his policy lost in the referendum of 1969, President Charles De Gaulle resigned.

The lesson of international experience with direct democracy is that Canada's political and constitutional problems are likely to be amenable to such mechanisms. Certainly the uses to which democratic devices abroad have been put are often of the same order of importance. It is also instructive to note several facts relevant to the Canadian case:

- The two most successful parliamentary systems, the United Kingdom and Australia, have used the referendum device and still retained the responsible government form.
- Three of the countries are federal. Two, Australia and Switzerland, use direct democracy at the federal, state, and local levels, and the U.S. uses it at the state and local levels. National consensus, rather than raw majoritarianism, is sought in the first two by combining thresholds for state and population approval levels. This is relevant to Canada, with its regional politics.
- Use of direct democracy may not appear to be a plebiscite on the national leader, and hence less threatening to leaders in a parliamentary system like that of Canada (in contrast to the leadership in a presidential system), because the Prime Minister is not directly elected by the whole population.[19]

Constituent Assemblies

Directly elected constituent assemblies such as Premier Wells (in part) and Reform leader Manning (in whole) are advocating are rarer in international use than are those chosen by other means. The other means of choosing constituent assemblies are indirect election (members elected by state or provincial legislatures), constitutional conferences (delegations from the existing national government, if existent, and the constituent units), representative legislative committees (like the Swiss Diet of 1848), and constitutional commissions (commissions of public figures or experts).[20] However, there is no good reason why they cannot work in Canada as they have worked elsewhere. The box on the following page lists the directly elected constituent assemblies of recent history.[21]

The delimitation between directly and indirectly elected constituent assemblies is sometimes an artificial one for the purposes of citing direct democracy precedents. Often, indirectly elected forums for constitutional discussion can approach the spirit of those directly elected. Indirect elections were the case in the United States (1787), Australia (1891, 1897-98, 1973-85), India (1946-49), Pakistan (1947-56), and Germany (1948).

The spirit of democracy that can pervade a constituent assembly has been ably presented by Professor James Gray Pope,[22] who argues that Canada needs the type of "republican moments" that the United States has had in its history instead of using the "politics as usual" approach that features *ad hoc* political party and interest group bargaining and a disinterested public. The United States has

---

Directly Elected Constituent Assemblies

Newfoundland (1946). The Newfoundland National Convention was mandated by the British government and popularly elected in 1946 by constituency to consider the form of government to replace the commission government that had existed since 1934. The Convention's report did not include Confederation with Canada as an option; but this option was included by Britain and ultimately approved after two referendums in 1948.

Spain (1977). The Spanish Cortes elected in 1977 after a long era of dictatorship under General Franco was in effect a constituent assembly. It devised a constitution that received legislative approval, ratification by referendum, and finally royal approval in 1978.

Nicaragua (1984). After the Somoza regime was ousted in 1979, a national assembly was elected in 1984 with one of its primary duties to draft a new constitution, which came into effect in 1987.

Namibia (1989). Elections for a constituent assembly to draft a new constitution for a future independent Namibia took place in 1989. It was finished in 1990.

known republican moments – extremely intense public involvement in constitutional matters – in the Constitutional Convention of 1787, the adoption of the "Reconstruction Amendments" from 1864 to 1870, and Roosevelt's mobilization of popular pressure on the Supreme Court to achieve the judicial revolution in economic policy in the 1930s. Amendments that required super-majorities, that is, consensus, were of little use when deep conflict reigned and made change imperative. Republicanism triumphed. In today's language, republicanism "emphasizes civic virtue over narrow self-interest, direct citizen participation over representative government, collective moral choice over instrumental rationality, and community over individual autonomy."[23]

Canada can know these moments, too. In fact, says Pope, they can be achieved by the use of the constitutional convention as an extra-legal method of constitutional change, analogous to the extra-constitutional means of change used in the U.S. Parliament would call such a convention, convention delegates would be elected on a non-partisan basis along the lines of broad and fair democratic participation, and they would propose a set of constitutional amendments. As well, the convention could use referendums as a way of bypassing the unanimity requirement in the amending formula in the Constitution Act, 1982, if it is hindering change; but referendums themselves, without conventions, are not sufficient to achieve republican politics. The advantages would be heightened political legitimacy, the breaking of constitutional logjams, and the creation of a new national myth out of a constitutional event. Here we have a very coherent union of many different threads of direct democracy.

Changes in Political Culture

A final category of argument for plebiscitarian democracy is simply that the dynamics of Canadian politics have changed, as have the political needs of the population. The parliamentary tradition in Canada flourished in an era of deference to authority and citizen quiescence. Those conditions no longer hold in what has become known as the "Charter era" of citizen activism, which is reflected in a growing distrust of the authority of the executive and legislative realms. Some specific aspects of the cultural shift are here outlined.

Party Discipline and Bloc Voting

One distasteful trend for many Canadians is the high degree of bloc voting that takes place in Parliament. The slavish devotion to party discipline in Commons and Senate votes is more severe than in the British[24] or Australian parliaments, and certainly is unlike the American Congress.

Party discipline has become less acceptable to many Canadians. It is not conducive to fair play in the electoral and parliamentary arenas. It gives too great an inroad to majoritarian interests in the country and downplays the concerns of representatives of less populous areas. It allows the governing party to give disproportionate rewards to its own partisans or favoured regions without fear of suffering immediate consequences. It discourages the disclosure of information to the public, and in the parliamentary context such bloc voting encourages the manipulation of rules and procedures against parliamentary minorities.

This sense of political imbalance was caught by the remarkable report of the Citizens' Forum on Canada's Future (Spicer Commission). It said that Canadians perceived party discipline as a "major constraint on the effectiveness of elected officials in representing constituents' views and in controlling a government agenda which may be out of touch with citizens' concerns."[25] Suggestions for less party discipline are thus likely to strike a sympathetic chord with many Canadians.

Regionalism and Intrastate Federalism

Regionalism is, and always has been, a primary fact of life for Canadian policy-makers, and the national institutions of government have been expected to reflect the needs of the regions. However, until now, radical change in the nature of the representative institutions to achieve regional input was not actively considered.

One new institutional expression of regionalism in Canada has been termed "intrastate federalism." It is usually differentiated from "interstate federalism" in political science literature. *Intrastate federalism* refers to "arrangements by which the interests of regional units – the interests either of the government or of the residents of these units – are channelled through and protected by the structures and operations of the central government."[26] *Interstate federalism* refers to the relations between the federal and provincial governments and the distribution of powers and resources between them. The traditional dialogue in Canada has been along interstate lines, but intrastate demands, sparked originally because of disputes over resource rents, began to take equal billing with the former in the constitutional disputes of the late 1970s.

The intrastate critique has been succinctly described (if not completely accepted) by Smiley and Watts. The intrastate assumptions are that centralization and majoritarianism have characterized national institutions; that the lack of an outlet for territorial-based interests in the central government has weakened its legitimacy and authority; that reforms to achieve representativeness of central institutions are preferable to a whole-scale decentralization of power in the context of interstate federalism; that federal-provincial conflict has arisen from the present unreformed national structures; and that the dual representation of Canadians – as members of both federal and provincial communities – is necessary because it encourages consensus politics rather than the present divisive majoritarian politics.[27] Intrastate federalism has profoundly affected the debate on institutional responsiveness in Canada. Its pervasiveness as a cultural reality is seen in the growing popularity of a triple-E Senate.

Non-Territorial Interests

Territorial interests are not the only ones implicated in the debate on institutional reform. The lack of representation of women in the executive, legislative, and judicial branches of government has been a common and regrettable fact of Canadian political life. By 1994 women comprised only 18.0 per cent of the membership of the House of Commons (fifty-three MPs) and formed an all-time high of 17.4 per cent of the federal cabinet (four of twenty-three ministers). The first woman, Madame Justice Bertha Wilson, was appointed to the Supreme Court only in 1982, and by 1994 there were still only two women on the Court (Madame Justice Claire L'Heureux-Dubé and Madame Justice Beverley McLachlin), Wilson having retired in 1991.[28] Women first ministers were unheard of before Premier Rita Johnston of B.C. in 1991 and Prime Minister Kim Campbell in 1993, neither of whom was elected as a first minister. Women are demanding equal access to these and other decision-making centres for a wide range of reasons: representation by population, different life experiences, the necessity of role models, and to prevent the overlooking of women's interests.[29] The dissatisfaction of the National Action Committee with perceived inadequacies of gender representation in a reformed Senate was a major reason for its initial opposition to the Charlottetown Accord.

Aboriginals did not have the right to vote in federal elections until 1960, and the institutional provisions for their representation leave much to be desired. The geographical dispersion of Natives in Canada condemns them to minority status in most federal ridings and an estrangement from national politics. The question of Aboriginal representation was a bargaining chip used by Aboriginal groups in the Charlottetown negotiations. As well, the Royal Commission on Electoral Reform and Party Financing was solicitous of the needs of the First Nations in its recommendations for a threshold of representation for them in the Senate and House of Commons. The current Royal Commission on Aboriginal Peoples can be expected to contribute to the debate on the sufficiency of institutional responses to Natives in Canada. It has been suggested that one response (among many needed) might be to adopt a suitable variation of the New Zealand model of Aboriginal representation. In New Zealand's Parliament, four of the ninety-one seats are set aside for Maori people, who have the option of voting in one of four Maori districts, which together include the entire country.[30]

The Decline of Political Parties as the People's Brokers

One cause of the estrangement of Canadians from institutions is the usurpation of traditional party functions by intermediary groups. The functions one normally associated with political parties throughout most of Canadian history are now the domain of other bodies – interest groups, ethnic organizations, regional organizations, and even government bureaucracies. To these have devolved the functions of policy advocacy, regional voice, and brokerage politics. If the parties were as involved in the day-to-day concerns of Canadians as they were in the past, citizens might be more forgiving of their various idiosyncrasies. However, with leadership being the only single uncontested function left to parties, their deficiencies with respect to the operation of national institutions are, increasingly, not looked upon with as much leniency.

The philosophical and political argumentation is eloquent: our political institutions need plebiscitarian democracy to meet the expectations of Canadian citizens and to match international progress. The fact is, we have borrowed selectively, to our detriment. We imported the Westminster model from Britain and neglected to modify it to suit a diverse federal country. We should have borrowed aspects of the American and Australian senates, and taken lessons from the populist instruments of America, Australia, Britain, France, and Switzerland. We should have studied the thought of American Progressives and European political philosophers sympathetic to citizen participation. We did not. However, a new generation of Canadians realizes that we now must.

Notes

1. Carole Pateman, *Participation and Democratic Theory* (London: Cambridge University Press, 1970), p. 26.

2. John C. Calhoun, *A Disquisition on Government* (New York: Liberal Arts Press, 1953).

3. Reginald Whitaker, *Federalism and Democratic Theory*, Discussion Paper No. 17 of the Institute of Intergovernmental Relations, Queen's University (Kingston, Ont., 1983), pp. 41-42.

4. See, for example, Patrick Boyer, *The People's Mandate: Referendums and a More Democratic Canada* (Toronto: Dundurn Press, 1992), p. 47.

5. Howard McConnell, "The Case for a "Triple E" Senate," *Queen's Quarterly*, 95, 3 (1988), pp. 683-98.

6. *Ibid.*

7. Premier Clyde Wells, "Notes for remarks by the Honourable Clyde K. Wells, Premier of Newfoundland and Labrador, to the Special Colloquium of the School of Public Administration," Carleton University, Ottawa, Ontario, June 5, 1991, p. 8. Emphasis added.

8. Roger Gibbins, *Regionalism: Territorial Politics in Canada and the United States* (Toronto: Butterworths, 1982), p. 48.

9. Campbell Sharman, "Second Chambers," in Herman Bakvis and

William M. Chandler, eds., *Federalism and the Role of the State* (Toronto: University of Toronto Press, 1987), p. 95.

10. David Kilgour, *Inside Outer Canada* (Edmonton: Lone Pine Publishing, 1990), p. 211.

11. Sharman, "Second Chambers," p. 96.

12. As noted in Boyer, *The People's Mandate*, pp. 42-45.

13. Canada, Royal Commission on Electoral Reform and Party Financing, *Final Report*, vol. 2 (Ottawa: Minister of Supply and Services Canada, 1991), p. 236.

14. Peter Studer, "The Limits of Direct Democracy: The Experience of Switzerland," in H.V. Kroeker, *Sovereign Peoples or Sovereign Governments?* (Halifax: IRPP, 1979).

15. Royal Commission on Electoral Reform, vol. 2, p. 237.

16. *Ibid.*

17. Austin Ranney, "United States of America," in David Butler and Austin Ranney, eds., *Referendums* (Washington, D.C.: American Enterprise Institute, 1978), pp. 77 ff.

18. Boyer, *The People's Mandate*, p. 144.

19. Vincent Lemieux, "The Referendum and Canadian Democracy," in Peter Aucoin, ed., *Institutional Reforms for Representative Government* (Toronto: University of Toronto Press, 1985), p. 127.

20. Patrick Fafard and Darrel R. Reid, *Constituent Assemblies: A Comparative Survey* (Kingston, Ont.: Queen's University Institute of Intergovernmental Relations, 1991), pp. 5-6.

21. The sources for directly elected constituent assemblies are two excellent studies: Fafard and Reid, *Constituent Assemblies*; Patrick Monahan, Linda Covello, and Jonathan Batty, *Constituent Assemblies: The Canadian Debate in Comparative and Historical Context* (North York, Ont.: York University Centre for Public Law and Public Policy, 1992).

22. James Gray Pope, "Some Possible Lessons for Canada of the United States' Experience with Major Constitutional Change," *McGill Law Journal*, 37, 1 (1992), pp. 1-26.

23. *Ibid.*, p. 4, n. 6.

24. Andrew Heard, *Canadian Constitutional Conventions: The Marriage of Law and Politics* (Toronto: Oxford University Press, 1991), p. 80.

25. Canada, Citizens' Forum on Canada's Future, *Report to the People and Government of Canada* (Ottawa: Minister of Supply and Services Canada, 1991), p. 102.

26. Donald V. Smiley and Ronald L. Watts, *Intrastate Federalism in Canada* (Toronto: University of Toronto Press, 1985), p. 4.

27. *Ibid.*, ch. 2.

28. Lynn Smith and Eleanor Wachtel, *A Feminist Guide to the Canadian Constitution* (Ottawa: National Advisory Council on the Status of Women, August, 1992), pp. 16-18. See also "Judges' reasons for leaving bench are varied," *Globe and Mail*, August 10, 1992; and recent editions of *Canadian Parliamentary Guide* (Toronto: Globe and Mail Publishing).

29. Smith and Wachtel, *A Feminist Guide*, p. 23.

30. Peter Hogg, *Is the Canadian Constitution Ready for the 21st Century?* Study No. 1 of the Background Studies of the York University Constitutional Reform Project (Toronto: York University Centre for Public Law and Policy, 1991), p. 25.

Chapter 10

Radical Institutional Change
Is a Prescription for Disaster

Radical institutional change of the direct democracy type amounts to a tyranny of majoritarianism. It equates to politics without leadership. The nominal leaders simply pass along decisions to be made by the masses in order to stay in power. It also encourages and exacerbates the tendency to make public policy by public opinion poll. Legislators become people-pleasers and regulators. The great and honourable tradition of the lawmaker, a cornerstone of Western civilization, fades into obscurity.

The arguments against radical institutional change follow some of the same categories as those used by the proponents of direct democracy, although not completely. For example, it is simply not tenable to depend so much on the experience of other countries when trying to achieve a secure constitutional future for one's own country. Culture, history, and other factors militate against such reliance. The radical proponents also overlook the significant possibilities inherent in moderate institutional reform.

Philosophical Arguments

The philosophical arguments for direct democracy are muted by the realities of the twentieth century. Democracy is a sacred trust, and the main issue in much writing is how to improve it or redefine it for modern times. This issue of redefinition is the crux of the attack on the idea of plebiscitarian democracy.

Yet such redefinition must revisit the past in search of inspiration. The classic argument between "delegate" and "trustee" theories of representation is relevant to any discussion of direct democracy. The *delegate theory*, which forms one leg of populist thought, holds that the legislative member must be largely a conduit for majoritarian public opinion. It is usually supplemented with a call for mechanisms for direct citizen involvement in the public policy process. It is usually counterpoised against the argument for *trustee representation*, whereby the legislative member is expected to use his or her own best judgement on behalf of the greater community good. Any abdication of this responsibility is considered detrimental to the public interest.

Edmund Burke gave a defence of the trustee approach that has withstood the passage of more than two centuries. His speech to the electors of Bristol uttered in 1774 maintained that sacrificing one's judgement as a representative amounted to a betrayal of the needs of the constituent. The representative should be moved by longer-term considerations of national needs instead of the more transitory parochial needs of the present. "Parliament is not a congress of ambassadors from different and hostile interests," he said; "Parliament is a deliberative assembly of one nation, with one interest, that of the whole." [1]

Another classic defence of representative democracy was that of James Madison. His Federalist Number 10 essay drew a distinction between a pure democracy and a republic in a way that is useful to our current debate. The pure democracy, in which a small number of citizens "assemble and administer the government in person," was not free of faction, and indeed would facilitate its spread, often sacrificing the interests of the weaker party. A republic, a representative scheme of government in which a small number of elected members were delegated by the majority the right to govern, was a better way to avoid factionalism since patriotic and just men could be least expected to sacrifice the true interest of the country to "temporary or partial considerations." Even better was an "extensive republic," one that covers more citizens and territory, and provides less probability of a common motive for some citizens to invade the rights of others. The multiplicity of parties and interests makes such invasion less possible. Madison thereby provides one of the most compelling cases for representative government, one integrating the public interest and minority rights.[2] By contrast, it is significant that few plebiscitarian writers demonstrate any concern about the needs of minorities.

Contemporary Canadian plebiscitarian logic tends to ignore national minorities. To be sure, Preston Manning includes the notion that each linguistic part of Canada will have separate constituent assemblies, but this is his only bow to minority interests, and it has harmful overtones of national disunity. Nowhere does Manning mention minority interest protection in his calls for referendums or initiatives, however; and his recent diluting of the thresholds needed for approval in referendums and constitutional amendments toward a simple majority of provinces (in *A New Canada*) betrays a certain insensitivity to Quebec, or to any other province or group of provinces whose needs are different from those of the rest of the country.

Some philosophic principle needs to be added to assure minority interests in the proposals for radical institutional change. Contrary to what some advocates of the plebiscitarian school may hold, they may not be operating purely in the spirit of John C. Calhoun and his concurrent majorities. Neither Wells nor Manning mentions an explicit veto for Quebec, or for any other region/province, in their constitutional or policy referendum proposals, and Wells would even get rid of the "unanimity category" of the Canadian amending formula. The Reform Party does not include a suggestion for a "double majority" of Francophones in Senate passage of matters related to language, culture, and civil law, as does Wells. However, the Newfoundland Premier's categories for application of the double majority are too narrow to be of use in protecting areas of interest to a Quebec nationalist.

One stream of Canadian political philosophy sees intermediary organizations as protectors of minority rights. David Laycock, one of Canada's more insightful critics of the Reform Party, takes issue with Reform's redefinition of populist democracy.[3] He finds it perverse that the Reformers claim a direct lineage to earlier populist democrats and yet undermine their contributions to Canadian politics. In particular, he takes issue with the antagonism to intermediary organizations or "special interests" endemic to right-wing populist movements like the Reform Party. It is clear from the context of Preston Manning's speeches that by "special interests" he means feminist lobby groups, Native organizations, organized labour, and especially public-sector unions, language and ethnic groups supported by Canada's long-standing multicultural policy, and the management of nearly all state agencies and Crown corporations. "In general terms . . . a special interest is seen as any group that asks for or benefits from government agencies' efforts to marginally offset the operation of market principles in the distribution of social benefits, resources and opportunities."[4]

Canadian populist theory (Social Credit excluded) traditionally turned to democratic organizations to weaken exploitative state-corporate alliances. Direct democracy makes no sense to Laycock, as it would not have to earlier populists, if divorced from widespread participation in farm, industrial, and community organizations. The Reformers, on the other hand, draw a conscious link between their direct democracy platform and their plans to replace the welfare state with voluntary and private provision. Laycock's argument is that:

> citizens, organized group representatives and state bureaucrats all learn from their participation in real dialogues. This is assuming that all participants can draw on some necessary resources, count on being involved in subsequent related discussions, and are genuinely assured that their participation is influential, not ritualistic and decorative for purposes of regime legitimation. While not everyone affected by a policy can contribute to a decision on it in this fashion (this can't be Rousseau's General Will in action), real accountability of decision-makers and an efficient capture of the value of all participants' efforts would easily excede the simple, illusory

sense of majoritarian determination that comes from a referendum vote.[5]

In relation to referendums in general, one would do well to examine what James S. Fishkin calls the three essential and coequal conditions for a fully realized democracy: *political equality* (equal consideration to the preferences of each citizen), *non-tyranny* (avoidance of policies that impose severe deprivations, where there are harmless alternatives), and *deliberation* (as complete as possible information about the track the debate has taken).[6] It is necessary to realize these goals simultaneously – something many democratic theorists have tried but failed to do. The notion of democracy inherent in the referendum, however, "neglects the deliberation needed to make democratic choices meaningful. We have moved to achieve political equality, but at the cost of sacrificing deliberation."[7]

The Flaws in Hypothetical Thinking

Hypothetical thinking pervades the thinking of the some plebiscitarian advocates, and it is not clear-mindedness. For example, according to Wells, the blanket spread of regional development policies designed for specific underdeveloped areas is the major reason that the federal regional development policy has failed to erase disparities.[8] The wealthier areas of the country have a greater ability to take advantage of the federal programs. They have an advantage because the numerical dominance of central Canadian legislators provides an incentive to design programs in that fashion.

Institutional explanations, however, are not the single factor to explain something so complex as regional disparity. For example, locational economics seems a logical place to start. Kenneth Norrie says that industrial underdevelopment may not stem from federal economic policies but from the natural operation of a market economy. Hinterland regions do not become industrial manufacturing centres in market economies.

Profit maximizing industries locate where the sum of materials acquisition, production and distribution costs is minimized. For most types of secondary industries only the latter costs differ substantially over alternative locations. Since distribution costs are minimized by locating close to the major markets for the product there is a tendency for industry to agglomerate around already established population centres. The geographically peripheral areas of the country are just not feasible sites to naturally attract most types of secondary industry. Their advantage lies rather with the further processing of locally available resources where there is a large weight loss, with the provision of certain kinds of inputs into resource industries and with the production of some consumer goods for the local market.[9]

The whole notion of arguing by analogy is a dangerous one in politics and history. Richard E. Neustadt and Ernest R. May have argued that reasoning from analogies in political decision-making is not necessarily wrong, but it is often done inappropriately.[10] They suggest five categories of analysis when making analogies. First, one disassembles the situation of the decision-maker into the *known,* the *unclear,* and the *presumed.* Then one clearly establishes the *likenesses* and the *differences* between the seemingly analogous situations. All of this is done in written form to heighten clarity. Their review of American defence and diplomatic policy finds that by not being rigorous about categorization, leaders have committed several inappropriate analogies in policy-making.

In the Canadian case, one is asked to believe (for the purposes of showing the benefits of a triple-E Senate) that there is a working analogy between the acrimonious federal-provincial relations of the seventies and the politics-weary, debt-ridden intergovernmental relations of the nineties. Before we are asked to believe that Senate reform is the key to better relations, perhaps we should be shown that relations are just as "bad" as they were in the old days. This type of analysis is usually lacking; McConnell's examples of conflict, for example, are drawn mostly from the Trudeau era.

A reader of David Hackett Fischer's *Historians' Fallacies*[11] will recognize the possibility of a number of fallacious arguments in the statements of the plebiscitarians. To state that it is inevitable that Canada with an unreformed Senate experiences regionally imbalanced national spending is an example of "the fallacy of the metaphysical question": a question that cannot be solved before settling some metaphysical issue like the nature of inevitability or reality, which is plainly beyond the scope of most mortals. There is also the problem of the "reductive fallacy," which involves replacing complex causes with simple ones, for example, saying that citizen alienation is due to representative government instead of a multiplicity of twentieth-century maladies. An additional shortcoming in the hypothetical argumentation of plebiscitarians is the "fallacy of the mechanistic cause." This "treats the various components of a social situation or of any organized system as though they were detachable, isolable, homogeneous, independently operative and therefore susceptible of being added to or subtracted from the causal complex, increasing or decreasing the result by that amount."[12] Because senators have acted as unifiers of federal and state governments in Australia and the United States, one might hold that they would act so in Canada. However, it just may be that the overwhelming tradition of party discipline in Canada would force elected senators in a reformed institution to act as MPs do at present.

The hope that intergovernmental relations would be conducted better than they had been in the past also seems to be misplaced. The subconscious wish that the federal-provincial squabbles of the past several decades could have been ameliorated, if only there had been a better mechanism in place, is not realistic.

Ronald L. Watts has outlined a convincing case that even Senate reform will not replace executive federalism as the centrepiece of Canadian intergovernmental relations.[13] His argument is based on a comparative analysis of both parliamentary and non-parliamentary federations around the world. His contention is that the union of parliamentary institutions and federalism yields executive federalism as a matter of course. *Parliamentary federations* develop intergovernmental institutions and relations quite distinct from those of the non-parliamentary variant. Parliamentary federations (Canada, Australia, Germany, India, and Malaysia) feature intergovernmental summitry, specialist intergovernmental agencies, dominant cabinets, and a tendency for framework-type intergovernmental agreements. *Non-parliamentary federations* (the United States, Switzerland) do not.[14] Two specific factors contribute to executive federalism in Canada: policy interdependence and executive dominance. The clear implication for Canada, especially in light of the Australian experience, is that "Senate reform may moderate its operation and impact but will not eliminate executive federalism."[15]

International Experience

International experience does not demonstrate the universal applicability and benefits of plebiscitarian models. Countries with some of the most advanced models of direct democracy also have some of the lowest turnouts in elections. In terms of voter turnout, the U.S. and Switzerland ranked eighteenth and nineteenth, respectively, among the nineteen major democracies of the world in the 1970s and the 1980s.[16] In addition, their turnout rate has been progressively dropping for decades. In Switzerland, voter participation in elections dropped close to 25 per cent from the 1940s (71.7 per cent) to the 1980s (47.5 per cent). Likewise, the United States, which hit a modern peak of 62.8 per cent in 1960, averaged 61.9 per cent in the 1960s and slid to 54.4 per cent and 51.9 per cent in the following two decades.[17] In recent times, the turnout rate for American presidential elections was 53.1 per cent in 1984, 50.1 per cent in 1988, and 55.2 per cent in 1992. Non-presidential election years saw turnouts only in the high thirties for most of the 1970s and 1980s.[18] The voter turnouts for recent Canadian general elections were: 1984 – 75.3 per cent; 1988 – 75.3 per cent; 1993 – 69.6 per cent.

The Royal Commission on Electoral Reform and Party Financing (the Lortie Commission) found that a variety of factors affected voter turnout in the advanced democracies. None of these factors related to aspects of plebiscitarian democracy. The most important factors explaining turnout were proportional representation, which got an average turnout of 82 per cent versus 73.6 per cent for plurality systems like Canada's; a competitive party system, which will entice more voters than a non-competitive one; the voters' perception that their vote will directly affect the formation of a government, rather than having coalition politics affect it; and the existence of a single legislative chamber, which attracts more voters than bicameral systems, allegedly because voters perceive they will have more effect in single (unicameral) contexts than in the more compromise-oriented politics of bicameral legislatures.

Two other factors are the day of the election (Sundays get more than Canada's usual Mondays) and compulsory voting laws. Australia, Belgium, Italy, Greece, Luxembourg, and Costa Rica all have compulsory voting; in the 1970s and 1980s the first three led the democratic world with 90 per cent or better turnout records. [19] The implications are obvious. If one wants to engage citizen participation, then reform of the electoral and party systems, not direct democracy, may be the way to go about it. The record of the Americans and Swiss suggests a definite danger in accelerating rates of dependence on plebiscitarian instruments, which may overwhelm or even alienate voters with the complexities of decision-making. Fishkin notes that despite frequent mass disinterest in America, "the number of referendums on the ballot has increased extraordinarily, particularly in the western states. In 1990, there were at least sixty-seven proposals on statewide ballots, the largest number since 1932." [20] The other surprise is finding that a bicameral legislature can actually turn off voters, which is certainly not a finding that triple-E advocates would like to boast about.

Also notable is the obvious conclusion that Fafard and Reid reach in their exhaustive study of international experience with constituent assemblies – that such assemblies are an exception. Most countries use special commissions or parliamentary committees in attempts to renew the constitution. [21] If international practice is any guide, then there is surely something instructive in the fact that most countries view constitutional amendment by constituent assembly as either too risky or not beneficial enough.

The Canadian Political Culture

One can make a number of objections or limiting qualifications to the idea of direct democracy as it relates to Canadian political culture. First, the advocates do not understand the Westminster tradition and its possibilities. Second, they do not understand the realities of national unity. Let us review the harm that each element of radical reform would do to the Canadian political fabric.

Senate reformers do not always consider political factors. C.E.S. Franks has noted the incompatibility of an elected Senate with several aspects of Canadian politics. Prime ministers, cabinets, and provincial premiers are likely to resent a new institutional competitor and, he implies strongly, might sabotage it. [22]

The relaxation of party discipline and bloc voting in Parliament would likely help to destroy the central rationale for major parties in Canada – to get things done efficiently and effectively. Coalition politics would be a likely result. Canadians wisely distrust coalitions, opting instead for large, homogeneous parties, which they view as durable and capable of providing strong leadership. Canadians, despite some increase in litigiousness resulting from the Charter of Rights and Freedoms, are still culturally different from Americans, for example, and value leadership over delay and disunity at the heart of government. Relaxation of party discipline would also weaken the ability of governments to arrange compromises that balance the needs of different areas of the country.

Referendums, initiatives, and recalls are not in keeping with the realities of parliamentary government and national unity in Canada. The conscription referendum of 1942 pitted Quebec and the rest of Canada against each other and the Charlottetown Accord referendum of 1992 rekindled hostilities against Quebec that had just begun to settle down after the rancorous Meech Lake Accord debate. Referendums can be inconclusive because of vague or convoluted wording, as was the case in the Quebec referendum of 1980, and lead to repeats of serious policy or unity disputes.

The Lortie Commission rejected both referendums during national elections and the recall of sitting MPs as being foreign to Canadian political tradition. The former would strip elections of their meaning; moreover, the idea ignores the policy ferment that frequent turning-out of governments has produced in Canada. As for recall, this would make the Prime Minister and cabinet disproportionately vulnerable because of the constituency basis of election and would weaken the system of representative government for no demonstrable benefit.[23]

There are significant disadvantages to the constituent assembly as a forum for far-reaching policy development. One is that it weakens the legitimacy of federal and provincial legislatures. It implies that representative and responsible government has failed and is unequal to the task(s) before us. The Beaudoin-Edwards Committee, which examined the process of constitutional amendment in Canada, could find no good reason for having a separate set of elections for the purpose of electing a constituent assembly.[24] Another argument against constituent assemblies is that they tend to work best where there is significant consensus on the nature of needed political and constitutional change.[25] This is plainly not the case in Canada. Quebec is not likely to let its province-centred view of Canada be bargained away by non-cabinet members; and Canada's First Nations, having achieved recognition of inherent self-government by the intergovernmental route, are not going to opt for another forum that may not be as certain to repeat the practical and theoretical gains of the Charlottetown Accord, which in large measure remain as concrete gains despite the referendum defeat of that Accord.

Finally, the versatility of responsible government in Canada's version of the Westminster tradition must be stressed. The "legislative implications" of responsible government have been interpreted to include measures that allow legislative influence on, but not direct participation in, public policy-making. Among these measures are:

- disclosure of executive plans and priorities;
- strengthened legislative committees;
- those "that otherwise give the legislature the power to check the freedom of movement of the executive, without checkmating it."[26]

There are countless opportunities for Canadians to reform the operation of responsible government in Canada without destroying its vitality. They should avail themselves of the opportunities.

Direct, or plebiscitarian, democracy will always have its adherents. It tends to appeal to those constantly in search of the novel and unexplored. Yet it does not have the same track record as traditional representative and responsible government in Canada. The latter has endured, in fact flourished, throughout Canadian history. To diminish it now would threaten a variety of peoples and sectors in Canadian society and would endlessly confuse citizens. Like strong drink, plebiscitarian democracy is best consumed in small doses, if at all.

Notes

1. Edmund Burke, speech to Bristol constituents, in James Prior, ed., *Burke's Works*, Volume I (London: Bell and Daldy, 1871), p. 446.
2. James Madison, The Federalist Number X, in Max Beloff, ed., *The Federalist: Or, The New Constitution*, by Alexander Hamilton, James Madison, and John Jay (Oxford: Basil Blackwell, 1948), pp. 41-48.
3. David Laycock, "Institutions and Ideology in the Reform Party Project," paper presented at the meeting of the Canadian Political Science Association, Carleton University, June 6, 1993.
4. *Ibid.*, p. 4.
5. *Ibid.*, p. 25.
6. James S. Fishkin, *Democracy and Deliberation: New Directions for Democratic Reform* (New Haven: Yale University Press, 1991), ch. 4.
7. *Ibid.*, p. 25.
8. Premier Clyde Wells, "Notes for remarks by the Honourable Clyde K. Wells, Premier of Newfoundland and Labrador, to the Special Colloquium of the School of Public Administration," Carleton University, Ottawa, Ontario, June 5, 1991, p. 6.
9. Kenneth H. Norrie, "Some Comments on Prairie Economic Alienation," *Canadian Public Policy*, II, 2 (Spring, 1976), p. 213.
10. Richard E. Neustadt and Ernest R. May, *Thinking in Time: The Uses of History for Decision Makers* (New York: The Free Press, 1986).
11. David Hackett Fischer, *Historians' Fallacies: Toward a Logic of Historical Thought* (New York: Harper and Row, 1970).
12. *Ibid.*, p. 178.
13. Ronald L. Watts, *Executive Federalism: A Comparative Analysis* (Kingston, Ont.: Queen's University Institute of Intergovernmental Relations, 1989).
14. Their intergovernmental relations are fragmented, vertical, functional, and centred on the national legislature.
15. Watts, *Executive Federalism*, p. 18.
16. Jerome H. Black, "Reforming the Context of the Voting Process in Canada: Lessons from Other Democracies," in Herman Bakvis, ed., *Voter Turnout in Canada* (Toronto: Dundurn Press, 1991), pp. 83-84.
17. *Ibid.*, p. 80.
18. United States, U.S. Bureau of the Census, *Statistical Abstract of the United States: 1993* (113th edition) (Washington, D.C.: Superintendent of Documents, Government Printing Office, 1993), table

No. 455, p. 284. See also "Low Voter Turnout Prompts Concern on the Hill," *Congressional Quarterly Weekly Report*, April 2, 1988, p. 862.

19. Black, "Reforming . . . the Voting Process," pp. 83-84.
20. Fishkin, *Democracy and Deliberation*, p. 58.
21. Patrick Fafard and Darrel R. Reid, *Constituent Assemblies: A Comparative Survey* (Kingston, Ont.: Queen's University Institute of Intergovernmental Relations, 1991), p. 45.
22. C.E.S. Franks, *The Parliament of Canada* (Toronto: University of Toronto Press, 1987), pp. 200-01.
23. Canada, Royal Commission on Electoral Reform and Party Financing, *Final Report*, vol. 2 (Ottawa: Minister of Supply and Services Canada, 1991), ch. 9.
24. Canada, Special Joint Committee of the Senate and the House of Commons, *The Process for Amending the Constitution of Canada*, chaired jointly by Hon. Gerald Beaudoin, Senator, and Jim Edwards, MP (Ottawa, June 20, 1991), p. 50.
25. Edward McWhinney, *Constitution-making: Principles, Process, Practice* (Toronto: University of Toronto Press, 1981).
26. Christopher Dunn, "A Note on the Meaning of Responsible Government," *Canadian Parliamentary Review*, 11, 3 (1988), p. 13.

PART SIX

Does Canadian Social Democracy
Have a Future?

Is there anything left of the Canadian left? It is one of the ironies of social democracy in Canada that its demise has been so often predicted while its vitality is simultaneously proclaimed. The following chapters will elaborate both the case for predicting a healthy future for this ideology and the counter-arguments in the other direction. Here we will examine the essence of Canadian social democracy, one of the most ephemeral or hard to define of the contemporary ideologies.

The problems surrounding social democracy in Canada are not difficult to grasp. The most influential political exponent of social democracy in Canada, the New Democratic Party (NDP), has formed the government in a number of Canadian provinces (see Table 1). Yet, until the Rae government took power in Ontario in 1990, it had been shut out of the powerful industrial provinces of central Canada. Even here, the unique electoral dynamics that

Table 1
CCF/NDP Provincial Governments

Province	Years	Premier
Saskatchewan	1944–61	T.C. Douglas
	1961–64	Woodrow Lloyd
	1971–82	Allan Blakeney
	1991–	Roy Romanow
Manitoba	1969–77	Edward Schreyer
	1981–88	Howard Pawley
British Columbia	1972–75	Dave Barrett
	1991–	Mike Harcourt
Ontario	1990–	Bob Rae
Yukon Territory	1985–92	Tony Penikett

allowed it to grasp power with a slim plurality of votes seem unlikely to repeat themselves. It is stretching credibility to conceive of an NDP government in Quebec, although the Parti Québécois exhibited some social democratic characteristics within its nationalist framework in the 1970s.

The NDP has never come close to forming a federal government. As Table 2 demonstrates, it has hovered about the 18-20 per cent range in popular vote in recent decades. Its seat representation has been regionally concentrated, giving it the appearance of a regional party, although it has a substantial electoral presence in the various provinces. Particularly alarming for party adherents was its performance in the 1993 federal general election, when it received only 6.9 per cent of the popular vote and nine seats. The Gallup Poll of February 7-14, 1994, saw the NDP garner only 4 per cent of decided voter support, its lowest showing in the previous decade.

Arguments about the future of social democracy are typically diverse, covering history, philosophy, political culture, economics, and the comparative study of other world movements. Yet the particular context of each country is also of vital importance.[1] The words "social democracy," "democratic socialism," and "socialism" are used synonymously here.

Table 2
Federal Election Results, 1878-1993

Election Year	Party Forming Federal Gov't	Total Seats	Conservative Seats	Votes (%)	Liberal Seats	Votes (%)	Progressive Seats	Votes (%)
1878	Con.	206	140	53	65	45		
1882	Con.	211	138	53	73	47		
1887	Con.	215	128	51	87	49		
1891	Con.	215	122	52	91	46		
1896	Lib.	213	88	46	118	45		
1900	Lib.	213	81	47	132	52		
1904	Lib.	214	75	47	139	52		
1908	Lib.	221	85	47	135	51		
1911	Con.	221	134	51	87	48		
1917	Con. (1)	235	153	57	82	40		
1921	Lib.	235	50	30	116	41	65	23
1925	Lib.	245	116	46	99	40	24	9
1926	Lib.	245	91	45	128	46	20	5
1930	Con.	245	137	49	91	45	12	3
1935	Lib.	245	40	30	173	45		
1940	Lib.	245	40	31	181	51		
1945	Lib.	245	67	27	125	41		
1949	Lib.	262	41	30	193	49		
1953	Lib.	265	51	31	171	49		
1957	Con.	265	112	39	105	41		
1958	Con.	265	208	54	49	34		
1962	Con.	265	116	37	100	37		
1963	Lib.	265	95	33	129	42		
1965	Lib.	265	97	32	131	40		
1968	Lib.	264	72	31	155	45		
1972	Lib.	264	107	35	109	38		
1974	Lib.	264	95	35	141	43		
1979	Con.	282	136	36	114	40		
1980	Lib.	282	103	33	146	44		
1984	Con.	282	211	50	40	28	Reform	
1988	Con.	295	169	43	83	32	Seats	Votes (%)
1993	Lib.	295	2	16	177	41	52	19

(1) Wartime Coalition.
SOURCE: Hugh J. Thorburn, ed., *Party Politics in Canada*, 6th edition (Scarborough: Prentice-Hall, 1991); for 1993, Elections Canada, *Official Voting Results: Synopsis, Thirty-Fifth General Election*, 1993 (Ottawa: Chief Electoral Officer, 1993).
Percentages may not add up to 100 due to rounding.

Table 2 *(continued)*

CCF/NDP		Social Credit		Reconstruction		Other	
Seats	Votes (%)	Seats	Votes (%)	Seats	Votes (%)	Seats	Votes (%)
						1	2
						2	2
						7	9
						1	
						1	
						1	2
						1	
							3
						4	6
						6	5
						6	4
						5	3
7	9	17	4	1	9	7	3
8	8	10	3			6	7
28	16	13	4			12	12
13	13	10	4			5	4
23	11	15	5	*Créditiste*		5	4
25	11	19	7	Seats	Votes (%)	4	2
8	9	0	2				1
19	14	30	12				
17	13	24	12				
21	18	5	4	9	5	2	1
21	17	0	1	14	5	0	1
31	18	15	8			1	1
16	15	11	5			1	1
26	18	6	5			0	2
32	20	0	1	*Bloc*		0	2
30	19			*Québécois*		1	
43	20			Seats	Votes (%)	0	4
9	7			54	14	1	4

Defining Social Democracy

One of the difficulties in dealing with the concept of social democracy is the problem of definition. A century ago the term stood for what would today be termed Marxism. Most analysts today will concede, however, that social democracy is a reaction against the Marxist revolutionary tradition. In spite of this important qualification, there is still a great deal of theoretical vagueness to the term. A review of some definitions will demonstrate the latitude of the term. To some extent, of course, the definitions overlap.

Social Democracy and Other Ideologies

One generic definition is that of Padgett and Paterson, who stress the ideological compromise among communism, socialism, and liberalism inherent in the term.

> Social democracy is a hybrid political tradition composed of socialism and liberalism. It is the product of a division in the socialist tradition between those who seek to realise socialist ideals within the institutions of liberal capitalist society (social democrats) and those who remain outside those institutions with the objective of superseding them through revolutionary force (communists). In particular, social democrats are fully committed to participation in the electoral process and in parliamentary democracy. Indeed, social democracy is often referred to as 'parliamentary socialism.' Social democracy is inspired by socialist ideals, but is heavily conditioned by its political environment, and it incorporates liberal values. The social democratic project may be defined as the attempt to reconcile socialism with liberal politics and capitalist society.[2]

Other authors also define social democracy in terms of a relationship to other ideologies. Maurice Duverger situates social democracy on a continuum between the catch-all pattern of bourgeois parties and the exclusive, disciplined organization of communist parties.[3] Gosta Esping-Andersen defines social democracy as "a movement that seeks to build class unity and mobilize power via national legislation."[4] However, later, he also compares the communist and socialist methods of party organization. The social democratic party does not stress proletarian or working-class membership, but alliances.

> Whereas the vanguard [communist] party admits only recruits who are willing to adhere to its manifesto, the social democratic party is prepared to align its program in response to current requirements for alliance formation. For communist parties, program dictates parliamentary power; for social democratic parties, parliament dictates program.[5]

The Philosophical Roots of Social Democracy

Social democracy has also tended to be defined in terms of philosophical objectives. Stanley Knowles observed that the progress toward democratic socialism was not a final goal but a continual striving for dignity, social justice, and freedom in the political and economic spheres.[6] Geoff Dow stresses social rights:

> In abstract terms, social democracy is an assertion that all citizens of a particular society are entitled, by reason of citizenship, to share equally in the standards of living which that society is capable of delivering. Social rights in this sense imply significant transgressions on the liberal principle that societal progress is best achieved when individual effort is rewarded directly and that social criteria for economic activity are normally illegitimate.[7]

Program as Definition

The final way of defining social democracy is in terms of program, that is, as a constellation of related policies for which the party stands. This approach is used by those who study consistencies in the historical record of specific social democratic parties.

The post-war pattern in social democratic policies, speaking generally, has focused on a handful of specific themes. Jim McAllister has summarized them as (1) redistribution of wealth to eliminate poverty and economic disparities; (2) public economic control and ownership by means of nationalization, equity, or regulation; (3) extension of economic democracy by political means – central planning; and (4) public participation to dilute the power of the bureaucracy and special interests, especially the wealthy.[8]

Others that might well be added to this list are progressive taxation regimes, the "mixed economy" of capitalist, co-operative, and public institutions, and extensive political and civil rights.

Situated within the larger international context, social democracy is chiefly a European phenomenon, and the countries most important to socialism in Canada are the northern ones – Germany, Britain, and Sweden – and to a lesser extent the southern European countries.

The Evolution of Social Democratic Thought

The evolution of modern democratic socialism starts with the so-called "Revisionist" school of Eduard Bernstein and proceeds over a century to the substantial results of the Swedish school. The particular historical circumstances in which the parties found themselves had a profound effect on the content of social democratic thought.

The Revisionists

The German "Revisionists," led by Eduard Bernstein, believed in evolutionary, not revolutionary socialism. Their contributions to democratic socialism are important because they began a powerful new tradition in socialism that was to make it much more palatable to the West. Their critique is multifaceted. They criticized Marx's view that control of finance and productive industry would be increasingly concentrated. They perceived the working conditions and labour laws to be steadily improving, due to the political activities of labour. The middle class was not disappearing, as the *Communist Manifesto* had predicted, but was beginning to expand as it included former members of the working class. Class warfare was not inevitable; it could be prevented by increasing democracy in general throughout society. A gradual improvement in the lot of the working class could be achieved by parliamentary socialist parties, strategic political alliances, and public enterprises.

The Fabians

The Fabians were the English answer to the popularity of socialism at the end of the nineteenth century. Unlike the continental variety, however, it was not inspired by Marxism but by indigenous intellectuals who acknowledged their philosophical debts to liberalism. Founded in 1884, the Fabian Society attracted such luminaries as Sidney and Beatrice Webb, G.B. Shaw, and H.G. Wells. It suggested that the road from capitalism to socialism could be a peaceful, evolutionary one, accomplished by the growth of technological efficiency, moral education, and sharing. The socialism they had in mind featured public and co-operative enterprises, economic planning by experts, and social control of wealth. The Fabians were committed to spreading their ideas in a variety of contexts and had a significant impact on the British Labour Party.

Guild Socialists

The Guild Socialists were another stream of British socialism and flourished before and after the First World War. Led by G.D.H. Cole and S.G. Hobson, the Guild Socialists advocated the ownership of industry by the state and the management of it by guilds of national and local workers who would have some say in determining the organization and output of production. The concept was designed to prevent bureaucratization and alienation of the worker. It was not of long duration as a movement, but it made important contributions to later thinking about industrial democracy.

Swedish Social Democracy

In the 1930s a great deal of intellectual ferment took place in European social democratic circles. One of the most thoroughgoing intellectual reformulations of social democratic thought was undertaken in Sweden. The leading theorist of the Swedish Socialist Labour Party (SAP), Ernst Wigforss, pioneered the integration of deficit financing, Keynesian economics, full employment, and welfare expenditures into social democratic thinking.

It was partly these innovations and partly the example of political longevity that attracted the attention of international observers, including those in Canada. The SAP remained in power in an unbroken string of victories from 1932 to 1976 and from 1982 to 1991. It is also noteworthy in the Canadian context that the Swedish model was a source of inspiration for some leaders of the NDP, including Ed Schreyer, Premier of Manitoba from 1969 to 1977.[9]

Post-War Social Democracy

After the Second World War, the various social democratic parties undertook similar measures while in power or at least advocated them while in opposition. There were three central themes to the social democratic programs.[10] The first was socialization of the means of production. This would subordinate the economy to national needs and also give socialist parties the power to deal with their opponents in the private sector on a basis of equality. The second was economic planning, intended to provide full employment and regulation of the private sector. The third was social security. The British and Scandinavian social democratic parties also popularized the concept of "citizenship rights." This meant that, following the logic of social theorist T.H. Marshall, a solidaristic society could be promoted by the provision of universality and uniform benefits in social welfare programs.[11]

Social Democratic Hegemony

Stephen Padgett refers to the 1960s and 1970s as the period of "social democratic hegemony." Strong socialist governments continued in power in Sweden and Austria (from 1945); German social democrats entered the Grand Coalition in 1966 and later formed the government from 1969 to 1982; and in Britain, Labour was in power from 1964 to 1970 and from 1974 to 1979.

> Success was based in large part on a new conception of social democracy which harmonized with the economic orthodoxies of the day, growth management and Keynesian interventionism. . . .
>
> For social democrats the elimination of poverty was inextricably bound up with economic growth. Growth was vital, not only for its own sake, but for the completion of the social citizenship state which was a central element in the new conception of social democracy.[12]

The New Left

While not at the forefront of many social democratic parties, and in some cases in outright opposition to them, the New Left was instrumental in bringing about a re-evaluation of many elements of the social democratic project. It was a loosely defined movement that criticized the bureaucratization of the state and Old Left parties, and was also hostile to the timidity of the Keynesian and state socialist solutions of the past. It promoted more thoroughgoing democratization and redistribution of resources. The New Left, with uneven success, tried to redefine mainstream social democratic practice in terms of decentralization, local and worker control, and public input into policy-making.

The Keynesian Breakup

The decline of the Keynesian consensus after the OPEC oil price increases of the early 1970s and the decline of U.S. economic leadership set in train a series of crises for Western social democracy. Unable to rely fully on the expansion of capital to achieve the aims of full employment and welfare state financing, social democratic governments as well as others had to rely on wage restraints, expenditure controls, and economic policies aimed at controlling inflation. There followed a period of crisis management and subsequent loss of clarity of identification for democratic socialism since the welfare state and free collective bargaining were part of the movement's traditions. [13] Social democracy is still trying to come to grips with this problem.

Nevertheless, there were significant victories for democratic socialist parties in this latest period, notably by the Swedish SAP in 1982, the French Socialist Party in 1981 in the elections for President and Parliament, Greece's socialist party PASOK in 1981 (until 1989) and again in 1993, Spain's PSOE in 1982, and the regaining of power by Norway's Labour Party under Gro Harlem Brundtland in 1986 and by Denmark's social democrats in 1993. As of August, 1994, victories by the left in upcoming elections in Sweden and Finland seem imminent, and the British Labour Party far outdistances the Conservatives in the polls.

The Development of Canadian Social Democracy

Social democracy in Canada has experienced changes analogous to those experienced elsewhere. It has reacted to electoral difficulties with reformulations of its basic doctrine. Its various leaders (see Table 3) have had a significant influence on steering the party toward successive reformulations of party policy.

Table 3
CCF-NDP Leaders

CCF Leaders
J.S. Woodsworth 1932-42
M.J. Coldwell 1942-60
Hazen Argue 1960-61

NDP Leaders
Tommy Douglas 1961-71
David Lewis 1971-75
Ed Broadbent 1975-90
Audrey McLaughlin 1990-

The Regina Manifesto

The Regina Manifesto of 1933 was an important milestone in the development of Canadian socialism. It was the statement of principles of the Co-operative Commonwealth Federation (CCF) formed that year. One approach sees the Manifesto as the work of intellectuals associated with the University of Toronto and McGill University and united in a Fabian-inspired organization called the League for Social Reconstruction. Another stresses that the Manifesto's provisions derived largely from earlier positions taken by the United Farmers of Alberta and prairie labour parties at a Calgary conference of 1932. Certainly its creation climaxed the opening stages of the socialist movement's unification movement, which had begun with the Calgary Program of 1932 – indeed, with a decade of electoral activity by the new leader, J.S. Woodsworth.[14]

The Manifesto was intended to supply a Canadian vision of socialism to replace the conflicting and sometimes inappropriate versions that Canadians had borrowed from Europe. The document wove a blend of themes from various sources. Like the Fabians, the CCF declared itself hostile to the excesses of capitalism and the "domination and exploitation of one class by another"; and it similarly committed itself to a peaceful road to a socialist government. It denounced the increasing concentration of power in the hands of the financial and industrial minority. Periods of "catastrophic depression" were inevitable in the capitalist system and should be rectified by a "planned and socialized economy in which our natural resources and the principle means of production and distribution are owned, controlled and operated by the people." Much of the Manifesto had a centralist edge. It recommended a National Planning Commission to co-ordinate the economy, a central bank, a "National Investment Board" to control credit, nationalized banks and insurance companies, a constitutional amendment establishing federal labour legislation to standardize worker protection and social insurance benefits, and socialized health services. As well, it noted that the constitution should be amended to give the federal government the power to deal with national economic problems. The Manifesto also suggested the abolition of the Senate, the pursuance of disarmament and the avoidance of imperialist wars on the international scene, a commission of social experts to monitor social reforms, and an emergency program of public works to solve the immediate and debilitating problem of mass unemployment.

But perhaps the most famous promise of the Regina Manifesto – to eradicate capitalism – was the one that was the most naive and problematic element of the package. The promise was inconsistent with the tone of the rest of the document and the outlook of party leaders, including Woodsworth, and it became a theoretical millstone around the necks of successive CCF and NDP leaders for the next several decades.

The Winnipeg Declaration

A redefinition of Canadian social democratic thought came with the Winnipeg Declaration of 1956. The Declaration was a hotly debated alteration to CCF principles that had actually been set in motion at the national convention in 1950. Such was the hold on the imagination of the party of the Regina Manifesto that it delayed the act of redefining for this substantial period.

Important developments had made a reformulation of basic principles imperative. The mainstream parties had much success baiting the anti-capitalist rhetoric of the Manifesto in election campaigns. The electoral fortunes of the party had failed to live up to the earlier wartime expectation of imminent success. International communism had given socialism a bad name with its takeover of regimes in Asia and Eastern Europe.

The Winnipeg Declaration is a conundrum for Canadian socialism: it has been seen both as a substantial departure from the CCF roots and a continuation of the essential parts of the tradition. There were in fact elements of both. The Manifesto and the Declaration each tried to establish a middle way between liberal individualism and radical socialism. Both criticized the concentration of wealth and corporate power and the need to overcome it by careful social planning. A full-employment economy was another common characteristic.

One major departure was the less strident language: it "made no use of the terms 'socialization', 'social ownership', 'exploitation', or 'class', and the number of negative references to capitalism diminished from 17 to 1. While there were more positive references to 'socialism', half were modified with the word 'democratic'. . . ."[15] Although it was still to be an important instrument, the scope of public ownership was implicitly reduced and more emphasis was placed on the mixed economy of public, private, and co-operative enterprise. There was a clearer effort to distinguish democratic socialism from its unwelcome totalitarian connotation, and a greater emphasis on disarmament and international development.

The Program of "The New Party"

The New Party Declaration of 1961 was essentially a very detailed plan of a later twentieth-century welfare state. The statement made a thinly disguised appeal to middle-class voters to adhere to the party, while establishing a special connection to "farmer and labour, cooperative and social democratic movements for which so many Canadians have striven in the past." It softened its economic stance and expanded the social and cultural prescriptions offered by the established left in Canada. It recommended the social programs that would later be adopted, with some pressure from the left, by the federal Parliament. These included a national medical plan, expanded social security, more generous and portable pensions, expanded federal financial involvement in the education field, and various measures to enhance the affordability of housing for lower-income people. It bowed to burgeoning provincialism and Quebec nationalism by emphasizing provincial autonomy, the existence of two national cultures, and institutions and meetings to facilitate co-operative federalism and help replace the centralist solutions the CCF had seemed to prefer. On the economic front, the familiar solutions of the CCF, such as public and co-operative ownership of utilities and resources and social planning, could be found, but there appeared more emphasis on a wider variety of less intrusive instruments, such as taxation and regulation. Attacks on corporate concentration were now wrapped in the cloak of nationalism as the dangers of unchecked foreign investment, much of it American, were cited.

The New Party Declaration, essentially, was an attempt to put a new face on a party that had achieved no growth in electoral success during the post-war period of economic growth and rising living standards. Indeed, the CCF had lost seventeen seats in the House of Commons in the 1958 federal election (see Table 2). Four years later, in the next election, the facelift was complete as the CCF had become the New Democratic Party, which sought with some success to appeal to a broader base of voter support.

The Waffle Manifesto

The Waffle manifesto of 1969 tried to swing the pendulum back toward the radicalism of the Regina Manifesto. It was unabashedly socialist, stating that "capitalism must be replaced by socialism, by national planning of investment, and by the public ownership of the means of production." It also incorporated the New Left themes of anti-imperialism and participatory democracy. Socialism, economic independence, and participatory democracy were all crucially interrelated. "The major threat to Canadian survival today," said this manifesto from the left wing of the NDP, "is American control of the Canadian economy. The major issue of our times is not national unity but national survival, and the fundamental threat is external, not internal." Canada's participation in the joint U.S.-Canada defence system precluded an independent international role, and the ownership of the Canadian economy by Americans meant the continuance of corporate concentration and the ignoring of social needs and regional disparities. The Waffle recommended common institutions committed to the national survival of the English and French "nations" in Canada. It also advocated worker participation in management, and related measures such as the "extensive public control over investment and nationalization of the commanding heights of the economy, such as the key resource industries, finance and credit, and industries strategic to planning our economy." The Waffle attempt to redirect NDP objectives and strategy soon alienated the NDP leadership, who dissociated themselves from this splinter group. The radical left drifted away from party activism and, in some cases, the party. Votes were more important than ideology. Nonetheless, the short-lived Waffle served to reinvigorate the NDP with a sense of purpose and direction.

Putting People First

The next major policy document was *Putting People First*, prepared by the party's Policy Review Committee and presented to the Halifax Conference of 1991. Implicitly to counter the imagery of a centralized command economy in the communist style, the report places a great deal of emphasis on the concept of economic democracy. Central planning and massive public enterprise are to be avoided as one extreme just as unalloyed capitalism is to be avoided as another extreme. Public enterprise and regulation of corporations need to be seen as part of a greater variety of democratic instruments in both the public and private sectors. These include such institutions as worker co-operatives, community-based development corporations, and "social capital funds" that invest in the economy but have broader objectives. The latter include registered pension fund plans controlled by labour and management or by labour alone, investment funds directed by labour, and the use of public pension plans to achieve economic control or other social purposes. The report also recommends that measures be taken to democratize state institutions and large corporations through various forms of worker and/or community participation.[16]

To deal with globalization and trade, this report suggested both national and global answers. One approach is to regulate international trade to prevent "social dumping," that is, the gaining of comparative advantage by other countries through substandard wages and working conditions. This could be achieved either through strengthened international organizations or with an international "social charter." Canada, the report stated, should set conditions about in-Canada production levels, employment, and value-added (further processing to enhance product value) to its participation in and openness to the international economy. It needs also to build a high-productivity industrial sector. The federal state should therefore undertake important infrastructural policies, such as government procurement to favour Canadian research and development, and a mandatory training tax/obligation on employers to overcome worker training deficiencies. Industrial policy would dictate trade policy, not the other way around. The stage was set for the election of 1993.

Notes

1. In each country the shape of political forces differs. It is therefore necessary to examine questions like the following: Has the neo-conservative wave sweeping the West affected Canadian socialism? Are there political implications in the debt load felt by most developed economies and especially in Canada? How different is Canada's political culture from other contexts in which socialism has had to contend for power? Has the late twentieth-century phenomenon of the shrinking middle class come to affect Canada and its political parties as well? Has the post-materialist politics proclaimed in Europe and America appeared in Canada as well?

2. Stephen Padgett and William E. Paterson, *A History of Social Democracy in Postwar Europe* (London and New York: Longman, 1991), p. 1.

3. Maurice Duverger, *Political Parties* (London: Methuen, 1964).

4. Gosta Esping-Andersen, *Politics Against Markets: The Social Democratic Road to Power* (Princeton, N.J.: Princeton University Press, 1985), p. 10.

5. *Ibid.*, p. 8.

6. Stanley Knowles, *The New Party* (Toronto: McClelland and Stewart, 1961), p. 93.

7. Geoff Dow, "What Do We Know about Social Democracy?" *Economic and Industrial Democracy,* 14 (1993), p. 11.

8. James A. McAllister, *The Government of Edward Schreyer: Democratic Socialism in Manitoba* (Montreal: McGill-Queen's University Press, 1984), pp. 4-5.

9. Interview with Premier Schreyer in the *Winnipeg Tribune,* July 5, 1969, reprinted in Paul Beaulieu, ed., *Ed Schreyer: A Social Democrat in Power* (Winnipeg: Queenston House Publishing, 1977), p. 190.

10. Padgett and Paterson, *A History of Social Democracy,* pp. 12-21.

11. *Ibid.,* p. 19.

12. Stephen Padgett, "Social Democracy in Power," *Parliamentary Affairs,* 46, 1 (January, 1993), p. 107.

13. Padgett, "Social Democracy in Power," p. 111.

14. Alan Whitehorn, *Canadian Socialism: Essays on the CCF-NDP* (Toronto: Oxford University Press, 1992), pp. 38-39. See also Kenneth McNaught, *A Prophet in Politics: A Biography of J.S. Woodsworth* (Toronto: University of Toronto Press, 1959), p. 264.

15. Whitehorn, *Canadian Socialism,* p. 50.

16. *Putting People First: Toward a Fair, Environmentally Sustainable and Democratic Economy,* A Report Prepared by the Federal New Democratic Party Policy Review Committee, June, 1991, pp. 8-10, 12-14.

Chapter 11

The Strength and Value of
Social Democracy in Canada

Canadian social democracy has a future. To paraphrase Mark Twain, its demise has been vastly exaggerated. Our argument for the vitality of social democracy will touch on a number of categories. We will examine the political base for social democracy, cultural-ideological considerations, philosophic arguments, international lessons, and policy arguments.

The Political Base

All the theorizing in the world would be in vain if the electoral base of the NDP were not secure. Although the 1993 election results were undeniably traumatic for the party, the popular vote in the elections of 1953, 1957, and especially 1958 was hardly encouraging for the CCF. The movement at that time bounced back and ascended to a new plateau in the polls. In 1987 the NDP ranked first in the public opinion polls and NDP leader Ed Broadbent was Canada's most trusted politician. Social democracy, and the political party carrying the social democratic banner, will continue to be a major factor in Canadian politics for a number of reasons.

The Union Affiliation

The organizational link between the NDP and Canada's labour unions has been an ambiguous blessing. It has offered an important electoral base for the social democratic movement. Yet there is no doubt that improvements could be made. Even though the NDP needed the symbolic support of the labour movement to an increased extent in the sixties and seventies, the rules for affiliation of labour scarcely changed over the CCF pattern. Some argue that they should, to give the party a better chance at the polls.

The CCF originated, as its last name plainly indicates, as a federation. No one sector, be it labour, farmers, or socialists, was to dominate, a condition that made strategic sense and responded to the demographics of Canadian society in the 1930s.[1] Adherence to the early CCF was by groups, not individuals, and the fact that affiliation of groups could only occur at the provincial level prevented a role for national unions in the party. In the later 1930s, the party, forced to specify what kinds of association were desirable, adopted the British Labour Party model: affiliating unions agreed to accept the party's constitution and paid per capita membership dues. However, unlike Labour in Britain, affiliation was to occur at the level of the union local and not at the regional or national levels. As well, the CCF did not adopt the Labour-style bloc representation in party governance and bloc voting rights at conventions: constituency organizations had far more representation in the party hierarchy than did labour, in order to prevent the appearance of labour dominance. The founding of the NDP retained the prohibitions against bloc voting and representation, and the overwhelming weight given to constituency members in representation at conventions. National and regional labour organizations were allowed in theory but discouraged in practice. Since considerable labour effort had gone into the new party's foundation, the continuity seems at first confusing; but as Archer says, "the main purpose of affiliation is to provide a 'cue' to union members that there is an important link between the party and organized labour."[2]

In fact, to a certain extent the cue has been remarkably successful. Chi and Perlin found that the percentages of unionists voting for the NDP in the 1965 and 1968 elections was twice and three times the rate for non-unionists: 26.9 per cent versus 14.9 per cent in 1965 and 30.9 per cent versus 11.6 per cent in 1968.[3] Reviewing the party identification and vote in the 1979 and 1984 elections, Keith Archer found in his sample that members of affiliated unions were three to four times more likely to vote NDP than non-unionists and significantly more likely to vote NDP than members of non-affiliated unions. Only the low rate of union affiliation mars this picture, but Archer's public choice approach suggests strongly that this is largely due to structural reasons (which are reversible).

Archer's analysis, in this respect, offers hope to the NDP. Rejecting political culture analyses of the strength of the CCF-NDP, such as that by Horowitz, he maintains that the key to greater strength for the party lies in the organizational incentives that the party offers. At present the pay-off for affiliation is low because union locals receive very few convention delegates compared to the other sectors, because the job of maintaining contact with the locals is so huge, and because the size of locals is so small that even if several joined, the overall effect of labour in the party would be only slightly changed. In spite of the difficulties labour has experienced in the affiliation process, it has nonetheless had significant results and is one of the forces that can help to stabilize the partisan fluidity of recent Canadian politics in favour of the NDP.[4] The implicit message is: change the incentives to increase the pay-off for union affiliation.

Middle-Class Rage

Another significant electoral base that beckons social democracy is the middle class, defined as earning between 75 and 150 per cent of the national average income. By any objective standard, the Canadian middle class is in a state of crisis.[5]

- As a percentage of the population, the middle class has declined from about 39 per cent of the population to about 32 per cent.
- The after-tax income of the average Canadian family, at $42,612 in 1991, was down 4.3 per cent from 1980.

- The middle quintile of Canadian income earners felt the brunt of the 1990-93 recession, seeing a decline in income of 3.7 per cent in comparison to 2.3 per cent and 1.2 per cent for the bottom and top quintiles, respectively.
- There were one million fewer people in the middle class in 1990 than there were in 1967.
- Personal income tax took close to 20 per cent of the average Canadian's pay in 1991, compared to 15.4 per cent in 1980, and most people were not in a position to claim the capital gains tax exemption introduced by the Mulroney Conservatives.

These are the figures driving the "middle-class rage" that currently dominates Canadian politics. This anger has resulted in a sense of disengagement from "politics as usual." According to surveys in 1993 by the Canadian polling firm Environics, "just 18% of Canadians express any confidence in their political leaders – only 1% have a lot – down from 52% in 1976, the year wages began stagnating in Canada."[6]

A modern protest party will capitalize on the middle class as a central component of a political strategy. In the Canadian general election of 1993, the Reform Party expressed the sense of alienation gripping the suburbs and small communities of Canada. NDP partisans were baffled by the phenomenon of their supporters deserting a left-wing party for one on the other end of the spectrum. However, the very fluidity that provoked this movement can again be harnessed to the left. The NDP must adopt a variant of the Clinton strategy of 1992, which involved accommodating the anxieties of the Ross Perot constituency (expressed eloquently in Kevin Phillips's 1992 book *Boiling Point*) while not abandoning a progressive platform.

The Electoral Record

One strong argument about the future of the NDP is its past. The party has a strong provincial electoral record that indicates both a vital regional presence and a strong possibility of transfer of voting allegiance to the federal level. Figures compiled by Rand Dyck on the percentage of popular vote and seats in provincial elections from 1960 to 1990 demonstrate that the party has a very strong base

Table 1
NDP Success: Percentage of Popular Vote, Total Seats, and Percentage of Seats Won in Provincial Elections, 1960-1990

% of NDP Vote, 1960–1990		Total NDP Seats		% of NDP Seats 1960–1990	
Sask.	43.9	Ont.	256	Sask.	51.3
B.C.	38.0	Sask.	248	Man.	38.2
Man.	33.1	Man.	196	B.C.	36.1
Ont.	26.1	B.C.	184	Ont.	23.2
Alta.	17.5	Alta.	37	Alta.	6.2
N.S.	11.4	N.S.	16	N.S.	3.7
Nfld.	4.8	Nfld.	1	Nfld.	.2
N.B.	4.1	N.B.	1	N.B.	.2

SOURCE: Rand Dyck, *Provincial Politics in Canada* (Scarborough, Ont.: Prentice-Hall, 1991), p. 631.

in Saskatchewan, British Columbia, and Manitoba in terms of popular vote. There was also a rough equivalency between the popular vote and the percentage of seats gained over the thirty-year period in Saskatchewan, Manitoba, B.C., and Ontario.

Ontario proved that a base of 26 per cent of the popular vote over a thirty-year period was enough to boost the party to a plurality victory in the Ontario election of September 6, 1990. The NDP increased its 1987 popular vote by about 12 per cent, to reach 38 per cent (compared to 32 per cent for the incumbent Liberals and 23 per cent for the Conservatives). Of course, with the distortions introduced by the single-member plurality system, the NDP went up to 74 seats (from 19), swamping the Liberals at 36 seats and the Conservatives at 20 seats.

Aggregated figures show that there is in fact a relationship between the provincial strength of the party and its federal showing. Of the federal elections from 1935 to 1988, the CCF-NDP garnered an average national vote of 17.2 per cent and a total of 257 seats. However, the average CCF-NDP vote over this period in British Columbia and Saskatchewan was 32.4 per cent, in Manitoba, 25 per cent, in the Northwest Territories and Yukon, 24.6 per cent (where elections were contested), and in Ontario, 20 per cent.[7] In spite of the party's poor showing in the 1993 election, there is a strong bedrock of support waiting to be wooed back to the party.

Policy Arguments

A variety of important policy arguments support the continued vitality of Canadian social democracy. The NDP has shown a capacity to adapt that was missing in the original CCF. Over a short history it has managed to accommodate itself to many new social and philosophical streams and such major shifts as Keynesianism, post-materialism, and anti-bureaucratism. It has outlasted its contemporaries (for example, Social Credit, the Reconstruction Party, and various Communist parties). The mark of a living and vital ideology is not dedication to an ossified set of beliefs but a lack of fear of change. The following section will show the various political challenges the NDP has faced over its long duration and how it reacted to them in the form of policy manifestos.

The Meaning of the "New Party"

Canadian socialists were quick to recover from the failure of programmatic renewal that the Winnipeg Declaration represented. They reacted to a number of important factors. The first factor compelling such introspection was the disastrous showing of the party in the general election of 1958. The Diefenbaker sweep of 1958 proved particularly harmful to the CCF, leaving it with only eight seats (from twenty-five) and a less significant but still disappointing shift in popular vote from 10.7 to 9.5 per cent. The second factor was the support of a newly formed labour central, the Canadian Labour Congress. It came into being as the result of the uniting of the Trades and Labour Congress with the CCF-sympathetic Canadian Congress of Labour in 1956. The CLC soon indicated that it saw the need for a new political instrument for the left. Still another factor was social and demographic in nature. Canadian society at the time of the Regina Manifesto had been heavily rural and the middle class was relatively small. In the intervening years, the country had become more urban, industrialized, and middle class in nature. The need for more of an overture to Quebec, where the party's support had been nominal only, was also an important reason for change.

A fourth factor was the perceived need for programmatic renewal in rhythm with the broader democratic socialist movement. Certainly in this respect the New Party Declaration of 1961 is important, but so is the preliminary work by party intellectuals Stanley Knowles in 1957 (*The New Party*) and Michael Oliver in 1961 (*Social Purpose For Canada*), both of which were intended as frameworks for the party in the tradition of the work of the LSR.[8] The contributors to *Social Purpose For Canada* were instrumental in establishing the ideological framework of the founding declaration of the New Democratic Party, and they in turn had been influenced by the broader revisions of Western social democratic thought.[9] Authors J.C. Weldon and Michael Oliver were particularly representative of the new "revisionist" approach in Canada. They established that the favoured nostrums of traditional social democrats, such as nationalization and centralized planning, were less defensible in managerialist capitalism and less imperative when an interventionist state could deliver sufficient jobs and social services. A Canada Development Fund, intended to mobilize capital and decrease dependence on American investment, and cooperative federal-provincial planning approaches were ideas that the NDP document borrowed from these authors as well as from another leftist intellectual, Pierre Trudeau.[10]

The Waffle

The Waffle manifesto, drawn up by nationalist and socialist members of the NDP, was entitled "For An Independent Socialist Canada." Its influence was substantial, despite its lack of comprehensiveness, and would outlast the short life of the Waffle.

By the end of the sixties, a number of factors had conspired to spark a re-evaluation of the Parliament-centred, gradualist approach of the NDP. The primary one, ironically, was not Canadian, but American: the Vietnam War. Popular American mobilization against the war demonstrated to youth everywhere that they could successfully mobilize as a self-conscious entity for progressive ends. National liberation struggles in the Third World provided a moral model, if not a political one, for the Canadian left. Coinciding with this was a spirit of contestation that flourished in farm, labour, and women's groups. A rebirth of Canadian nationalism was also a galvanizing factor for the left. In the face of the increasing level of foreign, especially American, investment in Canada, the matter of investment controls became the paramount concern among an intellectual faction of the left in Canada. The confluence of these factors led to the formation of an informal grouping in 1969 within the NDP, called the "Waffle," and to the generation of a statement of principles at the federal NDP convention of that year in Winnipeg. After some internal turmoil, the Waffle was forced to disband as a semi-formal component within the party.

However, the legacy of the Waffle was important. It sparked a significant reassessment in a number of unions in regard to their international domination. It put foreign domination of the Canadian economy on the front pages and provoked more nationalistic legislation from the Liberals (with the support of the NDP) to rectify the situation. Its emphasis on radicalism and organizing prevented the party from becoming too conservative and losing its reason for being. Lastly, it kept the word "socialism," and its respectability, alive.

Putting People First

Many societal changes faced the party when it began soul-searching under the leadership of its first new leader in fifteen years, Audrey McLaughlin. *Putting People First* was the attempt to come to grips with the changed ideological and economic world, and to do it in keeping with the consensual approach favoured by McLaughlin. To adjust to the new populism and to answer the problem of alienation from the political process, the paper styled itself "a framework for discussion" and was not to be "imposed from above."[11] It was, accordingly, "received" rather than passed or adopted in the manner of traditional CCF-NDP manifestos.

Changes in Canadian society affected the party. Due in part to the substantial dialogue that the Waffle had engendered within the party and in part to the "post-materialist ethos" of the intervening years, the NDP found itself having to address a new brand of problems, among them, women's issues, the environment, consumer protection, and gay and lesbian rights. This offered both the possibility of an expanded voter base and a programmatic problem as the party tried to balance it with the traditional interventionist-statist orientation favoured by old-line party and labour leaders.

From the mid-seventies until the early nineties, the NDP had to contend with "neo-conservatism" (a more accurate term would be "neo-liberalism"), a political movement that attacked the very basis of the party's platform. Neo-conservatism advocated a coherent and comprehensive philosophy of privatization, deregulation, the end of the welfare state, and smaller government. The philosophy was never implemented fully, but it had a powerful influence on provincial governments in all the western provinces and on the federal Conservative government (1984-93). Antagonism to neo-conservatism was behind the successes of the NDP in British Columbia and Saskatchewan.

International economic and political factors also proved daunting. Globalization, the increasing international mobility of capital, posed a great challenge for a party that had focused on domestic solutions to control monopolies and international corporations. The Canada-U.S. Free Trade Agreement (FTA) of 1988, with its "level playing field" philosophy of less restrained market forces, was another policy challenge for the NDP, whose trade policy had combined multilateralism and intervention in the marketplace. Shortly after the FTA came into effect, the North American Free Trade Agreement (NAFTA) was negotiated and the party had to enunciate a trade vision – later to appear in *Putting People First.* International political factors, such as the continuing need to distance the movement from the discredited economic vision of the communist states, were also a challenge. The document's emphasis on local control addressed this issue.

In summary, then, the NDP has faced a dizzying array of challenges and established coherent and valuable responses. If one is searching to judge its value, one obvious measure suggests itself. The best form of flattery is imitation, and the socialist movement has been flattered indeed. Liberal governments have borrowed some of its most popular and important policies from the NDP : the welfare state, socialized health care, the Electoral Expenses Act, and Petro-Canada. The 1993 platform of the Liberal Party had heavy social democratic overtones. The programmatic renewal process of the NDP is valuable not only for the party, but for the country as a whole.

Political Culture

One of the strongest arguments for social democratic vitality in Canada is the so-called "Hartz-Horowitz thesis." This is a novel explanation of ideological development in Canada. Based on a combination of idealist and dialectical assumptions, the approach gets its name from the work of two outstanding North American social scientists, Louis Hartz and Gad Horowitz. It began with the work of Louis Hartz, who elaborated the "fragment thesis" in two books called *The Liberal Tradition in America* and *The Founding of New Societies*. Gad Horowitz, realizing that Hartz and his disciples had conflated the American and Canadian cases, added some important qualifications to the fragment thesis in a ground-breaking 1966 article. [12]

The Hartzian approach was to study new societies founded by Europeans as "fragments" thrown off from Europe. A fragment was a smaller society coming from an older, more powerful European one. The fragment does not participate in the historical ideological spectrum of the mother country. It participates in only a chosen part of that spectrum and relives the old battles over and over again. The underlying assumption of the fragment approach is that ideological development takes place in a chronological order from feudal (or tory) to undemocratic liberalism to democratic liberalism to socialism. Hartz attributed the existence of socialism to the prior existence of feudal or tory values in a society: toryism would combine with liberalism to produce socialism.

Gad Horowitz adopted the Hartzian method but rejected Hartz's conclusions with regard to Canada. In doing so, he established a fundamental thesis of English-Canadian political culture. He typified the political culture of English Canada as basically liberal, but with significant tory and socialist streams or "imperfections," that is, weaker but still important elements arising from a variety of factors in Canadian history. These included the introduction of the United Empire Loyalists into Canada after the American Revolution, the immigration of radical labour elements to Canada from 1815 to 1850, and the interplay of toryism and socialism.

The fact that there is a mixture of ideological elements in the English-Canadian cultural mix implies some important things for the Canadian party system. Some of them are revealed in the course of Horowitz's argument, which is pitched at distinguishing the relative weights of Canadian and American socialism. Rather than the CCF being a mere agrarian protest movement and the NDP a "liberal" party, as Hartz reasoned, the CCF-NDP has been a minor socialist party at the federal level and a majority party at the provincial level. The Canadian socialist movement is "influential" and "legitimate."[13] Horowitz's evidence is convincing.

So strong is the socialist element in Canada that the major federal parties have had to reflect it in their respective platforms and policies; similarly, of course, the tory element has to be reflected in policy when the attack is from the right. Both the Liberals and the Conservatives therefore have "business liberalism" as their main ideological element, but it is not an American-style monolithic liberalism; it has to acknowledge the tory and socialist streaks in the political culture. The Liberal Party over history has been the most adept at mixing liberalism, toryism, and socialism. Due to socialist influence, the Liberals are less individualistic than they might be, recognize the need for collective action, advocate the reconciliation of classes, and merge on certain issues with the CCF-NDP. The Conservatives, likewise, have a "red tory" stratum in the party that indicates a socialist influence.

Socialism has such a hold on the Canadian reality that it has generated province-specific fragment explanations as well. One notable one is the contribution of Nelson Wiseman on the pattern of prairie politics.[14] Gordon S. Galbraith has also explained the British Columbia political tradition in fragment terms, calling B.C. a "fragment of Edwardian Britain" at the time of foundation.[15] Although the work on Ontario's political culture has not stressed fragment theory, the existence of a socialist element could be inferred from the prior existence of a thriving toryism and the liberal base, and validated by the subsequent periodic strength of the party provincially.

Philosophical Arguments

Socialism is, of course, an ideology, not a philosophy. Yet most ideologies have some basis in philosophy – a broader world view with the ultimate objective of understanding the world. Ideologies, on the other hand, are plans for changing the world or maintaining the status quo, based on the perceived needs of society. Sometimes the line between ideology and philosophy is a thin one. Existing in a political-philosophical context heavily influenced by liberalism, Canadian socialist thought occasionally has been enriched by its encounters with progressive liberalism.

Redistribution

One writer who has established a powerful rationale for the redistributive state, and who has struggled to weigh the values of equality and liberty, is American philosopher John Rawls.[16] Although the NDP or other social democrats have never claimed Rawls as one of their own, his work approaches some themes in the ambivalent fashion of Canadian socialists. (It was Stanley Knowles, after all, who, when describing the program of the New Party, attempted to establish a middle way between strict socialist economic equality and the liberal equality of opportunity by calling for the party to pursue "greater equality."[17])

Rawls manages to accommodate both equality and liberty by serially ordering two principles of justice, that is, by assigning the first principle a priority over the second. The first is that "each person is to have an equal right to the most extensive basic liberty compatible with a similar liberty for others."[18] This means that citizens should have equal civil liberties of the traditional sort, such as freedom of speech, of voting, of due process, and so forth. The second is that "social and economic inequalities are to be arranged so that they are both (a) to the greatest benefit of the least-advantaged, and (b) attached to offices and positions open to all under conditions of fair equality of opportunity."[19] This means that distribution of income, wealth, authority, and opportunity is not arranged to maximize total efficiency or the principle of utility. Instead, a just system is one that allows the more-favoured individual to prosper only if doing so allows the condition and prospects of the least well-off individual to improve (a situation that Rawls calls the "difference principle"). In other words, the system must move to a greater equality than would result from the normal interplay of social forces. The inequalities of birth and natural endowment – which are undeserved – cannot be used as a justification for having *some* suffer deprivation for the benefit of the *entire community* or for any member of it.

Even the method of arriving at this conclusion is one that social democrats might find congenial. Rawls asks us to take the perspective of the equal citizen (the first principle) and of the least favoured individuals in society (the second principle). This is accomplished by a number of rhetorical devices, one of which is the "veil of ignorance" and a four-stage sequence to applying justice to political institutions. One is asked to assume he/she knows nothing about his/her own particular social circumstances in order to choose basic principles of justice, and next to judge the fairest constitutional arrangements; then the veil is progressively lifted as one moves from the legislative to the administrative arrangements. Constitution-making should concern itself with the first principle of justice and the next stages with the second principle. While this is not a complete social democratic rationale for political reform – the NDP, it will be recalled, advocated that a "social charter" be included in the constitution during the Charlottetown Accord negotiations – it is a valuable starting point.

Anti-elitism

A closely related approach is to argue that there is a natural human tendency to resist elitism and undue concentrations of power. Social democratic movements are reflexively anti-elitist, Bryan Gould contends, comparing them to the insufficient alternatives. His analysis, although written about the British social democratic situation, is of relevance to Canada. All capitalist economies develop inequalities, and as long as they do there will be room for the type of approach that Gould describes:

> My contention is that every society has a natural tendency to distribute power unequally, and, in most cases, to concentrate power in a few hands. In all societies, those who are stronger, cleverer, richer, luckier, will acquire power at the expense of others in society and will then use that power to entrench their privileged positions.

The other ideologies will not make any attempts to deal with this problem in a serious way. Conservatism, liberalism, and totalitarianism validate or otherwise enforce elitism. Socialism, on the other hand, is an alternative to concentrations of power in the market or bureaucracy.

Only the socialist will consciously resist it and counteract it, by creating institutions and rules and collective action that constantly seek to reverse that otherwise inevitable phenomenon. That is why socialism is about political democracy and civil rights, about redistribution and equality, about common or social ownership, about breaking down the advantage the wage bargain gives the employer.[20]

However, the instruments used are not important, says Gould. State ownership need not be a major preoccupation of socialists. Even the market can be used to achieve the aim of diffusing power, as long as the parties to the transactions are put in a more equal position. If one examines the intellectual writings of the new social democracy in Canada or Europe, one will find an attitude much like the above as a moral foundation.

International Lessons

One of the lessons that is apparent from a review of comparative politics in the Western world is that broad currents of history seldom occur in isolation from each other. The European shift to social democratic governments in the immediate post-war context was a general phenomenon, and had an echo in the wartime popularity of the CCF. The "New Left" phenomenon was simultaneously short-lived and influential in most Western countries. The rise of the neo-conservative movement in the seventies and eighties was similarly coincidental and widespread. If social democracy has a future in the developed world, it is likely to have a future in Canada.

Relative Strengths of Social Democratic Parties

Table 2 shows the mean electoral support of party groupings in the Western European countries in the 1980s. It demonstrates that of all the party families, the socialists were leading contenders in all but a few countries. Socialist parties were the clear electoral leaders in Sweden, Denmark, and Spain. They were roughly neck and neck for electoral support with rightist parties in Austria, Belgium, Finland, Luxembourg, Norway, Greece, and Portugal. They followed, but not by much, the leading rightist parties in France,

Table 2
The Party Families in the 1980s: Mean Electoral Support, by Country, % of Vote

	Communists	New Left	Socialists	Greens	Agrarians	Liberals	Christian Democrats	Conservatives	Extreme Right	Nationalist & Regionalist	Other*
Austria	0.7	—	45.4	4.1	—	7.4	42.2	—	—	—	—
Belgium	1.4	—	28.0	6.1	—	21.1	27.8	—	1.3	12.3	—
Denmark	0.9	14.4	31.9	0.7	11.4	5.6	2.4	26.0	—	—	6.5
Finland	13.9	—	25.4	2.7	25.2	0.9	2.8	22.9	—	5.3	0.6
France	12.4	—	35.0	0.9	—	—	42.7†	—	6.5	—	—
Germany	—	—	39.4	5.1	—	8.9	45.9	—	—	—	—
Iceland	15.3	7.8	17.1	—	20.0	—	—	38.4	—	—	—
Ireland	—	3.9	8.9	0.4	—	3.5	(33.9)‡	45.9	—	1.3	0.7
Italy	28.3	4.0	16.4	1.2	—	6.9	33.6	—	6.4	1.7	5.8
Luxembourg	5.1	—	32.3	6.8	—	17.5	33.3	—	—	—	—
Netherlands	1.1	3.7	31.0	—	—	25.5	36.6	—	0.6	—	—
Norway	0.9	6.8	37.4	—	6.6	3.4	8.7	35.1	—	—	—
Sweden	5.6	—	44.5	2.9	12.2	10.8	2.4	21.1	—	—	—
Switzerland	0.9	3.5	21.2	3.9	11.1	30.1	22.2	—	3.2	3.7	2.2
United Kingdom	—	—	29.2	—	—	23.9	—	42.4	—	—	—
Greece	12.1	—	43.5	0.2	—	—	—	41.8	—	—	—
Portugal	16.0	—	28.7	—	—	(27.3)‡	6.9	—	—	—	19.1
Spain	6.1	—	43.5	—	—	4.6	2.2	25.9	—	5.2	6.6
Mean (all countries)	6.7	2.5	31.0	1.9	4.8	11.0	16.7	19.0	1.0	1.6	2.3
Mean (excluding Greece, Portugal, Spain)	5.8	2.9	29.5	2.3	5.8	11.0	19.5	18.3	1.2	1.6	1.1

*The criterion for inclusion is that the party must win at least 1 per cent of the vote or one parliamentary seat. †Includes liberals, Christian democrats, and secular conservatives. ‡Figures in parentheses indicate that the classification of the party concerned was ambiguous.
SOURCE: Michael Gallagher, Michael Laver, and Peter Mair, *Representative Government in Western Europe* (Toronto: McGraw-Hill, 1992). Reproduced with permission of McGraw-Hill.

Table 3
Western European Social Democrats:
Electoral Performance, % of Vote

	1950s	1960s	1970s	1980s	Parties Competing in 1980s
Austria	43.3	45.0	50.0	45.4	Socialist party
Belgium	35.9	31.0	26.6	28.0	Socialist party (PS + SP)
Denmark	40.2	39.1	33.6	31.9	Social Democrats
Finland	25.9	26.9	25.1	25.4	Social Democrats
France	25.9	18.6	22.1	35.0	Socialist party, Left Radicals
Germany	30.3	39.4	44.2	39.4	Social Democrats
Iceland	19.5	15.0	14.8	17.1	Social Democrats, Social Democratic Federation
Ireland	10.9	14.8	12.7	8.9	Labour party
Italy	18.0	19.4	14.4	16.4	Social party, Social Democrats
Luxembourg	37.1	35.0	35.4	32.3	Social Workers party, Independent Socialist party*
Netherlands	30.7	25.8	31.9	31.0	Labor party
Norway	47.5	45.4	38.8	37.4	Labor party
Sweden	45.6	48.4	43.7	44.5	Social Democrats
Switzerland	26.0	26.0	25.7	21.2	Social Democrats, Autonomous Socialist party
U.K.	46.3	46.1	39.1	29.2	Labour party
Mean	32.2	31.7	30.5	29.5	

*The party has not contested all elections in the 1980s.
SOURCE: Michael Gallagher, Michael Laver, and Peter Mair, *Representative Government in Western Europe* (Toronto: McGraw-Hill, 1992), p. 61.
Reproduced with permission of McGraw-Hill.

Germany, and the Netherlands. Table 3 illustrates the relative stability in the socialist vote in the past four decades in Austria, Finland, Iceland, Netherlands, and Sweden, the ascending support in France and Germany, and descending support in only a minority of countries. The lesson is a simple one: if many countries experiencing approximately equal conditions of socio-economic change can choose social democracy as a safeguard factor, and choose it consistently, the possibility is strong that Canadians may ultimately do the same.

Electoral Expectations

One useful lesson to learn from international social democratic movements is that it helps to have modest expectations about ultimate electoral success. The relatively quick provincial successes notwithstanding, the sixty years of lack of federal socialist governments in Canada is bound to be discouraging to partisans unless one remembers the slow rise of international social democracy.

The times between inauguration of the movement and ultimate electoral success are in some cases substantial.[21] Sweden proved the quickest European success, taking twenty-eight years from party formation in 1889 to the first short minority government in 1917, but forty-three years to its first government as senior member of a coalition in 1932 and seventy-nine years to a majority government in 1968. In Norway, the socialist party waited forty-one years to form an eighteen-day government in 1928, forty-eight years for junior status in a coalition in 1935, and fifty-eight years to form a majority government in 1945, then remaining in power continuously until 1963. In Britain, Ramsay MacDonald's first Labour minority government came in 1924, forty-three years after the formation of the Social Democratic Federation in 1881, and the first majority government came only in 1945, sixty-four years after formation. The German Social Democratic Party had its first incarnation in 1869; it was fifty years to involvement in government in 1919, ruled in coalition with the CDU/CSU from 1966 to 1969 and in coalition with the FDP from 1969 to 1982, but it has never by itself formed a majority government. It took the Austrian Social Democrats eighty-two years to form a majority government, although they led coalition governments from 1945 to 1966. Of course, there are exceptions to the general story: Australia's social democrats gained power only twenty-two years after party foundation. The vitality of the movement and its contribution to national life are watched closely, and occasionally these factors are rewarded with a quick popular mandate. Generally, however, it is a longer wait.

The Context of Party Politics

Another set of lessons that can be gleaned from a comparative international review is that the context sometimes explains the relative difficulty or success that social democracy experiences at election time. Lynn McDonald cites the formidable difficulties that have befallen socialist parties in Canada in comparison to those across the world. One important contextual problem is access to the media. The balance so necessary in a free press is noticeably lacking in Canada, as opposed to Europe.

> Every country of Western Europe has some paper at least sympathetic to, if not actually supportive of, its social democratic party. Neither Canada nor the United States has one. The result is that social democratic politicians can count on reasonable coverage of their views in some papers. Problems they take seriously will be taken seriously. . . . Television coverage of social democratic parties is also probably better in Europe.[22]

The media help to set the public policy agenda in Canada, and a crucial element of the debate is being denied Canadians. Social democracy might have a better chance in Canada with a freer press that reflects a broader ideological range rather than one that maintains the hegemonic liberal ideology.

Another lesson from the international scene concerns the electoral system. Canada's plurality system may have the capacity to understate the strength of the socialist movement in the public imagination. As McDonald notes: "Few social democratic parties have made it to government without a system giving them some proportional representation while they build their forces. The only clear exceptions are Britain, Australia, and New Zealand, all of them countries with a more radical political culture and stronger labour organization."[23]

How Canadian socialists deal with this lesson is, of course, ambiguous. The single-member plurality system has the capacity to take a plurality and turn it into a government party situation, so it offers certain advantages to a tentative social democratic movement. On the other hand, such a system can give an exaggerated and potentially fatal impression of electoral irrelevancy in some parts of the country, such as Atlantic Canada and Quebec, and prevent the party from attaining a national image. Probably because of the double-edged nature of this issue, Ed Broadbent was convinced to suggest a combination of both systems for Canada. He suggested the enlargement of the Commons by 100 seats, with twenty to be allocated to each of the five "regions" of Canada, regional representatives being allowed from each party according to their percentage of the regional vote.[24]

The Method of Programmatic Renewal

An international review of social democracy can shed light on the problem of programmatic renewal. Inevitably, all parties have to modernize their programs, and the skill with which they approach this task can sometimes help their political fortunes. Those who fear that Canadian social democrats may lack models or inspiration for programmatic renewal need only look at successful examples such as Germany and Sweden.

All social democratic parties have not been equally successful in the renewal process. Hodge argues, for example, that the German SPD (Social Democratic Party) was able rather painlessly to renew its program (with the revisionist and coalitionist Bad Godesberg Program of 1959) because of the lack of an overarching point of contention in its platform, whereas the British Labourites divided seriously between the Gaitskellites and the fundamentalists, concentrating on the nationalization issue (represented by Clause IV of the old 1918 Program) to the single-minded exclusion of most others.[25] "Programmatic renewal [for the SPD] was neither a principled crusade nor a reckoning with history; it was a bureaucratic and semantic enterprise."[26] In a similar vein, the Swedish Social Democrats have established a certain rhythm to program renewal that has allowed them to stay in power for most of the modern era. The revisions of the original 1897 program (1911, 1920, 1944, 1960, 1975, 1990) seem recently to have gotten into a fifteen-year cycle. The original program has never been completely rewritten; it is merely added to incrementally, a process that has "probably eased the traumatic nature and controversies surrounding revision [and has] also softened discontinuities."[27] The lesson for the NDP is that manifestos are strategic instruments, not eternal statements of principle.

The Content of Programmatic Renewal

Social democracy in Canada is likely to succeed because the world-wide social democratic movement is so rich in ideas and alternatives to the crisis-oriented capitalist order. The alternatives are attractive for a number of philosophical and electoral reasons. They are also attractive because they have successfully been put into practice and are therefore an inspiration for comparative public policy students. The most interesting contributions are perhaps those of the Swedish Social Democrats.

In the fifties and sixties, the *solidaristic wage policy* (also known as the "Rehn Model" after its originator, economist Gosta Rehn) involved national-level labour negotiations between capital and labour. The level of profitability in the most productive companies of a sector would determine the level of wage settlements throughout the sector, forcing out the less productive companies and discouraging inflation. The *activist wage policy*, to some extent necessitated by the solidaristic policy, involved large-scale retraining and labour mobilization. "Rehn's technically brilliant scheme reconciled the requirements of profitability and rationality in a capitalist economy with the demands of the trade unions for full employment and high wages."[28] These and other measures also demonstrated an important modern principle for social democrats: "Control over the functions of capitalist ownership . . . is more important than socialization of property per se."[29]

The 1975 SAP program revision introduced the notion of radical reform – "economic citizenship" – by way of politics.

> Whereas the orthodox scheme [of socialist thought] presupposes that welfare and the good life can arise only after the socialization of production, Swedish revisionism holds that political and then social reforms can create the conditions for economic transformation, step by step. "Political citizenship" [universal suffrage] must precede "social citizenship," [the welfare state] and these are in turn indispensable for the third stage, "economic citizenship." Workers must be emancipated from social insecurity before they can partake effectively in economic democracy.[30]

The most important aspect of economic democracy was the participation of employees rather than government *per se* in capital formation by way of "wage-earner funds," an innovation named the "Meidner Plan" after its originator, Rudolf Meidner.[31]

The 1990 party program is perhaps the most interesting revision yet. The Swedish "third way" has come to mean the midpoint between provision by the private sector and by centralized public bureaucracies. The 1990 program is a fresh approach to new and old problems.[32] Rather than choose between the post-materialist and materialist approaches to politics, the SAP has accommodated both. It accepts that the key social division in the future may in fact be the split between intellectual and non-intellectual workers, but it claims that this division overlaps with and reinforces traditional class cleavages. In a new departure (reminiscent of Rawls) the party has chosen a "solidaristic working life policy" that aims at improving the lot of workers experiencing the most hazardous and monotonous working conditions as a first priority, analogous to the way that the solidaristic wage policy improved the wages of the poorest paid in particular sectors.

Implications for Canada

The net implications for Canada of such innovations are difficult to predict. Certainly there is a great deal of cross-fertilization of ideas among members of the Socialist International, to which the NDP belongs; and Canadian socialists are bound to consider the Swedish departures (and those of other socialist parties) with great interest. Readers will note a certain similarity between the collective funds idea of the 1991 NDP document *Putting People First* and earlier Swedish plans, and one of the authors of the document has noted its indebtedness to the Meidner Plan.[33]

Canadian social democracy has demonstrated its resilience at many junctures in Canadian history. It will draw upon its considerable strengths to surmount the difficulties it now faces. It is in the interest of the people of Canada and not just the immediate personnel associated with the movement that it survive. It represents an important part of our political culture, reflects the needs of a threatened middle class, and is anti-elitist without pandering to the lowest common denominator. Canadian social democracy is part of a great international movement that shows no signs of disappearing.

270 Canadian Political Debates

Notes

1. Keith Archer reminds us that "In 1931, 28.6% of the work force was employed in agriculture and 33.8% in secondary production. As well, only 15.3% of the non-agricultural work force was unionized; about half of these workers belonged to the TLC." Keith Archer, *Political Choices and Electoral Consequences: A Study of Organized Labour and the New Democratic Party* (Montreal and Kingston: McGill-Queen's University Press, 1990), p. 12.
2. *Ibid.*, p. 25.
3. N.H. Chi and George C. Perlin, "The New Democratic Party: A Party in Transition," in Hugh G. Thorburn, *Party Politics in Transition* (Scarborough, Ont.: Prentice-Hall, 1979), p. 179.
4. Archer, *Political Choices*, ch. 6.
5. The following figures are from Edward Greenspon, "The Incredible, Shrinking Middle Class," *Globe and Mail*, July 31, 1993. Similar figures are available in Gordon Betcherman, "The Disappearing Middle," in Daniel Drache, *Getting on Track: Social Democratic Strategies for Ontario* (Montreal and Kingston: McGill-Queen's University Press, 1992), pp. 124-35.
6. Greenspon, "The Incredible, Shrinking Middle Class."
7. The statistical summaries are from Table 1 in the Appendix to Alan Whitehorn, *Canadian Socialism: Essays on the CCF-NDP* (Toronto: Oxford University Press, 1992), pp. 262-64.
8. Stanley Knowles, *The New Party* (Toronto: McClelland and Stewart, 1961); Michael Oliver, ed., *Social Purpose For Canada* (Toronto: University of Toronto Press, 1961), pp. vi-vii.
9. Neil Bradford, "Ideas, Intellectuals and Social Democracy in Canada," in Alain G. Gagnon and A. Brian Tanguay, eds., *Canadian Parties in Transition: Discourse, Organization and Representation* (Scarborough, Ont.: Nelson Canada, 1989), pp. 85-87.
10. *Ibid.*, p. 87.
11. *Putting People First: Toward a Fair, Environmentally Sustainable and Democratic Economy*, A Report Prepared by the Federal New Democratic Party Policy Review Committee, June, 1991, p. 2.
12. Gad Horowitz, "Liberalism, Conservatism and Socialism in Canada: An Interpretation," *Canadian Journal of Economics and Political Science*, 32, 2 (1966), pp. 143-71.
13. *Ibid.*, p. 150.

14. Nelson Wiseman, "The Pattern of Prairie Politics," *Queen's Quarterly*, 88, 2 (Summer, 1981), pp. 298-315.

15. Gordon Galbraith, "British Columbia," in David J. Bellamy, ed., *Provincial Political Systems* (Toronto: Methuen, 1976), pp. 62-75.

16. John Rawls, *A Theory of Justice* (Cambridge, Mass.: Belnap Press, 1971).

17. W. Christian and C. Campbell, *Political Parties and Ideologies in Canada*, Third Edition (Toronto: McGraw-Hill Ryerson, 1990), p. 206.

18. Rawls, *A Theory of Justice*, p. 60.

19. *Ibid.*, p. 83.

20. Bryan Gould, "What's left of the left?" *New Statesman and Society*, May 3, 1991, p. 15.

21. The following section owes much to Chapter 4 of Lynn McDonald, *The Party That Changed Canada: The New Democratic Party Then and Now* (Toronto: Macmillan of Canada, 1987).

22. *Ibid.*, p. 138.

23. *Ibid.*, p. 134.

24. William P. Irvine, *Does Canada Need A New Electoral System?* (Kingston, Ont.: Queen's University Institute of Intergovernmental Relations, 1979), pp. 62-63.

25. Carl Cavanagh Hodge, "The Politics of Programmatic Renewal: Postwar Experiences in Britain and Germany," *Western European Politics*, 16, 1 (January, 1993), pp. 5-19.

26. *Ibid.*, p. 11.

27. Diane Sainsbury, "The Swedish Social Democrats and the Legacy of Continuous Reform: Asset or Dilemma," *Western European Politics*, 16, 1 (January, 1993), p. 42.

28. Stephen Padgett, "Social Democracy in Power," *Parliamentary Affairs*, 46, 1 (January, 1993), p. 108.

29. Gosta Esping-Andersen, *Politics Against Markets: The Social Democratic Road to Power* (Princeton, N.J.: Princeton University Press, 1985), p. 23.

30. *Ibid.*, p. 22.

31. Sainsbury, "The Swedish Social Democrats," pp. 44-45.

32. Most of the following description of the program is from *ibid.*, pp. 48-56.

33. Andrew Jackson, "The Last, Best Left?" *Studies in Political Economy*, 37 (Spring, 1992), p. 165.

Chapter 12

The Irrelevance of Social Democracy in Canada Today

Canadian social democracy does not have a future, at least not the future envisaged in its own past. It has squandered the opportunities it once had, and it is a victim of its own contradictions. This chapter will examine the political base, political culture, philosophy, international lessons, and policy arguments to demonstrate that social democracy as we know it has become an anachronism in Canada today.

The Political Base

The political base for social democracy in Canada has always been extremely fragile, and it has recently disintegrated. The reasons are several.

The Union Affiliation

The union affiliation is an albatross for the NDP. It gets all the blame for being the lackey of big unions without actually having big unions – or small, for that matter – as close partners. In fact, the detrimental nature of the link is such that it should have long ago been abated; it was recently, in Britain.

The stronger tendency for unionists to vote NDP, as noted by Keith Archer, is, on first blush, good news for the party. It is, of course, marred by the fact that only a distinct minority of NDP-affiliated unionists voted for the NDP in the first place. Even among affiliated unionists, the NDP was second to the Liberals in 1979 and second to the Conservatives by an even wider margin in 1984. This tendency is also marred by the extremely low rate of affiliation of union members with the party. The high mark of affiliation was in 1963, when 14.6 per cent of union members were affiliated with the party through affiliated locals, but the rate had slipped to 7.3 per cent by 1984.[1]

The example of the British Labour Party seems applicable, with qualifications, to the Canadian situation. In the fall of 1993, the Labour Party's annual conference voted to end the bloc voting by union executives that had given them such a major influence in the party's selection of candidates. The new arrangement, promoted heavily by new party leader John Smith, was that unionists would have to join the party individually to have the right to vote. Unions will still have significant influence in the party, but the change will bring the party closer to "the political reality that every second union member no longer votes Labour, and that collectively organized labour is a diminishing political force in Britain."[2] Surely it is significant that the very party that served as the model for the affiliation rules of the CCF-NDP should now begin to turn away from union affiliation. Rather than actively questioning the affiliation matter after their 1993 defeat, however, the party entered into a two-year joint study with the labour movement itself to chart the future course of the party. The lack of realism in this strategy speaks for itself.

The Effect of Deindustrialization

Canada is not immune from the international trend toward deindustrialization, nor from its attendant effects. Deindustrialization
means the replacement of mass production industry as the motor
force of the economy by the services sector. As deindustrialization
proceeds, Francis Fox Piven notes, working-class parties wane.[3]
Workplace solidarity came naturally in the factories of heavy
industry, where similar conditions engendered common political
attitudes; in smaller post-industrial employment environments
characterized by irregular schedules, solidarity is harder to achieve.
Workers do not settle in the same homogeneous communities and
fraternize to the same degree as during the heyday of industrialism.
As well, Piven says, the twin analyses of power that previously
motivated working-class parties no longer are applicable:

> The once-stirring idea that the working class could organize
> to wield power over industrial capitalism has lost its force as
> industrial capitalism has reorganized domestically and dis-
> persed globally, disorganizing the working class and escaping
> its leverage. Similarly the idea that workers could transform
> their societies by the power they exercised as citizens in the
> democratic nation state has lost credibility, because the
> nation state seems only one player, and often a minor player,
> in a world dominated by international market organizations.[4]

Although worker solidarity was never as pronounced in Canada as
throughout Western Europe, the same general dynamics have surfaced in Canada. As well, the relative weights of the nation-state
and industrial capitalism are further affected by free trade arrangements that take the tools for social transformation increasingly out
of the hands of government.

The Unstable Coalition

The coalition politics that dominates the NDP at present is inherently unstable. Single issues seem to have the capacity to destroy
the credibility of provincial NDP governments and to reflect nega-
tively on the federal wing of the party.

The British Columbia NDP alienated its "green" wing with its decision to appease the union wing and allow cutting of substantial parts of old-growth forest in Clayoquot Sound in the early nineties. The Ontario NDP government in 1993 attempted to appeal to middle-class voters and reduce the provincial deficit by $2 billion; it established a broad "social contract" that overrode public-sector collective bargaining agreements and alienated both public and private unions while decreasing the popularity of the party. In Saskatchewan, the NDP government was more popular than its two socialist neighbours, but its budget cuts were also unpopular. The NDP has not learned the lesson of several Canadian parties and severed relations between the federal and provincial wings. As a result, the federal party got blamed at the polls for the alleged sins of the provincial parties. This dynamic is likely to repeat itself until the party is only a pale reflection of its former self and no longer a viable national actor – the 1993 general election scenario.

Middle-Class Rage

The NDP may have an intellectual grasp of "middle-class rage" (see Chapter 11), but right-wing parties like the Reformers are a more authentic political voice of the embittered middle class. The middle class blames big government and special interests for the tax crunch it has experienced. The 1993 general election saw close to three times as many people vote Reform as NDP (18.7 per cent for the Reformers as opposed to 6.9 per cent for the NDP). Reform got to this stage by promising an elimination of the federal deficit, then estimated to be $35 billion, in three years; $19 billion was to disappear because of specific program cuts and $16 billion was to come from economic growth. The NDP waffled on the question of deficit size and how to reduce it, and was rewarded appropriately at the polls. Reform is aiming to form the next government; it is significant that the NDP talks only of political survivalism.

The popularity of the NDP has suffered also as result of its apparent preoccupation with special interests. One of the selling points of the Reformers is their contention that interest groups have come between what should be a direct relationship between governors and governed; the special interests, in addition, demand expansion of public spending and taxation, as they get their way with the public purse. The NDP shows no sign of coming to grips with this problem. In fact, it rejoices in its relations with the "popular sector." It will continue to pay the price at the polls.

Policy Arguments

A host of policy arguments indicate the tenuous hold on reality that social democrats have in Canada. The lack of "connectedness" to the real needs of Canadians does not bode well for the socialists.

Poverty of Ideas

The current socialist approach to public policy in Canada is marked by confusion and a poverty of ideas. One has only to look at the recent literature on party policy – and this, it should be noted, is from those *sympathetic* to the party – to find this theme explored. Bradford and Jenson, for example, have used the expression "contentless populism" to describe the modern outlook of the NDP. The party in the 1984 and 1988 elections used language devoid of traditional social democratic concepts and relied on polling and marketing techniques to drive the party platform. As a result, the party could not formulate a clear programmatic alternative to the bourgeois parties in economic and constitutional matters.[5]

In a way the demise of the Waffle a full generation earlier had thrown the progressively bourgeois nature of the NDP program into relief. The Waffle did not last as a permanent feature of the NDP. In 1972 the Ontario NDP effectively began the process that ended the Waffle's life in both that province and in Canada. There were too many mutual antagonisms and inconsistencies. The NDP was a party that focused on socialism achieved by the parliamentary route; the Waffle believed that socialism grew as a result of mobilization and militancy. The NDP rejected the Waffle emphasis on Quebec self-determination in favour of constitutional negotiation over the province's grievances. In addition, the party believed it had moved beyond reliance on a few instruments like nationalized industries and economic planning to achieve its socialist goals, while the Wafflers emphasized these very methods for change. Lastly, there were personal reasons.[6] With the ejection of the Waffle, the party lost a vital source of renewal and was indeed to become a shell for contentless populism.

Internal Fragmentation

The reason for this inability to establish a distinctive program lay in the internal pluralism of the party. There has been a continuing series of disputes between the western and central Canadian wings of the party, between the populists and labourites, and between liberal progressive revisionists and extra-parliamentary socialists. Contentless populism in fact began in the 1972 election, as the party sought to recover from the divisions of the Waffle episode. The lesson of the era was that populism was a way of avoiding the divisive search for an alternative political and economic framework while reacting to the traditional union conservatism on questions like economic nationalism and the two nations concept.[7]

The Lack of Constitutional Credibility

The party has lacked credibility on constitutional issues. The NDP has become a marginal actor in the constitutional debates in Canada because it has avoided dealing with the three competing "legacies" in the intellectual heritage of the party, says ex-Waffle member John Richards.[8] These legacies are:

- *British Fabianism,* which believes in centralized political power to overcome the concentrated economic power of the monopolies, and, with F.R. Scott's influence, a pan-Canadian francophone policy and entrenched bill of rights;
- *the Saskatchewan legacy,* emphasizing the realism borne of governing experience, the need for provincial financial and policy autonomy, and preference for parliamentary protection of rights over entrenchment of them;
- *the American legacy,* which translates the positive state into justiciable rights and has recently expanded the rights dialogue to include the notion of "collective entitlements" for groups, a notion that appeared in the Ontario NDP government call for a "social charter."

Although Richards treats the NDP's constitutional crisis as merely a microcosm of the larger national crisis of Canadian identity and its internal party debates as important contributions to the larger debate, this is plainly not the case. The national party was so racked by its internal divisions that it made practically no distinctive contribution to the constitutional packages of 1981, 1987, and 1992. It simply went along with whatever national government package there was, regardless of its Liberal or Conservative origin, or whether the package was relatively centrist-populist, as in 1981, or provincialist-elitist, as in 1987 and 1992. The Canadian public can certainly be forgiven for assuming then, as now, that the party is not a player.

Political Culture

Closely related to philosophical arguments (to be discussed later) are considerations of the approaches necessary to reach the Canadian body politic. Those who hold out hopes for the continued vitality of social democracy based on cultural arguments are optimistic indeed, for Canada, much like the United States in many ways, is basically liberal.

After an exhaustive study of Canadian public policy that integrates cultural, historical, and ideological perspectives, Ronald Manzer describes Canada as having a "liberal public philosophy."[9] It has been decisively shaped, he says, by British and American liberalism, although Catholic conservatism and non-Marxian socialism have had some, albeit less, influence. The basis of the public philosophy in liberalism, even if this liberalism is internally divided between economic and ethical (developmental) liberalism, has some important policy implications. Social policy, for instance, can never go far beyond the liberal emphasis on individual responsibility and effort. "Given varying individual efforts in the pursuit of individual rewards, unequal outcomes are inevitable; and collective material prosperity depends on defending this inequality."[10] This means that socialist approaches to welfare and development, which aim at redistribution of economic power through public ownership and redistribution of wealth, are not central to the Canadian public philosophy.

It should also be noted that the Hartz-Horowitz thesis, and its contention that socialism is alive and well in Canada, has not been spared from criticism. H.D. Forbes sheds doubt on the validity of Horowitz's claim to a sweeping historical generalization. "Horowitz develops his analysis of the Canadian political tradition around the 'hard fact' that socialism is stronger in Canada than in the United States. . . . [but the] treatment of socialism in North America is vulnerable to the observation that this ideology was once much stronger in the United States than in Canada, a difference that can easily be related to Canada's Tory traditions, with unsettling effect."[11] Even a fellow fragment theorist, Kenneth McRae, thinks that the socialist (and tory) effects Horowitz identifies are minor. Canadian and American ideological underpinnings are basically liberal. The founding of the NDP marked the absorption of socialist thought into the liberal tradition.[12]

Once one stands back and contemplates the alternative explanations for socialist parties in Canada, the fragment approach and the case for the continuing health of socialism seem less convincing. The early vitality of the socialist movement could have been due to the percentage of British ex-Labourites in the population, a condition that no longer holds. The parliamentary system, which promotes the formation of disciplined political parties, could have encouraged the formation of a third party by entrenching the policy inflexibility of the older parties. The demographic makeup of the population that Archer says pertained in the early 1930s certainly played a role; but the dwindling of the working class and the agricultural sector diminished the appeal of a socialist party.

Some argue that pragmatism, rather than ideology, marks the English-Canadian approach to political choice. Gibbins and Nevitte used cross-national attitudinal survey data to compare the ideological structures of English Canada, Francophone Quebec, and the United States. Canadians, relative to Americans, displayed a "relative lack of ideological coherence and structure," even more so in the case of French Canadians. There was an apparent "wariness of ideological rigidity," which might have had something to do with the importance of such "non-ideological" matters on the Canadian national agenda as the constitution and federal-provincial relations.[13] This does not appear to offer solace to socialist ideologues.

Philosophical Arguments

One cannot go far in examining socialism without coming to grips with its unfortunate philosophic faultlines. Millions of Canadians have gone through this exercise, and doubtless there will be more. The most objectionable aspect of contemporary social democratic thought in Canada is its preoccupation with redistribution.

The NDP and Redistribution

Redistribution has always been a preoccupation of the NDP. In the 1993 election, for example, the party pledged to halt cuts to federal transfers to provinces for welfare and education, to establish a national day-care system with 600,000 spaces, to expand new housing by means of a $100 million program, to expand student loans, and to pay for these programs with simultaneous deficit reduction created by increased corporation and wealth taxes and defence cuts.[14] The NDP has basically deformed the welfare state from a protective mechanism to one aiming at social transformation – most notably, greater equality of income – through redistributive measures.

The Problem with Redistribution

Marc Plattner criticizes the philosophical approach of Rawls and other advocates of redistribution.[15] They tend to ignore the crucial aspect of effort and concentrate simply on redistribution of income and wealth; but it is unfair to allocate equal benefits to individuals who have shared costs (labour or effort) unequally. Even the unequally endowed should have to make an equal effort to justify their sharing in community benefits, but this is not a part of the redistribution philosophy. Neither is the contention that harder work justifies greater reward. As well, the unequal distribution of natural talent or ability, even though it is arbitrary, should not be considered a common asset and the resulting benefits shared, because any other formula is bound to be just as arbitrary. There is also a fundamental logical inconsistency in the difference principle. (The difference principle is explained in Chapter 11.) Allowing an economic incentive to the wealthier to maximize income by a great amount if the benefits of the poorer also increase would move the system away from equality and toward wealth maximization – which is unavoidable in any case. Another consideration is that the redistribution ethic is not self-executing; it is subject to the political forum, where every citizen votes in accordance with self-interest.

Last, the accountability requirements that come with the disbursements of public money are bound to require intrusions into the details of private lives. "It is difficult," says Plattner, "to see how the private sphere can retain its autonomy when wealth is regarded as communal."[16] Most of these arguments could be applied rather effortlessly and accurately to the NDP, especially at the federal level.

The Canadian public has never endorsed the redistribution goal, except to a limited degree on a regional basis. The defeat of the Charlottetown Accord, with its "social and economic union" charter offering heavy hints about redistributional equity, is but one example of this.

International Lessons

The lessons from an international perspective are of a different nature than supporters of social democracy would offer. They focus not so much on party dynamics and more on the effects of the international political economy.

The Effects of Globalization

The phenomenon of globalization presents a potent threat to social democracy both in Canada and around the world. This trend toward world markets for production, sourcing, and labour has harmful implications for the very instrument that the social democrats place so much faith in, that is, the nation-state. By the end of the 1980s, Patricia Marchak argues, the nation-state was relatively powerless before the transnational corporation, which extended the meaning of private property to include aspects other than the traditional fixed natural assets or industrial assets.

> Over the post-war era, and especially since about the mid-1960s, property rights have been claimed and effectively extended to non-material things. The right to a return on investment, the right to profits, and the right to move capital out of regions where it has accumulated were among these. Such rights exceeded their territorial location. Governments that are fixed in space and property rights that exceed that space no longer form a coherent political and economic unity.[17]

282 Canadian Political Debates

The standard social democratic response to this phenomenon, indeed, the response of Marchak herself, is to extend controls over capital at the international level. However attractive this is in theory, the fact remains that the possibility of such a regime being established is remote indeed.

The Free Trade Issue

The free trade issue has shown how irrelevant the NDP is to the debate on responses to international economics. The shortcomings of the party's economic policy were admitted even by party insiders. Andrew Jackson notes that in the 1988 election in the party "there was no consensus over a coherent alternative to the neoconservative project of growth through continental economic integration and wholesale deregulation. Indeed, many in the leadership believed that the NDP had so little credibility on economic policy that economic issues, including free trade, were best avoided entirely."[18] In fact, this was what happened as the party chose to emphasize a bland "ordinary Canadians" theme, allowing the Liberals to seize the free trade issue and to grab second place in the polls from the New Democrats.

Unlike European social democrats, who have come to terms with the notion of supranational economic institutions and have even pushed for supranational reforms like charters of economic and social rights, the Canadian NDP has not kept pace with the notion of a borderless world. It based its 1993 election platform on antagonism to NAFTA and failed to ignite public opinion. The public, of course, had already adjusted.

The Swedish Model

Basing one's hope for renewal of the social democratic project internationally on the alleged innovativeness of Swedish social democracy is irrational, essentially because the Swedish welfare state is in the process of substantial modification under the centre-right coalition of Carl Bildt. Compromise measures such as cuts in sickness benefits and housing subsidies, as well as in the level of foreign aid, have been put in place. Given public support for the measures, a planned bout of privatization and tax cuts are yet to come.[19] Many in Sweden think it is high time such measures were enacted, since the Swedes have the world's highest taxes (55 per cent of gross domestic product compared to the European norm of 40 per cent, 42 per cent for Canada, and 34 per cent for the United States) and a general value-added tax of 25 per cent.[20] As well, the significant portions of the welfare state left intact are presenting serious difficulties for the government in its attempt to reduce the country's deficit.

The future of social democracy is a bleak one indeed. Perhaps one would be rash to forecast the total demise of a movement that has been such a major actor in the past. However, given the almost insurmountable obstacles that socialism now faces, it would be doubly rash to forecast the reappearance of anything like its past glories.

Notes

1. Keith Archer, *Political Choices and Electoral Consequences: A Study of Organized Labour and the New Democratic Party* (Montreal and Kingston: McGill-Queen's University Press, 1990), ch. 3.
2. Paul Koring, "Power of unions cut by British party," *Globe and Mail*, October 2, 1993.
3. Francis Fox Piven, "The Decline of Labour Parties: An Overview," in Francis Fox Piven, ed., *Labour Parties in Postindustrial Societies* (New York: Oxford University Press, 1992).
4. *Ibid.*, pp. 8-9.
5. Neil Bradford and Jane Jenson, "Facing Economic Restructuring and Constitutional Renewal: Social Democracy Adrift in Canada," in Piven, ed., *Labour Parties in Postindustrial Societies*, pp. 190-211.
6. See Dennis Gruending, *Promises to Keep: A Political Biography of Allan Blakeney* (Saskatoon: Western Producer Prairie Books, 1990), p. 57.
7. Bradford and Jenson, "Facing Economic Restructuring," p. 202.
8. John Richards, "The NDP in the Constitutional Drama," in Douglas Brown and Robert Young, eds., *Canada: The State of the Federation, 1992* (Kingston, Ont.: Queen's University Institute of Intergovernmental Relations, 1992), pp. 159-82.
9. Ronald Manzer, *Public Policies and Political Development in Canada* (Toronto: University of Toronto Press, 1985), p. 188. Manzer (p. 13) defines a public philosophy as "a set of political ideas and beliefs that enjoy widespread acceptance in a political community and serve as principles to guide and justify government decisions."

10. *Ibid.*, p. 72.
11. H.D. Forbes, "Hartz-Horowitz at Twenty: Nationalism, Toryism and Socialism in Canada and the United States," *Canadian Journal of Political Science*, XX, 2 (June, 1987), p. 314.
12. Kenneth McRae, "The Structure of Canadian History," in Louis Hartz *et al.*, *The Founding of New Societies* (Toronto: Longmans, 1964), p. 273.
13. Roger Gibbins and Neil Nevitte, "Canadian Political Ideology: A Comparative Analysis," *Canadian Journal of Political Science*, XVIII, 3 (September, 1985), 577-98. They said these issues were "not easily or traditionally organized through the left-right optic" (p. 598). It must be noted that the survey sample was limited: it included 364 senior American undergraduates surveyed in 1979 and 558 senior Canadian undergraduates surveyed in 1983.
14. "A Voter's guide to the issues," *Globe and Mail*, October 2, 1993, p. A5; "Where the major players stand," *Maclean's*, October 18, 1993, p. 29.
15. Marc F. Plattner, "The Welfare State vs. The Redistributive State," *The Public Interest*, 55 (1979), pp. 28-48.
16. *Ibid.*, p. 47.
17. M. Patricia Marchak, *The Integrated Circus: The New Right and the Restructuring of Global Markets* (Montreal and Kingston: McGill-Queen's University Press, 1991), p. 262.
18. Andrew Jackson, "The Last, Best Left?" *Studies in Political Economy*, 37 (Spring, 1992), pp. 162-163.
19. Peter Cook, "Requiem for the Welfare State," *Globe and Mail*, October 3, 1992.
20. *Ibid.* Cook bases his figures on OECD reports.

PART SEVEN

Are Canada's Interests Served by North American Economic Integration?

The question of the appropriate degree of economic integration with other countries has been one of the most controversial issues in the history of Canada. In fact, the issue even predates the founding of modern-day Canada; British and colonial politicians had to struggle with the question of the American economic giant to the south a century and a half ago. The arguments for and against increased economic integration tend to fall into predictable categories: trade considerations, economic benefits, international development, and Canadian national integrity.

The arguments presented here will be in more summary form for the Canada-U.S. Free Trade Agreement (FTA) than for the North American Free Trade Agreement (NAFTA). The FTA debate is becoming more of historical than of practical interest, but NAFTA, with its broad accession clause, has the possibility to

285

generate a new debate on trade issues every time a new member seeks to join the agreement.

The Different Forms of Regional Economic Integration

There are many types of economic integration, all of which can be seen as parts of a continuum of options arranged according to the degree of integration and co-ordination of national economic policies. It should be added that these forms of integration are explicitly sanctioned by Article XXIV of the General Agreement on Tariffs and Trade (GATT).

* A *free trade area* is a comprehensive agreement between countries for the elimination of all trade barriers of a tariff and non-tariff nature on almost all goods and services. Members of such an area may levy their own tariff rates and impose other restrictions on goods from third countries (non-partner countries). Such agreements also typically allow members to restrict movements of capital and labour within the trade area.

* A *customs union* is a free trade area whose partners are united against external trade rivals. Member countries agree to remove all barriers to trade in goods and services at the same time as establishing a common trade policy (tariffs and related matters) against third countries.

* A *common market* is a customs union with freedom of movement of capital and labour added. Common markets approximate the type of economic union that most federal countries have, but allow their members to retain significant political sovereignty.

* A *monetary or currency union* is a common market sharing a single currency and subject to the monetary policy of a central bank and possible harmonization of broad economic policies.

* An *economic union* is the most advanced or integrated form of union, calling for the harmonization of almost all national economic policies and laws. Its inner logic leads in the direction of advanced political union.

Canadians have never seriously considered the more extreme forms of economic integration because of their wish to retain the independence that would be lost in the more advanced forms of regional economic unity. Even the idea of free trade has seemed too radical a departure from traditional trade patterns. The remarkable fact about Canada is that until very recently it has been the exception to the world-wide tendency for regional trade groupings of various degrees. Until it entered the Canada-U.S. Free Trade Agreement Canada was the only advanced trading nation without secure access to a trading bloc of more than 100 million people.

Debate still ensues about the reasons why Canada entered the FTA in 1989, after such a long history of resisting the notion of comprehensive free trade. One rationale often mentioned was to avoid aggressive U.S. trade policy. Growing protectionism in the U.S., due to trade deficits and unemployment, was putting U.S. market access at risk for Canadians. Dholakia argues that regional economic integration occurs over time as trade and investment links become more intensive between countries. A transnational coalition of core, ascendant business interests becomes impatient with the expensive trade restraints between them, pushes for a formal free trade area in which they stand to gain enormously, and acts in co-operation with political champions of their cause in a "parallel political marketplace": this was how the FTA, NAFTA, and the EC came about. [1] Richardson attributes the introduction of the FTA partially to the increasing strength of Canadian finance capital and partially to the increasing weakness of Canadian labour and agriculture. [2] William Watson says there is some merit to the argument that the Conservatives "stumbled into it, more or less unwittingly": the options of the status quo, sectoral free trade, and a new GATT round had all been foreclosed by the time they got into office in 1984. [3]

One other alternative explanation is simply that Canadian public opinion swings back and forth between desires for more and for less economic integration with the Americans. Canadians have been fundamentally ambivalent about their economic relationship with the United States. The weight of integrationist sentiment gradually wins out, however. Table 1 shows how the pendulum of public opinion has carried trade policy with it over the last century and a half.

Table 1
The Pendulum of Canada–U.S. Bilateral Trade Relations, 1854–1989

Closer Continental Economic Integration	*Less Continental Economic Integration*
RECIPROCITY TREATY OF 1854 The 1854 treaty established free trade between the BNA colonies and the United States in a small range of primary goods such as timber, grain, fish, meat, dairy goods, flour, and coal. The deal excluded manufactured items. The treaty was negotiated by the British as a logical consequence of their adoption of a free trade policy in 1846 and the ending of the system of imperial preferences. As permitted under the terms of the treaty, the U.S. abrogated the treaty on March 17, 1865, effective March, 1866. U.S. hostility had derived from, surprisingly, the Cayley–Galt tariff increases (1858 and 1859) on manufactured goods, as well as alleged British sympathy with the South in the U.S. Civil War, 1861–65. DRAFT RECIPROCITY TREATY OF 1874 This stillborn treaty involved free trade in the primary products covered earlier by the 1854 treaty and also manufactured products of an extremely broad variety: agricultural goods, wood and leather manufacture, locomotives, steel, paper, and others. The British government approved the treaty but not the U.S. Senate, which was convinced to reject it by protectionist business forces in U.S.	BRITISH NORTH AMERICA ACT, 1867 In addition to political and military advantages, a federal union offered important potential economic gains. Even before the Americans ended the Reciprocity Treaty, its precarious nature had been recognized by colonial politicians. Its termination left two alternatives: either renegotiate with Congress or hasten the progress of the Confederation talks begun in 1864. The former suffered a setback in late 1865 when Canadian emissaries Galt and Howland had to refuse an offer of a free list of worthless items in exchange for American access to inshore fisheries. Britain showed no willingness to reopen preferential tariffs. Interprovincial commerce was the best available option. Federation would allow for an internal ''common market,'' the opening of new territories for resources and markets, and the financing of transportation infrastructure useful for any future trading arrangement in America. THE NATIONAL POLICY OF 1879 American protectionism engendered Canadian protectionism. Canada undertook a policy of import substitution for the next half-century (with some deviation). Tariffs were raised to protect Canadian producers and jobs, along with a shorter-term emphasis on immigration and railway-building. An important effect of the tariff policy was the impetus given to the establishment of branch plants and subsidiaries by foreign companies, who thereby avoided the tariff wall.

Table 1 *(continued)*

Closer Continental Economic Integration	Less Continental Economic Integration
THE RECIPROCITY AGREEMENT OF 1911 Based on entreaties from western farmers and responding to the historical free trade sympathies within the Liberal Party itself (the Liberals since the mid-1800s had been free-traders and had run on the issue in the 1891 general election), Prime Minister Laurier negotiated free trade with the Americans. This time, the Americans had made the initial overture. The agreement included tariff-free entry on many natural products and substantially reduced duties on U.S. tractors and farm implements entering Canada. The agreement was largely aimed at the agricultural sector and expected to be relatively non-controversial.	THE RECIPROCITY ELECTION OF 1911 The 1911 election was to prove a huge symbolic victory for those Canadians wishing less formal economic integration with the U.S. Ontario businessmen led a successful public relations campaign against the agreement, warning of losing the imperial tie as a result of a continental trade arrangement. However, self-interest was a powerful motivator. Central Canadian business had gained by the National Policy. It was afraid the policy would be in danger if reciprocity were expanded to a wider range of goods in the future. They were also mistrustful of the Americans' relative commitment to a long-term trade partnership.
THE CANADA–U.S. TRADE AGREEMENTS OF 1935 AND 1938 The 1935 and 1938 trade agreements amounted to tariff reductions rather than free trade. Once again, U.S. trade action spurred a counter-reaction in Canada. The trade agreements were a response to depression-era protectionism in America and marked the first tentative steps toward the end of the National Policy as the dominant model for industrial policy. They were the first successful comprehensive agreements between Canada and the U.S. since the Reciprocity Treaty of 1854. The 1935 deal rolled the tariff walls back to the 1920 *status quo ante*, but was constrained by the System of Empire Preferences. The 1938 deal narrowed the preference system for British manufactured goods in Canada and Canadian natural products in Britain, and lowered tariffs for American manufactured goods in Canada in return for increased access to the U.S. However, the United Kingdom was still a more important trading partner than the U.S. with 38 per cent of Canadian exports going to the former and 23 per cent to the latter in 1938.	THE REFUSAL OF FREE TRADE, 1948 As a recognition of the new post-war trade patterns – decreased trade with the United Kingdom and increased trade with the United States – and in the specific context of an exchange rate crisis, Canada entertained the idea of free trade with the United States. Tariffs would have been removed on a wide variety of goods. Prime Minister Mackenzie King decided not to proceed with the agreement for a number of considerations, not the least of which were the fears of radical change and of antagonizing pro-British sympathy in Canada.

Table 1   *(continued)*

Closer Continental Economic Integration	*Less Continental Economic Integration*
POSTWAR SECTORAL EXPEDIENTS After World War Two, Canada began a period of experimentation with forms of trade that offered sectoral advantages but stopped short of comprehensive integration with the U.S. (a) *Defense production-sharing agreement*: In 1958 Prime Minister John Diefenbaker negotiated an agreement with the Americans to allow Canadian suppliers to make bids for U.S. defence contracts and avoid American tariffs on defence goods. (b) *The Auto Pact of 1965*: The Canada–U.S. Automotive Agreement (Auto Pact), beginning in 1965, allowed for a "sectoral" free trade in automobiles and automobile parts. Some have termed it "managed trade," since U.S. autos could enter Canada duty-free providing certain safeguards for Canadian production were met.	POSTWAR DIVERSIFICATION ATTEMPTS Canada became alarmed at the growing dependence on trade ties with the United States. In 1955, 60 per cent of Canada's exports went to the U.S. and 73 per cent of imports came from the U.S. It attempted to offset this dependency, but not forcefully enough. (a) *Diefenbaker's diversion*: In 1957 Prime Minister Diefenbaker promised to divert 15 per cent of Canada's trade with the U.S. to Britain instead. The patent unworkability of this policy doomed it. (b) *Trudeau's "Third Option"*: In 1972, the Trudeau government reviewed its trade options and decided on a "third option" (trade diversification) apart from the status quo and apart from closer economic integration with the United States under free trade. It objected to free trade because it tended toward a customs or economic union; and these would threaten Canadian independence and reduce manoeuvrability in trading with third countries. In practice the major effect of the policy was an attempt to develop a tie with the European Economic Community (later the European Community), but only nominal progress was achieved.

Table 1 *(continued)*

Closer Continental Economic Integration	*Less Continental Economic Integration*
GENERAL AGREEMENT ON TARIFFS AND TRADE (GATT) Another post-war development that brought Canada and the U.S. closer together economically was, ironically, not a bilateral but a multilateral agreement. The GATT was signed in 1947 by Canada and twenty-two other nations (now 108) as an international commitment to trade liberalization. Since 1948 there have been eight rounds of negotiations, the most recent being the Uruguay Round, which began in 1986 and ended in 1993. The effect of the GATT has been to reduce tariffs substantially across the world. As a result, Canada–U.S. trade has also experienced gradual lowering of tariffs. By 1987, 95 per cent of Canadian imports from the U.S. were entering either duty-free or at less than a 5 per cent tariff rate; 80 per cent of Canadian exports to the U.S. were entering duty-free. The two economies continued to become more intertwined. By the late eighties, 75 per cent of Canada's exports went to the U.S. and 80 per cent of its imports were from the U.S., forming 25 per cent of total American exports. The pressure for a free trade agreement grew from this extreme degree of economic dependence.	THE SECTORAL FREE TRADE INITIATIVE By 1983 the Liberal government had become convinced of the inevitability of close economic ties with the United States. However, it wanted to adopt a more incremental approach to minimize adjustment costs. The government's position was outlined in a White Paper, *Canadian Trade Policy for the 1980s*: it would pursue sectoral free trade – in specific industries. Canada and the United States announced a joint study of sectoral free trade in steel, farm machinery, urban transit equipment, and computer services. There was no further progress in this matter for a variety of reasons: the government changed, Article XXIV of the GATT did not provide for sectoral trade, the Americans were indifferent, and "non-included" industries would have found the deal unjust.

SOURCES: Canada, Library of Parliament, Research Branch Economics Division, *The Idea of Canada–U.S. Free Trade* (Backgrounder) (Ottawa: 23 January 1985); Canada, Royal Commission on the Economic Union and Development Prospects for Canada, *Report* (Ottawa: Minister of Supply and Services, 1985); Economic Council of Canada, *Venturing Forth: An Assessment of the Canada–U.S. Free Trade Agreement* (Ottawa: Minister of Supply and Services, 1988); J.L. Granatstein, "Freer Trade and Politics," in Norman Hillmer, ed., *Partners Nevertheless: Canadian–American Relations in the Twentieth Century* (Toronto: Copp Clark Pitmar, 1989); Richard G. Lipsey and Murray G. Smith, *Taking the Initiative: Canada's Trade Options in a Turbulent World* (Toronto: C.D. Howe Institute, May, 1985).

The Canada-United States Free Trade Agreement

The FTA is a comprehensive agreement covering items that are standard to free trade agreements across the world, plus some others that are not. It included the standard measures such as tariff elimination and trade dispute resolution mechanisms. However, it was unlike the standard arrangements in that it included a "services" provision and was a departure from some practices of GATT, under which it operated. As well, it stirred controversy. Table 2 delineates the important issues of the FTA debate.

Tariffs. The agreement in article 401 provides for a three-stage reduction of all tariff barriers between Canada and the United States over a ten-year period ending January 1, 1998. The ten-year period is to allow the industries in the two countries to adjust to the new trading environment. Neither party may increase any existing customs duties or introduce new ones on goods "originating" in the other's territory except as provided for in the agreement. (Because of this terminology, strict conditions about "rules of origin" for goods have been added.)

In light of successive waves of GATT-inspired tariff reductions that have also reduced barriers between Canada and the U.S., the need for these tariff reductions may seem surprising. Tariffs, however, had not been universally reduced, and there were still some relatively high barriers in areas that had been considered sensitive to foreign competition by both countries in the past. The U.S. provided barriers to trade in petrochemicals and metal alloys and Canada did so for textiles and apparel. In some cases there had also been escalating tariffs on products with a resource base, meant to discourage further processing in the home country.

Rules of origin. Rules of origin provisions are included in recognition of the fact that this is a free trade agreement, not a customs union. Both countries continue to apply their own tariffs against imports from third countries. Since there could be a potential threat of either partner using cheap inputs from other countries to give an unfair advantage to its bilateral trade, specific rules were devised. These rules of origin identify the national source of the good.

There will be preferential treatment – or "area treatment" as the

Table 2
The Debate on the Canada–U.S. Free Trade Agreement

Pro-FTA	Anti-FTA
1. The alternative model to regional integration is nationalist protectionism: this is an inadequate model. Protectionist tariffs (and other barriers) encourage inefficient economies and discourage economies of scale, are a tax on consumers, perpetuate comparative disadvantage, and reflect non-economic criteria such as the power of organized groups.	1. One can oppose the FTA and not be protectionist *per se*. Nationalists see the need for a comprehensive industrial policy that would guide trade, rather than the other way around. Trade barriers would fall after the restructuring of the Canadian economy. Local research and development and performance requirements for multinationals are necessary first.
2. Trade diversion is unlikely to occur in the FTA area merely because of tariff reasons. Many variables are considered in investment decisions.	2. There could be a diversion of trade once tariff barriers are lowered. The incentive for branch plants to locate in Canada will be gone.
3. Government intervention has generally promoted inefficient economic policies in both the public and private sectors. The market orientation of the FTA is beneficial. For example, it will encourage investment in Canada and avoid disastrous energy policies like the National Energy Policy.	3. Comparative advantage can be manipulated through the exercise of a number of policies that involve public-private partnerships. The FTA guts many of these options, for example, foreign investment controls and government procurement preferences.
4. Since provincial governments were integrally involved in the drafting of the FTA, it was not reflective of any one governing party's agenda. Democracy reigns, in fact: the agreement can be abrogated with six months' notice.	4. The FTA is undemocratic. It entrenches a right-wing agenda and places it beyond the reach of a so-called sovereign Parliament.
5. The dispute settlement provisions offer Canada, and indeed the world, an important advance in international trade disputes. The FTA is a model for the GATT reform of dispute settlement. It replaces lengthy judicial proceedings with ten-month (maximum) binational panels, which will save litigants both trouble and expense. They will be more objective as well. It is unrealistic to expect a mere free trade agreement to result in derogations of sovereignty, like higher forms of integration, so this was the best situation possible. *Something* had to be done by Canada in the face of rising U.S. protectionism in the 1980s and beyond. As for the danger of "subsidy wars" threatening Canadian social programs, this is an unrealistic fear: GATT permits programs of universal application.	5. The dispute settlement provisions are inadequate. They are not binding; they reflect only a moral commitment to abide by one's own trade laws. They will involve increasing levels of bureaucratization. The definitions of "subsidies" and "dumping" are missing; hence there is an invitation to arbitrariness, especially on the Americans' part. The non-definition of subsidies raises the possibility that social programs and regional development programs could be included as subsidies.

accord refers to it – to goods obtained completely from North American sources. Area treatment will also be given to those third-country goods that incorporate significant Canadian or American content. To achieve this, they will have to have been significantly altered in one or both of the two countries, according to procedures outlined in the annexes to the agreement.

National treatment. National treatment means equal treatment: that the goods of either country will not be discriminated against once they are imported into the other. This does not mean that the goods necessarily have to be treated identically in the other country, but simply that there is no replacement of eliminated trade barriers by new internal arrangements of a tax or regulatory nature that are not also applied to the domestic good in question.

Agriculture. Agriculture is given slightly different arrangements. Like other sectors of the economy, agricultural products are subjected to article 401's schedule of a ten-year phase-in of tariff reductions. However, there is a "snapback provision" in article 702 that allows the temporary restoration of tariffs on fresh fruits and vegetables, when prices are depressed, over a period of twenty years. There was to be a mutual lifting of export subsidies on bilateral trade in agriculture and of controls established previously under meat import laws. However, as befit a politically sensitive sector, there was allowance for the continuance of marketing systems in dairy and poultry, price support and income stabilization programs, and certain income controls.

Energy. The most important energy products for the two countries are oil, gas, electricity, and uranium. They are subject to some changes intended to offset previous policy directions in Canada. The previous Liberal government had introduced a "two-price system" for oil and gas and had also undertaken a series of export restrictions as part of a nationalistic industrial strategy; one example of the latter was the export tax introduced under the National Energy Policy.

Article 903 states that there should be no export taxes for energy unless they apply domestically as well. Export restrictions are permitted but, under articles 409 and 904, are to be so arranged that they do not disrupt the normal pattern of trade between the two countries. The agreement introduces a "proportionality rule" to guide the restrictions on exports of energy products between the two countries. It states that one country must allow the other one access to the same proportion of total supply of the good that it had in the thirty-six-month period before the imposition of the restriction. The total amount of energy may be curtailed, but up to the same proportion must be exported. The Agreement on an International Energy Program is to govern the provisions in Chapter Nine on energy with regard to energy-sharing in conditions of national shortages. Licences, fees, or other measures are not allowed as methods of elevating export prices above domestic ones if the rationale for this is conservation or price stabilization.

There are other energy provisions as well. One relates to uranium, where in article 902 the Americans agree to eliminate their restrictions on the enrichment of Canadian uranium and the Canadians agree to eliminate their requirement that uranium shipped to the United States first be processed in Canada. Oil and gas exploration incentives are kept. The countries commit themselves to consultation on regulatory policy that may affect energy trade.

Automotive products. The FTA provided for the continuation of the Auto Pact, a Canadian-American agreement established in 1965 to provide for secure, duty-free access of new automobiles and auto parts. The Americans permitted duty-free entry to Canadian auto goods for which at least 50 per cent of full invoice cost was of North American content. Canada could import vehicles duty-free if Canadian content and value-added requirements were met; foreign producers manufacturing in Canada could import vehicles and parts duty-free if they exported amounts equivalent to the amounts imported and also increased Canadian value-added. In the FTA, the Auto Pact was retained but the membership in it was frozen at the "Big Three" North American automakers. The Canadian duty remissions for value-added by foreign producers were to be gradually eliminated but value-added commitments by the Big Three were retained. Assemblers will have to use a higher percentage of North American parts: the 50 per cent of invoice cost provision was dropped and replaced with one stipulating 50 per cent of direct production costs. This amounts to about a 70 per cent requirement on the old basis.[4]

Services, investment, and temporary entry. These matters are dealt with as a unit both because they are ground-breaking departures from standard free trade arrangements and because they are closely cross-referenced to each other as well as to other sections of the FTA. Article 1402 applies the practice of national treatment to the providers of commercial services. *Covered services* include that broad cross-section of transactions that are necessary complements to the production, sale, and distribution of goods. Examples of these include the work of engineers, accountants, financial experts, data processors, maintenance providers, and so forth. *Non-covered services* include those relating to transportation, basic telecommunications, medical and dental care, lawyers' services, and such government-provided services as health, education, and social services. National treatment in services does not mean, as noted above, identical treatment, only non-discriminatory treatment, and covers only new regulations in the service area. Governments will change immigration regulations to ensure mutual access to markets by nationals engaging in business travel and after-sales service.

In addition, the negotiators perceived a *liberal investment regime* to be necessary to complement the achievements made in the goods and services areas. National treatment is to be accorded in section 1602 to both Canadian and American investors in the establishment of new businesses. Once established, each country's set of Canadian- or American-owned corporations will be regulated according to the same rules; and the agreement forbids investment-related performance requirements like local content standards. There was to be a higher threshold for review of direct acquisitions of existing businesses by Canadian regulators: section 1607 targeted it as $150 million by 1992. Review of indirect acquisitions (buying of subsidiaries) is completely ended by the FTA.

Institutional and dispute settlement mechanisms. Canadians did not get the full extent of what they had desired in the Free Trade Agreement. What Canadians aimed for was a supranational institution, something like the Commission of the European Community, which could give independent judgements on trade disputes between the two countries. Canada also wanted protection from the increasingly troublesome American use of *countervailing* and *anti-dumping duties,* which protect against unfair subsidies and against a country selling goods in a foreign country at a price lower than that prevailing in the domestic market. Blunting of these instruments, which were quite in tune with GATT guidelines against unfair trading practices, was intended to ensure security of access. Instead of absolute security of access, however, Canada got relative security of access. As well, the two countries agreed to delay final determination of trade remedy laws until a period five to seven years hence.

What was established was a regime that distinguished between general dispute settlement, on the one hand, and special arrangements for countervailing and anti-dumping duties, on the other. For general disputes – that is, those arising from interpretation and implementation – Chapter 18 of the agreement establishes an institution called the Canada-United States Trade Commission and a series of procedures. The Commission itself is a ministerial-level consultation mechanism that holds annual meetings on an alternating basis in the two countries. Should negotiations and consultation fail, the Commission establishes compulsory arbitration with binding effect over interpretation of safeguard measures, or mutually agreed upon binding arbitration by a five-member binational panel, or an advisory panel to feed suggested solutions to the Commission. The so-called binding arbitration can in fact be ignored by one of the parties, giving the other the right to suspend the application of equivalent benefits.

For the special cases of countervailing and anti-dumping duties, Chapter 19 of the agreement replaces the much longer process of judicial review by domestic courts with review by a *binational appeal panel,* which must render its decision within a 315-day limit. Like the binational arbitration panels above, the appeal panel is a five-member body, with each country selecting two members and the Commission choosing the fifth member. The panel has the responsibility to ascertain whether or not relevant domestic trade remedy laws were correctly and fairly applied by the national authorities (National Revenue or the Canadian Import Tribunal, in Canada, and the Department of Commerce or the International Trade Commission, in the U.S.). There is also provision for an *extraordinary challenge procedure,* made up of judges, which can investigate conflicts of interest or manifest cases of injustice by the appeal panel.

The North American Free Trade Agreement

The North American Free Trade Agreement, with its provision of a market of 360 million people, establishes the largest trade zone in the world. It essentially applies the FTA arrangements to a wider continental arrangement involving Canada, the United States, and

Mexico, but it foresees the possibility of further partners joining under its "accession clause." Under NAFTA, Mexico will have to make the largest changes, since the other two partners have adjusted trade policy substantially already under the FTA. However, there are some qualitative changes in the new deal.

FTA-NAFTA Comparison

Despite their obvious similarities, the FTA and NAFTA feature some significant differences:

- NAFTA has an "accession clause" that allows other countries or groups of countries to join the agreement, subject to the approval and conditions of the NAFTA participants in place. The FTA did not have such a provision.
- NAFTA includes protection of "intellectual property rights" on a national treatment basis. This means the initiation of commitments by all members in the areas of copyrights, patents, and trademarks, among others, and the elimination of any discrimination in favour of local patent rights. The FTA had no such arrangements, although some critics argued that some "side deals" like that regarding pharmaceuticals amounted to the same thing.
- NAFTA allows governments to override trade agreements in order to protect the environment as long as doing so does not amount to a hidden trade restriction. The FTA had no such provision.
- The rules of origin for textiles and apparel are more restrictive in NAFTA than they are in the FTA. However, there will be expanded quotas for Canadian apparel and textiles entering the U.S. market that do not meet the North American preference rules.
- The institutional and dispute settlement mechanisms are clearer and more transparent (open) and enjoy much more thoroughgoing and extensive secretariat help under NAFTA.
- Financial services, land transportation, and specialty air services are included for the first time in NAFTA.
- As an innovation in investment matters, the agreement

accords national treatment to investors from NAFTA countries and "most favoured nation" (MFN) treatment to the
investors of other countries. (MFN treatment traditionally
has been a trade measure.)

- The definition of investment is broader in NAFTA, which
  includes portfolio investment as well as foreign direct
  investment. "This is a very important change insofar as it
  extends the coverage of Chapter 11 to an exponentially
  larger value of economic activity than was the case under
  the FTA."[5]

The Canadian government has felt constrained by domestic politics not to deviate too markedly in some areas from the status quo
established under the FTA regime. The similarities between NAFTA
and the FTA are several:

- The agreement retains the exemptions that Canada negotiated under the FTA for cultural industries – publishing,
  film and video, music and sound recording, broadcasting
  and cable – and extends it to Canadian-Mexican relations.
- The FTA commitments about Canadian-American energy
  trade are maintained in NAFTA.
- Neither agreement applies to large-scale export of water
  (i.e., "inter-basin transfers or diversions of water").
- Health and social services are not covered by either agreement. Provincial governments are not required to open
  health-care management systems to NAFTA country
  bidders.
- Neither agreement changes Canadian policy control over
  basic telecommunications.
- The review threshold for direct acquisition of Canadian
  businesses established in the FTA as $150 million is main-
  tained. Mexico has similar arrangements, with its initial
  review threshold set at $25 million and the same ultimate
  threshold as Canada's phased in over ten years.

Contents of NAFTA

Tariffs. The agreement in Article 302 eliminates almost all tariff
barriers between the three countries, in most cases over a transition
period of ten years. The parties will progressively eliminate

the tariffs in five or ten equal annual stages with some particularly trade-sensitive items requiring at least fifteen years. The agreement came into effect on January 1, 1994, and is to be almost fully implemented by 2003. The tariff eliminations only apply, of course, to goods that are North American in terms of agreed-upon rules of origin. Tariff reductions established under the FTA continue as scheduled. The parties could agree to an accelerated schedule for reductions, as they could under the FTA. Safeguards will allow both Canada and Mexico to reimpose duties ("safeguard measures") to counteract import surges.

Rules of origin. NAFTA attempted to establish rules of origin that were clearer and capable of uniform interpretation. Like those in the FTA, they were meant to provide benefits to goods wholly originating in the trade area or, in the case of goods incorporating non-regional materials, having undergone significant alteration in the trade area sufficient to qualify for a change in tariff classification. The preferential duties will be accorded on either of two tests: on the basis of percentage of North American content or on the basis of regional value content. (The latter, in turn, can be decided by either the "transaction value" method or the "net cost" method.) Special arrangements are made for automotive goods and parts, and for textiles and apparel.

National treatment. A commitment to national treatment following the GATT rules is an integral part of NAFTA. Goods exported from one NAFTA country to another will not be discriminated against, on the basis of origin, by the federal or sub-national governments of North America. All three countries may not apply export taxes unless they are also applied to domestic consumption; there are, however, some minor exceptions in the case of shortages of basic goods in Mexico.

Agriculture. NAFTA provides for separate U.S.-Mexico and Canada-Mexico agreements on agricultural goods, while retaining the FTA agriculture provisions. Yet the spirit of the FTA affects even the Canada-Mexico provisions: Canada's import quotas and tariffs, which form an integral part of the supply management system for poultry, eggs, and dairy products, are maintained and are matched by Mexico. Mexico will eliminate import licences and phase out tariffs on a wide variety of goods, making Canadian exports of grains, pork, potatoes, and processed foods particularly favoured.

Both countries retain the right, for ten years, to impose special tariff safeguards against surges in imports of certain categories of fruits and vegetables. All three countries loosely pledge themselves to eventually eliminating export subsidies in the NAFTA area, while the U.S. and Canada understand that they will not subsidize exports to Mexico except where faced with subsidized competition. For adminstration and monitoring purposes, there will be a trilateral commission on agricultural trade and two binational working groups.

Energy. Negotiators tried but failed to establish a North American energy regime that would closely resemble the FTA arrangements. The Mexican constitution prevents the country from accepting private investment in a good percentage of its energy sector. However, some important advances were made in the direction of liberalization. Mexico, like the other two partners, cannot engage in such restrictive trade practices as export taxes, duties, or charges unless they also apply domestically. There are new private investment opportunities in non-basic petrochemical goods and electricity generating facilities. The agreement aims at promoting a stable, non-discriminatory regulatory environment for energy matters by subjecting them to, among other things, the general rules of national treatment. The energy provisions of the FTA continue to pertain in matters relating to Canada-U.S. energy trade.

Automotive products. In the case of automobiles, NAFTA was an effort both to clarify the confusing regulations that had grown up around the administration of the Auto Pact and to open up the protectionist Mexican market. Each country pledged to eliminate duties on imports of North American automotive goods over a ten-year period. In the FTA version of the Auto Pact, of course, there had been a 50 per cent North American direct production cost rule to qualify auto goods for duty-free treatment, but the regulations were interpreted differently by Canadian and American trade officials. The most notable examples were the Honda and GM-CAMI cases of 1991-92 in which American trade officials disputed the contention that cars made in Canada actually qualified for North American status under the FTA. In NAFTA, there are clearer rules of origin for autos and auto parts and improvements in customs procedures to prevent recurrences of similar problems. There is also a hike in the North American content requirement to 62.5 per cent for light vehicles (cars and light trucks) and 60 per cent for other auto goods, introduced in two stages over two years. The protectionist Mexican Auto Decree would end with the transition period, thus permitting the auto parts manufacturers of all three countries to compete on an even footing.

Services and investment. NAFTA broadens the covered services category in the existing Free Trade Agreement to cover a wider variety of services. Transportation services and new types of professional services are included. The Mexican financial services sector will be open to Canadian companies; but the agreement does not open up the American financial services sector any further than it is already. However, the agreement excluded domestic trucking totally within national borders, and continued to exclude basic telecommunications (such as local and long-distance telephone calls), as well as government-provided services.

Institutional and dispute settlement mechanisms. The general institutional framework of the FTA continues, with the provisional aspect becoming a permanent one. There are similar divisions, namely general dispute resolution and special arrangements for countervailing and anti-dumping duties. For *general dispute settlement,* the agreement creates a trilateral trade commission with a permanent secretariat to serve it and its dispute settlement panels. The three countries jointly establish a roster of experts from which they can take members for the panels in an unusual manner designed to promote impartiality: a complainant country selects two roster members from the defendant country, the latter selects two members from the former, and the chair takes the fifth from the non-involved NAFTA country or from a country outside NAFTA. The special arrangements outlined in Chapter 19 of the FTA continue in NAFTA. Now, however, Mexico has also agreed to binational review panels for countervail and anti-dumping actions, rather than relying on judicial review. Each country, as in the FTA, retains the right to amend its own countervail and anti-dumping laws, and such amendments are subject, as in the FTA, to bilateral review and possible retaliation in the form of comparable legislation, regulation, or even termination of the agreement.

Finally, there is a new provision in NAFTA that allows for the creation of a *special committee to safeguard the panel process.* At the request of a complainant country, which alleges that another's domestic law has prevented the establishment, decision-making, or implementation of a panel's decisions, the special committee may investigate. A successful challenge may result in the suspension of the binational panel system by the complainant country if no rectification of the situation is forthcoming.

The Side Deals and After

NAFTA became embroiled in the dynamics of electoral politics, and a number of "side deals" and other arrangements emerged as compromise solutions to political problems. In the 1992 American election, presidential candidate Bill Clinton refused to accept the Bush version of the agreement without qualitative supplements on labour, environmental standards, and import surges (rapid increases in imports). This stand was meant to attract Democratic supporters who were either lukewarm or cold to the deal and to reposition the Democrats as qualified free-traders. In Canada, Kim Campbell became the new Conservative Prime Minister on June 25, 1993, after a Conservative leadership convention and found herself at the tail end of a series of tri-level negotiations on the side deals; as for the main deal itself, former Prime Minister Brian Mulroney had ensured its passage through the Conservative-dominated Parliament earlier that month. Her main concern became to minimize the impact of these side deals on Canadian sovereignty and trade, an aim not unlike that of President Salinas of Mexico. In August, 1993, the three governments agreed to side deals on the environment and on labour standards and import surges, the texts of which were released some time later.

The deals were not part of the main NAFTA agreement, enjoined the parties to obey their own laws, and were asymmetrical in some aspects. The North American Agreement on Environmental Co-operation established a tri-national North American Commission for Environmental Co-operation composed of a council, a secretariat, and a joint public advisory committee. The North American Agreement on Labour Co-operation established a tri-national North American Commission for Labour Co-operation that, like the environmental commission, had a council and secretariat, but it had no advisory committee, opting instead for a system of national administrative offices in each country. There was a qualified provision in the environment agreement allowing non-governmental organizations or persons to submit complaints of non-enforcement of environmental law to the commission for investigation, but in the labour agreement only governments can set analogous labour law investigations in progress. The dispute resolution provisions prescribe a detailed series of consultations that can end in an arbitration panel decision. A panel's job is to adjudicate disputes arising from a country's alleged failure to comply with its own labour and environmental laws and to recommend appropriate fines against governments or, if necessary, sanctions. Trade sanctions (quotas or tariffs) may apply to Mexico or the United States; but Canada is to be subject only to fines established by the relevant Commission and enforced by a Canadian federal court. Another special treatment for Canada is that the federal government cannot be held responsible for environmental or labour matters falling under provincial jurisdiction; conversely, it cannot normally challenge the other countries on matters outside its jurisdiction. The only labour matters liable to be brought forward for dispute resolution are those relating to occupational health and safety, child labour, and minimum wage technical standards. The rights to organize, to bargain collectively, and to strike are outside the sphere of both investigation and arbitration in the labour side deal.

Prime Minister Campbell called a general election for October 25. Trade, although not as central an issue in 1993 as it had been in 1988, was still a matter on which the Liberals under Jean Chrétien thought they could distance themselves from the government. Very early in the campaign the Liberals released what they referred to as the "Red Book" of campaign promises. It promised a review of the labour and environmental side deals and noted that their subject matter was best dealt with in a larger context. Accordingly, it committed the party to renegotiating the FTA and NAFTA to achieve a subsidies code, an anti-dumping code, a more effective dispute resolution mechanism, and the same energy protection as had been accorded Mexico.[6]

Not surprisingly, the new Chrétien government found the Americans unwilling to negotiate on the main or side deals. Instead, a month of negotiations resulted in tepid joint statements by all three NAFTA partners on subsidies, anti-dumping, and water exports, and a unilateral Canadian pledge on energy. The three made a non-binding pledge to establish a code on subsidies and anti-dumping by December 31, 1995; but, as U.S. Trade Representative Mickey Kantor pointed out, U.S. participation did not commit it to "any particular outcome."[7] The partners also clarified that NAFTA did not compel a country to export water resources or to exploit them for commercial use. The Canadian government pointedly issued its own declaration, stating that "in the event of shortages or in order to conserve Canada's exhaustible energy resources, the government will interpret and apply the NAFTA in a way which maximizes energy security for Canadians" and if necessary would establish strategic reserves.[8] This declaration was just as pointedly discounted by various sources as having no legal bearing on either the FTA or NAFTA.[9]

Notes

1. Nikhilesh Dholakia, "Integration of Markets and the Interplay of Interests: Understanding the Discourse about North American Free Trade Area," *Canadian Journal of Administrative Sciences,* 9, 2 (June, 1992), pp. 106-15.

2. R. Jack Richardson, "Free Trade: Why did it happen?" *Canadian Review of Sociology and Anthropology,* 29, 3 (August, 1992), pp. 307-28.

3. William Watson, "Canada-U.S. Free Trade: Why Now?" *Canadian Public Policy,* 13, 3 (1987), pp. 337-49.

4. Canada, External Affairs Canada, *The Canada-U.S. Free Trade Agreement: Synopsis* (Ottawa: External Affairs, December 12, 1987), p. 33.

5. Alan M. Rugman and Michael Gestrin, "Foreign Investment and NAFTA," *Policy Options* (January-February, 1993), p. 33.

6. Liberal Party of Canada, *Creating Opportunity: The Liberal Plan for Canada* (Ottawa: Liberal Party of Canada, 1993), p. 24.

7. "Liberals concede NAFTA fight," *Globe and Mail,* December 3, 1993.

8. *Ibid.*

9. "Cabinet set to okay NAFTA," *Globe and Mail,* December 2, 1993.

Chapter 13

The Value of NAFTA
to the Canadian Economy

The North American deal is thoroughly in keeping with progressive trade practices around the world and will assure Canadian prosperity for many years to come. The North American Free Trade Agreement has many of the same arguments in its favour as did the Canada-U.S. Free Trade Agreement. However, we shall not repeat them here, but instead concentrate on those particular benefits that flow from NAFTA. They relate to international trade patterns, economic benefits, international development, and Canadian national integrity.

International Trade Considerations

International considerations weigh heavily on Canadian trade policy-makers. These include several important areas, most notably the demonstration effect of NAFTA, the hub-and-spoke analysis, the role of other trade blocs, and the globalization phenomenon in general.

Demonstration Effect

It is sometimes maintained by opponents that NAFTA amounts to a regional trade bloc that will have the effect of discouraging global trade liberalization. This is not true. If anything, the agreement has an important demonstration effect: it shows the partners' support and encouragement for larger forms of economic integration. Such integration could be endangered if NAFTA diverted trade from the larger environment; if it harmed current efforts at multilateralism; or if it raised existing barriers to trade. However, the access clause is a guard against trade diversion, offering an inclusive rather than exclusive approach to trade, possibly hemispheric in nature; the GATT encourages comprehensive bilateral free trade, and the World Trade Organization that Uruguay Round negotiators established is based on the bilateral panel model of the FTA; and the negotiators, with the notable exception of the Auto Pact, resisted the temptation to misuse the rules of origin to shore up powerful economic interests. [1]

Hub and Spoke

Forestalling a hub-and-spoke trading pattern in the Western Hemisphere is another pressing consideration for Canada. One possibility is that the U.S. could become the predominant trade power – or hub – with Canada and other countries establishing separate – or spoke – arrangements with the U.S. on terms that are uneven and of benefit predominantly to the Americans. Now, with both the United States and Canada on an even footing vis-à-vis Mexico and with the access clause written in such a way as to preclude renegotiating the agreement every time a new partner wants to enter, Canadian interests are served.

Once having negotiated the FTA, it was largely common sense for Canadian policy-makers to ensure that Mexico did not get any better access to the U.S. market than Canada did, and, for that matter, that Canada would have equal access to Mexico as that accorded to the United States. A spoke arrangement was a distinct possibility, because when talks on a U.S.-Mexico deal began in the summer of 1990, Canada was not automatically considered a possible partner; in fact, Mexico was opposed to Canadian participation. Even after trilateral talks began in February of 1991, the U.S. chief trade negotiator warned that Canada could be dropped from the talks if its participation threatened to delay the negotiations.[2] Trade Minister John Crosbie noted the worry for Canada: "It might well be that if Canada were not involved in the enlarged free-trade area, important job-creating investment could well decide to go elsewhere."[3] One trade writer summed up the stakes this way:

> Mexico has 81 million people, the United States has 250 million and Canada 26 million. If the United States and Mexico strike a bilateral deal without Canada, companies looking at long-term investment opportunities might decide to put their money where the bulk of the population is, and that does not mean Canada.[4]

Globalization

Although it has a number of characteristics associated with it, the globalization phenomenon (as first enunciated by Theodore Levitt) simply means the emergence of global markets for standardized consumer products.[5] Multinational (or "transnational") companies downplay the importance of national policies and national preferences in their decisions about production, distribution, marketing, and standards, and think of the world as a single market. The multinationals are becoming the major actors in a hierarchical global industrial structure; the 600 or so transnational corporations have substantial shares of world trade and many national markets, and dominate over three subordinate tiers, namely medium-size multinationals, threshold multinationals, and purely domestic companies, each of which has access to progressively smaller national markets.[6]

Other characteristics associated with the term "globalization" include:

- world-wide disaggregation of production;
- specialization by subsidiaries;
- niche products;
- footloose approach to sourcing;

- growing importance of knowledge-based service industries.

Hart's generic description of globalization is that "economic rivalry is rapidly replacing political ideology as the defining factor in international affairs."[7]

Globalization does not necessarily logically dictate any one specific form of economic integration. However, most analysts agree that the increasing intensity of international competition that globalization entails necessitates a Canadian stance supportive of international rules, as opposed to international economic power. Canada as a middle-level power has always had to seek influence in international forums, both political and economic. Predictability is the major benefit of such arrangements. NAFTA is a positive development from Canada's perspective because it offers a secure framework for trade relations that will remain intact with the addition of new members and be the model for new international trade agreements.

Regional Trade Groupings

One of the distinguishing characteristics of the post-war period has been the substantial growth of regional trade groupings in Europe, Latin America, and the Far East. Although various observers describe the three major blocs in different ways, North America cannot afford to remain indifferent to the increased levels of world trade they account for.

Compared to Western Europe (the countries of the European Community and of the European Free Trade Association) and the Asia-Pacific region (Japan plus the countries of the Association of Southeast Asian Nations, as well as the newly industrializing countries of South Korea, Hong Kong, and Taiwan), North America is not flourishing. GATT statistics collected over the last two decades reveal the relative extent of slippage:

> North America [the U.S. and Canada] has experienced the largest relative decline in the share of world exports – five percentage points from 1970 to 1986. Its exports as a percentage of world trade have declined in every major region; bilateral Canada-U.S. trade has declined as a proportion of world

trade; and the region has developed a trade balance of equal but opposite magnitude to that of the Asia-Pacific region – a deficit equal to six percent of total world exports. [8]

Western Europe's relative share also declined, but this was compensated for by the increase in intraregional trade; and the Asia-Pacific region saw the most dramatic export growth. [9]

NAFTA is an eminently sensible strategic move for a trade group that has also seen its inter-bloc trade patterns change for the worst. Over the same period of the 1970s and 1980s, both North American exports and imports relative to the European Community declined markedly and there began a growing trade imbalance with the Pacific Rim countries. [10] North American integration may be the only workable medium-term alternative available in the face of such entrenched imbalances with other blocs. An import substitution strategy was tried by Mexico and abandoned with its entry into the GATT in 1986; economic nationalism has ceased to be a working concept in Canada; and the United States is deeply suspicious of the possibilities inherent in the multilateral route, at least for the present. As well, NAFTA offers the best demonstration model to effect multilateral reforms.

Other Economic Benefits

International trade considerations make a convincing case for NAFTA. However, when other economic benefits are also considered, the need for such an agreement seems overwhelming. The major economic benefits in question are the asymmetry in gains from the accord, sectoral advances, and the possibility of lower-cost inputs into the manufacturing sector.

Asymmetrical Gains

Both Canada and the United States have gained asymmetrically through NAFTA. As the government's White Paper notes, "NAFTA does not greatly change the access for the United States or Mexico to the Canadian market, but it does fundamentally change Canadian and U.S. access to the Mexican market." [11] There was not a level playing field in regard to access to the Mexican market. Much of the latter had been characterized by a number of trade blockages, the remnants of the country's hostility to international trade before 1986. There were Mexican import licences, government procurement preferences, restrictions on investment, and blockages to involvement in the services sector, all of which made doing business in Mexico a distinct problem. Now, practically the whole Mexican economy is open to Canadians and Americans – on a preferential basis.

There are important sectoral advances to consider as well. Mexico is a modernizing economy, and its population and economy are likely to want the kinds of goods that Canada produces on a competitive basis. Current trade between Canada and Mexico is relatively modest. However, the government's White Paper suggests that important advances in trade with Mexico could be made in several areas. The box on the following page indicates the former Conservative government's estimation of the best areas for trade growth with Mexico.

Manufacturing Inputs

Another advantage of NAFTA is the availability of cheaper inputs into the manufacturing process. About a quarter of Canadian exports are used in the manufacture of Canadian exports. If Canada did not belong to NAFTA, and thus missed out on the availability of low-cost manufacturing inputs from Mexico while the Americans enjoyed them, Canadian manufacturers would likely be much less competitive than their American counterparts. Exports would slide and Canadian jobs would be in jeopardy. The effects, moreover, would be cumulative. The more the Americans exported to the Mexicans, the greater would be their opportunity to increase economies of scale, and the greater would be the threat to Canada.[12]

On the employment side of the coin, it is wrong to imply, as some critics do, that an agreement like NAFTA is a direct contributor to Canada's employment problems, that relatively low Mexican wages threaten Canadian manufacturing, jobs, and wage levels. Some important facts have to be considered by Canadian critics of the agreement:

The Federal Case for
Trade with Mexico (1992)

- *agri-food products*: Mexico will not be self-sufficient in livestock or in meat in the proximate future; it will also need improved technology for fish harvesting and processing.

- *transport equipment*: Mexico is the fastest growing market for auto parts in North America, and sales of vehicles should grow even more with the lifting of the Mexican Auto Decree. As well, the tremendous transportation infrastructure program the Mexicans have undertaken to cope with growing urban populations offers inroads for the Canadian steel rail, locomotive, and rolling stock industries.

- *petroleum equipment and services*: PEMEX, the state petroleum monopoly, will be spending several billions of dollars in modernization of equipment and services, and Canadian energy specialists are allowed to compete for it under NAFTA.

- *mining equipment and services*: Canada is a world leader in mining technology, and Mexico badly needs to elevate its mine safety and environment standards.

- *telecommunications*: There is a growing market for suppliers of electronic components, telecommunications equipment, and computer software in Mexico.

- *environment equipment and service*: Public opinion is forcing Mexico to make its environmental regulation meaningful, and Canadian water treatment specialists and others are poised to make inroads.

- *industrial technology*: Canadian industrial technology is already competitive in Mexico; and the bulk of growth in this area is expected to come from imports.

- *consumer products*: Seventy per cent of Mexico's 85 million inhabitants are under thirty, and increasingly urbanized, offering prime targets for a variety of Canadian goods.

- *financial services*: Mexico has privatized and opened much of its banking, insurance, and securities sector to foreign competition, and Canada already has a strong presence in the area.

SOURCE: Government of Canada, *The North American Free Trade Agreement: An Overview and Description* (August, 1992), pp. vii-ix.

- Competitiveness is determined by more than labour costs. Also important are other factors of production and related considerations, including the cost of capital, capital productivity, knowledge and skill level of the labour force, transportation and communications networks, and product quality. Labour costs account for only 17 per cent of the average cost of production for Canadian manufacturers.[13]
- If wages were a determining factor in industrial location, their effect would have been felt already. The average rate of duty on Mexican imports into Canada is under 3 per cent, and about 80 per cent of Mexican goods enter Canada duty-free already.[14]
- The productivity of Canadian labour is six to seven times higher than that of Mexican labour.[15]

If low wages were such an important factor in the modern capitalist economy, countries such as Mexico would already have been industrial powers. Canada has little to fear from the Mexican challenge on the wage front.

International Development

One international argument for NAFTA is that the best way to promote Third World development is to encourage the spread of inclusive regional trade networks. Another is that the human rights, labour, and environmental records of new partners in NAFTA will improve as the force of public opinion comes to bear on the countries that lag behind the progress of the leaders.

The implications of NAFTA for Third World development are important indeed. It is instructive to consider that the impetus for NAFTA came in the first instance from a developing nation, Mexico. The interest in freer trade reaches far beyond the borders of Mexico, however. Chile, presently involved in a free trade agreement with Mexico, has expressed great interest in joining NAFTA. Its enthusiasm is closely matched by other nations. The most interested are the nations of the Mercosur free trade group (Argentina, Brazil, Uruguay, and Paraguay); Central American countries that have trade agreements with Mexico; and certain Caribbean nations that fear the loss of U.S. access after NAFTA.[16] These countries are more interested in trade as a development tool than they are in aid. They remember that free trade is the general promise the United States gave the thirty-one countries in the Western Hemisphere with which it signed framework agreements under the now stalled Enterprise of the Americas Initiative (in return for liberalized investment regimes).

So even within the hemisphere there is a powerful demonstration effect at work. But the growing popularity of the NAFTA model is more than a bandwagon phenomenon. It stems from a disenchantment across the continent with interventionism and protectionism, the former economic model of preference. Lipsey summarizes the new outlook in Latin America:

> The less developed countries obtain many advantages by getting into close economic relations with developed nations. Free trade in goods and services probably does not pose any great threat. Inward-looking, import-replacement methods of growth are generally discredited. Free investment flows offer a technology transfer that creates faster economic growth than can be achieved by creating one's own technology behind closed trade and investment barriers. Most importantly, a regime of liberalized trade and investment flows formalized in a free trade area treaty is an important check on future populist regimes which will promise short-term gains, through such income redistribution policies as lowering profits and raising wages, that will bring long-term losses. . . . the evidence from Latin America and Africa is that the easiest way to eliminate growth prospects is for a government to be interventionist with state-owned production and major redistribution schemes.[17]

The environmental and social progress that most North Americans would like to see flourish in the hemisphere is given an important impetus by NAFTA. Some critical environmentalists have overlooked the general tone of the main agreement as well as the several specific provisions that are sensitive to environmental issues. All three countries have committed themselves to promoting sustainable development in implementing the agreement. NAFTA accepts each country's right to adopt standards and sanitary and phytosanitary measures that exceed international standards, and certain international agreements (on endangered species, ozone-depleting substances, and hazardous wastes) may even take precedence over NAFTA provisions (provided they do not constitute disguised trade restrictions). Rather than depressing environmental standards, NAFTA may elevate the standards of member countries, especially in the case of Mexico. Canadians or Americans, for example, could block imports from Mexico that failed their domestic standards. Environmental issues will be investigated by a trilateral dispute panel, but the panel will be advised by environmental experts.

The side deal on the environment does not meet every perceived need identified by the green movement – which would in itself be a doubtful and unrealistic aim, to be sure – but it is a significant beginning. William Watson sees it as having a strong potential. The fact that the Environmental Secretariat has a relatively large staff, a wide mandate, and a supportive Advisory Committee invites activism. As well, "the obligation to consider requests from private parties and to publish most of what it produces – unless the Council disapproves, which it will do at risk of public criticism – can only reinforce a penchant for activism."[18] Gilbert Winham states that the tri-national environmental commission will keep environmental issues on the agenda and provide additional focus for environmental interest groups to lobby governments. "The creation of lobby-able international structures is not an insignificant achievement for non-governmental organizations."[19] President Clinton's threat to withdraw from NAFTA in the event of Canada or Mexico withdrawing from the environmental side deal implies a certain precedence of environmental agreements over trade agreements.[20]

The whole issue of labour and human rights is a very serious one in developing countries, and trade agreements should pay them some attention. Unlike environmental matters, however, labour issues were largely outside the main agreement, appearing only in its preamble and also in a Memorandum of Understanding on Cooperative Labour Activities signed between Canada and Mexico in May, 1992. The latter commits both governments to an exchange of information and technical assistance in the areas of labour market statistics, occupational health and safety, job training, and labour relations. This reflected a mainstream view that, in D'Aquino's words, "the best way to upgrade Mexico's labour standards is to encourage it to create better paying jobs and prosperity through freer trade and an open market."[21]

The labour side deal extends co-operation in labour matters. This deal is not as potentially activist as the environmental one, but it offers analogous opportunities for the experts on the secretariats to contribute to public policy. In addition, if informal consultation does not lead to enforcement of the domestic labour laws challenged by another NAFTA partner, an "Evaluation Committee of Experts" can be struck. The committee can issue public reports on such important issues as minimum wages, worker health and safety, equal pay between the sexes, and protection for migrant workers. Over time, the combination of international attention and the improved standard of living from enhanced trade will result in better labour laws, as has been the case in most countries. As for collective bargaining itself, this, plainly, is too important politically to be loosened from the bounds of national sovereignty.

Human rights are an analogous situation. In Mexico, as in some other areas of Latin America, human rights and civil liberties are dealt with in an extremely arbitrary fashion. As with labour issues, the question of rights is outside the bounds of the agreement *per se*; but the agreement will affect rights nevertheless. A Canadian government fact sheet on NAFTA gives the accepted wisdom on the question: "the strengthened, more prosperous economy that will result from the NAFTA will increase the Mexican standard of living, promote a higher level of education, and encourage individuals to take an active role in creating a more pluralistic society." This corresponds with the record of human rights in the more developed countries of the West.

Canadian National Integrity

National unity and integrity are unavoidable considerations that enter into almost every major public policy decision in Canada, and NAFTA is no exception. Careful consideration leads one to endorse the current course of economic integration in North America. In specific terms, NAFTA, like the FTA, responds to the aspirations of Quebec and perhaps weakens the argument for separatism. As well, the increasingly multicultural nature of Canada virtually dictates a more outward-looking trade perspective for Canada.

Quebec is a unique province that has often insisted on the right to undertake public policies designed by Quebecers for Quebecers.

The insistence on provincial autonomy has on occasion grated on the sensibilities of those in other provinces, who are distinctly more centralist in their federal orientations. With both free trade agreements, however, Canada experiences the happy coincidence of a major policy initiative that has not turned political representatives of the two charter groups against each other. In a country where the French-English duality is the most serious cleavage threatening national unity, this turn of events should be considered a master stroke of statesmanship.

Much of the activity of Quebec in the economic policy area has been spurred by a collective sense of urgency. In fact, it can be argued that this sense of urgency has allowed Quebec to serve as an early warning system for the impending economic realities that ultimately all Canadians had to face. Realizing that international competitiveness depended on a combination of access to markets and a knowledge-based economy, Quebec insisted on forward-looking policies:[22]

- the inauguration of Quebec trade offices abroad (the earliest in 1940);
- Quiet Revolution initiatives such as the nationalization of Hydro-Québec, the building of development funds through the Caisses de dépôts et placements du Québec, and public education breakthroughs;
- reacting to the lack of opportunities and capital for young Québécois educated during and encouraged by the Quiet Revolution by establishing the Quebec Stock Savings Plan;
- the formation of a social consensus, during and after the serious recession of the early eighties, that stressed the primacy of ensuring Quebec's international competitiveness.

NAFTA is a logical culmination of these developments. The shared vision of Quebecers is that of "a strong regional economy in a world-wide global market," and the opposite vision of a protectionist Canadian national market is simply a non-starter.[23] One of the surest ways to discourage Quebec membership on the Canadian ship of state is to deny it the economic tools it has deemed necessary for its cultural survival.

Alternately, free trade also acts as a glue for national unity because, once implemented, it discourages Quebec's exit from the Canadian national framework. Quebec, if it made a unilateral declaration of independence or opted for sovereignty-association, would most likely find itself outside the free trade framework looking in because it had not been a signatory to the original agreement(s). Its membership would not automatically be assured. As noted above, this would deprive Quebec of one of its most cherished positions in trade matters.

The hope of renegotiating its way back in after a political separation from Canada is such a risky affair that Quebec may not want to chance it. Rugman and D'Cruz are pessimistic that a sovereign Quebec could get as good a deal as it now has.

> The U.S. negotiators would be hostile to Quebec's subsidies to business, and Quebec would need to make major concessions in order to secure access to the U.S. market. Quebec has abundant energy and other resources, but there are few alternatives to the U.S. market, so for these exports Quebec's bargaining position is not as strong as that of a united Canada.[24]

The likelihood of trade concessions by a truncated Canada to help prop up the Quebec economy should not be automatically assumed, to say the very least. All in all, therefore, the free trade format has a unifying effect on Canadian federalism.

In addition, NAFTA is in tune with the world views of Canadians who are not of the original charter groups. Rightly or wrongly, Canadian immigration for the past few decades has emphasized possession of capital and entrepreneurial skill as determining characteristics in granting landed immigrant status. Authorities have interpreted the national interest as promoting a pro-business image for Canada. Potential new immigrants to Canada will be likely to be attracted to a country that is part of a broad regional framework where their investments can be accorded national treatment with those of other partner nations.

Economic integration initiatives like NAFTA offer positive benefits to Canada and to other trade partners. They promote efficiencies of scale, eliminate expensive and time-consuming *ad hoc* trade restrictions between nations, and discourage government interventionism. NAFTA in particular is in tune with the twin imperatives of globalization and global development. It embodies the historical logic of earlier movements toward Canada-U.S. economic alliances. It is not perfect; but to retreat from it now would be to return to a past imperfect.

Notes

1. "NAFTA and the world," *Globe and Mail*, editorial, March 2, 1993.
2. "FTA may be reopened," *Globe and Mail*, February 7, 1991.
3. "3-way trade talks set," *Globe and Mail*, February 6, 1991.
4. Madelaine Drohan, "Coming to terms," *Globe and Mail*, February 12, 1991.
5. Theodore Levitt, "The Globalization of Markets," *Harvard Business Review* (May-June, 1983), pp. 92-102, as cited in Edward A. Carmichael, Katie Macmillan, and Robert C. York, *Ottawa's Next Agenda: Policy Review and Outlook, 1989* (Toronto: C.D. Howe Institute, 1989), pp. 82-83.
6. Bryan B. Purchase, *The Innovative Society: Competitiveness in the 1990s. Policy Review and Outlook, 1991* (Toronto: C.D. Howe Institute, 1991), p. 50.
7. Michael Hart, "A Brave New World: Trade Policy and Globalization," *Policy Options*, 13, 10 (January-February, 1993), p. 4.
8. As cited and interpreted in Carmichael *et al.*, *Ottawa's Next Agenda*, p. 89.
9. *Ibid.*, pp. 88-89.
10. Dorval Brunelle and Christian Deblock, "Economic Blocs and the Challenge of the North American Free Trade Agreement," in Steven J. Randall, ed., *North America Without Borders? Integrating Canada, the United States, and Mexico* (Calgary: University of Calgary Press, 1992), p. 123. Here the authors mean Canada, the U.S., and Mexico when referring to North America.
11. Government of Canada, *The North American Free Trade Agreement: An Overview and Description* (August, 1992), p. v.
12. Leo-Paul Dana, "Why we must join NAFTA," *Policy Options*, 13, 2 (March, 1992), pp. 7-8.
13. Government of Canada, *North American Free Trade Agreement: The NAFTA Manual*, August, 1992.
14. *Ibid.* See also Thomas D'Aquino, "Why We Need NAFTA," *Policy Options* (January-February, 1993), p. 23.
15. D'Aquino, "Why We Need NAFTA," p. 23. David Ricardo (1814)

noted the importance of differences in relative labour productivity in establishing comparative advantage.

16. Peter Cook, "Continental Divide," *Globe and Mail* Report on NAFTA, September 24, 1992, p. C3.

17. Richard Lipsey, "The Case for Trilateralism," in Steven Globerman, ed., *Continental Accord: North American Economic Integration* (Vancouver: Fraser Institute, 1991), pp. 98-99.

18. William G. Watson, "Environmental and Labour Standards in the NAFTA," *Commentary*, no. 57 (Toronto: C.D. Howe Institute, The NAFTA Papers, February, 1994), p. 17.

19. Gilbert R. Winham, "Enforcement of Environmental Measures: Negotiating the NAFTA Environmental Side Agreement," paper presented at a conference on "Enforcement of International Environmental Agreements," La Jolla, California, September 30-October 2, 1993, p. 19.

20. *Ibid.*, pp. 19-20.

21. D'Aquino, "Why We Need NAFTA," p. 23.

22. Rita Dionne-Marsolais, "The FTA: A Building Block for Quebec," *American Review of Canadian Studies* (Summer/Autumn, 1991), pp. 245-52.

23. *Ibid.*, p. 250.

24. Alan M. Rugman and Joseph R. D'Cruz, "Quebec Separatism and Canadian Competitiveness," *American Review of Canadian Studies* (Summer/Autumn, 1991), p. 257.

Chapter 14

Canada Loses in NAFTA

The North American Free Trade Agreement is even worse than
was its immediate predecessor, the Canada-United States Free
Trade Agreement. Arguments against NAFTA fall under the
categories of international trade, economic benefits, international
development, and Canadian national integrity.

International Trade Considerations

NAFTA is not the inevitable result of international trade realities, as
some mainstream economists would have Canadians believe. In
the context of other regional groupings, the agreement may actually harm multilateralism. As well, hopes to avoid a "hub-and-
spoke" dynamic are misplaced. The threat posed by globalization
is misstated, as is that by other trade groupings.

The Dangers to Multilateralism

NAFTA is part of an unfortunate trend in modern trade relations to weaken the spirit and the progress of multilateralism. The effort expended on regional efforts may divert attention away from multilateral negotiations. There is also the disincentive to international trade liberalization created by powerful regional groupings. Protectionism thrives behind regional walls. Both the FTA/NAFTA and the EC have specific sectors that receive special tariff protection from outside competition: agriculture in the EC, automobiles and textiles in North America. Such protectionism can occasionally harm multilateralism directly, as when the EC's refusal to change its Common Agricultural Program (CAP) stalled the Uruguay Round in 1990. The "fall-back" security offered by regional groupings could actually promote an accelerating rate of growth in tariff and non-tariff barriers.

One associated flaw in NAFTA is that it violates the self-interest of middle-level powers. There can seldom be an equality of benefits when the economic power of the bargainers in a trade deal is uneven. As Gus Tyler has pointed out, throughout history free trade has been used as a myth to legitimize the unequal benefits accruing to the dominant power in economic networks, ranging from the British Empire to the post-war American economic hegemony. [1] The self-interest of countries like Canada lies primarily in the multilateral field. Under the rules of the GATT, Canada posted consistent trade surpluses with the U.S.

Hub and Spoke

The hub-and-spoke analysis offered by NAFTA proponents is also fundamentally inadequate. The simple fact is that rather than averting a hub-and-spoke dynamic, NAFTA will likely simply enhance the *present* hub-and-spoke arrangements. In both trade and investment matters, the intensity of the linkages between the three countries is uneven. The United States-Canada trade link is more intense than are those between the U.S. and Mexico and between Canada and Mexico, and the same pattern repeats itself for foreign direct investment. These patterns are likely to remain. [2]

Another problem with the hub-and-spoke analysis is that it assumes the likelihood of due process. The simple fact it overlooks is that the larger economic party in a trade arrangement nearly always wins, whatever the *formal* rules are. The formal rules may in fact only describe a fraction of the trade dynamics, the primary element of which is economic power. Both before and after the FTA, Canadian trade negotiators have only responded to a small proportion of U.S. countervail and anti-dumping actions with trade sanctions of their own because Canada only accounts for a small part of total U.S. exports in the first instance. Any Canadian retaliation would not have equivalent effect. As one trade official put it: "We spend a lot of time [instead] in Canada at different levels of government thinking about how to design subsidy programs to avoid U.S. countervail."[3]

Still another problem with the analysis is that, in its assumption that such an arrangement would result in investment diversion from the hub to the spokes, it attributes an extraordinary importance to market access as a criterion in location decisions for manufacturing plants. Market access to the maximum number of countries is only one consideration in investment decisions, some of the others being exchange rate imbalances, location of demand, costs of production, transportation, adherence to government regulations, and non-tariff barriers hindering access to the U.S.[4] In fact, as Grinspun notes, NAFTA hobbles Ottawa's ability to manipulate these factors to attract international investors.[5]

Rule of Law Ignored

Even when there are very specific rules in place, as in the FTA, the Americans have chosen whether or not they would obey them. This tendency drove one of the negotiators of the FTA to distraction. Gordon Ritchie has commented on the "extraordinary challenge" brought by the U.S. special trade representative after two unsuccessful American attempts in Canadian-invoked bilateral panels to justify protection from Canadian hog producers and pork processors. This challenge mechanism, a legal measure originally meant only as an emergency fall-back in the case of corrupt or illegitimate action by panels, revealed the potential inadequacy of the dispute resolution system in the face of American arbitrariness:

> The United States has presented an interpretation of the FTA system which is completely contrary to the text of the

agreement and to the understandings of the negotiators. In effect, the United States is maintaining that the binational panel system must not be allowed to constrain the arbitrary and often capricious functioning of the highly politicized system of American "fair trade" remedies.[6]

The American refusal to play by the rules had upset the basic assumption of the FTA and called into question the "fundamental basis" of the agreement.[7]

NAFTA compounds the difficulties that the FTA's dispute settlement arrangements involved. Despite the promises of American and Canadian negotiators to arrive at a more secure protection from the rather arbitrary trading practices of the U.S. within seven years, they and the Mexicans largely adopted the stopgap measures of the FTA. Research by the federal NDP revealed that as of September, 1992, of twelve cases heard by the binational panels under the FTA, Canada had lost seven outright, won four, and tied on one. Of these twelve, nine had been Chapter 19 disputes, with the U.S. winning five, Canada three, and one tie; three had been Chapter 18 disputes, and the U.S. had won two to Canada's one.[8] Canada was on the losing end of a process that it had accepted only under political duress and that was now permanently entrenched.

Canada will not be able to get a clear definition of allowable subsidies included in a subsidies code. "The U.S. will remain free to countervail Canadian exports which the U.S. deems to be 'subsidized,' even though many of the alleged subsidies are permissible under GATT, and securely provided for in the draft GATT [Uruguay Round] agreement."[9] Not only this, but the U.S. had managed to get the "extraordinary challenge" provision, the use of which had caused the concern of Ritchie, actually strengthened.

The Agenda of the Transnational Corporations

There is a danger posed by globalization, but it is not the one stated by NAFTA proponents. The danger is the globalization – or internationalization – of the influence of transnational corporations (TNCs), the new name for what used to be called multinational corporations. One notable group pushing for the deal was a business lobby called USA-NAFTA, headed by Eastman Kodak and American Express and including more than 1,000 companies, trade associations, and business groups. Although the group had been flouting U.S. legislation by not officially registering and allowing public disclosure of membership, it is safe to conclude that American TNCs are the most important partners in USA-NAFTA. Big business stands to make tens of billions of dollars in new trade and investment opportunities in NAFTA.[10]

From the perspective of business, NAFTA merely fixed up some of the loose ends left after the Canada-U.S. agreement. It benefited by the inclusion of services in the earlier bilateral accord, since the American service industry was world-powerful and was pushing for services to be covered in the new GATT round. It prevented the possibility of any reappearance of the nationalistic investment regime that Canada had initiated in the mid-1970s. It benefited by the proportionality rule in energy.

Yet U.S. transnationals were not yet satisfied. The advances they had made with the FTA were not yet in place in the multilateral setting. There were also some matters, like intellectual property rights, that had not been dealt with to the full extent possible in the FTA. NAFTA would be one important way to advance the broader TNC agenda. In hemispheric matters:

> the . . . basic agenda was the same – reform of intellectual property laws, unrestricted rights of establishment for American corporations including services companies, increased constraints on future government actions, and unfettered access to the region's oil reserves. The elimination of tariffs, the classic view of what trade agreements are about, was far down the list of objectives.[11]

Intellectual Property Rights: Drug Patents

Canadian drug patent legislation is an example of the extent to which intellectual property rights in such an agreement can trump a country's right to provide affordable health services to its citizens. The country's drug policy has been driven since the mid-1980s by the needs of the multinational drug companies.

Until 1969 drug inventions were subject to the same patent protection rules as other inventions: a seventeen-year prohibition on the duplication and sale of the drug. Legislation introduced by the Trudeau government in 1968 allowed for the duplication and sale before the expiration of the patent on drug inventions. Amendments to the Patent Act provided for compulsory licensing to import prescription drugs, effectively allowing firms to produce drugs similar to those of patent holders in exchange for royalties. This expedient spawned the growth of a vibrant domestic generic drugs industry and saved Canadians millions of dollars.

However, 1987 and 1993 saw the passage of Conservative legislation that first restricted and then ended the protection for Canada's generic drug industry. The 1987 legislation ended compulsory licensing and set the period of patent protection at seven to ten years. In 1993, Bill c-91 extended the full patent protection on new drugs to twenty years, retroactive to December 20, 1991.

The Conservative measures had been driven in both instances to assuage the TNCs. The first was a bargaining stance to sweeten the FTA deal for the American negotiators, even though Canada denied that drugs were a part of the bigger picture. The latter was even more transparent since the language and rationale of NAFTA, the Uruguay Round of the GATT, and Bill c-91 were basically identical for drug patents. The rationale was "intellectual property rights": that inventors deserve a long period of patent protection to recoup their research and development costs and incidentally advance the cause of technological and scientific progress while they are serving their own interest. The multinational drug companies, speaking through their lobbying organ, the Pharmaceutical Manufacturers Association of Canada (PMAC), also claimed that the legislation, by making Canada an attractive place to invest, would attract $500 million in new investment.[12]

The drug issue had broad practical and symbolic overtones. The Ontario government said that Bill c-91 would add another $1 billion to Ontario's health-care costs in the next decade.[13] Experts testifying before the Commons committee studying c-91 testified that the new investment foreseen by PMAC would be dwarfed by the additional cost to consumers of around $7 billion by the year 2010.[14] Bill c-91 was opposed by nine of ten Canadian provinces, with Quebec, anticipating new investment from the international companies, the only exception.[15] Roy Davidson, a former director of the federal merger and monopoly branch, called the legislation a "disaster" and a cave-in to the multinational drug companies. He said the claim that the legislation would spur new investment was inaccurate, since existing tax breaks for research and development, already among the most generous in the world, were responsible for existing investment; that 95 per cent of Canadian drug patents were foreign-owned, so the bill would result in a transfer of income to outsiders; and that the bill would lessen competition in the Canadian market.[16] American public interest activist Ralph Nader said that the bill would harm Canada's image as a "beacon" to other countries trying to control the major U.S.-based drug corporations, among them, ironically, the U.S. itself.[17] It symbolized every objectionable element of the free trade deals: foreign domination, weakening of the welfare state, consumer powerlessness, and the excesses of monopoly capitalism.

Economic Losses

The benefits that the proponents of NAFTA suggest are vastly overrated. It stands to reason that a deal so comprehensive will involve significant pockets where Canadian industry is not able to compete. There are, and will be, cases of asymmetrical losses of a major nature. Some areas of the Canadian economy will be particularly hard hit.

Asymmetrical Losses

NAFTA embodies uneven economic benefits that imply an existing hub-and-spoke approach. Special treatment is given to powerful American industries: the Big Three automakers, the textile and apparel sector, sugar, transportation, and transnational corporations in general. Significantly, Mexico got a much better deal than Canada in several important areas.

The Auto Pact provisions refer to "North American" content rather than Canadian content. This leaves the door open to the flooding of Canada with autos made in low-cost North American locations, most notably the Maquiladora area of Mexico.

The American textile and apparel industry was successful in turning aside one of the few Canadian success stories to come out of the FTA by initiating a restriction on the use of offshore goods, which had allowed the Canadian-owned apparel industry to make inroads to the U.S. market. The special exemption in the FTA that allowed foreign fabric to be used in wool apparel and qualify for a lower rate of duty under rules of origin was successfully lobbied against by the American Apparel Manufacturers Association.[18] In NAFTA, as well, both yarns and fabrics must originate in North America to qualify for duty preference; in the FTA, only fabrics were made to meet the requirement.

In addition, NAFTA allows the Mexicans to retain political control over energy matters that Canada abrogated in the FTA. NAFTA reserves control to the Mexican government over investments and activities in the oil, gas, refining, basic petrochemicals, nuclear, and electricity sectors. Eight basic petrochemicals remain under the exclusive control of PEMEX, the state energy monopoly, as well as the critical areas of oil and gas drilling and production.[19] Mexico successfully negotiated itself an exemption from the thirty-six-month "proportionality" requirement in energy export restrictions that Canada subjected itself to in the FTA.

The "Maquiladora" Threat

There is a looming crisis involved in NAFTA, and it is the threat to both Canada and the United States of Mexico's "Maquiladora" region. The Maquiladoras are foreign-owned, export-only plants in northern states of Mexico that assemble and export goods made from parts and supplies imported duty-free. Except for the auto and appliance industries of the interior, they are the motor force of the Mexican economy. They are in theory rendered anachronistic by NAFTA, but their numbers are increasing and their low-wage structure remains a lasting legacy. They threaten to degrade not only the manufacturing and wage structure of North America, but also the environmental and economic development of Mexico itself.

The Maquiladora name comes from the Spanish *maquilar,* a verb meaning to retain a portion of flour in exchange for milling wheat.[20] The formal name given by the Mexicans in 1965 to what became known popularly as the Maquiladora industries was the Border Industrialization Program. In keeping with the apparent image of mutual benefit, both the U.S. and Mexico passed legislation to facilitate an enclave economy in northern Mexico. The U.S. assessed duties on the basis of value added instead of actual value on goods assembled in Mexico. The Mexicans allowed duty-free entry of the goods to be used in the Maquiladoras. Mexico also allowed complete foreign ownership of business – the greatest part of it by U.S. transnationals, as it turned out – provided that all of its output was exported, although recent policy has permitted some servicing of the domestic market. The Mexican National Statistics Institute reported a 4.9 per cent rise in the number of Maquiladora plants in the first eight months of 1993 from the same period in the previous year, to 2,178, together with a 7.3 per cent rise in the number of workers, to 544,476, obviously in anticipation of the passage of NAFTA. The plants annually bring in $4 billion U.S. to Mexico, the largest source of income after oil. A survey by Wharton Econometric Forecasting Associates recently revealed that U.S. companies had a depressing effect on Maquiladora wages: their average wage was $1.73 U.S. per hour, as opposed to $2.17 U.S. an hour for Mexican manufacturers outside the region.[21] Even the latter figure was small compared to the average wage of workers in Hong Kong ($3.58), Korea ($4.32), Singapore ($4.38), and Taiwan ($4.42).[22]

Nor should Canadians be blind to the implications of the qualitative changes taking place in the Mexican work force. Gereffi notes that there is now a dual structure to the Maquiladora industries – the old-style and new-style Maquiladoras. The old style featured low-wage, labour-intensive piecework in areas like garment production and light manufacturing. The new style involves such sophisticated production processes as automobile-related manufacturing and advanced electronics and includes a higher degree of inputs from Mexico. The new-style Maquiladora features Japanese and European as well as American TNCs who find labour cost advantages important. As well, the Maquiladoras are starting to become competitive in the service industry as well, most notably in business and medical services.[23] The Mexicans are becoming more diversified and also more productive: productivity growth in Mexican manufacturing over the five-year period 1988-92 was twice the American growth rate.[24] Making stereotypes about lower productivity and limited attractiveness to foreign investors is therefore dangerous in the long run. As Andrew Jackson of the Canadian Labour Congress observes, "developing countries such as South Korea and Taiwan, which are a decade or so ahead of Mexico, now combine relatively low wages with very high levels of technological competence, and their manufacturing companies have at least as much access to highly educated scientists and engineers as do Canadian companies."[25] Canada does not necessarily have a long-term comparative advantage in high-productivity areas.

The Cheap Labour Threat

Free trade proponents maintain that the cheap labour in Mexico is not a threat to Canadian economic well-being, but they are wrong. The Mexican cabinet oversees a command economy run more like those of Southeast Asia than like the economies of Canada and the United States. Wages and prices have been controlled since 1987 in a system that co-opts both business and labour. This gives the Mexicans a distinct competitive advantage against the high-wage economies of its northern neighbours. Stanford has argued that the seven southeast American states have in effect – if not in trade law, which tends to reflect the needs of the corporate sector – established an unfair subsidy in international trade in the FTA through their right-to-work legislation and the lack of worker protection through state minimum wages.[26] The case can be made that the negotiators are allowing the same dynamic to repeat itself in NAFTA by the failure to include strong labour protections.

The U.S. Office of Technology Assessment (OTA), a congressional think-tank, warns of the theoretical possibility of depression engendered by making the competitive erosion of wages a central aspect of employment policy in an integrated continental economy. The present NAFTA could divert U.S. investment to Mexico because of the security it promises for investments, and Asian and European investors would follow once the physical infrastructure of Mexico begins to improve. Making an analogy to post-war America, when the low wages and low bargaining power of southern workers bid down the manufacturing wages and influence of workers in the northern and northeastern states, the OTA says that increased investment in Mexico could lead American employers to leverage the 20 million less-educated Mexican workers against less-educated Americans and successfully depress wages. It criticizes the neo-classical view that reduced wages create jobs; in fact, it says, lower wages could reduce demand and create unemployment.[27] The study does not deal directly with the effect on Canadian workers, but Canadian employers could not be indifferent to a situation in which it shared a trade zone with two low-wage competitors, and with similar results: a stalled Canadian economy.

Policy Instruments Foreclosed

An especially pernicious element of NAFTA is its foreclosing of the use of some traditional policy instruments on which Canada has come to depend. Canada's post-war history of industrial policy has been one of trying to wean the economy off its dependency on the export of raw and only slightly processed materials. To this end it has used a variety of mechanisms: the managed trade of the Auto Pact, regulation in transportation, regionally oriented subsidies, government procurement, and a host of others, all of which are now weakened or rendered obsolete by the FTA and NAFTA.

Canada is a country built in defiance of the marketplace. Canadian industrial policy has stressed government intervention in the marketplace. Jackson writes:

> The key point is that if we are to generate jobs in "winner" industries in Canada, governments must get involved. The elements of a necessary industrial policy include subsidies for research and development and investment in machinery and equipment; planned government and public-sector procurement to support Canadian-based companies; requirements on companies to process resources to an advanced stage prior to export; performance requirements on transnational corporations operating in Canada, managed trade in key sectors etc. Yet all of these active industrial policies are either prohibited or heavily restricted by the CUFTA/NAFTA model of economic integration.[28]

We are not likely to see any repeats of co-operative public-private success stories like Northern Telecom or the Canadian auto industry. In the regulatory field, the transportation provisions of NAFTA mean that "future Canadian governments will be unable to require that our exports and imports move over Canadian rail and port infrastructure, rather than the U.S. rail and port network, even though NAFTA, like the Canada-U.S. agreement, preserves the

U.S. reservation of intercoastal shipping for U.S. flagged ships."[29] All this hobbling of the Canadian state is likely to accelerate the losses undergone by Canadian industry.

International Development

Rather than aiding international development, as the proponents claim, NAFTA will impede it. It is an agreement between unequals, and very little has been done to soften the effect on its victims: labour, human rights, and the environment in Mexico and for other acceding partners in the future.

Violations of Labour Rights

Labour rights are not held in high regard in Mexico. To be sure, there are unions and labour confederations, but the most influential are "official" unions chosen directly by the government or the dominant party (since 1917) in what has essentially become a one-party state, the Institutional Revolutionary Party (PRI). There are also elaborate constitutional protections for labour, but these are overlooked in the collusion between government and the official unions.

The Mexicans ignore not only their own constitution but also the moral directions of international organizations. Warnock notes how the conventions of the International Labour Organization have been systematically violated. The *right to free association* is blunted by the general lack of freedom of workers to elect union leadership and the policy of not recognizing non-PRI unions practised by the PRI-appointed Boards of Conciliation and Arbitration. The *right to free collective bargaining* is harmed by the usual lack of worker votes on contracts negotiated for them and the prevalence of "protection contracts" promising labour peace that are often sold to companies by the official unions. The *legal right to strike* is virtually non-existent: the approval of the Boards of Conciliation and Arbitration, needed for unions to strike, is seldom given. Only 2.3 per cent of the 78,801 requests between 1982 and 1988 were approved. Torture and assassination of non-official labour activists is common. The *workers' right to non-discrimination* is denied when they are regularly expelled or lose jobs for criticizing the official unions.[30]

Those who argue that the labour side deal is an advancement for North American workers are simply missing the point. The side deal does not establish or elevate labour standards. It essentially only provides for study of them. Canada can only challenge in areas under its own direct federal labour jurisdiction, unless in the unlikely event enough provinces opt into the deal. Ian Robinson notes a glaring deficiency: it leaves untouched the basic asymmetry established in the main deal. The main deal establishes increased capital mobility and an increased corporate legal capacity to challenge economic regulations. This, in turn, will pressure national and provincial/state governments to constrain or reduce worker rights, which remain untouched by any corresponding international protections. Since the side agreement only provides for international review of domestic labour law (and a very limited range of labour law at that) there is nothing in the labour deal to prevent a country from actually *narrowing* labour rights. This is a clear and present danger especially in the case of Mexico.[31] The only way that labour could get as much mobility as capital would be for North America to establish a common market, and the Americans have no desire for this to happen; if anything, they want to stem Mexican migration to the United States.[32]

Violations of Human Rights

The government also participates in, or at best turns a blind eye to, the systematic violation of human rights. As with its record on labour and environmental issues, the Mexican authorities prefer outward demonstrations of sincerity to real reform, although occasionally international pressure has some incremental beneficial effect. One example of the latter was the spate of reformist activity that followed the release of a very critical report by the U.S. human rights group Americas Watch before the U.S. and Mexican presidents began negotiations on free trade. This led to Mexico establishing a National Human Rights Commission and, in 1992, amending the Mexican constitution to entrench its existence and to mandate each of Mexico's thirty-one states to establish state human rights commissions. However, the federal and state agencies have not fully complied with a great many of the Commission's recommendations; among the agencies is the federal attorney general's office, which is alleged to be involved in torture and illegal detention, among other serious charges, for which there have only been a smattering of prosecutions. A wide variety of human rights abuses continue to take place, and in November, 1992, the United Nations Committee Against Torture complained that the public officials implicated continued to operate with impunity.[33]

Violations of the Environment

NAFTA has no definite code of environmental protection included in its terms. This is lamentable, given that Mexico has allowed TNCs to operate there under environmental conditions that would not be allowed in their home countries. It is a practice of these corporations to escape costly environmental regulations by placing environmentally and occupationally hazardous activities in Third World countries.[34] Mexico is not about to start being more stringent in enforcing environmental protections under NAFTA simply because, along with labour costs, low environmental costs offer it a competitive advantage.

NAFTA's environmental problems spill over into Canada. There is nothing in the agreement or the side deals to prevent corporations from leaving Canada or the United States to take advantage of lax Mexican environmental standards. The bilateral panels hearing challenges to environmental laws, which are advised by environmental experts, are under no compulsion to follow their advice. In fact, there is a good chance they will be swayed more by trade than by environmental concerns. A related danger is the real one of levelling health or environmental standards to the lowest common denominator. Canada's often stricter regulations may be lowered, for example, by the adoption of U.S.-style "risk-benefit" assessment, which calls upon analysts to weigh economic benefits against risks from, say, pesticides and food additives.[35]

Nor is the environmental side deal any panacea for the environmental sections of the main deal. Like the labour side deal, it does not establish international environmental standards, applies merely to domestic law, and only provides for study of standards. The initial option of fines in the case of non-compliance with domestic law makes the state, not the polluters, suffer.

Lack of International Protections

Some of the deficiencies of NAFTA might not be so alarming if they were offset by international protections. Yet this is not the case. The European Community has a variety of valuable characteristics that are lacking in NAFTA. Its 1992 Single Market Plan has a social charter that establishes such rights as freedom of association, collective bargaining, minimum wage, social assistance, and training. It also has a development fund entitling EC countries with a per capita gross domestic product of less than 75 per cent of the EC average to receive assistance. The per capita GDP of Greece and Portugal is about half that of the EC average, and they therefore receive aid; yet Mexico, with less than 15 per cent of the per capita GDP of its northern neighbours, does not have the same deal in NAFTA.[36] "While the EC has established a conscious policy aimed at reducing inequality, NAFTA is more of a sink-or-swim exercise."[37] Arguments painting NAFTA as the salvation of the poor, which do not take into consideration the large debt-related net transfer of resources from Mexico and other Latin American countries toward the U.S. and Canada, are simply unrealistic; a program of debt-relief is arguably needed.[38]

Canada's National Integrity

The intrusion of the federal government into areas of provincial jurisdiction by virtue of its trade deals has done harm to the federal principle in Canada. This is evident on a number of fronts.

One affront to the federal principle in Canada is the use of imperative language in the implementation sections of the FTA and NAFTA. Article 103 of the FTA and Article 105 of NAFTA use virtually identical language to describe the responsibility of the national governments. Article 105 of NAFTA states that "the parties shall ensure that all necessary measures are taken in order to give effect to the provisions of this Agreement, including their observance, except as otherwise provided in this Agreement by state and provincial governments." This is remarkable. It flies in the face of past practice, by which the federal government usually added, and other countries and international organizations generally accepted, a more tentative "federal clause" to treaties it had negotiated that touched on provincial jurisdiction. This would give warning to fellow signatories that those treaty aspects relating to provincial responsibility would come into effect only with the approval of the provinces, and thus qualify Canada's international liability. Such a distinction between treaty negotiation and implementation was due to the reasoning of the Judicial Committee of the Privy Council in the *Labour Conventions Case* of 1937. The imperative or obligatory nature of the wording in Article 105 appears to assume for the federal government a power it does not have in constitutional law.

The Ontario government has been one of the most persistent critics of the constitutional aspects of the trade deals. In May, 1988, the Attorney General for Ontario, Ian Scott, tabled a legal analysis of the FTA that reviewed the implications of Article 103's mandatory language. It noted that "it contains no limits, whether of politics or of reasonableness."[39] It would upset the carefully constructed balance of Canadian federalism:

> The Agreement sets no limits on what the federal government is obliged to do in case of continued lack of compliance. Paramount legislation to override that of the province, the declaratory power, the disallowance power, the withdrawal of federal interlocking legislation in areas of joint regulation with the provinces, and the full scope of federal spending power can all be called on. These methods must be considered as part of the federal arsenal, with the Americans in a position to require the use of some or all of them. Failure to use any of them in the case of persistent non-compliance would itself constitute a breach of the Agreement on the part of Canada.
>
> As a result, the United States assumes the position of a third party at the constitutional negotiating table with federal government and the provinces. By insisting that Ottawa use all its rights to enforce the Agreement, it will be able to prevent compromises that might otherwise develop.[40]

Replace references to the Americans by the NAFTA partners, and the story is essentially the same in the more recent trilateral agreement. In fact, in 1993 the Ontario government threatened to launch a court case to challenge the federal constitutional intrusions embodied in NAFTA.

Interventionist provinces – and every province becomes attached to interventionism at some point – will be frustrated at the policy options that are foreclosed to them by the two deals. They close off the possibility of subsidies that contradict the national treatment principle. The provision for proportional U.S.-Canada sharing of energy resources during shortages cuts into a province's power to shape economic development policy. The inability to discriminate between Canadian and non-Canadian service providers for the service sectors opened under free trade will have an analogous effect.

The financial strains put on the federal health-care system by the NAFTA-associated Bill C-91 will place it on an escalating crisis curve. Poorer provinces will be unable to offer a national standard of care and the other provinces will be unable to share resources to the same extent as in the past.

In short, NAFTA is a poor deal for Canada. It amounts to a predatory arrangement that will aggravate rather than ameliorate the lot of the poor in Mexico and the underdeveloped Latin American countries that may later adhere to the agreement. It amounts to an economic bill of rights for American multinationals. It ignores the concerns of working men and women. It will accelerate the further deindustrialization of Canada without allowing the country to make full use of instruments that allowed it to grow in the first place. The important areas of public policy now forbidden to Canadian policy-makers will render the Canadian state more anachronistic and distant in the eyes of Canadians.

Notes

1. Gus Tyler, "The Myth of Free Trade," *Dissent,* 35 (Spring, 1988), pp. 212-18.
2. Lorraine Eden and Maureen Appel Molot, "The View from the Spokes: Canada and Mexico Face the United States," in Stephen J. Randall, *North America Without Borders: Integrating Canada, the United States and Mexico* (Calgary: University of Calgary Press, 1992).
3. Drew Fagan, "Canada to fight NAFTA side deals," *Globe and Mail,* May 19, 1993.
4. Richard Grinspun, *North American Free Trade Area: A Critical Economic Perspective* (North York, Ont.: Canadian Centre for Policy Alternatives, September, 1991), p. 10.

338   *Canadian Political Debates*

5. *Ibid.*

6. Gordon Ritchie, "The Free Trade Agreement Revisited," *American Review of Canadian Studies,* 21, 2/3 (Summer/Autumn, 1991), p. 211.

7. *Ibid.,* p. 212.

8. Memorandum, to Dave Barrett, Trade Critic, from Tom O'Brien, NDP Research, Federal NDP Party, 30 September 1992.

9. Bob White, "Average Canadian won't benefit from NAFTA," *The Financial Post,* August 31, 1992.

10. Details on USA-NAFTA are covered by the Associated Press in "Business mobilizes lobby group," *Globe and Mail,* February 16, 1993.

11. Ken Traynor, "The Origins of Free Trade Mania," in Jim Sinclair, ed., *Crossing the Line: Canada and Free Trade with Mexico* (Vancouver: New Star Books, 1992), p. 10.

12. As stated in the PMAC advertisement "Why Bill C-91 is good medicine for Canada," *Globe and Mail,* December 7, 1992, p. A7.

13. Jeff Sallot, "Drug bill symbolizes Tory trade strategy," *Globe and Mail,* December 7, 1992.

14. Drew Fagan, "Nader denounces drug plan as boon for multinationals," *Globe and Mail,* December 3, 1992.

15. Robert Sheppard, "Why not go to court over drug prices?" *Globe and Mail,* December 9, 1992.

16. Rod Mickleburgh, "Controversial drug bill receives royal assent," *Globe and Mail,* February 5, 1993.

17. Fagan, "Nader denounces drug plan."

18. David MacDonald, "The fabric of NAFTA: textile, apparel negotiations face major obstacles," *Winnipeg Free Press,* August 4, 1992.

19. Drew Fagan, "Nationalist symbol Pemex protected from NAFTA," *Globe and Mail,* September 24, 1992.

20. As noted by Jim Carlton of the *Wall Street Journal* in "Not-so-jolly Green Giant casts a long shadow," *Globe and Mail,* September 24, 1992.

21. As cited *ibid.* For other information on the Maquiladoras, see Gary Gereffi, "Mexico's Maquiladora Industries and North American Integration" in Randall, *North America Without Borders,* pp. 137-38; Jim Sinclair, "Cheap Labour, Cheap Lives," in Sinclair, *Crossing the Line,* pp. 52-65; and "More maquiladoras start up in Mexico," *Globe and Mail,* November 22, 1993.

22. "The Mexican Worker: Smart, Motivated, Cheap," *Business Week,* April 19, 1993, p. 84.

23. Gereffi, "Mexico's Maquiladora Industries."

24. "The Mexican Worker," p. 84.
25. Andrew Jackson, "NAFTA and the Myth of 'Win-Win,'" *Policy Options* (January-February, 1993), p. 27.
26. Jim Stanford, *Going South: Cheap Labour as an Unfair Subsidy in North American Free Trade* (Ottawa: Canadian Centre for Policy Alternatives, December, 1991).
27. United States Congress, Office of Technology Assessment, *U.S.-Mexico Trade: Pulling Together or Pulling Apart?* (Washington, D.C., 1992).
28. Jackson, "NAFTA and the Myth of 'Win-Win,'" p. 26.
29. Bob White, "Average Canadian won't benefit."
30. John Warnock, "For unions and workers, Mexico's no paradise," *Globe and Mail*, October 5, 1992.
31. Ian Robinson, *North American Trade As If Democracy Mattered* (Ottawa and Washington, D.C.: Canadian Centre for Policy Alternatives and the International Labor Rights Education and Research Fund, September, 1993), p. 43.
32. Mel Watkins, "Afterword: The NAFTA Side-Deals," in Duncan Cameron and Mel Watkins, *Canada Under Free Trade* (Toronto: Lorimer, 1993), p. 286.
33. As noted in Ellen L. Lutz, "Human Rights in Mexico: Cause for Continuing Concern," *Current History* (February, 1993), pp. 78-82.
34. Zen Makuch, "Free Trade and the Environment," in Sinclair, *Crossing the Line*, p. 73.
35. Tony Clarke, "NAFTA: a new constitutional trap," *Globe and Mail*, December 18, 1992; Makuch, "Free Trade and the Environment," p. 71.
36. Drew Fagan, "Salvo of cheap shots fired over free trade," *Globe and Mail*, February 16, 1993.
37. *Ibid.*
38. Grinspun, *North American Free Trade Area*, pp. 17-19.
39. Ontario, Attorney General for Ontario, *The Impact of the Canada/U.S. Trade Agreement: A Legal Analysis* (May, 1988), p. 92.
40. *Ibid.*, p. 88.

PART EIGHT

Does Canada Need
Official Bilingualism?

Seldom has a single policy raised so much controversy as that pertaining to Canada's official languages. Moreover, it is a durable controversy. There has been a steady level of debate on official bilingualism since it was introduced in 1969. This debate is balanced, as well. It has detractors and supporters in both French and English.

The next two chapters present the case for and against the current regime of language and culture policy in Canada. To understand the nuances of the arguments, however, it is useful to review some basic historical and constitutional facts. The most controversial aspects of the policies are statutory in nature – legislation passed in the sixties, seventies, and eighties – but all the legislation has occurred within a specific constitutional context. The policies are an amalgam of constitutional and statutory elements. Paradoxically, the statutory elements are more controversial than the constitutional ones. Table 1 gives a quick overview of the most important of both in the area of the official languages of Canada.

Table 1
Landmarks in Canadian Bilingualism

1867 *British North America Act, 1867.* The BNA Act, now renamed the Constitution Act, 1867, mentions language rights in only one section and in a restricted context. Section 133 of the Act provides that English and French can be used in the debates and business of the legislatures of Canada and Quebec, and in courts established under their authority. Records and journals of the Canadian Parliament and Quebec legislature must be bilingual.

1963 *Royal Commission on Bilingualism and Biculturalism.* The "B&B Commission," as it came to be known, operates from 1963 to 1971. It recommends the establishment of an Official Languages Act and a Commissioner of Official Languages to oversee its implementation.

1966 *Bilingualism Policy in the Canadian Public Service.* Prime Minister Pearson enunciates a qualified statement that Anglophones and Francophones should work in the language of choice and initiates a bilingualism bonus for clerical staff engaged in bilingual work.

1969 *Official Languages Act.* The Official Languages Act receives unanimous support from all parties in Parliament and becomes law. It establishes that federal public services be delivered in one or other of the official languages of Canada where numbers warrant, creates the Commissioner of Official Languages to implement aspects of the Act, and authorizes the creation of bilingual districts.

1973 *Parliamentary Resolution on Official Languages.* Parliament reaffirms the principles of the Official Languages Act. The federal Treasury Board designates bilingual districts where both languages are to be languages of work. (This arrangement is never implemented.)

1982 *Constitution Act, 1982.* The Constitution Act, 1982, is a schedule to the Canada Act, 1982, the instrument that patriates the Canadian constitution. It includes the Canadian Charter of Rights and Freedoms, part of which constitutionalizes (or in some cases, reconstitutionalizes) aspects of the official languages of Canada. It says that English and French are the official languages of Canada and New Brunswick and accords the right to minority language education where numbers warrant.

1988   *Official Languages Act, 1988.* The 1988 Act reaffirms the directions of the 1969 Act and expands the government's commitment to official language minorities across the country. It allows for application for judicial remedy to the Federal Court and also recognizes the principle of Canadian duality.

Constitutional Bilingualism

There are two major constitutional elements of bilingualism in Canada, the Constitution Act, 1867, and the Constitution Act, 1982. Section 133 of the Constitution Act, 1867, is the original statement of the bilingual nature of government in Canada and Quebec. It enabled the use of either English or French in the Canadian Parliament and the legislature of Quebec, mandated that records and journals of the two jurisdictions were to be in English and French, and allowed either language to be used in the courts established by authority of Canada or Quebec. Section 23 of the Manitoba Act, 1870, essentially replicated the Quebec provisions of section 133 for the new province of Manitoba.

The next constitutional mention of official languages in Canada is in the Canadian Charter of Rights and Freedoms, which forms part of the Constitution Act, 1982. Sections 16-22 (Official Languages of Canada) and section 23 (Minority Language Education Rights) of the Charter both duplicate and add to the bilingualism provisions of the Constitution Act of 1867.

The similarities between the 1867 and 1982 Acts are obvious upon examination. For example, sections 17-19 of the Charter replicate the language of section 133 with regard to the use of English and French in parliamentary debates and records and in courts established by Parliament. As well, section 21 provides that nothing in sections 16-20 abrogates or derogates from any other constitutional protections for language, meaning that guarantees in sections 133 of the 1867 Act and section 23 of the Manitoba Act are secure.

There are also departures. In the words of Mr. Justice Beetz in *MacDonald v. City of Montreal,* section 133 was a constitutional minimum, an historical compromise that "has not introduced a comprehensive scheme or system of official bilingualism, even potentially, but a limited form of compulsory bilingualism at the legislative level, combined with an even more limited form of optional unilingualism at the option of the speaker in Parliamentary debates and at the option of the speaker, writer, or issuer in judicial proceedings or processes."[1] The Charter provisions, however, are qualitatively different. Sections 16 to 23 entrench the concept of Canadian duality in the constitution of Canada.[2] Not only is there linguistic equality, but also a commitment to advancing the equality of status or use of French in the case of federal and New Brunswick jurisdictions.

In addition, New Brunswick is now included in the list of constitutionally bilingual jurisdictions. The provisions applying to the federal government are replicated for New Brunswick. Contrary to the 1867 constitution, Quebec is not explicitly included in the official languages section, due to the opposition from the separatist government of Quebec at the time, for whom a bilingual vision of Canada was simply not acceptable. However, Quebec was still bound by section 133, as is Manitoba by section 23 of the Manitoba Act. Canada therefore has three bilingual provinces, which have arrived at this state by slightly different constitutional routes. Still another change is the addition of the obligation of bilingual services to the responsibilities of government, in section 20, which goes far beyond the provisions of section 133. Any member of the public has a right to services in English or French from the central office of an institution of the Parliament or government of Canada subject to the provisos that there is significant demand for the services and that it is reasonable to demand bilingual services due to the nature of the office. New Brunswickers can communicate in either language with any provincial office without the above qualifications holding.

One last major difference is the minority language education rights elaborated in section 23. To be sure, education rights had been mentioned in section 93 of the 1867 Act, but these pertained to those rights enjoyed by the denominational, not linguistic, minorities in the founding provinces at the time of Confederation.

Section 23 outlines minority language education rights and the conditions under which they can be enjoyed in any province of Canada. Canadian citizens may have their children receive primary and secondary school education in English or French in a province (1) if the parents' first language learned and still understood is that of the English or French minority of the province where they reside (the *mother tongue clause*); (2) if the parents received primary school education in Canada in the language that is the minority language in the province where they reside and in which they desire the child to be educated (the *Canada clause*); (3) if one of the children has already received or is currently receiving primary or secondary school education in English or French anywhere in Canada, the citizen has the right to have all his/her children receive primary or secondary instruction in the same language (the *sibling clause*).

The application of the mother tongue clause to Quebec is dependent, under section 59, on the authorization of the legislative assembly or government of that province. Quebec has not yet given such authorization. The net practical effect is that the children of immigrant parents are streamed into French-language education in Quebec.

The foregoing should not lead one to conclude that the federal government alone has the constitutional jurisdiction to legislate in matters of language. Each level of government has such power to the extent that language is incidental or ancillary to a matter falling under that government's competence in the division of powers. However, the respective governments must respect the language guarantees that are not subject to alteration. In other words, they cannot derogate from, only add to, the language rights included in the Constitution Acts of 1867 and 1982.[3]

Statutory Bilingualism

Statutory bilingualism, that is, the application of bilingualism policies by ordinary laws of Parliament or the legislatures, or by regulations made pursuant to legislation, is the present focus of most bilingualism opponents. The two most notable examples at the federal level are the Official Languages Act, 1969, and the Official Languages Act, 1988. There are also other, less significant examples. Together they constitute the three prongs of the federal government's policy: language of service, language of work, and balanced participation of each language group.

The *Official Languages Act of 1969* heralded a new attitude of *rapprochement* between the French and English language groups in Canada. It also served as a model for some aspects of the official languages sections of the Charter of Rights and Freedoms. Section 2 of the Act stated that "The English and French languages are the official languages of Canada for all purposes of the Parliament and Government of Canada, and possess and enjoy equality of status and equal rights and privileges as to their use in all the institutions of the Parliament and Government of Canada."[4] The Act established that federal services were to be provided to the public in both official languages where there is significant demand. Documentation of a general nature from federal executive agencies was to be in English and French, reversing a decades-old trend of *de facto* English unilingualism in the federal service. Court judgements and issuances of quasi-judicial agencies were to be in both languages. The post of Commissioner of Official Languages was created to monitor the implementation of the Act. The Act provided for the creation of bilingual districts, but they were never created due to the political difficulties involved.

The *Official Languages Act of 1988* was more than a simple reaffirmation of the 1969 Act. It was the culmination of a number of factors, including allegations of deficiencies in the former Act, the effect of the Charter of Rights and Freedoms, and the record of judicial decisions dealing both with the 1969 Act and language matters in general. Qualitative changes were made in the federal language legislation.

Of course, there are similarities in the legislation of 1969 and of 1988. There is an emphasis on assuring language of service in the two official languages if there is significant demand. In matters of criminal law, a person giving evidence is to be allowed to give it in either official language, as before. There is also a continuation of the post of Commissioner of Official Languages as a major actor in the federal language regime.

One significant aspect of the 1988 Act was the broadening of the objectives of the legislation. In a sense, the new legislation merely ratified what had already become broader aims in a series of incremental steps over the intervening decades. In 1973, Parliament adopted a resolution adding the objectives of working in one's own language and also of balanced participation of the English and French language groups to that of language of service in the language of one's choice. These objectives had also come to be included in the annual reports of the Commissioner. In fact, Keith Spicer, Canada's first Commissioner of Official Languages (1970-77), has revealed that he decided "to bluff the idea of language of work into the Act's absolutely vague Section 2" on the suggestion of NDP leader David Lewis, "and found that nobody dared disagree."[5]

Accordingly, the 1988 Act, section 34, says that English and French are the languages of work in all federal institutions and all officers and employees have the right to use either official language.[6] To give meaning to balanced participation, section 39 specifies that both language groups will have equal opportunities for employment and advancement and that the "composition of the workforce of federal institutions tends to reflect the presence of both the official language communities," taking into consideration the specific nature of the institution in question.[7]

There were several other differences.[8] They can be summarized concisely:

- The 1969 Act, as revealed by a series of judicial decisions,[9] was of a declaratory nature rather than executory. This meant that the Act merely declared the equality of the two languages instead of putting into place a distinct regulatory scheme to guarantee such equality. The 1988 version, in contrast, clearly allows any person who has made a complaint to the Commissioner in respect to rights and duties mentioned in the Act to apply to the Federal Court for a remedy. Remedy may also be granted by the Commissioner himself or the Commissioner may appear before the Court on behalf of someone who has applied for remedy (section 78).

- The 1969 Act did not enjoy primacy over other federal enactments, whereas section 82 of the 1988 Act provides for such primacy. Parts I to IV of the 1988 Official Languages Act prevail over other Acts of Parliament (except for the Canadian Human Rights Act) to the extent that the other Acts are inconsistent with them. This gives the 1988 Act a quasi-constitutional nature that the earlier Act did not have.

- There is a preamble in the 1988 Act, which was not available in the 1969 Act; the preamble is designed presumably to assist in interpretation.
- The 1988 Act is far more specific than the 1969 version, no doubt to aid in the implementation of the language legislation. The definition of federal institution now clearly includes Parliament and excludes the Yukon and Northwest Territories.
- The new Act drops the idea of bilingual districts used in the former Act.
- Unlike in the earlier Act, the federal government in the new Act commits itself to enhancing the vitality of French and English minority language communities (Part VII).
- In the new Act, there is a specific bureaucratic co-ordinator for official language programs in the guise of the Treasury Board (section 46).
- The Commissioner of Official Languages has additional responsibilities designed to assist him or her in ensuring recognition of the status of each of the official languages (sections 55-75).

Some pertinent statistics on the general status of the French and English languages in Canada are presented in Tables 2 and 3. These tables offer the most recent publicly available official data from the reports of the Official Languages Commissioner of the trends in official languages between the 1981 and 1991 censuses. The preliminary figures show a continued decline in the health of Canada's official language communities. Proponents and opponents of official bilingualism draw opposite conclusions from these figures.

Table 2
Population by Mother Tongue, Canada, Provinces, and Territories, 1981 and 1991

		Total Number (000s)	English (000s)	(%)	French (000s)	(%)	Other Languages (000s)	(%)
Canada	1981	24,303	14,961	61.5	6,253	25.7	3,129	12.9
	1991	27,297	16,837	61.7	6,647	24.4	3,813	14.0
Nfld.	1981	568	561	98.7	3	0.5	5	0.8
	1991	568	560	98.6	3	0.5	5	0.9
P.E.I.	1981	123	115	94.0	6	4.9	1	1.1
	1991	130	122	94.2	6	4.5	2	1.2
N.S.	1981	847	794	93.7	36	4.2	18	2.1
	1991	900	842	93.6	37	4.1	21	2.3
N.B.	1981	696	454	65.1	234	33.6	9	1.3
	1991	724	471	65.1	243	33.6	9	1.3
Quebec	1981	6,438	707	11.0	5,312	82.5	419	6.5
	1991	6,896	667	9.7	5,669	82.2	560	8.1
Ontario	1981	8,625	6,695	77.6	475	5.5	1,455	16.9
	1991	10,085	7,722	76.6	505	5.0	1,858	18.4
Manitoba	1981	1,026	741	72.2	52	5.1	233	22.7
	1991	1,092	819	75.0	51	4.7	222	20.3
Sask.	1981	968	776	80.1	25	2.6	167	17.2
	1991	969	833	84.2	22	2.2	134	13.5
Alberta	1981	2,238	1,817	81.2	62	2.8	359	16.0
	1991	2,546	2,100	82.5	58	2.3	388	15.2
B.C.	1981	2,744	2,257	82.2	46	1.7	442	16.1
	1991	3,282	2,643	80.5	52	1.6	588	17.9
Yukon	1981	23	20	87.6	1	2.5	2	9.9
	1991	28	25	88.8	1	3.2	2	8.0
N.W.T.	1981	46	25	54.1	1	2.7	20	43.2
	1991	58	32	55.2	1	2.5	24	42.3

NOTE: Multiple responses were divided equally among the languages reported.
SOURCES: Statistics Canada; Commissioner of Official Languages, *Annual Report, 1992*, Table II.1.

Table 3
Population by Home Language, Canada, Provinces, and Territories, 1981 and 1991

		Total Number (000s)	English (000s)	(%)	French (000s)	(%)	Other Languages (000s)	(%)
Canada	1981	24,083	16,355	67.9	5,940	24.7	1,788	7.4
	1991	26,994	18,439	68.3	6,290	23.3	2,265	8.4
Nfld.	1981	564	560	99.3	1	0.3	3	0.4
	1991	564	560	99.2	1	0.2	3	0.5
P.E.I.	1981	121	117	96.6	4	3.1	0	0.4
	1991	128	125	97.3	3	2.4	0	0.3
N.S.	1981	840	807	96.1	24	2.9	9	1.1
	1991	891	858	96.3	22	2.5	11	1.2
N.B.	1981	689	468	67.9	217	31.5	5	0.7
	1991	716	489	68.2	223	31.2	5	0.7
Quebec	1981	6,369	784	12.3	5,276	82.8	309	4.9
	1991	6,810	759	11.1	5,655	83.0	397	5.8
Ontario	1981	8,534	7,311	85.7	332	3.9	891	10.4
	1991	9,977	8,500	85.2	318	3.2	1,159	11.6
Manitoba	1981	1,014	868	85.7	31	3.1	114	11.3
	1991	1,079	947	87.7	25	2.3	107	9.9
Sask.	1981	956	885	92.5	10	1.1	61	6.4
	1991	976	921	94.4	7	0.7	48	4.9
Alberta	1981	2,214	2,025	91.5	29	1.3	160	7.2
	1991	2,519	2,305	91.5	20	0.8	194	7.7
B.C.	1981	2,714	2,480	91.4	15	0.5	219	8.1
	1991	3,248	2,910	89.6	15	0.4	323	9.9
Yukon	1981	23	22	95.7	0	1.0	1	3.3
	1991	28	27	96.7	0	1.4	1	1.9
N.W.T.	1981	46	29	63.0	1	1.4	16	35.7
	1991	57	38	66.8	1	1.6	18	32.0

NOTE: Data were reconciled and multiple responses were divided equally among the languages reported.
SOURCES: Statistics Canada; Commissioner of Official Languages, *Annual Report, 1992*, Table II.1.

Notes

1. [1986] I SCR 460 at 496. As quoted in Gerald-A. Beaudoin and Ed Ratushny, *The Canadian Charter of Rights and Freedoms,* 2nd edition (Toronto: Carswell, 1989), p. 655.
2. André Braen, "Language Rights," in Michel Bastarache, ed., *Language Rights in Canada* (Montreal: Les Éditions Yvon Blais, 1987), p. 43.
3. Beaudoin and Ratushny, *The Canadian Charter of Rights and Freedoms,* ch. 15.
4. Official Languages Act, RSC 1970, c. O-2, s. 2.
5. Keith Spicer, "How the Linguistic World Looked in 1970," *Language and Society* (Summer, 1989), p. R-10.
6. In order to provide work environments that are conducive to the use of either language, workers are to be provided with appropriate work instruments and services, as well as access to automated data processing and data communication systems in either language; and supervisors and management groups are to be able to communicate in both official languages with officers and employees of the institution (section 36).
7. Official Languages Act, RSC c. 31, s. 39(I).
8. The sources for the following are the Acts themselves; the Hansards (debates in the Commons) at second reading of the Official Languages Act, 1988, from February 8, 1988, to March 7, 1988, especially the address by Jean-Robert Gauthier, February 8, 1988, pp. 12707-13; Canada, Library of Parliament, Research Branch, *Official Languages Act (1988),* Backgrounder by Jean-Charles Ducharme (Ottawa, October, 1988); and D. Martin Low, "The Roots of Change: Legal Sources of the 1988 Official Languages Act," *Language and Society* (Summer, 1989), pp. R-25, R-26.
9. The most notable is *Association des Gens de l'air du Quebec Inc. v. The Honourable Otto Lang* [1977] 2 FC and [1978] 2 FC 371.

Chapter 15

Official Bilingualism Saved
A Foundering Nation

Canada was foundering before it adopted its current bilingualism and multiculturalism policies. Canada was undergoing the greatest crisis of its history by ignoring, albeit unconsciously, its founding myth. The historical relations between the English and French had been poor and showed no signs of significant improvement. Policy implementation of the official languages policy has proved imperfect; but it has achieved the greater goal of national unity. The vastly improved language rights were arranged so as to be in balance with the more traditional civil liberties. Canada borrowed wisely but not unthinkingly from its international neighbours and in 1971 added the new dimension of multiculturalism to bilingualism, to make Canada a world leader in fostering tolerance.

Founding Myths

Myths can never be proved or disproved. That is their nature. The way to judge a myth is by its effect. Does it animate the imagination of a significant amount of people? Does the myth contribute to social peace? Does it reflect concrete needs? The founding myths of Canada that are of definite value are those of dualism and individualism, and they are the myths upon which were built the values of bilingualism and multiculturalism. Without adherence to these values, Canadians might as well give up on a united Canada and begin negotiations on sovereignty-association, or whatever the new name for Quebec separation is these days.

Canadian Dualism

Canadian dualism has not been taken seriously throughout most of the country's history except in Quebec. It is significant, however, that when the dangers of national disintegration became apparent after the rise of separatist forces in Quebec, dualism became the posture of most committed progressive federalists in both English and French Canada. There was, and is, no other alternative to the past English-Canadian pattern of domination and the prospect of separation.

This was the apparent conclusion of the government of Canada when it established the terms of reference for the Royal Commission on Bilingualism and Biculturalism. The terms committed the Commission "to recommend what steps should be taken to develop the Canadian Confederation *on the basis of an equal partnership between the two founding races,* taking into account the contribution made by the other ethnic groups to the cultural enrichment of Canada and the measures that should be taken to safeguard that contribution."[1] The social reality of more than two ethnic groups was not to be ignored, but neither was the background of the founding constitution of the country, the British North America Act. As Pierre Trudeau was to observe trenchantly, the difference between the other ethnic groups and the English and French groups was that the latter had the ability to terminate Canada's existence.

Duality in Pre-Confederation History

Some of the most important political thinkers have recognized the dualist dynamic in Canadian history. Historian G.F.G. Stanley, for example, saw a compact or "pact" between the two peoples of Canada as the foundation of political unity in this country. Yet it was not a legal contract, not an Anglo-French agreement entered into with the intention of legal enforcement; it was more like "a gentleman's agreement, an understanding based upon mutual consent, with a moral rather than a juridical sanction."[2]

The idea of a compact between races was integral to the Confederation agreement; but it had become a tradition, even a convention of Canadian constitution-making, long before then. The Quebec Act of 1774 amounted to a social contract between the French Canadians and Britain. It provided the juridical basis for a French fact that already existed, recognizing French civil law, liberalizing religious privileges, and providing for French Canadians to be part of the civil government. The Constitution Act of 1791 created two separate provinces, Upper Canada and Lower Canada, on an ethnic basis. This was designed to bring about colonial unity but had the additional effect of reconsecrating the French fact in Canada. The Act of Union of 1840 brought an unintended form of federalism to the united province; by denying the French the initial advantages of representation by population, it strengthened the resolve of the French to hold onto the gains of 1774 and 1791 and to seek new methods of maintaining control over their own political destiny, such as dual ministries and the principle of the "double majority" in passage of legislation vital to the interests of one of the linguistic groups.

Confederation and the Duality Principle

By the time of Confederation, then, the principle of duality was well established. It was strong enough to deter English Canadians from pursuing their dream of a legislative union and to force them to negotiate a precise federal arrangement to replace the obtuse form that had limped along under the Act of Union. The principal actor on the French side was George-Etienne Cartier, who in the negotiations had "succeeded in maintaining the fundamental principle of the entente between the two racial groups in Canada, equality of race, equality of religion, equality of language, equality of laws."[3] However, the implications went beyond these matters to include implications for amendment.

The next step was as easy as it was logical. Since both races were equal, a decision taken, an agreement arrived at by the equal partners on the fundamental character of the new constitution, could not be changed without the consent of each. It was, in fact, a treaty, a compact binding upon both parties. This was a view which scarcely roused a dissenting voice in the Canada of 1865.[4]

The racial compact became political-geographic in nature, transformed into a compact between provinces, at the Charlottetown and Quebec conferences, because of the tendency to identify racial groups and geographical areas. Belief in this historic pact has always been stronger in central Canada than in other regions, but nevertheless it has introduced an element of rigidity and inflexibility in the Canadian constitution that will endure.

Henri Bourassa and Canadian Dualism

If the program of one of Canada's great visionaries, a man whom Pierre Trudeau has called among "the most brilliant parliamentarians Canada has ever known,"[5] had been followed, Canada would have been spared much conflict. Henri Bourassa was a pan-Canadian nationalist in the dualist sense. In his lifetime he served as an MP, a member of the Quebec legislature, the founder (in 1910) of the influential Montreal newspaper *Le Devoir,* and an outspoken critic of Canada's identification of its own interests with those of the British Empire, especially in matters of defence.

Bourassa's contribution to Canadian political thought is his renewal and sanctification of the notion of Canadian dualism. Bourassa and his followers believed that the two cultures, French and English, were equal. In order to combat British influence, Bourassa proposed a new Canadian political nationality built on cultural dualism. The whole of Canada, not just Quebec, should be home to French Canadians: Canada should be a bilingual and bicultural state from sea to sea, with minority rights respected throughout the country.

There is a direct line of descent from Bourassa to the pan-Canadian policies of Trudeau. Bourassa's spiritual heir as an editor of *Le Devoir* was André Laurendeau, the man whose influence had led to the establishment of the Royal Commission on Bilingualism and Biculturalism. The legacy of Bourassa and Laurendeau, says Douglas Verney, was the "establishment of Pan-Canadianism as the official ideology of the government of Canada," culminating in the passage of the Official Languages Act of 1969.[6] However, it was not the traditional Quebec view of pan-Canadianism, for it stressed participation in federal politics and a willingness to accept (English-Canadian) majority rule. Minority status was not acceptable; equality of language and culture was.

New Statements of Dualism

In the Meech Lake and Charlottetown attempts at constitutional change, there was strong evidence that their failure rested on the degree to which they threatened the dualist vision of Canada. The accords indicated quite plainly that the alternative to the bilingualism policy was a fragmented Canada. In May, 1987, Pierre Trudeau's denunciation of the inward-looking Quebec nationalism inherent in the Meech Lake Accord, and the Accord's threat to official bilingualism, galvanized opposition to the agreement across Canada.[7] The Charlottetown Accord was defeated in a general constitutional referendum in 1992, partly due to public perceptions that the trade-offs Quebec had won in the bargaining were too exorbitant. Few proposals to alter the regime of official bilingualism were seriously entertained. In short, a program that a mere generation ago had seemed radical to many is now seen as a basic minimum requirement for political peace in Canada.

French-English Relations in Confederation

In addition to being consonant with the dominant theories of Canadian Confederation, the current language regime was required for reasons of historical redress. Governments at both the federal and provincial levels had offended constitutional law and simple social justice on language matters since Confederation. Canada did not have bilingual bank notes until 1937. French Canadians were vastly underrepresented in the federal bureaucracy. At some point the pattern had to be broken and reparations made to Canada's French Canadians and, as we shall see later, to the other cultural groups in the country. *One can safely say that if the federal government had not acted, no other jurisdiction would have.*

With the exception of New Brunswick, no province has shown a consistent long-term commitment to assuring its citizens an equality of public service, public employment, or participation for French and English citizens. Even if a province had made headway in one of these categories, it would be a cause for jubilation. Such is not the case.

Quebec

The case of Quebec is instructive. Rather than take the high road in the face of Anglophone intolerance to official language minorities elsewhere, it chose to mimic the intolerance. As Table 1 shows, Quebec attempted to come to terms with its bilingual and bicultural element but gave up on the effort beginning in 1974. In spite of advances made in 1993 under Bill 86, Quebec remains a province where French is the only official language.

Table 1
Quebec Language Landmarks

Bill 63 (1969). Introduced by the Union Nationale government, An Act to Promote the French Language allows parents to choose English or French as the language of instruction of their children.

Bill 22 (1974). The Liberal government of Robert Bourassa introduces the Official Language Act, which purports to make French the official language of public administration and commerce. It also provides for language tests for students wishing to be exempted from schooling in French.

Bill 101 (1977). A major initiative of the new Parti Québécois government, the Charter of the French Language is an attempt to remake Quebec society. It makes French the official language of the Quebec legislature and courts. English-language legislation is no longer officially valid. The "Quebec clause" restricts instruction in English to children whose parents or siblings themselves received primary instruction in English in Quebec. The language of commercial signs is deemed to be French.

Blaikie No. 1, 1979. The Supreme Court of Canada invalidates the sections of Bill 101 on the language of legislation and the courts.

Blaikie No. 2, 1981. The Supreme Court of Canada clarifies that section 133 of the 1867 Constitution Act applies to cabinet regulations and rules of court.

Schools Case, 1984. The Supreme Court of Canada invalidates the Quebec clause of Bill 101 because it collides directly with the "Canada clause" of the Charter.

Ford Case, 1988. The Supreme Court of Canada rules that Bill 101's restrictions on the use of English in commercial signs was an infringement on the freedom of expression guarantee in the Charter and hints at a solution in the predominant but not exclusive use of French in commercial signs.

Bill 178, 1989. Relying on the fact that freedom of expression is subject to the section 33 override clause of the Charter, Premier Bourassa's Liberal government invokes the latter to amend the Charter of the French Language to prevent the use of any language other than French on outdoor commercial signs, while allowing bilingual indoor signs under certain circumstances.

Bill 86, 1993. The Bourassa government, citing Supreme Court decisions and a report of the United Nations human rights committee, introduces legislation to amend the Charter of the French Language. It allows the use of English on outdoor advertising, the introduction of English-immersion classes in French-language schools, and temporarily relaxes regulations for children of English-speaking immigrants in Quebec who want to obtain instruction in English.

Manitoba

The other provinces have histories of intolerance toward official language minorities that are worse than Quebec's. The history of Manitoba is particularly unfortunate. Much was expected of Manitoba in terms of the *épanouissement* of French-Canadian language and culture. Far from being a successful test case and model to other provinces, Manitoba showed the ugly face of Anglo intolerance in Canada. The province was willing to abrogate unilaterally the constitution of the country in language matters. It moved only when forced to by the Supreme Court and refused broader protections for bilingualism negotiated in the political realm.

Section 23 of the Manitoba Act was similar to section 133 of the BNA Act, yet, contrary to the constitution, the Manitoba legislature passed the Official Language Act of 1890, which purported to make English the official language of the province's legislature and courts. For good measure, the legislature abolished separate schools as well; this also hurt the French since the majority were Catholic. Only in 1967 was some half-hearted reversal of the pattern in evidence with the province's amendment of education legislation to provide at least half a day of instruction in French.

Almost a century went by before court challenges by the Franco-Manitobans were finally successful. In 1979 the *Forest* decision of the Supreme Court declared the 1890 Official Language Act unconstitutional. Coincident with the release of the *Forest* decision, the Court came down with *Blaikie No. 1* (see Table 1), which because of constitutional wording also applied to Manitoba. Dissatisfied with the rate of compliance with the two decisions, Roger Bilodeau launched a test case in 1980 asking the courts to strike down two unilingual English statutes. This provoked the Manitoba government to try a political settlement with the Société Franco-Manitobaine and the federal government regarding French services. There would have been a constitutional amendment protecting the French language and, later, expansion of services in French across the province. The public reaction to this was so hostile that the Manitoba cabinet shelved the idea. Meanwhile, the federal government, anticipating a decision in the Bilodeau case, launched a reference on the broader question of the validity of post-1890 Manitoba statutes. Not surprisingly, the Supreme Court, in the *Manitoba Language Rights Reference* (1985), ruled them invalid. It, however, granted them temporary validity and imposed deadlines for the translation of Manitoba statutes and rules of court into French.

Saskatchewan and Alberta

Saskatchewan and Alberta are other examples of provinces that do not honour the bilingual compact at the founding of our country. These provinces were originally part of the Northwest Territories, and the governing act before the granting of provincehood was the Northwest Territories Act. Language rights parallel to those in Quebec, Manitoba, and at the federal level were granted in section 110 of the Act. In 1891 Parliament modified section 110 to provide the legislative assembly of the Territories with the ability to alter the language of the legislature, courts, and records and journals. Some attempt was made to do this but the proper methods were not followed by the territorial politicians.[8] When Parliament created Alberta and Saskatchewan in 1905, it provided in section 16 of the Alberta Act and the Saskatchewan Act, respectively, that all laws, orders, and regulations then in force should continue subject to their repeal or alteration by the Parliament or provincial assembly. Neither legislature repealed section 110, although both continued to pass legislation only in English.

In the *Mercure* case of 1988, the Supreme Court found that, in fact, the original 1877 bilingual language rights still pertained in Saskatchewan and that, similar to the case in the *Manitoba Language Rights Reference*, the statutes of Saskatchewan were invalid. The difference between the two provinces was that the language provisions were entrenched in the constitution and could only be changed by constitutional amendment, whereas they were not part of the constitution in the case of Saskatchewan. Since section 110 provided for the possible repeal of bilingualism by the legislature, the language rights could be changed simply by the ironic method of a bilingual statute validating in *post hoc* fashion a century of English-only legislation.

The government quickly initiated legislation to make English the only official language. However, it allowed for the use of French in the legislature and before certain courts, and provided for the translation of selected statutes. No arrangement was made for French-language services in health care, social services, or municipal services; and marked progress in minority language education rights seems to have resulted only from the effect of section 23 of the Charter.[9]

Alberta acted in similar fashion to Saskatchewan. It also passed bilingual legislation in 1988 to negate the requirement for bilingualism in the legislature, courts, and records, since the *Mercure* decision apparently applied to it as well. (The Supreme Court's *Pacquette* decision of 1990 settled the question for good, replicating the earlier Saskatchewan finding.) The Alberta legislation, however, was more restrictive in the case of the courts and government publications.[10]

Ontario

There has been a long history of intolerance toward Francophones in Ontario, with some progress being made in recent decades. It is not unreasonable to argue, however, that the recent progress is partly due to the demonstration effect of the federal government and the moral onus put on the province by the B&B Commission.

In 1912 the government adopted Regulation 17, which for fifteen years largely abolished the teaching of French in Ontario schools. It made English the only language of instruction after three years of public school and limited the teaching of French to one hour a day. The genesis for this was a sudden growth in the number of French settling in eastern Ontario and their pressure for bilingual schooling and possibly official bilingualism; Regulation 17 and subsequent judicial interpretation confirmed recognition only of Catholic schools, not French schools, and the crisis demonstrated that Ontario was not willing to accept the principle of Canadian duality.[11]

Yet, under pressure from federal authorities and public opinion, Ontario began to make progress in the late 1960s. In 1969, legislation authorized the creation of French public schools; in 1970, legislative rules were changed to permit French in the Provincial Parliament; in 1975, the province began French services in courts, later to be expanded; in 1984 it acknowledged the right of Franco-Ontarians to French-language education.[12] In 1989, Bill 8 took effect. The French Language Services Act acknowledged the right to speak French in the House and to receive French services in certain designated areas. In addition, certain health and social services institutions must provide bilingual services, much like in Quebec.

Ontario's efforts in promoting French-language services, however, do not extend to the municipal level. In contrast, Quebec, through Bill 101 (section 113), allows for municipal governments to offer services in both English and French. Some 100 Quebec municipalities have announced their intention to do so. In Ontario, 31 municipalities have declared themselves bilingual, while another 41 have said that they are "unilingual" English.[13]

The progress made to date, however, has still not resulted in Ontario declaring itself a bilingual province, as the B&B Commission had recommended a generation before.

New Brunswick

The province of New Brunswick is Canada's only officially bilingual province. Even here, however, as Savoie notes, "one is hard pressed to find more than a handful of initiatives promoting the province's official languages policy over the past twenty years that saw the light of day without direct federal encouragement and financial support."[14]

The Francophone minority of New Brunswick, constituting about one-third of the population, did not receive official recognition until the late sixties when the government complied with recommendations of the B&B Commission. In 1968 the legislative assembly passed the New Brunswick Official Languages Act, declaring English and French to be the province's official languages. Legislation, oral debates, and written proceedings of the legislature are in both languages. The Act provided for bilingualism in the language of service, the right to French-language education, and the right to use either language in the courts. Municipalities could adopt the language regime of their choice. In 1981 legislation (popularly known as Bill 88) recognized the equality of the two language communities.[15]

Subsequently, two constitutional amendments have entrenched official bilingualism for New Brunswick. The Constitution Act,

1982, essentially constitutionalized the Official Languages Act. As noted previously, the federal and New Brunswick provisions were virtually identical, with the slight difference that any government or legislative office in New Brunswick was to offer the bilingual service, not simply do so on the basis of "significant demand" as in the federal provisions.

In March, 1993, another constitutional amendment was proclaimed. It had been part of the Charlottetown Accord, but with its failure the federal and New Brunswick governments decided to undertake a bilateral amendment of the type permitted under section 43 of the Constitution Act, 1982. The amendment constitutionalizes 1981 New Brunswick statutory arrangements (Bill 88). It says the two linguistic communities have equality of status and equal rights and privileges, which include distinct educational and cultural institutions, and commits the legislature and government to preserve and promote the equality of status and institutions of the two groups.

So what exists in Canada are highly abbreviated language rights that exist in large part because of federal pressure and example. Ottawa, Quebec, Ontario, and New Brunswick are the only jurisdictions that offer anything approaching satisfactory service. The Atlantic provinces and British Columbia offer minimal services at the will of government, while Saskatchewan and Alberta have turned their backs on their historical bilingual responsibilities. Manitoba has come to symbolize the ill will and lack of generosity in English Canada. Canada needs a bilingual regime and it needs the federal government to be resolute in its commitment to the two languages.

Policy Implementation

Important things need to be mentioned about the implementation of the bilingualism policy. It includes a significant element of choice, as opposed to coercion; it has resulted in French representation in, as opposed to domination of, the civil service; the cost of the policy is relatively modest; and the policy has consistently polled majority support among Canadians.

Choice, Not Coercion

Opponents of the policy usually portray it as highly coercive. The more uninformed call it a program to bilingualize all of Canada. The more subtle call it a measure to cheat unilingual Anglophones of career opportunities. Rather than being coercive, the program as implemented since 1969 merely calls for freedom of choice for Canadians in the language of service and the language of the courts. Institutions of the federal government have to be bilingual, but not individuals. The legislation does not force provinces or municipalities to provide bilingual services; it applies only to the federal level.

Representation, Not Domination

Of course, some federal employees have to be bilingual to make the policy work. The question is whether or not the number of positions or the degree of bilingualism is excessive and unfair to Anglophone job aspirants. The answer can only be no.

Linguistic categories in the federal public service have been kept to four since the early seventies: bilingual, English essential, French essential, and either/or. The percentage of federal positions designated bilingual has been under 30 per cent for the last five years. In 1993 the percentage of bilinguals was 29.0 per cent; English essential was 59.4 per cent; French essential was 6.4 per cent; and either/or was 5.2 per cent. These proportions had changed since 1989 by only a fraction of a percentage point each. The absolute numbers of bilingual positions changed, it is true, from 61,741 in 1989 to 63,882 in 1993, but so had the total number of positions in the service, from 210,294 to 220,403.[16]

Moreover, the geographic distribution of the positions (measured in 1993) is appropriate, given the distribution of official language groups in the country. In western Canada, there was the same percentage of minority official language public servants (those having the minority official language as their first official language spoken) in government as there was percentage of minority population of the total population (2.2 per cent); and bilingual positions (positions that have an English-French bilingualism requirement but whose incumbents may have either French *or*

English as their first official language spoken) formed 3.3 per cent of total public servants in the West. In Atlantic Canada, the French official language minority is slightly underrepresented in the public service (10.8 per cent) relative to its percentage of the population (12.2 per cent); and the percentage of bilingual positions is 14.9 per cent. The National Capital Region and Quebec have the highest number of positions allocated to bilingual positions (55.6 per cent and 52.2 per cent respectively).[17] Given the nature of a national government, which should balance the interests of all the country, and the preponderance of French in Quebec, these arrangements are only logical and natural.

As to the federal service itself, the degree of bilingualization should not suggest a blockage to unilingual official language speakers. Many bilingual positions are open to unilinguals who are willing to undertake training in the other official language. Therefore the positions are in some cases "theoretically" bilingual, a target set in the expectation that the unilingual, most often an Anglophone, will learn enough of the other language. Research has shown that the federal government is not draconian, to say the least, in its enforcement of the policy.

The upper echelons of the service, access to which is highly symbolic to Anglophone Canadians, have not been overrun by Francophones. Gerard Pelletier, the Secretary of State who first introduced the Official Languages Act, sees the accusation of inequality at the top as the most damaging and the most inaccurate charge against the Act.

> Had bilingualism become a practical necessity for the "more rewarding" civil service jobs . . .? Yes, but in practice, only for the francophones. In twenty years, I never met a single deputy-minister who did not speak English. . . . And today, the upper echelons of whole departments are still filled with totally unilingual anglophone civil servants, who are in no way serving "a life sentence to job immobility." The civil service has made a lot of progress in French, even great strides in some sectors. But English unilingualism is doing very well, thank you.[18]

In some respects, in fact, the Francophones have not yet achieved their proportionate share of representation in the federal service. On an overall basis they have, of course. As Table 2 in the

Part Eight introduction shows, 24.4 per cent, or about 6,647,000 of the Canadian population in 1991, claimed French as a mother tongue, and 61.7 per cent, or about 16,837,000, claimed English. In 1992, 26.7 per cent of employees in all federal institutions said French was their first official language and 72.3 per cent said English. (Some did not specify, which explains the lack of rounding.) In the public service itself (that is, just counting departments, and not Crown corporations, agencies, the armed forces, and the RCMP), the figures were 71.9 per cent English and 28.1 per cent French.[19]

Continuing Problems

Francophones are still underrepresented in senior management and in the technical and scientific and professional groups of the federal public service. Anglophones in 1992 accounted for 77.3 per cent of senior management positions in the public service and Francophones constituted the other 22.7 per cent. However, slight progress is being made: in 1986 the percentages were 80.2 per cent and 19.8 per cent, respectively. In the two other employment categories the percentages by 1992 had moved only by a fraction toward more Francophone representation, at 77.3 per cent English and 22.7 per cent French in scientific and professional, and at 78.6 per cent English and 21.4 per cent French in technical.[20]

The Cost Question

The matter of cost has exercised a great many of the opponents of official bilingualism. It need not. There are important considerations here. One is that the relative amount spent on official languages is fairly low compared to other expenses. Another is that the resources are evenly spread.

In 1992-93 the Official Languages Program cost $656 million. Of this amount, only $319 million went to fund the "internal" developmental and service programs of the federal government itself. The rest, $337 million, went to "external" programs of aid to other governments and to associations. Lest one think that official bilingualism is creating a budgetary sink-hole, one should compare internal Official Languages expenditures of less than a third of a billion to the annual federal budgetary expenditures of $161 billion and federal public debt of $457 billion. Clearly, the cost of bilingualism is not the cause of the crisis in public finances. The cost of the internal program is about the same as the cost of the Atlantic Canada Opportunities Agency or federal grants to municipalities.[21] Not very many people suggest that we save money by eliminating *them*. As the federal government is fond of reminding Canadians, the program only costs each Canadian about 3.5 cents a day.

The other consideration to remember is that no one is building an empire on the language policy. The Commissioner of Official Languages administers a fraction of the total amount, about $13 million. The resources are spread out. Official minorities of both languages benefit from the expenditures. The English of Quebec depend heavily on the federal financing they receive from Ottawa. The external funding provides aid to around 100,000 Anglophone students in Quebec and 158,000 Francophone students outside Quebec, in both cases for minority language education; it also helps 2.7 million youth learn English or French as a second language.[22] The money for these items amounts to over 11 per cent of the total amounts that the federal government transfers to provinces for education.[23]

Unachieved Results?

Some opponents of the official languages policy look at census statistics like those in Tables 2 and 3 (Part Eight introduction) and declare evidence of assimilation and, accordingly, the failure of the official languages policy. This is faulty logic. What they do imply is the failure of the ethnocentric, selfish policy of generations of Anglophones in Canada that has resulted in such a state of siege for Francophones in Canada that many of them are contemplating a separate country.

What is more, the same statistics can be interpreted in different ways. One of these ways is as an alarm bell. They signify the growing crisis in Canadian duality: hence the need not only to redouble efforts, but also to invent new ways to achieve historic goals. Ignored, these statistics will be the symbol used by Quebec separatists to achieve the dismemberment of Canada.

The statistics, as well, do not indicate total failure or cause for gloominess. They show a growth in the number of Francophones measured both by mother tongue and by the more rigorous indicator of home language. They show that French is holding its ground in Quebec at 82-83 per cent as measured by both indicators. In addition, as suggested by the Commissioner of Official Languages, the numbers themselves are indicative of a critical mass. "Clearly, 6.6 million Francophones, including 978,000 outside Quebec, remain numerically far more significant than any other non-English language community. There are more Francophones in Canada than there are in Switzerland and Belgium combined."[24]

Public Opinion

Public opinion has come onside for the policy of official languages. Some survey results of the 1990s will tell the tale:

- Environics, State of the Nation poll (May, 1990): "Please tell me if you agree or disagree that French and English should be Canada's two official languages." (Seventy-two per cent agreed.)
- Globe and Mail/CBC News poll (April, 1991): "Do you think the federal government should continue to provide services to the public across the country in both English and French?" (Sixty-nine per cent said yes.)
- Angus Reid poll (January, 1992): "Officially Canada is a bilingual country with both French and English as official languages. What do you think about official bilingualism? Would you say you strongly support, moderately support, moderately oppose or strongly oppose official bilingualism?" (Sixty-five per cent strongly or moderately support.)[25]

Of course, some polls give lower approval ratings for the policy. Reviewing the effect that the nature of the poll question had on responses about the languages policy in general, researchers at the Office of the Commissioner of Official Languages have concluded that "references to the federal language policy as 'bilingualism' without an accurate portrait of what the Official Languages Act does and does not say, tend to elicit higher proportions of negative responses."[26] The Commissioner thus has to do a more intensive job of public education.

International Models

When Canadians discuss official languages policy, they often raise the possibility of adopting a different approach based on international models. One quite popular idea is *territorial bilingualism,* as opposed to bilingualism based on the personality principle. Territorial bilingualism would constrict the application of official bilingualism to specific territories, or regions of the country, often as a function of numerical concentration of the linguistic group in question, or of local choice of languages, or both. The *personality principle,* which applies on an even basis across the country based on demand by individuals, is rejected as being too cumbersome or too divisive. Yet it is instructive to return to the reasoning of the B&B Commission on the question of territoriality versus personality. The Commission saw possibilities in each, but finally decided the personality principle was most appropriate to the Canadian situation.

Canada and the Territorial Model

Of the countries that, like Canada, had committed themselves to the principle of linguistic equality – Belgium, Switzerland, Finland, and South Africa – Belgium and Switzerland best exemplified the territorial principle. The two advantages of the territorial approach were that "the minority language is guaranteed priority in some areas and a large majority of the total population may be served in its own language."[27] However, this attraction was offset by the simple fact that the official language minorities were not concentrated, but widely scattered across the country. As well, if tradition were any guide, application of the territorial principle with federal bilingual institutions in the centre might well convince provinces to adopt unilingualism. This in turn could lead to majority rights and the oppression of official language minorities. Territoriality was therefore not appropriate to the B&B Commission.

On the other hand, the Commission felt the personality principle had important positive possibilities. It could not be a personality principle as extensive as that of South Africa, which adopted it as a result of significant linguistic interpenetration and a high level of bilingualism both within and outside of the civil service. The level of bilingualism in Canada, however, was 12 per cent in the mid-sixties (as compared to 66 per cent in white South Africa) and Canada's official language minorities constituted less than 14 per cent of the population in nine of the ten provinces (compared to a 23-39 per cent range in provincial populations in South Africa).[28] Consequently, the Commission suggested a system of official bilingualism for Canada, Ontario, New Brunswick, and Quebec and a system of bilingual districts, based on modifications of the Finnish bilingual communes idea, for other areas of Canada where numbers warranted.

Institutional Bilingualism

In fact, it would probably be more accurate to term the actual policy adopted in Canada as *institutional bilingualism* rather than the personality principle. Canadians have received a great deal more services in both official languages, but the government has always premised its policies, even its constitutional amendments, on the basis of "significant demand."

Canadians are realistic enough to temper their language demands as a function of language population concentrations. Thus, the government has pursued a common-sense policy of increasing the number of bilingual positions, enhancing second-language and minority language education, and effectively bilingualizing the National Capital Region. Institutions, not societies, have been bilingualized. Canadian pragmatism and common sense prevail in federal language policy.

Notes

1. Canada, Royal Commission on Bilingualism and Biculturalism, *A Preliminary Report of the Royal Commission on Bilingualism and Biculturalism* (Ottawa: Queen's Printer, 1965), p. 151. Emphasis added.
2. G.F.G. Stanley, "Act or Pact – Another Look at Confederation," *Annual Report of the Canadian Historical Association* (1956), p. 2.
3. *Ibid.*, p. 12.
4. *Ibid.*
5. Donald L. Johnston, ed., *Pierre Trudeau Speaks Out on Meech Lake* (Toronto: General Paperbacks, 1990), pp. 23-24.
6. Douglas V. Verney, *Three Civilizations, Two Cultures, One State: Canada's Political Traditions* (Durham, N.C.: Duke University Press, 1986), p. 235.

7. Pierre Trudeau, "Say Goodbye to the Dream of One Canada," *Toronto Star*, May 27, 1987.

8. C.A. Sheppard, *The Law of Languages in Canada*, Study 10 of the Royal Commission on Bilingualism and Biculturalism (Ottawa: Information Canada, 1971), p. 85.

9. Donald J. Savoie, *The Politics of Language* (Kingston, Ont.: Queen's University Institute of Intergovernmental Relations, 1991), p. 13.

10. *Ibid.*, p. 14.

11. Verney, *Three Civilizations*, p. 277.

12. "Federal and Provincial Linguistic Dates," *Language and Society* (Summer, 1989), pp. R-31, R-32.

13. Savoie, *The Politics of Language*, p. 11.

14. *Ibid.*, pp. 20-21.

15. In an Act called, not surprisingly, the Act Recognizing the Equality of the Two Official Linguistic Communities in New Brunswick.

16. Canada, Commissioner of Official Languages, *Annual Report, 1993* (Ottawa: Minister of Supply and Services Canada, 1994), Table III.12.

17. *Ibid.*, Table III.13. The "first official language spoken" was used to determine official language populations.

18. Gerard Pelletier, "1968: Language Policy and the Mood in Quebec," in Thomas S. Axworthy and Pierre Elliott Trudeau, eds., *Towards a Just Society: the Trudeau Years* (Markham, Ont.: Viking, 1990), p. 218.

19. Commissioner of Official Languages, *Annual Report, 1992*, Table III.4.

20. *Ibid.*, Table III.6.

21. *Ibid.*, Table III.17.

22. Canada, Office of the Commissioner of Official Languages, *Official Languages: Some Basic Facts* (Ottawa: Minister of Supply and Services Canada, 1992), p. 16.

23. Commissioner of Official Languages, *Annual Report, 1992*, p. 91.

24. *Ibid.*, p. 16.

25. The various polls are cited *ibid.*, p. 10.

26. *Ibid.*, p. 11.

27. Canada, Report of the Royal Commission on Bilingualism and Biculturalism, Book I: *General Introduction: The Official Languages* (Ottawa: Queen's Printer, 1967), p. 83.

28. *Ibid.*, p. 84.

Chapter 16

The Founding Myth and Bilingualism

Canada's bilingualism policy is ill-advised and ill-conceived. It is founded on a flawed version of the founding myth. It has exacerbated tensions between the two main linguistic groups in Canada. The implementation of policy has been confused and contradictory. As well, international experience, such as it is, shows us that territorial solutions to language questions are best.

Founding Myths

The most disagreeable aspect of the official languages policy is its implicit use of "duality" as the founding myth of Canada. To be sure, French-English relations are important in Canada. Yet, it is a distortion of reality to claim that this was the sole basis for creating Canada. The duality theory is bad history and bad politics.

Dualism as Bad History

The duality theory is, first of all, bad history. There may have been aspects of an intercultural *entente* at work before Confederation, but the Constitution Act of 1867 was certainly not a pact between linguistic groups. F.R. Scott has attacked the notion of dualism in the 1867 Act.[1] The only direct mentions of Quebec in the Act, he says, were intended not to enlarge the autonomy of Quebec but to impose restrictions on it in order to protect minority rights. The Protestant minority in Quebec was protected in section 80, which provided for special votes in the Eastern Townships, and by the extension of the principle of minority denominational education rights to Quebec as well as to Ontario in section 93(2). The English minority was protected by making the legislature and courts of Quebec bilingual in section 133. Other sections recognized the bicultural nature of Canada, as in section 94, where Quebec is excepted from the potential delegation of property and civil rights to Ottawa, and section 98, where Quebec judges are to be chosen from the provincial bar. However, these restrict rather than add to Quebec autonomy.

On the division of powers question, there was in 1867 no impediment to the transfer of powers to the federal Parliament by constitutional amendment. As well, the 1867 division of powers is identical for all provinces. There are no special powers allocated to Quebec in recognition of its cultural characteristics or the need to preserve them. In fact, where provincial autonomy and minority rights have the potential to clash in the constitution, minority rights are privileged. Ottawa is allowed to legislate on education rights to safeguard denominational minorities in section 93(4); and the disallowance power of section 90 is, on the face of it, a check on the arbitrary use of provincial power.[2]

Dualism as Bad Politics

The duality theory is also bad politics. It ignores the importance of the Aboriginal peoples in shaping Canadian history. It relegates the multitude of ethnic groups who came later in history to the status of second-class citizens. It could also impede the merit basis for public service employment.

English-French Relations in Confederation

Relations between the English and French have been worsened, rather than ameliorated, by inauguration of the official languages policy because it responded to the definition of the Quebec crisis espoused by English-Canadian intellectuals, not to that of Quebec nationalists. As Kenneth McRoberts has demonstrated, Trudeau's hostility to nationalism led to espousal of a language regime for Canada that was roughly based on the policy of "personality principle" bilingualism. This corresponded to the agenda of the English-Canadian intelligentsia, which had an ideology – a pan-Canadian nationalism – designed to defeat Quebec nationalism and restore Canadian unity.[3]

Official Bilingualism as Ideology

Because the bilingualism policy was an ideology, its various operational failures could be forgiven. What was important was the message. First, the language policy was premised on individual rights: individuals, not collectivities, could claim privileges, a stance that corresponded with English-Canadian hostility to collective rights. Second, the uniformity of language rights throughout Canada would avoid the unpleasant option of according any "special status" to Quebec. Quebecers ultimately would be able to experience opportunities throughout the country. Third, it was an Anglo-driven policy. English Canadians felt that their actions, rather than the constitutional plans of Quebec nationalists, could save Canada. As McRoberts says, "the bilingual vision of Canada has only a loose relationship to the reality of language use in Canada; it derives its force from other considerations."[4]

Since it is preoccupied with the national crisis as defined by English Canadians, official bilingualism is doomed to be a peripheral measure. In fact, with the hostility to significant Quebec-sensitive reforms offered in the Meech Lake and Charlottetown Accords, the bilingualism policy now appears to be a threshold, a ceiling beyond which English Canada is not likely to move. This makes the bilingualism policy a prison rather than a possibility.

Official Bilingualism and Unilinguals

One rather surprising thing for English Canadians to realize is that unilingual Francophones, many of them in Quebec, have just as much reason to be hostile to the policy as unilingual Anglophones. One reason is that it implies continuing injustice to unilingual French-speaking individuals seeking posts in the federal service. Given the continuing numerical inferiority of Francophones in Canada, says Quebec nationalist Georges Mathews, "bilingualism would always be necessary for a francophone who wants access to the upper reaches of the Canadian public or parapublic service, while an anglophone could be unilingual."[5]

A second reason is that the policy has unfortunately fostered the cult of the official language minority.[6] This makes it seem like the future of the country is ineluctably linked to the linguistic survival of relatively few scattered minorities across the country. This rationale is not only a flagrant abuse of logic; it also seeks to bolster a losing cause. Nothing will stop the trend toward Anglicization of most of the French minorities outside Quebec. A look at the French "home language" figures of Table 3 (Part Eight introduction) is enough to lead to this conclusion for all provinces except New Brunswick. Concerned Francophones are ultimately likely to come to the same conclusion: that the best place to protect the French language is in the province of Quebec. This makes most of the federal official languages policy superfluous.

Policy Implementation

Not only are the historical and logical bases of official bilingualism flawed, but its implementation is as well. Important objectives of the policy are not realized, and the program is inordinately expensive for the little it achieves.

Unrealized Objectives

If one interprets the major objective of the official bilingualism policy since 1969 to be the vitality of the official language communities (an objective finally made explicit in the 1988 Act), then the most recent census figures must be cold comfort. Preliminary results of the 1991 census,[7] combined with Tables 2 and 3 in the Part Eight introduction, show:

- a percentage decline of mother tongue Francophone communities in most provinces, especially in the prairie provinces and P.E.I.;
- a net decline in the Quebec mother tongue Anglophone community;
- a decline in the proportion of Canadians reporting French as the principle home language from 24.7 per cent in 1981 to 24.1 per cent in 1986 to 23.5 per cent in 1991, although there is an increase in the numbers speaking French. This latter increase no doubt derives from an increase in the number of mother tongue Francophones, from 6.253 million in 1981 to around 6.647 million in 1991;
- whereas 29 per cent of mother tongue French spoke English more often at home in 1981, the figure had changed to 35 per cent by 1991, indicating an increase in the rate of language shift;
- the percentage of those Canadians reporting themselves bilingual did not climb significantly from 1986 to 1991 (16.2 to 16.3 per cent) despite an absolute increase of 342,495 bilinguals.

It is true that certain advances have been made on other objectives, such as service and language of work, and these, of course, have been meticulously detailed by the reports of the Commissioner of Official Languages. However, if the percentage of those actually speaking the endangered language is going steadily downward, then something is plainly not working. The emperor, in this case, has no clothes.

The statistics suggest that *territorial unilingualism,* something like that of Switzerland or of Belgium, is inevitable for Canada. (Additional arguments for this will be made in a later section.) The problem with the federal "personality principle," as McRoberts suggests, rests not in its strategic imperfections but rather in the linguistic structure of the country.[8] Outside of the "bilingual belt" – the regions in Ontario and New Brunswick that border Quebec and have a significant proportion of Francophones, and where both French and English continue to thrive – unilingualism is the fate of the rest of the country.

Pierre Fournier cites evidence that one of two Francophone youth outside Quebec does not receive the French-language education promised in the Charter of Rights. Francophone parents are subjected to a variety of administrative harassments or inadequate resource bases from provincial governments, despite findings that the lack of a Francophone educational infrastructure is key to assimilation of Francophone minorities.[9]

Recognition of duality, if considered another implicit objective of the policy, has not been realized. The steady decline in the percentage of Francophones means that their political clout is on the wane. As Richard Joy comments, Quebec, previously the national example of successful bilingualism, no longer is, and its alleged indifference to the Quebec Anglophones has reduced the support of the English-speaking majority for the official languages policy.[10]

The Cost Question

It is in the government's interest to underestimate the cost of bilingualism. The actual costs are much higher. Thomas Flanagan makes a convincing case.

> The widely quoted figure of $13.00 a year, or 3.5 cents a day, for each of us, is a gross underestimate. It refers only to translation, interpretation, and training. It excludes the $800 a year bonus for thousands of bilingual civil servants, and the more than $250,000,000 that is transferred to the provinces for related purposes, including second language education and the support of minority language lobby groups. It also excludes the expansion of the federal civil service: when someone is away on language training, a replacement must be hired.
>
> There are additional large costs for the private sector. Crown corporations such as Air Canada and Petro Canada have been privatized, but they still labour under expensive bilingualism requirements. Canada's labelling regulations, apart from the trivial complaint of French on cereal boxes, are a barrier to the importation of goods and help to raise costs. I know of no estimate of the true cost of bilingualism, but it must be at least $1 billion a year in federal tax revenues, plus expenses imposed upon the private sector.[11]

It makes no sense to pursue a program that offers such slight benefits, especially when the fiscal situation of the country is in such desperate shape. The official languages program, rather than being a national priority, is an expensive testimony to the quirky national vision of one of Canada's most controversial prime ministers.

The official languages program, moreover, offers incentives for its own internal growth that should alarm Canadian taxpayers. William D. Gairdner sees the incentives to bilingual and multicultural organizations as of one cloth.[12] That is, they are attempts by politicians to segment an undifferentiated electorate in order to maximize votes. The leadership of the new or renovated interest group at the centre of this action trades influence for subsidies. This dynamic is both expensive and ultimately destructive to national unity, in the sense that it tends to destroy common denominators that bind a country together. While his analysis is different from that of Gairdner, Leslie Pal's evidence leads one to conclude that the Official Language Minority Group program from 1970 to 1982 had the effect of stimulating the creation of groups. A government report found that "of a sample of 325 organizations that submitted applications in 1981-82, fully 72 per cent had been established during the life of the program (since 1970) and that 40 per cent of these had been set up in the preceding five years."[13]

International Models

Another line of criticism of the official bilingualism policy sees it ignoring the lessons of other countries with analogous language situations. In the light of international experience, current federal policies have a pernicious effect.

Language, the Provinces, and the Constitution

One group drew lessons for the constitutional status of languages at the provincial level from abroad. The Task Force on Canadian Unity (Pépin-Robarts Task Force) liked the Swiss example. The federal level guarantees service in any of the three official languages of the country, French, Italian, or German. The cantons (provinces) are able to establish their own languages of service and of work. The Task Force likewise thought that each of the eleven jurisdictions of Canada should be free to respond to the unique conditions facing them. This meant amending the constitution to delete the responsibilities falling to Quebec under section 133 and to Manitoba under section 23. (The report of the Task Force came down in January, 1979, so it does not mention New Brunswick's constitutional status.) The rights of the French and English minorities would be met not by constitutional obligations, but by relying on the generosity of the majorities under ordinary legislation and social consensus.[14]

Swiss and Belgian Models

Jean Laponce says that Canada chose the wrong model – namely Finland – rather than the one that is most appropriate – Switzerland.[15] His analysis is an interesting one, based on a distinction between *diglossic bilingualism* and *bilingualism without diglossia.* Diglossic bilingualism is the bilingualism of people whose two languages do not "meet," meaning that they are used in different circumstances deriving from their different social roles. The languages usually collaborate with one another because individuals want them confined to specific contexts – for example, sacred versus secular or local ethnicity versus the wider community. Bilingualism without diglossia is the bilingualism of people, on the other hand, whose languages do "meet": the languages are associated with all social roles and social contexts and are hence in competition for dominance. Language preferences tend to become associated with differences in political power: the two language groups share power unevenly, or asymmetrically. With some exceptions, the dominant group generally tries to impose bilingualism on the minority, which in turn attempts to retreat into a territorial concentration and linguistic isolation to reduce its contacts with the dominating force.

Examples of each abound. German Swiss exhibit diglossic bilingualism. They speak local Swiss German at home and in cantonal legislatures and standard German in the national legislature. Local dialects and national languages are also the case in parts of India and Africa. Non-diglossic bilingualism is the case when Flemish Belgians feel compelled to speak French, when French Canadians speak English, and when Francophones use the dominant German in the Swiss federal bureaucracy.

Non-diglossic situations are therefore distressing and insecure for minority languages. The question is how to deal with that insecurity – on a territorial or a personal basis. The Swiss and Belgian models, based on territorial bilingualism, offer iron-clad security to language groups. In Switzerland, the linguistic borders are unchangeable at the cantonal level while multilingualism is the case at the federal level. The integrity of the territory is guaranteed against linguistic encroachment; citizens from elsewhere are expected to yield to the language of the canton. The cost of having collective rights dominate over personal rights is offset by the benefit of linguistic and cultural stability. The same dynamic exists in Belgium, with modifications: a Flemish Flanders, a French Walloon, and a bilingual capital, Brussels.

Canada, on the other hand, chose the option with less security for the minority, that of Finland. Finland has a Finnish-speaking majority and a Swedish-speaking minority. If the Swedish-speaking minority falls below 8 per cent in the local commune, there is unilingual service in Finnish; above it, bilingualism is the rule. There is, however, less relative security in this model, as the safety for Swedish lies only in bilingualism and is also dependent on population thresholds.

The irony of the Canadian situation is that, whereas the federal government policy is largely built on the Finnish model, whatever stability there exists is a result of the predominantly territorial model adopted by Quebec. Bill 101 has reduced language tensions among Francophone Quebecers and diminished the pressure for separation. The Swiss model – juxtaposing unilingual areas – is better for Canada.[16]

Kenneth D. McRae, although he plainly admires it greatly, does not recommend the complete transplantation of the Swiss system to Canada. However, he does advise careful study of successful multilingual systems, like that of Switzerland, that have moderated linguistic conflict to a greater extent than has Canada. The Swiss example offers some intriguing principles for Canadian consideration: (1) the absence of a centralized language plan; (2) the use of need rather than symmetry as the guideline for federal financial assistance to language groups; (3) absence of federal-cantonal overlap in language jurisdiction; (4) a policy of non-involvement by each canton in the language policies of other cantons; (5) little government promotion of individual bilingualism; and (6) the confluence of simultaneous political loyalties to the Confederation, the canton, and to the linguistic-cultural group. Consideration of the Swiss case might lead Canadians to adopt a federal language policy quite different from the one that has dominated for years. [17]

Language and the Division of Powers

John Richards weaves arguments from international experience with others to present an argument for an explicit division of powers over language in the Canadian constitution. [18] He hopes that Canada does not repeat the mistake of England, which defeated Home Rule for Ireland in 1886 and gave rise to a bitter nationalist movement and, ultimately, to independence for the Irish Free State in 1922. The combination of the official bilingualism policy and the refusal to recognize a special jurisdiction for Quebec in language matters has had the effect of denying it a kind of linguistic home rule. What has resulted is a harmful form of "linguistic free trade." [19]

Needed, he says, is an explicit division of powers over language. The case for decentralization of major aspects of language to the provinces, and especially to Quebec, is compelling. Without public intervention, the social contract of Confederation would be broken and majority rule would be lost within Quebec. (Richards manages therefore to combine the dualist theory and territorialism, unlike many other critics of the federal policy.) Pragmatism as well dictates a predominant provincial role. People tend to value language over economics, as the U.S.S.R. taught us. In addition, the positive discrimination inherent in a Quebec-centred policy may actually contribute to Quebec's economic productivity by removing a source of artificial discrimination against Francophones.

Richards is not definitive about the exact shape of the division of powers. It would look something like the "distinct society" provisions of the Meech Lake Accord (provided they allowed language policies that favoured French over English in Quebec) or the solution provided by the Pépin-Robarts Task Force some years before. He also provides for an unspecified federal jurisdiction in language. One imagines that he would not be very far from the writers sympathetic to the Swiss or Belgian models.

The official languages policy is untenable on grounds of history, policy, statistics, and the experience of successful multilingual regimes in the world. It is time for federal policy-makers to face facts and introduce something better. Ideology masquerading as language policy must give way to common sense.

Notes

1. F.R. Scott, "Areas of Conflict in the Field of Public Law and Policy," in Mason Wade, ed., *Canadian Dualism* (Toronto: University of Toronto Press, 1960), pp. 81-105.

2. *Ibid.*, pp. 82-83.

3. Kenneth McRoberts, "Making Canada Bilingual: Illusions and Delusions of Federal Language Policy," in *Federalism and Political Community* (Peterborough, Ont.: Broadview Press, 1989), pp. 160-61.

4. *Ibid.*, p. 163.

5. Georges Mathews, *Quiet Resolution: Quebec's Challenge to Canada* (Toronto: Summerhill Press, 1990), p. 23.

6. *Ibid.*, p. 31.

7. As cited in Canada, Commissioner of Official Languages, *Annual Report, 1992* (Ottawa: Minister of Supply and Services Canada, 1993).

8. McRoberts, "Making Canada Bilingual," p. 157.

9. An unnamed study of the Official Languages Commission [presumably the federal one] cited and analysed in Pierre Fournier, *A Meech Lake Post-Mortem: Is Quebec Sovereignty Inevitable?* (Montreal: McGill-Queen's University Press, 1991), p. 101.

10. Richard J. Joy, *Canada's Official Languages: The Progress of Bilingualism* (Toronto: University of Toronto Press, 1992), p. 5.

11. Thomas Flanagan, "Should official bilingualism be scrapped? Yes!" *Western Report*, 7, 5 (March 16, 1992), p. 16.

12. William D. Gairdner, *The Trouble With Canada* (Toronto: Stoddart, 1990), ch. 15.

13. Cited in Leslie A. Pal, *Interests of State: The Politics of Language, Multiculturalism and Feminism in Canada* (Montreal: McGill-Queen's University Press, 1993), p. 155.

14. Canada, Task Force on Canadian Unity, *A Future Together: Observations and Recommendations* (Ottawa: Minister of Supply and Services Canada, January, 1979), pp. 48-52.

15. J.A. Laponce, "Reducing the Tensions Resulting From Language Contacts: Personal or Territorial Solutions?" in David Schneiderman, ed., *Language and the State: The Law and Politics of Identity* (Cowansville, Quebec: Les Éditions Yvon Blais, 1991), pp. 173-79.

16. *Ibid.*
17. Kenneth D. McRae, "Precepts for Linguistic Peace: The Case of Switzerland," in Schneiderman, ed., *Language and the State*, pp. 167-72.
18. John Richards, "The Case for Provincial Jurisdiction over Language," in John Richards, François Vaillancourt, and William G. Watson, *Survival: Official Language Rights in Canada*, "The Canadian Round Series" on the Economics of Constitutional Renewal, No. 10 (Toronto: C.D. Howe Institute, 1992), pp. 9-56.
19. *Ibid.*, pp. 21-22, 25.

Index